American Creed

American Creed
Philanthropy and the Rise of Civil Society
1700–1865

KATHLEEN D. McCARTHY

The University of Chicago Press
Chicago and London

Kathleen D. McCarthy is professor of history and director of the
Center for the Study of Philanthropy at the Graduate Center of the
City University of New York. She is the author or editor of five
other books, including *Women's Culture: American Philanthropy
and Art, 1830–1930* published by the University of Chicago Press,
and *Women, Philanthropy, and Civil Society.*

The University of Chicago Press, Chicago 60637
The University of Chicago Press, Ltd., London
© 2003 by The University of Chicago
All rights reserved. Published 2003
Printed in the United States of America

12   11   10   09   08   07   06   05   04   03   1   2   3   4   5

ISBN: 0-226-56198-4 (cloth)

Library of Congress Cataloging-in-Publication Data

McCarthy, Kathleen D.
    American creed : philanthropy and the rise of civil society,
1700–1865 / Kathleen D. McCarthy.
        p. cm.
    Includes bibliographical references and index.
    ISBN 0-226-56198-4 (cloth : alk. paper)
        1. Charities—United States—History—18th century. 2. Non-
profit organizations—United States—History—18th century.
3. Civil society—United States—History—18th century.
4. Charities—United States—History—19th century. 5. Nonprofit
organizations—United States—History—19th century. 6. Civil
society—United States—History—19th century.   I. Title.
HV91.M375 2003
361.7'63'097309034—dc21

                                                2002009734

⊗ The paper used in this publication meets the minimum
requirements of the American National Standard for Information
Sciences—Permanence of Paper for Printed Library Materials,
ANSI Z39.48-1992.

To the International Fellows
of the Center for the Study of Philanthropy
The Graduate Center
City University of New York

Contents

Acknowledgments

One of the happiest tasks in writing a
book is thanking the people who helped along the way. I am extremely
grateful to everyone who assisted me on this journey.

Any historian will tell you how vitally important archivists are to our
work. I have benefited greatly from the wisdom and the assistance of the
staffs of the Pennsylvania Historical Society, the New-York Historical Society, the New York Public Library, the Schomburg Center for Research in
Black Culture, and the American Bible Society, where Mary Cordato was
particularly helpful. I especially want to thank Phillip Lapasansky and his
outstanding staff at the Library Company of Philadelphia. Their kindness, help, and efficiency played a vitally important role in my ability to
finish this research.

Many colleagues and friends read some or all of the manuscript in
various stages of its career, including Kenneth Arnold, Benjamin Barber,
Carol Berkin, Martin Burke, Charles Clotfelter, Virginia Hodgkinson,
Stanley Katz, Thomas Kessner, Barbara Leopold, Charles William Maynes,
Louis Masur, Eugene Miller, Dan Moore, John Morning, James Oakes, Joel
Orosz, Colin Palmer, Bhikhu Parekh, Frances Fox Piven, Kathryn Kish
Sklar, James Allen Smith, Francis X. Sutton, and Sidney Verba. Their good
counsel immeasurably improved the book; any remaining errors of fact
or interpretation are entirely my own. I also particularly want to thank

Thom Thurston for his help in devising the formula for converting current to constant dollars.

Several students did yeoman service in gathering information and providing leads over the years, including Angelo Angelis, Erica Ball, Dorothy Browne, Scott Gac, Tevah Platt, Shawn Savage, Ariel Rosenblum, and Oleg Vinogradov. Adam Reichmann deserves special thanks for his ongoing assistance, and for the many enjoyable hours we have spent debating the merits and shortcomings of Andrew Jackson.

My staff has been incredibly supportive over the years, and I am deeply indebted to them not only for their service, but for their constant encouragement and good cheer. Barbara L. Leopold, Eugene Miller, Amal A. Muḥammad, William Amory Carr, Leah Obias, and Tevah Platt have contributed more than they know to the completion of this book.

Last, but not least, are the people who keep us going, especially during a long-term project such as this. Many people have shared their ideas, their kindness, and their encouragement with me while I was writing this. Magda Ratajski, James and Valerie Smith, Barry Gaberman, Malcolm and Katharine Richardson, Elizabeth Sackler, Peter and Helene Kloehn, Ron and Valerie Chernow, Elizabeth Boris, Virginia Hodgkinson, and even Sam Waterston, with whom I had a fascinating discussion one night about the difficulties of capturing the spirit of Thomas Jefferson—all contributed to this book. My mother and my dear A. have also helped more than they can ever know—and yes, I am very grateful!

Finally, this book is dedicated to the International Fellows of the Center for the Study of Philanthropy. We will have over sixty alumni from around the world by the end of 2002. Many of these young people have become an indispensable part of my life, a fact that came home with stunning clarity in the aftermath of the terrorist attacks on September 11. Several of them were in immediate and constant contact, questioning, consoling, and mourning with me in the aftermath of that terrible assault on the city we love. And so, a special and most heartfelt thanks to the Fellows who virtually held my hand and wept and prayed with me on those first days: David Barnard (South Africa), Gunita Bullite (Latvia), Myrna Cacho (the Philippines), Angela Calvo (Colombia), Ben Cele (South Africa), Alex Chakhunashvili (Georgia), Noshir Dadrawala (India), Marwa El-Daly (Egypt), Sunny Ho (Taiwan), Jung Rin Kim (Korea), Rosario Leon (Peru), Esther Lethlean (Australia), Marina Liborakina (Russia), Natalya Kaminarskaya (Russia), Svitlana Kuts (Ukraine), Ritu Mohan (India), Otieno Aluoka N. Ogolla (Kenya), Esther Plemper (the Netherlands), Bhavna Ramrakhiani (India), Jack Shen (Taiwan), Maina Singh

(India), Andrés Thompson (Argentina), Gisela Velasco (the Philippines), Anahi Viladrich (Argentina), and Xolani Zungu (South Africa). These young people are shaping the contours of civil society around the world today. They constantly inspire me, teach me, and always make me proud.

Introduction

Shortly before Thomas Jefferson died, he wrote his own epitaph. Setting aside his two terms as president, his vice presidency, and his diplomatic roles, he singled out three accomplishments for which he wished to be remembered: "Author of the Declaration of American Independence, of the Statute of Virginia for religious freedom, and Father of the University of Virginia." Perhaps realizing that his heirs might think the inscription incomplete, he cautioned that they were to add "not a word more," for, as he explained, these were the legacies by which "I wish most to be remembered."[1]

Jefferson's enigmatic epitaph provides a Rosetta stone for tracing the rise of civil society—that broad range of institutions and activities that fall between the family and the state—during the nation's youth. The egalitarian ethos embodied in the Declaration of Independence set the stage for the development of a public culture that was broad enough and generous enough to accommodate a steadily growing stream of competing interests and associations. The notion of religious freedom that Jefferson helped to promote enhanced the growth of civil society by spawning thousands of new groups in its wake. And his success in building the University of Virginia exemplified the ways in which a single individual, working outside elected office, could use his time and talents to shape public policies and institutions. Over the course of the country's history, the faith in egalitarian ideals, religious freedom, and the

1

right to engage in civic activism have constituted an enduring American creed.[2]

This book traces the evolution of these ideals from the eighteenth century to the Civil War. Unlike the political revolution, America's associational revolution occurred with minimal fanfare. Explicit references to voluntary associations are absent from the country's key political documents: the Declaration of Independence, the Constitution, and The Federalist. Instead, faith in the value of individual benevolence stemmed not from the political events that surrounded the republic's creation, but from the concept of republican virtue; not from the enumerated powers of government, but from the liberties guaranteed; not from Jefferson's legislative achievements, but from his legacy and those of his contemporaries as private citizens. His epitaph both recorded and celebrated this invisible revolution.

Over the ensuing decades, voluntary organizations sprawled across the American landscape in increasing numbers, promoting a constellation of new endeavors. The pages that follow examine the factors that fostered the expansion of the charitable, educational, welfare, advocacy, and religious nonprofit organizations that came to constitute America's "third sector," as well as the individual philanthropy (the gifts of time, money and/or valuables) that supported them. Within this framework, the terms "voluntary association" and "nonprofit organization" refer to institutions that were (1) institutionalized (rather than ad hoc gatherings such as mobs), (2) private (i.e., "institutionally separate from government"), (3) non-profit-distributing (i.e., with revenues reinvested in programs, rather than given to founders or trustees), (4) self-governing, (5) voluntary, and (6) primarily of public benefit. Political parties, which are less distinct from governmental operations than other associations by virtue of their mission (i.e., electing their members to public office) are excluded under this definition, as are paramilitary groups that promote their version of public benefit through physical violence and coercion in lieu of peaceful, organizational means.[3]

My central argument is that it is not possible to understand the meaning of American democracy without understanding civil society. Nor is it possible to understand civil society without understanding the role of nonprofit organizations and the philanthropy—broadly defined to include giving *and* voluntarism—that sustains them.[4]

As such, the focus here is on the social, political, and economic impact of giving and voluntarism between the eighteenth century and 1865, rather than the detailed histories of the specific institutions these activities created, which can be found elsewhere. Because giving and voluntarism were broadly based, taken together they afford a useful lens for studying one of the major ways in which white women, free blacks, and white male elites collectively built institutions and participated in public policymaking, providing a yardstick for measuring fluctuating levels of public influence over time.[5]

A definition of philanthropy that couples giving with voluntarism may at first glance seem startling. In the twentieth century, the term has become synonymous with giving, particularly the enormous gifts of men like John D. Rockefeller, Andrew Carnegie, or [to give it a more contemporary spin] George Soros and Bill Gates. Ironically, this definition, this coupling of lavish generosity with lavish wealth which has come to symbolize the essence of philanthropy would have puzzled most nineteenth-century Americans, particularly in the decades before the Civil War. For them, the term meant giving *and* volunteering, the personal excursions that large numbers of Americans regularly made into charity, communal self-help, and social reform, mingling their donated time and often modest sums for public ends. Rather than the privilege of the few, it was the practice and prerogative of the many. Black social activists, white abolitionists and educational patrons, even female labor reformers adopted the term, defining themselves as "philanthropists and lovers of equal rights" in their campaigns. If we abandon our contemporary biases and follow their lead on the basis of *their* definitions, the import of these activities changes dramatically. Rather than the exclusive realm of privilege and wealth, it leads directly onto the public stage on which men and women, rich and poor, black and white publicly contested for authority and power during the nation's youth.[6]

It also drew them into the market and political activities. Popular perceptions of the role of philanthropy and nonprofit organizations are often veiled in mythologies. Most studies present the nonprofit sector as a separate sphere, a prop to government, a counterweight, or a forum for public discourse and civic bonding, but rarely as an inherent part of governmental or market operations per se. Both historians and political scientists have traditionally tended to view the social landscape in tripartite terms, with government, the for-profit economy, and nonprofit organizations occupying separate spheres. By this line of argument, nonprofits test while government enacts; when government moves into an area of charity, education, or social welfare activity, "private" actors are ultimately "crowded out."[7]

This interpretation assumed political import in the 1980s, as cam-

paigns to dismantle the welfare state were cast as a quest to return the
country to its historic roots, when public and private responsibilities were
supposedly pristinely separate, and local citizens cared for their own, *on
their own*. The upshot was that many nonprofits embraced income-gener-
ating activities to make up for the anticipated shortfalls in government
funding, sparking contemporary concerns that the sector had "lost its
soul," that it had compromised its traditional, altruistic mission in the pursuit of economic gain. During the 1990s, congressional efforts surfaced to
limit the amount of social advocacy—broadly defined—that nonprofits
with public funding could engage in. Taken together, these events raised a
number of intriguing historical questions. Was there a golden age when
American charities operated independently from government and the for-
profit economy; was there a time when social advocacy was politically circumscribed, and if so, what were the results?

New theoretical issues also emerged in the 1990s, as scholars such as
Robert Putnam devoted increasing attention to the role of civil society in
differing national contexts. Putnam argued that regions with large numbers of voluntary associations will be more democratic and have higher
levels of civic engagement and economic development, while those with
stunted associational networks will be more hierarchical, and more rooted
in the rule of force, rather than the rule of law. By this interpretation, associational life is one of the keys to "making democracy work." When citizens withdraw from these activities, when they begin "bowling alone,"
civil society, social capital, and societal well-being decline.[8]

These are the issues that this volume seeks to address: (1) the interrelationships among the government, the market, and the voluntary sphere,
(2) the impact of earlier efforts to limit social advocacy, and (3) the extent
to which philanthropy historically fostered economic development and
democratic participation. Beginning in the eighteenth century, it traces
the ways in which ordinary men and women, both black and white, as well
as economic and political elites used their gifts of money and time. Within
this framework, philanthropy and nonprofit organizations played four key
roles. First, they assumed *the power to define*, by creating institutions—
charities, Bible societies, schools, abolitionist and moral reform organizations—that shaped "the public interpretation of reality." Some initiatives
defined "the other," publicizing the needs of particular groups such as
widows and small children, and placing those needs—however accurately
or inaccurately interpreted—on public agendas. Others institutionally
defined their backers, becoming vehicles for the assertion, refutation, and
reformulation of the hegemonic interpretations of different groups. They

also became engines for the creation of social capital by forging communities of like-minded peers and strengthening the bonds of civic engagement and social reciprocity among their members. According to Putnam, the essence of social capital is trust, and the ability to work collectively for the common good. In the minds of many observers, this in turn provides a vital source of community cohesion, and the wherewithal to peacefully pursue democratic aims and economic development. The antithesis of social capital is cast in Hobbesian terms: societies held together by violence, coercion, and force rather than a common faith in the rule of law. This study examines the ways in which voluntary associations served as both mechanisms for constructing and challenging the parameters of gender, class, and race and as laboratories for democracy and communal action.[9]

Second, philanthropy and nonprofits fostered what we now call *"public-private partnerships"* and popular governance: those areas of "active participation ... in ruling and being ruled" where private citizens outside elected office took a direct hand in governmental affairs. Participation in the creation and management of charitable and educational ventures enabled at least some citizens to participate in the allocation of public resources by winning appropriations of money, land, and in-kind services for their institutions and constituencies. These activities afforded a more inclusive definition of the country's political culture by opening significant quasi-governmental roles for voteless citizens, such as middle-class white women. The history of American philanthropy reveals the extent to which it was not a discreet area of enterprise and the extent to which the lines between "public" and "private" activities were historically blurred and constantly redrawn.[10]

Philanthropy and voluntary associations also promoted *social advocacy.* The right to petition was a First Amendment guarantee, enabling even disfranchised groups to spark legislative discussions and educate elected policymakers about their causes and concerns. Other First Amendment guarantees of freedom of assembly and speech cleared the way for organizations to monitor, criticize, and reform governmental activities. For many Americans, efforts such as these constituted the essence of democracy in an often undemocratic age, allowing even citizens of modest means and without the vote to shape public policymaking agendas and pursue legislative change. The public sphere that they created was a highly contested arena in which voluntary associations provided mechanisms for channeling conflict between disparate groups as they competed for authority and power. By defusing situations before they exploded into physical combat, associational activities provided a vital "safety valve" for popular discontent, enabling often very different groups to live in relative harmony as they vied for political power and the right to define the nation's agenda.

The final element examined here is the sector's *economic function:* its least studied, least understood role. Social capital theorists such as Putnam argue that voluntary associations promote economic development by fostering the trust that encourages citizens to work together and to pool their funds in joint investments. Yet there are more immediate implications that this interpretation overlooks. Voluntary associations created jobs, manufactured and sold goods, and patronized local tradesmen, all of which helped to spur economic growth. They also had a direct impact on economic development by serving as magnets for capital formation, attracting and generating funds that were invested in loans and business ventures, as well as charitable and educational institutions and publications. In effect, philanthropy helped to foster market values through associational sales and investments in business development and public works, as well as social causes. Seen from this vantage point, the history of American philanthropy provides a fresh lens for assessing the scope and nature of the market revolution and the country's transition to capitalism. Moreover, the pursuit of "communal" capitalism—including the ability to generate profits through what would now be termed nonprofit entrepreneurship—often resulted in expanded political and economic roles for volunteers and trustees. Rather than "separate spheres," philanthropy, governance, and the economy were inherently linked.[11]

The early national and antebellum years provide an ample laboratory for testing these hypotheses: (1) that philanthropy and voluntary associations played an important role in the social construction and reconstruction of the boundaries of gender, class, and race, (2) that the lines between public and private activities were blurred and constantly redrawn, (3) that the public sphere was a hotly contested arena that afforded a "safety valve" for popular discontent, a function vital to the maintenance of civil peace and public governance in a heterogeneous society, (4) that philanthropy and the market were historically linked, and that (5) taken together, these phenomena constituted a driving force of American democracy, economic development, and civil society, providing a valuable perspective for assessing the collective history of elite and nonelite actors over the course of the country's history.

American philanthropy and civil society passed through three distinct phases between the Revolution and the end of the Civil War. The first, which ran from the 1780s to the late 1820s, was a period of slow but steady growth, as an increasingly heterogeneous array of citizens built their local

organizations into a national infrastructure for charity, mutual aid, and reform, a trend fostered by colonial precedents, the revolutionary language of
individual rights, and religious disestablishment. The American penchant
for associationalism was given an added push by the religious revivals of the
Second Great Awakening, and the creation of a national organizational infrastructure in the second decade of the nineteenth century, set in place by
a diverse array of Bible, tract, Sunday school, and missionary societies
known as the Benevolent Empire, and the rise of independent black denominations beginning with the African Methodist Episcopal Church in
1816. By 1820, a broad framework for civil society had been built on the
bedrock of Protestantism, bringing men and women of even modest means
into the public arena.

These developments are presented through a series of roughly chrono-
logical chapters. Chapter 1 examines the impact of colonial precedents and
the Revolution through Benjamin Franklin's career. Although male elites
were active in building charitable and educational enterprises throughout
the colonies, Franklin's efforts provide a particularly revealing example of
the intersection of the market, the government, and philanthropy in the
colonial era, and the contested rise of social advocacy in the aftermath of
the war. Chapter 2 focuses on the development of the first charities and
asylums created by white female elites such as Isabella Graham. Beginning in the 1790s, these efforts drew their backers into a variety of social,
economic and political activities, broadening the concepts of republican
virtue and female citizenship. Chapter 3 compares the differential civic
and economic roles played by (predominantly, but not exclusively white)
Protestant, Catholic, and Jewish women's philanthropy, and examines the
reasons why Protestantism emerged as the key catalyst to the growth of
civil society in the second decade of the nineteenth century. The emphasis
here is on evangelical organizations such as the American Bible Society;
the first Jewish women's benevolent associations; and the first asylums,
convents, and schools created by American Catholic nuns such as Mother
Seton. Chapter 4 examines the growing regional disparities between
Northern and Southern philanthropy between 1790 and 1840, focusing on
giving patterns and the broader economic impact of charitable and educational endowments and wealthy nonprofit organizations such as mutual
savings banks. Chapter 5 takes a different slant on religious and regional
philanthropy, tracing the impact of African American Protestantism in
mobilizing Northern black communities for social reform. Their first major, coordinated campaign emerged in 1816, in response to the efforts of
the federally funded, privately managed American Colonization Society

(ACS) to deport free blacks to Africa. This chapter details the ways in which black-led anticolonizationist initiatives publicly pitted former slaves like Absalom Jones and Richard Allen against the programs and prerogatives of a host of slaveholding political luminaries, underscoring the leveling potential of civil society.

The second section of the book explores the clash of two competing visions of how the country should be governed during the antebellum years. During the heyday of "Jacksonian democracy" in the 1820s and 1830s, a concerted effort was set in motion to reduce public support for the poor and to curb the public policymaking authority of the most politically volatile strain of social advocacy, abolitionism. These years also marked the simultaneous growth of universal white male suffrage and mass-based social reform. Although often depicted as a high-water mark of American participatory democracy because of the expansion of the franchise, from the perspective of civil society Jackson's administrations marked a democratic trough in terms of civil liberties and access to public resources at the local level. Ironically, Alexis de Tocqueville's insight that voluntary associations were vital to American democracy recorded a system under duress, marking the convulsive birth pang of a new, far more inclusive national political culture. Far from a golden age, the Jacksonian era ushered in one of the most volatile eras in American history, a period scarred by violence, vigilantism, and civil disobedience.[12]

Chapter 6 focuses on Andrew Jackson's presidency to examine the political implications of the growing differences between Northern and Southern philanthropy, and their impact on the federal Indian removal campaigns and abolitionism. While the Indian removals sparked the first nationally coordinated female petition drives—efforts choreographed through the churches and the religious press—abolitionist clashes brought one group of Northern reformers into volatile federal contests over slavery, civil liberties, and First Amendment guarantees. Chapter 7 focuses on these contests. The abolitionist movement was far from monolithic, and different groups responded to local, state, and federal opposition in different ways. While black philanthropy created a distinctive political culture through secular charitable, educational, and mutual aid groups in the face of racist rioting and antiabolitionist aggression during Jackson's regime, many abolitionists subsequently moved from peaceful efforts to the endorsement of violence and insurrection following years of federal unresponsiveness and hostility. Chapter 8 explores the social and economic impact of Jacksonian-era and post-Jacksonian-era governmental policies on white female-controlled charities and advocacy campaigns, from female moral, labor, and suffrage reform to Dorothea Dix's legislative crusades of the 1850s.

The conclusion briefly discusses the impact of the Civil War, and the ways in which philanthropy reshaped the contours of civil society during and after the hostilities. Northern and Southern white and African American participation in three major public-private initiatives—the United States Sanitary Commission, the Freedmen's Bureau, and soldier's aid societies—brought new groups into partnerships with the federal government for the first time and laid the groundwork for a more inclusive public arena throughout the country.

Far from a tale of unimpeded progress and inevitable triumph, this is a story of gains won, rescinded, and reclaimed. This, then, is a book about the ebb and flow of democracy and the exercise of power: who wielded it, toward what ends, and how Americans ultimately created an enduring civil society.

PART ONE

The Rise of Civil Society

1

Forging the Creed

❦❧

"We hold these truths to be self-evident, that all men are created equal; that they are endowed by their creator with certain unalienable rights, that among these are life, liberty, and the pursuit of happiness." Few phrases have been invoked as often or as fervently as this section of the Declaration of Independence. Between the Revolution and the Civil War, it became a mantra for reform, used by men and women, black and white, elites and laborers to promote their causes and their rights. To quote Jefferson's biographer, Joseph Ellis, "the entire history of liberal reform in America can be written as a process of discovery, within Jefferson's words, of a spiritually sanctioned mandate for ending slavery, providing the rights of citizenship to blacks and women, justifying welfare programs for the poor and expanding individual freedoms."[1]

It was an unanticipated legacy. When Jefferson wrote the declaration, voluntary associations were almost exclusively the province of white male elites. Two decades later, African American mutual aid societies were evolving into the nucleus of the black church, and the first women's charities were seeking charters in Philadelphia and New York. Over the ensuing years, a growing array of groups would create charities, participate in state and federal policymaking and economic development, compete for public funding, and forge distinctive political cultures uniquely their own.

It was a stunning transformation, born of colonial precedents, revolutionary ideals, and the ideas and actions of the statesmen who led the Revolution. One man, in particular, exemplified the trends that set America's associational revolution in motion: Benjamin Franklin. While Franklin forged a highly visible model for combining philanthropic, public, and market activities for communal ends, his fellow revolutionary leaders—men such as Thomas Jefferson and James Madison—minted much of the egalitarian rhetoric, the religious libertarianism, and the philosophical backing behind the American creed. Franklin's career illustrates the ways in which the scaffolding for American civil society was built over the course of the eighteenth century, including early examples of the ways in which associations built social capital among men of middling means, public-private partnerships, market activities, and a broadened mandate for social advocacy.

Colonial Precedents

Franklin's career heralded a new chapter in a transatlantic philanthropic revolution that began with the Reformation. Earlier historians such as W. K. Jordan and David Owen ably traced the evolution of English beneficence from donations to voluntarism. As Jordan explains, the creation of the Anglican Church and the dissolution of monastic properties under Henry VIII ushered in a new era in secular giving by wealthy merchants in the middle of the sixteenth century. By the seventeenth century, Puritan businessmen had become the country's most generous donors, moved by religiously bound notions of stewardship and the desire to apply their riches to the solution of social ills. The embourgeoisement of British philanthropy entered a second stage in the seventeenth century, as men of still more modest means began to pool their resources and time to create voluntary associations and broadly based subscription drives. Some turned to mutual aid while others used their donations to set up hospitals, charity schools, and colonial libraries, efforts inspired by the rise of joint-stock companies (which popularized the idea of pooled funds), a growing faith in progress, and personal piety. By the time of Franklin's birth in 1706, ample precedents for associational activity were flourishing in England, and a few fledgling ventures had been introduced into the colonies by innovative clerics like Boston's Cotton Mather.[2]

At first glance, Franklin seemed an unlikely philanthropist. Unlike the aristocratic Jefferson, he was born into humble circumstances, one of seventeen children of a Boston chandler. Rather than inheriting his wealth, he became the quintessential self-made man. He was also a man of his times, and his *Autobiography* provides significant clues to the origins of his lifelong fascination with philanthropy through his literary tastes. According to Franklin, three works were particularly influential: *Bonifacious: An Essay upon the Good*, by Cotton Mather; Daniel Defoe's *Essay upon Projects;* and Plutarch's *Parallel Lives of the Noble Greeks and Romans.*

Bonifacious was a clarion call for social activism. Massachusetts already had a well-defined rationale for philanthropic stewardship in the idea that citizens were duty bound to share their wealth with their communities. In effect, personal wealth and public gain were ideologically linked. Mather extended this notion of civic duty to include voluntarism. Toward this end, he urged his readers to embrace "an unfainting resolution to *do good*" through the creation of societies of "Young Men Associated." Rather than focusing on elites, he sought to mobilize men of all ranks, both young and old. "A *little* man may do a great deal . . . of *good!*" Mather exclaimed. "It is possible the *wisdom* of a *poor man*, may start a proposal, that may *save a city*, serve a nation!"[3]

Readers were offered a list of suggestions for possible activities, most of which were based on British precedents, ranging from efforts to curb sinful behavior through "Reforming Societies, or Societies for the Suppression of Disorders" to charity schools. Missionary work among foreigners, Catholics, soldiers, sailors, and Indians was also recommended, as were the creation of tradesmen's libraries, colleges, and seminaries.

Although Mather's book failed to evoke much of an upsurge of voluntarism aside from a few short-lived ventures in New England, Franklin fastened on his ideas, secularized them, and made them his own. To quote one of his many biographers, he transformed the notion of associated public service into "a kind of religion." As he later admitted, *Essay upon the Good* inspired him to "set a greater value on the character of a *doer of good*, than on any other kind of reputation."[4]

Like Mather, Defoe offered a menu of potential activities, from insurance schemes to schools for women. Unlike Mather, however, he rooted these activities in self-interest. Carefully sidestepping the idea that one could buy one's way into heaven through good works, Mather gloweringly warned: "when you have done all the *good* that you can, reckon yourself well paid . . . if you are not *punished* for what you do. In short, be insensible to any *merits* of your performance." Conversely, Defoe emphasized the ties between "*Publick Good*, and *Private Advantage*." By linking public service to self-interest, Defoe's work underscored the possibilities for doing well by doing good—lessons not lost on the ambitious Franklin.[5]

Plutarch cast the theme of service in more patriotic terms. Histories of ancient Greece and Rome fueled the transatlantic fascination with republican ideals that so profoundly shaped the thinking of the revolutionary generation. Republicanism was predicated, among other things, on a set of values that stressed simplicity, patriotism, integrity, valor, and a love of justice and liberty, ideas popularized in the writings of seventeenth-century English "country" writers such as James Harrington and eighteenth-century critics such as John Trenchard and Thomas Gordon. Republican theorists stressed the need for a virtuous citizenry ready to set aside personal honors and gain for the good of the community. Luxury went hand in hand with corruption and vice in this scenario, undermining the societies in which they were tolerated. In the process, republicanism helped to forge a new definition of manhood, one that moved beyond men's traditional roles as heads of households by linking individual virtue to public service in pursuit of the common weal.[6]

Although seldom interpreted in this light, Franklin's *Autobiography* can be read as a primer in republicanism. Franklin was a man obsessed with virtue: its practice, its achievement, its results. For him, virtue was a quarry to be stalked through charts and graphs to monitor behavior, and countless rules and maxims for subduing the all-too-human desire to grasp, to sin, and to offend. The *Autobiography* was also a primer in manly conduct. Notions of republican virtue were inevitably presented against the foil of an insidious feminized "other." Republican theorists continually invoked the trinity of luxury, effeminacy, and vice in their cautionary treatises. To be virtuous, self-abnegating, and dedicated to the common welfare, therefore, was to be a *man*. Franklin embraced these ideas and translated them into a variety of associational experiments, beginning with the Junto.

Founded in 1727, Franklin's circle of "Leather Apron Men," or Junto, borrowed liberally from Mather, Defoe, and Plutarch to forge a new kind of "volitional community" composed of fictive kin. It was a novel experiment. Voluntary associations were just beginning to surface in the North American colonies by the early eighteenth century. Aside from Mather's ill-starred ventures, Boston had recorded two groups by the time the Junto was founded, the Scot's Charitable Society, a mutual aid association that dated from 1657, and the Episcopal Charitable Society, founded in 1724. Newport also had a volunteer fire club, created two years later. The Junto was distinguished by its novel blend of self-help and civic aims, and by the relatively humble status of its members, most of whom were ambitious apprentices like Franklin. To quote Gordon Wood, this was an era when "mechanics and others who worked with their hands were thought servile and totally absorbed in their narrow occupations, and thus . . . having no leisure for public service." The Junto refuted this idea.[7]

For Franklin, public service was both an avocation and a necessity. At sixteen, he fled his family and an unhappy apprenticeship under his brother, James, who managed the Boston newspaper, the *Courant*. The split occurred after the youngster anonymously published his "Silence Do-Good" letters under a pseudonym. Ironically, the popular series was aimed at the pious Mather, causing the stricken cleric to damn the essays as efforts to "blacken and burlesque" his reputation and to urge local magistrates to monitor the *Courant*, surveillance that ultimately landed Franklin's brother in jail for contempt. Perhaps as a hedge against future incarceration, after his release James published the *Courant* under his brother's name, signing a bogus discharge on Benjamin's contract of indenture to make the arrangement seem legitimate. When the paper prospered under the younger brother's editorship, rivalries flared, and Benjamin began to push to be released from his apprenticeship in earnest, signed papers in hand. James ultimately capitulated, but he retaliated by blacklisting the youngster among other Boston printers. Unable to find work, Franklin decided to leave, a decision which brought him to Philadelphia in 1723.[8]

Franklin's unconventional behavior could have cost him his career. Bereft of kin, even letters of introduction and an adequate supply of cash, he effectively cut himself off from most traditional sources of professional, emotional, and financial support that a young man of his station could rely on in starting his career. His rendition of his subsequent adventures is a picaresque novel in miniature. Shortly after landing in Philadelphia he was befriended by the governor, who sent him on a disastrous excursion to London, where the young printer found himself nearly penniless. He ultimately found work in the printing houses of London, returning to Philadelphia in 1726, first as an apprentice and journeyman, then as the publisher of the *Pennsylvania Gazette* in 1729.

Cut adrift from his own family at a point in his career when kinship networks were often the primary determinant of one's failure or success, Franklin crafted his own circle of "brethren" to fill the void. In the process, he began to recast the boundaries between public and private affairs by drawing his fellow apprentices away from the isolation of their individual workshops and into the public sphere of social service and action. The association embraced a variety of aims. At one level, it was an informal university, where members discussed weekly reading assignments on history, ethics, literature, and science. At a time when a classical education was an indispensable credential of elite status, these activities provided members with a means of hurdling social distinctions—an advantage rarely available to young men of their station.

Junto members coupled self-education with public service and self-help. Weekly meetings began with a series of questions concerning everything from business trends to public needs. In addition to discussing reading assignments, members pooled information on recent business failures and coups, the personal foibles and gains of individual citizens, worthy deeds, and ideas for ways "in which the Junto may be serviceable to *mankind.*" Queries were also made about individuals' needs and how their fellow members might be of assistance. It was a highly successful alliance, lasting over three decades. Rather than extend the original circle, Franklin ultimately encouraged each member to start a group of his own, to better promote "our particular interests in business . . . the increase of our influence in public affairs, and our power of doing good."[9]

More than a club, the Junto was a template for the creation of social capital, the trust that enables individuals to work collaboratively to benefit themselves and the larger society. It was certainly an important prop to Franklin's career. In addition to pooling information and contacts, members lent the funds that enabled him to set himself up as the editor of the *Gazette,* a function normally filled by kin in an era when cash was scarce and loans from strangers both risky and difficult to obtain. The meetings provided items for the columns of his paper, and inside information on emerging business trends. They also served as a crucible for many of the public ventures that burnished Franklin's reputation, such as the Library Company of Philadelphia, the city's first subscription library (which ultimately resided in the State House, bolstering Franklin's "private" organization with public housing); the American Philosophical Society, a pancolonial community of intellectuals, scientists, and inventors; and the Union Fire Company, the city's first volunteer fire brigade. In the words of one observer, the Junto "was his benevolent lobby for the benefit of Philadelphia, and now and then for the advantage of Benjamin Franklin." It was also the template for a lifetime of good works.[10]

Government Funding and the Commonwealth Ideal

Despite his personal generosity, Franklin harbored a glowering dislike of public poor relief, which he deemed the wellspring of indolence, idleness, and prodigality, attitudes that presaged the Draconian poor laws of the 1820s. In his estimation, public support for the poor offered "a premium for the encouragement of idleness." "Giving mankind a dependence on any thing for support in age or sickness, besides industry and frugality during youth and health," he gloomily predicted, "tends to . . . promote and increase . . . the very evil it was intended to cure." Franklin's dictum was that the "best way of doing good to the poor is [by] . . . driving them *out* of it." Yet he was quick to draw on public support for his own philanthropic ventures, patterns codified in English law and rooted in colonial necessity. In an era of limited personal fortunes and public expenditures, Franklin realized that collaboration was imperative.[11]

Perhaps the most ingenious example of Franklin's skill at cobbling together public and private support was his work on behalf of the Pennsylvania Hospital for the Sick Poor. Initially proposed by Dr. Thomas Bond, the hospital was the first of its kind in North America. Because of its novelty, Bond had difficulty in raising funds and turned to Franklin for help. Franklin publicized the venture in the *Pennsylvania Gazette*, launched a subscription drive, donating twenty-five pounds from his own pocket, and drafted a petition to the Pennsylvania Assembly (he was the clerk) when the fund-raising campaign began to falter.

A shrewd judge of character, Franklin was well aware that the assembly would be reluctant to grant public funds. When his petition was denied, the printer introduced an alternative plan for a two-thousand-pound matching grant, which readily passed since the legislators knew that public donations and enthusiasm had flagged. As Franklin explained, "the Members who had oppos'd the Grant . . . now conceiv'd they might have the Credit of being charitable without the Expence." Much to their surprise the money was quickly raised through the enticing prospect that "every man's donation would be doubled." "I do not remember any of my political manoeuvres the success of which gave me . . . more pleasure," the printer chortled.[12]

Franklin also managed to wrangle a grant from the Pennsylvania Assembly for the academy that later became the University of Pennsylvania. Here, too, private donations from Philadelphia and England were coupled with "considerable" grants of land from the Pennsylvania Assembly. Public support for colleges and universities had ample colonial precedents. Harvard received both public and private funding beginning in the 1630s, including substantial government grants for capital improvements in the middle of the eighteenth century. Yale was given more than twenty thousand dollars by Connecticut's colonial government over the first half of the eighteenth century, as well as receiving a fifteen-hundred-acre parcel of land. King's College in New York also received substantial windfalls from public sources over the course of Franklin's lifetime.[13]

Like colleges, colonial charities were often jointly funded. Both Boston and Philadelphia turned the management of their municipal work-houses over to private groups, blending tax monies with private dona-tions, practices repeated in most of the larger colonial cities. In the case of Philadelphia's Bettering House, "public and private philanthropy were so completely intertwined as to become almost indistinguishable." Public charity in Penn's colony was initially limited, with religious organiza-tions taking up the slack by augmenting municipal aid with support for their own members. The colony's poor law was strengthened in 1749, en-abling towns like Philadelphia to receive gifts and bequests from individ-uals for poor relief. By midcentury, growing numbers of Philadelphians were living on the edge of subsistence, plagued by seasonal unemploy-ment and inadequate wages, which inspired a group of Quaker mer-chants to form the Committee to Alleviate the Miseries of the Poor in 1762. Four years later they received a municipal charter for the Bettering House, coupling private donations with public poor relief funds through work programs for the destitute. They were also empowered to receive loans, gifts, and bequests to replace the city's dilapidated almshouse. In-come generation figured into their plans as well, as inmates picked oakum, cobbled shoes, and produced cloth and nails to offset the costs of their care. Ventures such as these illustrate the extent to which the lines dividing private, governmental, and market activities were blurred in colonial society. Because tax revenues were limited and colonial bureau-cracies small, "most public action . . . depended upon private energy and private funds."[14]

Charters played a key role in consolidating these alliances. Granted on a case-by-case basis by state legislatures, charters such as those of the Pennsylvania Hospital and the University of Pennsylvania were devised as contractual relationships between governments and individual citizens. While America would be flooded with chartered businesses and charities in the nineteenth century, colonial charters were more sparingly granted and laced with clauses limiting their duration and the amount of capital the institutions could control.

They derived their authority from English common law and the com-monwealth ideal which defined chartered institutions as organic exten-sions of the state. The public nature of these documents was starkly underscored in England, where businesses were barred from receiving charters for a century between the passage of the Bubble Act of 1720 and its repeal in 1825. During the interim, charters were granted for one pur-pose: to create "agencies of government . . . for the furtherance of community purposes." In return for promises to execute specific projects for which the state lacked sufficient resources, corporate bodies were given public funds, access to lottery monies, and the right to collectively hold property and bequests. If the organization was able to generate profits in the pursuit of public ends, it was entitled to those funds as well, an "enticement for which the members would tax themselves and manage the coveted enterprise efficiently."[15]

The commonwealth ideal, the notion that public and private interests were blended under the sanction of a charter, infused Franklin's associational work, providing legal authority and support for a variety of privately initiated civic improvement schemes. It also undergirded the long-standing colonial practice of earmarking public funds for ostensibly private charitable and educational ventures, coupling public and private resources, donations, tax monies, earned income, and voluntarism in order to maintain public services in an era of limited taxes, limited government, and limited surplus cash. Born of necessity, the commonwealth ideal provided a mechanism through which nonelected citizens (particularly rising members of the elite, like Franklin) could influence public priorities and the direction of public expenditures within their communities.

Philanthropy and the Market

While charters blurred the boundaries between philanthropy and the state, "nonprofit entrepreneurship" (i.e., profit making by and for nonprofit ventures) linked philanthropy to the marketplace, trends epitomized in Franklin's career. As in the case of "public-private partnerships," colonial imperatives reinforced the ties among giving, voluntarism, and profit making. However, unlike for-profit businesses, nonprofit charities, hospitals, and schools reinvested their income in their services and operations, rather than distributing them to their subscribers, donors, and trustees. Moreover, these revenues were often vital for their continued existence. Few, if any, colonial charities or colleges could subsist entirely on a single source of income, be it donations or government support. Most followed the pattern of the Bettering House, cobbling together a varied portfolio of resources that coupled private and public donations with income-generation activities, such as tuition fees or the sale of such marketable items as textiles or shoes. In a few instances, these profit-making schemes reached unusual proportions, as illustrated by Franklin's dealings with the charismatic revivalist George Whitefield.

It was an odd alliance. Franklin was an avowedly secular being and therefore hardly a candidate for conversion. Nevertheless, the two men forged an enduring friendship cemented by their common entrepreneurial bent, their shared cosmopolitanism, and their commitment to philanthropy.

Whitefield was one of the most influential leaders in the Great Awakening, the transatlantic religious revival that inspired unprecedented numbers of conversions in the second quarter of the eighteenth century. Tremors of religious enthusiasm were felt in areas of the Northeast as early as the 1720s, stirred by the preaching of gifted ministers such as Jonathan Edwards. While most, like Edwards, confined their efforts to their local regions, Whitefield aggressively marketed his writings in England and across the breadth of the colonies to underwrite his revivals.

His efforts capitalized on the surge of consumerism that swept both sides of the Atlantic in the eighteenth century. To quote his biographer, Whitefield used ideas as "commodities," coining a new genre of "entrepreneurial evangelicalism." For publishers such as Franklin, Whitefield's arrival was a windfall. Sermons and religious journals were extremely popular in the 1730s, with some selling thousands of copies. Whitefield sold his own works through his London offices, evangelical societies, and partnerships with publishers such as Franklin. As historian Frank Lambert explains, Whitefield was a "hot commodity" whose works often became "bestsellers." "For many printers, the revivalist's writings constituted a significant portion of their business." Indeed, "in the peak revival year, 1740, Whitefield wrote or inspired thirty-nine titles, or thirty percent of all works published in America," outperforming even Franklin's own best-selling *Poor Richard's Almanack.*[16]

The cleric was an inveterate entrepreneur, vending commercial goods as well as religious writings to fund his charities. When he arrived in Philadelphia in 1739 with a "shipload of manufactured goods," Franklin advertised their auction in the *Pennsylvania Gazette*. The preacher also brought boxes of publications that Franklin distributed colony-wide through his networks of partners and former apprentices. For Franklin, the revivalist represented "a marketable product and a competitive edge."[17]

In return for the right to distribute his works, Franklin made generous contributions to Whitefield's charities, some of which were invested in a five-thousand-acre site the cleric acquired on the Delaware River for a school for blacks and a community for English evangelicals. Franklin advertised the school and solicited funds on Whitefield's behalf. Whitefield also bought a five-hundred-acre plantation in South Carolina to support his orphanage in Georgia and made donations to Eleazer Wheelock's Indian school in New England, Gilbert Tennent's Log College in Princeton, Harvard, and Franklin's Philadelphia Academy.

But the centerpiece of the revivalist's charitable empire was Bethesda Orphanage, which he founded outside of Savannah, Georgia. The history of Bethesda provides eloquent testimony to the ways in which even the best intentions can go awry when too deeply enmeshed in the scramble for gain. Whitefield initially planned to support the orphanage through donations, but then decided to make the institution self-supporting. Toward that end, he immersed himself in transatlantic merchandising to generate sufficient funds to ensure the asylum's independence from outside control, whether by colonial or religious officials. Although the orphanage was constructed on donated land from Georgia's colonial government (in yet another instance of public support for an ostensibly private charity), Whitefield built it into a charitable fiefdom, offering a striking example of the ways in which public and private donations intermingled with commercial revenues. In addition to income from his writings, he eventually secured a ship to import European goods for sale in American markets. He even tried his hand at manufacturing cotton textiles at the orphanage until the Georgia trustees censured the scheme as a violation of the English Navigation Acts. The story's most bizarre twist came when the cleric sought to persuade Georgia's colonial officials to allow him to import slaves—which was prohibited in Georgia before 1750 by law, if not entirely in practice—to bolster the asylum's fortunes while Christianizing the slaves. This truly was a case of paving the road to hell with good intentions. Whitefield's misguided generosity ultimately ended in disaster. The orphanage drifted into insolvency after his death, the buildings were destroyed in a hurricane in 1790, and the land and holdings were liquidated by the trustees. The only enduring legacy was his role in helping to legitimize the introduction of slavery into Georgia, where the "peculiar institution" emerged in some of its most brutal forms.[18]

Revolutionary Ideals and the Rise of Social Advocacy

During the colonial era, the growth of private philanthropy helped to define new communities and build social capital through associations like the Junto; it became embedded in the market through nonprofit entrepreneurship, a practice exemplified by Franklin's dealings with Whitefield; and it provided a new wrinkle on the political culture of cities like Boston and Philadelphia by blending citizen initiatives with public support in the provision of public services. The Revolution opened a new chapter in the history of American philanthropy by drawing citizen groups into the policymaking arena through social advocacy. Here, too, Franklin's career provided a significant marker of this trend.

It was a contested innovation. Charitable and educational ventures such as Franklin's aroused little controversy; rather than seeking fundamental social or political change, they enhanced the status quo. Advocacy was a different matter. The war unleashed a flood of egalitarian rhetoric and a zeal for liberty that was difficult to contain, raising uncomfortable questions about who should rule, and who should populate the public stage. What distinguished civil society from civic disorder? "Who should govern? How much dissenting opinion could be tolerated? What was the appropriate balance between liberty and order, freedom and government? What sorts of controls were necessary to preserve the political union?" Issues such as these reverberated throughout early national and antebellum years. The task of the Revolutionary leaders, to quote Kimberly Smith, "was to decide how the people would participate in government, which was not at all self-evident."[19]

Two factors, in particular, broadened the arena for citizen participation during the revolutionary era: religious disestablishment and the development of an egalitarian political philosophy. Penned by Thomas Jefferson in 1777 and passed with James Madison's aid in 1786, Virginia's Statute for Religious Freedom opened a new era in the history of American religion. Most of the colonies had Protestant state-supported churches at the time of the Revolution, ranging from the Church of England in Virginia to Congregational churches in New England. The extent to which civil rights were linked to religious observances varied from state to state. In Virginia, for example, laws making heresy a punishable crime were still on the books in the 1780s, although rarely enforced. The colony also had a sizable Methodist population that openly dissented from the doctrines of the Church of England.

Jefferson's aim in severing Virginia's Anglican congregations from state support was not to stem religious observance, but to make these practices a matter of individual conscience. The wording of the Act for Religious Disestablishment made his position unequivocally clear: "To compel a man to furnish contributions of money for the propagation of opinions which he disbelieves and abhors, is sinful and tyrannical." Instead, citizens should "be free to profess . . . their opinions in matters of religion" without affecting "their civil capacities." It proved a convincing argument. The Virginia bill was the first in a string of disestablishment laws that culminated in legislation eradicating the last of the state churches in the middle of the nineteenth century.[20]

Disestablishment had a profound impact on the social geography of American civil society. By building a "wall of separation" between church and state, Jefferson shifted churches into the voluntary sphere, placing all denominations on a level playing field in the competition for parishioners and funds. Shorn of public support, they began to compete for members, lacing the country with parishes and networks for fund-raising, proselytizing, and reform. This in turn provided an enduring institutional framework for social mobilization, drawing women and men of differing races and stations into the voluntary sphere.

Ideas played a role as well, including Madison's celebrated essay, "Federalist Paper Number 10," written in 1787 to convince a reluctant electorate to endorse the Constitution. "Federalist 10," as it is commonly known, dealt with the question of whether a large republic could survive, or whether it would falter on the shoals of factional sparring. The men of Madison's generation were deeply cynical about the corrupting influence of power. In a republic, it was argued, the balance of power could easily be tipped by competing groups, each pursuing its own ends. Freedom to associate meant freedom to challenge, to contest, and to persuade. In authoritarian regimes these rights were ruthlessly repressed. The problem for Madison's generation was how to unleash the forces of liberty without unleashing the destructive potential of "factions."

Madison's essay addressed the issue head-on. "Factions," as he defined them, included "a number of citizens . . . who are united and actuated by some common impulse of passion." The capacity of cabals to wreak political havoc was unquestionable. Although they could be curbed by "destroying the liberty which is essential to [their] existence," Madison cautioned that such a remedy would be "worse than the disease. Liberty is to faction what air is to fire, an aliment without which it instantly expires."[21]

The solution was to control the effects, rather than allowing liberty to be stillborn. "Extend the sphere and you take in a greater variety of parties and interests," he predicted. In the process, it will become "less probable that a majority of the whole will have a common motive to invade the rights of other citizens, or if such a common motive exists, it will be more difficult for all who feel it to discover their own strength and act in unison with each other." Although designed as a model for controlling political interests, Madison's essay had implications for religious and secular associations as well. As he explained, religious freedom "arises from that multiplicity of sects, which pervades America, and which is the best and only security for religious liberty in any society."[22]

The question of who should govern and who should participate assumed added urgency in the new republic, as groups such as the Democratic-Republican societies and Franklin's Pennsylvania Abolition Society began to engage in social advocacy. Prior to the war, mob action had often been the primary means by which average citizens called attention to their grievances and needs, but the broadly based citizen boycotts of British consumer goods that bubbled up on the eve of the war suggested a new possibility. The boycotts provided "political instruments open to persons of 'all ranks,'" as well as "a concept of virtue that included any man or woman capable of economic self-restraint, and . . . new interpretive communities based on shared secular interests." Sparked by political events, these opportunities just as quickly vanished, extinguished by the lack of permanent organizational bases to sustain them.[23]

Bolstered by colonial precedents and revolutionary libertarianism, the immediate postwar years became a period of associational experimentation, leaving many Americans hard pressed "to distinguish between lawful and unlawful resistance to legislative authority." Essentially debating and self-study groups, Democratic-Republican societies cropped up in several Northern and Southern states in the early 1790s, a trend their detractors linked to the radical Jacobin political clubs of the French Revolution. Yet far from being subversive, they constituted early examples of what in twentieth-century parlance would come to be known as political watchdog groups. Under their auspices, artisans and local elites gathered to study public documents and to assess the performance of elected officials, publicly monitoring and criticizing government activities. As members in Addison, Vermont, explained, "we are convinced that the present political state of our country, calls for the rational, wise and vigilant attention of its citizens." Toward that end, they vowed to "study the Constitution, to avail ourselves of the journals, debates, and laws of Congress," and to track "the conduct of individual officers in the discharge of their trusts, whether in Congress . . . the executive or [the] judiciary."[24]

The Whiskey Rebellion brought these groups into direct conflict with the federal government. Ignited in 1794, the protest flared across the western Pennsylvania frontier. It was born of long-standing grievances. Frontier life was both perilous and poor, as European-American and Indian civilizations grated against each other in the wilderness, exacting an often harsh toll. As atrocities escalated, frontier settlers called for increased mil-

itary support, which was not forthcoming from the Washington administration. Instead, the government levied an excise tax on the local staple,
whiskey, threatening to lower still further an already marginal standard of
living. When the frontiersmen protested by refusing to pay the levy, Treasury Secretary Alexander Hamilton persuaded Washington to call out the
troops.[25]

He and Washington traced the source of the unrest to the Democratic-
Republican societies. Determined to quash popular resistance to federal
policies, Washington lashed out at these "self-created societies" in his annual address to Congress in November of 1794, arguing that they would
"destroy the government of this country" if left unchecked. Branding
them "incendiaries" and enemies of public order, he sought to have them
muzzled and curbed. Others defended the groups. Rather than condemning the societies as extralegal associations, Madison derided Washington's
stance as "the greatest error of his political life." Countering the president's charges that the groups promoted "Mob and Club Government,"
Jefferson professed shock that Washington "should have permitted himself to be the organ of such an attack on the freedom of discussion, the
freedom of writing, printing and publishing."[26]

Washington's censure provoked a congressional debate about the scope
and limits of American citizenship, particularly as it applied to the political pronouncements of propertyless laborers. Several Federalist congressmen agreed with Washington's reading, castigating the societies'
activities. In the words of one historian, "Everywhere they looked they
found self-governing individuals making their way across the landscape, a
sight that unleashed their worst fears of anarchy and destruction." Others
demurred, arguing that "Every government under Heaven hath a tendency to degenerate into tyranny. Let the people then speak out. *Why not
let them speak out?*" Madison coolly summarized the dilemma, noting,
"opinions are not the objects of legislation." Although the societies vanished almost as quickly as they appeared, they established an important
precedent for broadened citizen participation.[27]

Franklin catalyzed an equally lively debate in 1790. The printer ended
his public career at the helm of the Pennsylvania Abolition Society (PAS),
a Quaker venture created in 1775 and reorganized under Franklin's presidency twelve years later. One of a number of state-based antislavery societies that emerged in the wake of the Revolution, the PAS promoted a
variety of aims, from documenting manumissions as a hedge against the
kidnapping of freedmen by slave catchers to helping African Americans to
secure schooling and jobs. Franklin drafted the society's "Plan for Improv-

ing the Condition of Free Blacks" in 1789, including legal assistance, manumission registration, and efforts to prevent kidnappings. The "Committee of Employ" was empowered to help in finding jobs and aiding aspiring black businessmen. Comparable committees were created to provide schooling, moral instruction, and apprenticeships.[28]

The society also endorsed gradual emancipation. Toward this end, it petitioned Congress "to countenance the restoration of liberty to those unhappy men, who alone, in this land of freedom, are degraded into perpetual bondage." Submitted in 1790, the memorial provoked a sharp debate on the legality of associational petitions. While some felt that "Congress ought not to refuse to hear the applications of their fellow-citizens," others were less sanguine. Representative Tucker of Virginia, in particular, feigned surprise "to see another memorial on the same subject," following on the heels of a similar Quaker petition, "and that signed by a man who ought to have known the Constitution better." Franklin obviously knew the Constitution better than Congressman Tucker, and so presumed to exercise a fundamental First Amendment right.[29]

Both petitions stimulated animated discussions about constitutional guarantees, states' rights, the slave trade, the legality of petitions, and the boundaries of congressional authority. An exchange between Georgia's representative, James Jackson, and New Jersey's Elias Boudinot summarized the differing points of view. In response to Jackson's query about the legality of petitions submitted by a specific group, especially when Quakers opposed the war as pacifists, and Southerners fought, Boudinot countered, "It is not because the petition comes from the society of Quakers that I am in favor of the commitment, but because it comes from citizens of the United States." Franklin's missive was ultimately referred to the Committee of Correspondence, whose members were bombarded with PAS literature on the evils of slavery and the horrors of the middle passage. Members of the PAS also publicized the ensuing congressional discussions, monitoring their progress from the galleries during the debates.[30]

When the committee ruled that Congress could not intervene in the internal affairs of the states, Franklin penned his final satire. Likening Congress to a mythical Algerian assembly, and his own memorial to a request to end the taking of Christian slaves by Algerian pirates, he concluded: "The Divan came to this resolution: 'The Doctrine, that Plundering and Enslaving the Christians is unjust, is at best *problematical;* but that it is the interest of this State to continue the Practice is clear; therefore let the Petition be rejected.' And it was rejected accordingly."[31]

Although the plea was declined, the petition itself established a signifi-cant precedent. As in the case of the Democratic-Republican societies, a vitally important principle was tested in these early debates, casting the political parameters of associational activity in broadened terms. It was a contested evolution, one that presaged future battles as new groups pooled their time and contributions to gain a voice in public policymaking. It also provided an eloquent capstone to Franklin's career. While the printer's first publications, his "Silence Do-Good Letters," marked the birth of a new associational culture at the beginning of the eighteenth century, his antislavery satire marked the legitimation of social advocacy at the cen-tury's end.

When Franklin died in 1790, an array of new actors was poised at the edges of the public sphere, ready to stake their claims for participation and authority much as Franklin had in his youth. Over the course of his life-time, the practice and prerogatives of philanthropy had substantially widened, encompassing institutional development, alliances with govern-ment, nonprofit entrepreneurship, and reform. Through its actions and its ideas, Franklin's generation sparked a revolution within the revolution, creating a civil sphere in which the meaning and practice of citizenship and democracy would continually be tested, contested, and refined. Forged in the idiom of republican manhood, it was about to receive a decidedly feminine reiteration.

2

The Feminization of Republicanism

Isabella Graham was an unlikely heir
to Franklin's activism. A Scottish immigrant, Graham had endured a period of intense poverty after her husband died in 1773, leaving her with
three children and a fourth about to be born. When she returned to her
once-wealthy family she learned that they, too, were destitute. She eked
out a marginal existence with her father and her children, maintaining
them by opening a girls' school near Edinburgh with the aid of a local patron. When she emigrated to the United States in 1789, she supported her
family through a similar venture in New York. Graham's piety ultimately
led to her financial salvation when her school became affiliated with the
Cedar Street Scottish Presbyterian Church, where her daughter met and
married Divie Bethune, a wealthy merchant.

In 1797, Isabella Graham spearheaded the creation of one of the country's first female-controlled charities, the Society for the Relief of Poor
Widows with Small Children. In part, her ability to do so stemmed from
the status conferred by her daughter's marriage. But her association also
reflected her belief that women, as well as men, had a right and a responsibility to address public needs. Although barred from participation in
elected office, Graham confirmed through her activities that women had a
legitimate place in the public sphere, a notion that permeated the secular
charities explored in this chapter and those of the religious groups discussed in chapter 3.

Beginning at the threshold of the nineteenth century, a small but growing number of privileged women such as Graham used their charities to
recast the parameters of republicanism, collectively reclaiming the rights
denied them by custom and common law. Historians have tended to emphasize "republican motherhood" as the Revolution's primary legacy for
women. Briefly stated, this was the notion that the country needed educated mothers to raise virtuous citizens, giving white women a new political role, at least rhetorically. Far less studied have been the ways in which
the first women's charities created a political and economic space for
female enterprise, challenging misogynistic stereotypes and forging a
feminized version of the republican credo of public service, personal self-
sacrifice, and individual virtue. Like the rise of the Democratic-Republican societies, white women's philanthropy provided a test of the breadth of
revolutionary gains.[1]

A "Most Heroick" Enterprise: The Rise of Women's Charities

Two kinds of female-controlled charities were created for women and
children in the 1790s: asylums and charities providing employment and
outdoor (noninstitutional) relief. Prior to that, although elite women were
sporadically tapped for donations, they did not build enduring institutions
themselves. For example, Benjamin Franklin solicited funds from wealthy
widows and women of substance to pay for a shipment of medical supplies
for the Pennsylvania Hospital. His granddaughter, Sarah Franklin Bache,
helped to coordinate a wartime fund-raising drive that raised seventy-five
hundred pounds from sixteen hundred donors for Washington's troops in
1780, stimulating comparable efforts in other states that ultimately included such prominent political spouses as Martha Washington, Martha
Jefferson, and Abigail Adams. Born of wartime imperatives, these efforts
quickly dissolved at war's end.[2]

This pattern began to change at the end of the century as more enduring female-controlled charities appeared in seaboard cities such as Philadelphia and New York. Although their efforts were sometimes resisted—
Anne Parrish, a young Quaker who helped to found Philadelphia's Female
Society for the Relief of the Distressed in 1795, confessed that "None seem
to understand my language. . . . I believe they are afraid that I shall be singular, and led astray"—these early pioneers were able to create a "space"
for their activities because public funds were limited and the needs were
great. They had their work cut out for them. Estimates place the ratio of
women on Philadelphia's relief rolls between 86% and 91% during the

early nineteenth century. While groups such as Philadelphia's Female Hospitable Society traced the sources of female poverty to immigration and substandard wages for seamstresses, the death of a spouse often played a substantial role as well. As Christine Stansell points out, widowhood was virtually synonymous with impoverishment in this era, a fact that was immediately apparent to women like Graham.[3]

Religion also had an impact. Beginning in the 1790s, mounting waves of religious enthusiasm swept across the western frontier with the first tremors of the Second Great Awakening. Over the next century, repeated revivals would speed the growth of evangelical Protestantism, building a welter of national denominations in the wake of disestablishment. Women played a central role in these developments. As churches lost their public funding, their congregations became increasingly "feminized": estimates place the percentage of female converts in northeastern revivals as high as 70% between 1795 and 1815, giving women a commanding presence in a growing variety of Protestant institutions that provided new opportunities for public roles, patterns discussed more fully in chapter 3.[4]

Although some of the first women's charities were founded by denominational coalitions of Protestant laywomen such as Graham, most were initially secular in tone. Some, like the Boston Female Asylum, relied on local ministers to preach charity sermons to help them raise funds, but this does not seem to have translated into the kind of heavy-handed proselytizing that marked the asylum programs of the 1830s and 1840s. Religiously diverse boards further underscored their ecumenical character. In Philadelphia, for example, several Jewish women were founding members of the nonsectarian Female Association for the Relief of Women and Children in Reduced Circumstances, and founders and officers of the Philadelphia Orphan Asylum. One of these pioneers, Rebecca Gratz, later became a leader in the development of Jewish women's charities as well, creating the Female Hebrew Benevolent Society in 1819 and the nation's first Hebrew Sunday School Society in the 1830s.

Other charities were built by Quakers like Anne Parrish. Quaker women occupied a unique position within their congregations, participating in business meetings and even establishing national and pancolonial reputations as preachers. To quote Rebecca Larson, "since an authentic ministry rested solely on the 'charismatic' authority of divine inspiration rather than on the 'traditional' authority acquired through academic training and ecclesiastical ordination, women's religious leadership was legitimized on the same basis as men's." Quaker women were also encouraged to take the lead in poor relief, since George Fox, the sect's leader, felt they were more attuned to the needs of the destitute, and this laid the groundwork for the institutional developments of the 1790s.[5]

Both Quakerism and evangelical Protestantism were firmly rooted in the transatlantic imperatives that fueled the career of the charismatic Whitefield. Similarly, Graham drew on her experience in organizing the mutual benefit Society for the Relief of the Destitute Sick in her native Scotland to introduce a new genre of female philanthropy in New York. Civic imperatives provided a hospitable environment for transplanting these innovations. Rather than raising taxes to build a larger almshouse, public officials in selected cities and rural areas began to work with emerging women's charities such as Graham's to aid the female poor. Philadelphia's first white women's charities included Parrish's Female Society, Gratz's Female Association for Poor Women with Children, and the Magdalen Society. Created in 1795, the Female Society provided relief for impoverished black and white women and managed a house of industry where mothers received food, day care assistance, and wages for spinning linen and flax. The Female Association and the Magdalen Society also distributed relief, found emergency housing, and helped needy women to secure public aid.

Graham initiated comparable services in New York. In addition to the society that she had helped to found in Edinburgh, the inspiration for the Society for the Relief of Poor Widows with Small Children (the "Widows' Society") came indirectly from her son-in-law, Divie Bethune. A wealthy Scottish émigré, Bethune was a member of the St. Andrews Society, a mutual aid association that distributed charity to Scots who had fallen on hard times. Joanna Bethune, Graham's daughter, persuaded her mother of the need for a similar service for women, giving rise to the Widows' Society in December, 1797. In the process, she helped to lay the groundwork for a parallel female empire of philanthropy to complement the growing variety of male-controlled institutions forged by men like Benjamin Franklin and Bethune.[6]

Her timing was fortuitous. Within months, the city was racked by yellow fever, leaving many "respectable, industrious women" with neither work nor food. As Graham later recalled, "house rents were going on, while every industry was at a stand." Those who could flee did so, "leaving every thing in their houses, and, on their return, found nothing remaining but naked walls." Within months, over 190 subscribers and approximately one thousand donors of one-time gifts had come forward with donations.

Graham captured the sense of emergency in a letter to a friend, confiding that "the poor increase fast: emigrants from all quarters flock to us, and when they come they must not be allowed to die for want."[7]

Many apparently did die over the following disease-laden summers, and in 1806 Joanna Bethune and a group of younger women founded the city's first orphanage. Inspired by Franklin's description of an orphan asylum at Halle (yet another example of the transatlantic scope of the emerging philanthropic culture), it was one of several children's homes that dotted the eastern seaboard after the turn of the century. In addition to Bethune's venture in New York, similar institutions appeared in Boston in 1800, Savannah, Georgia, in 1801, Norfolk, Virginia, in 1804 and Petersburg, Virginia, Fayetteville, North Carolina, Philadelphia, Baltimore, and Natchez, Mississippi, over the course of the ensuing decade.

Charleston's asylum lay at the far end of the patriarchal spectrum, serving as a harbinger of the more circumscribed roles that Southern female philanthropy would play as the century progressed. Begun as a patriotically inspired "institution of national virtue," the South Carolina orphanage was created in 1790 to house the offspring of revolutionary casualties. Backed by both public and private donations, it was run as a municipal institution under the control of a board of male appointees. Women stayed on the sidelines, accorded perfunctory roles as "lady commissioners" and donors. Unlike many of their counterparts to the north, Charleston's largest charities fell "within the political sphere, a realm reserved to men."[8]

Asylums founded after the turn of the century evinced a different pattern. In predominantly rural states such as Virginia and North Carolina, the transfer of responsibility for poor relief from church vestries (which had traditionally distributed public relief funds) to public authorities produced a variety of results. Publicly appointed overseers of the poor and county almshouses ostensibly assumed these obligations in the wake of disestablishment. In reality, North Carolinians boarded paupers with families, sold them to bidders, and encouraged private charities to take up the slack, in some instances with public funding. Thus, the Female Orphan Asylum Society of Fayetteville was officially accorded the task of caring for and apprenticing dependent children by the Cumberland County authorities in 1813. In Petersburg, one of Virginia's largest towns, the task of poor relief fell largely to women (although men assumed primary responsibility for fund-raising until 1829). Here, as in other areas, they built on almshouse precedents to create smaller, safer, more feminized asylums of their own.

For many impoverished women, incarceration in the public almshouse must have been a terrifying prospect. The poor, the debauched, children, adults, the elderly, and the insane were all crowded together in these institutions, and the deranged were often kept in cellars, cages, and cells, occasionally sharing their quarters with the aged and youngsters. Over eight hundred paupers and public charges were warehoused in New York City's poorhouse in 1798, leading Graham to confess that she was "very uneasy about our dear country."[9]

While epidemics such as the yellow fever that swept New York in 1797 created widows and orphans, urbanization went hand in hand with increasing numbers of female-headed households and female poor. For those not born of wealth, the lack of a breadwinner often meant a precipitous decline into poverty, since aside from teaching, the occupations available to women were generally among the lowest paid. Difficult on one's own, the problem was compounded if there were children, and this was an era of substantial families. Estimates place the average percentage of female-headed households in Philadelphia at approximately 15% between 1790 and 1860 (as opposed to almost 20% in 1986). And impoverished women—the majority of whom were widows—constituted the city's largest pool of welfare recipients.[10]

The relief that women's organizations were able to offer in this setting was only partial, and often far more a palliative than a solution. Indeed, their insistence on visiting each recipient to ensure "her moral character, her situation, her habits and mode of life . . . so that assistance may not be extended to the vicious and idle, when it is due only to the honest and industrious." at first glance smacks of a smug moral superiority on the part of these early charity workers.[11]

But from the trustees' perspective, these were not only valuable, but indispensable criteria. Because their funds were generally limited, solicitation far from pleasant, and the needs both great and growing, tests of morality became a guideline for choosing between one applicant and another. Moreover, public relief payments were meager, often "barely sufficient to purchase bread for a large family." The presence of a small but growing number of charities earmarked specifically for women would have enabled at least a few of the more creative widows, mothers, and unemployed laborers to knit together a minimal supply of food, clothing, rent money, and jobs. And, as the directors of these organizations continually pointed out, their charities helped to keep at least some out of the almshouse.[12]

Republicanism, Charters, and Citizenship

White women's charities also gave new meaning to the rhetoric of republicanism and widened political roles. Historians have been quick to point out that discussions about the role of republicanism in the new nation were "primarily a male discourse," emphasizing the subordination of self-interest for the public weal. Indeed, John Adams's curt dismissal of Abigail's oft-cited injunction to "remember the ladies" underscored the extent to which men of his generation ridiculed the notion that women—even literate and politically astute women—might aspire to a measure of shared responsibility in the nation they were creating. Indeed, normally liberal thinkers such as Thomas Jefferson recoiled from the "deprivation of morals" that might result from women's presence at male gatherings. Men of Jefferson's ilk believed that "women must always be excluded from public deliberations and offices," ceding the public arena to men.[13]

Abigail Adams's tart response to her husband's refusal to take her proposals for women's political parity seriously captured the tenor of annoyance that many women may have felt in being consigned to the political sidelines with such cursory nonchalance. "I can not say that I think you very generous," she wrote, "for whilst you are proclaiming peace and good will to Men . . . you insist upon retaining an absolute power over Wives. But you must remember that Arbitrary power is like most other things which are very hard, very liable to be broken—and notwithstanding all your wise Laws and Maxims we have it in our power not only to free ourselves but to subdue our Masters, and without violence throw both your natural and legal authority at our feet."[14]

One of the barriers that seemed to preclude women's participation in the public realm of republican virtue, aside from the lack of suitable outlets before 1790, was the issue of valor. In the Roman republic, which provided one of the most compelling models for the American experiment, the highest form of citizenship was giving one's life for one's country. In the words of historian Linda Kerber, the ultimate test of a man's patriotism was his "willingness and ability to risk his life for the republic; women are not part of political associations, nor do they guarantee the security of the republic by their valor; therefore . . . they can not be considered political beings."[15]

In Abigail Adams's estimation, any interest women might take in the "publick Welfare" would have to be "most Heroick." But a few women, like the directors of the Widows' Society, did manage to devise—and publicize—a genre of female valor through their charities. Their annual report in 1800 emphasized this point by underscoring the fact that "four of the Society's board, at the risk of their lives, remained in the city" during the yellow fever epidemic of 1799. This was not a casual gesture. Death from yellow fever came quickly and brutally, which is why Washington's administration decamped during the Philadelphia outbreak of this highly contagious disease in 1793. Yellow fever was endemic in New York at century's end, as were scarlet fever and smallpox. For those who tarried in the city during these disease-ravaged summers life was grim. To quote Graham, "those spared by the pestilence were ready to perish by famine." Graham and her colleagues were aware of the political significance of their gesture in legitimizing women's charities, and adamant in their insistence that it be recognized. As the society concluded in its report on the epidemic, "every candid observer must allow the extensive usefulness of this institution."[16]

A second way in which women's charities legitimized their authority by building on republican rhetoric was their use of what we would now term the nonprofit form. Although republicanism stressed the idea that commerce and virtue were incompatible, the notion of "moral capitalism" and nonprofit entrepreneurship demonstrated the ways in which income generation for public purposes could serve republican ends. Women's organizations gave these activities a new twist. Because their organizations distributed the revenues they generated to charity, rather than to their officers and subscribers—and in a few instances these revenues were fairly considerable—they underscored the extent to which their backers were "free from ... the petty interests of the marketplace," even when they engaged in commercial activities. In effect, like the concept of "moral capitalism," nonprofit organizations resolved the inherent tensions between profit making and republicanism by providing mechanisms for capital accumulation and investment that eschewed personal gain.[17]

Participation in organizations such as these gave women a modicum of financial authority and a political identity that individual married women lacked. Membership in a chartered nonprofit organization enabled wives to collectively own and alienate property, a right denied them under the English common law doctrine of *femme coverte*. Indeed, women's inability to control property was one of the primary rationales for excluding them from direct political participation, in the belief that "only men secure in their property could be virtuous." To quote historian Pauline Maier, corporate charters had the "capacity to empower individuals whose resources were unequal to their imaginations."[18]

Charters enabled organizations to "make binding rules for self-government, to function in law as a single person with the right to hold property and to sue and be sued—and so to protect its assets—and to persist after the lifetimes of its founding members." Under the commonwealth ideal, "corporations were considered 'agencies of government' . . . for the furtherance of community purposes." Attaining a charter was a political act, with each petition considered on a case-by-case basis by state legislatures. To win their charters, white women used the same right of petition that was guaranteed under the First Amendment. Although "the most primitive of political mechanisms," petitioning opened the way to public roles in the provision of municipal services.[19]

Women's use of the right to petition was itself of recent origin. According to Linda Kerber, women's petitions were "virtually unknown" before the 1770s. Their success in using this device to gain charters for their charities raises an interesting question. Much of the literature on charters stresses the contested nature of these grants. Originally, the granting of charters was by authority of the crown, and only sparingly practiced. Some colonies and cities were chartered—Massachusetts was a prime example—as well as selected eleemosynary institutions such as Harvard. The remaining examples were primarily commercial monopolies, such as the East India Company.[20]

Concerns about the use of this device flared in the new republic, coming to a flash point when Alexander Hamilton sought a federal charter for the Bank of the United States. Jefferson was adamant in his opposition to Hamilton's proposal, arguing that such a measure would be "against the laws of mortmain, . . . against the laws of alienage, . . . against the laws of Monopoly" and beyond the powers "delegated to the United States, by the Constitution." Jefferson's response has colored scholarly discussions of the granting of charters more generally with the argument that the lines dividing public and private social action, business, government, and social welfare were still so indistinctly drawn that all charters were viewed as potential monopolies and threats.[21]

Women's groups were often able to secure charters because many of their officers had ties to influential male elites. More important, they provided needed services for cash-starved and overburdened governments. In effect, they subsidized the state by cutting social service costs through their contributions of money and time. In return, female trustees won an enlarged stake in public governance and forged tangible partnerships with state and local governments even though they themselves lacked the vote. Because their help was needed, their philanthropy was not only tolerated but encouraged.

In 1802, the Society for the Relief of Poor Widows became the first chartered women's charity in New York, five years after it began operations. For Graham, it was a hard-earned vindication since, as she explained, when the organization began it had been "the jest of most, the ridicule of many, and it met the opposition of not a few. The men could not allow our sex the steadiness and perseverance necessary to establish such an undertaking."[22]

Petersburg's women justified their quest for a charter in terms of disciplining defaulting subscribers, arguing that their organization might perish unless they were empowered to "punish refractory members." Boston's women pursued their charter on the basis of their need to legally control the Female Asylum's resources. When local legislators tried to dissuade them, they held their ground, and the charter was granted in 1803. A subsequent report hinted at the difficulty of their negotiations, noting the "prejudices and obstacles which an undertaking so novel and so little understood was calculated to excite."[23]

These prejudices were occasionally echoed in the press. One editorial under the nom de plume of Curtius likened the founders' audacity to the "bold and masculine imagination of Mary Wolstoncraft," an early advocate of women's rights. In pursuing a charter, he claimed they had "far out step'd the modesty of sex," threatening "the peace of society," and "the regularity and harmony of families." It would have been far better, in Curtius's imagination, if they had stayed in their own domestic spheres, safely insulated from masculine pursuits and the direction of property. Despite such misgivings, within little more than a decade elite white women's charities held charters across the country. As the president of Newark's Female Charitable Society, Hanna Kinney, explained in 1816, it was an "age of wonders, when the liberal dare to devise liberal things, [and] applications to legislators by females to become incorporate bodies" were no longer "novelties."[24]

The success of the Isabella Grahams and Hanna Kinneys of this era symbolized the weakening ties of patriarchalism in the decades after the Revolution—an admittedly incomplete shift, but an important change nonetheless. The appearance of female-controlled charities marked a "deep change" in American society. From a vertically oriented society bound by patriarchal hierarchies of community and kin, America was becoming a land in which "mental communities" of aspiration of concern linked neighbor to neighbor in new ways. Yet how democratic was this change?[25]

The research of the past three decades has cast substantial doubt on the old egalitarian mythologies that once surrounded the Revolution. Rather than opening opportunities, it is now clear that in many areas it rigidified class lines, particularly in cities like Boston and Philadelphia. It is also clear that the pioneers who received the first crop of charters for women's charities were well connected enough to influence legislators to take their petitions seriously. In every city from Petersburg to Boston, the pattern of elite participation seems to have been the same. In Boston, for example, Sarah Bowdoin relied on her wealthy husband for help in drafting the female asylum's petition and shepherding it through the legislature. A detailed analysis of the three hundred subscribers who backed the Boston Female Asylum—a list that included Abigail Adams—reveals that only 8% were married to skilled artisans, and only 1% had spouses who reported less than $500 ($4,567 in 2000 dollars) worth of taxable property. The bulk of these backers (50%) were married to petty proprietors or merchants, with another 24% wedded to professionals. Most of these families reported incomes in the upper echelons of Boston's wealth, with 37% recording estates worth $1,000–$5,000, 25% in the $5,000–$10,000 range, and almost a third (31%) with between $10,000 and $50,000 ($91,000–$456,700 in 2000 dollars) worth of property.[26]

Some were related to leading political figures. For example, one of the founders of the Petersburg asylum, Jane Taylor, was the sister of Supreme Court justice John Marshall. Alexander Hamilton's widow played a prominent role in New York, where she helped to found the city's first private asylum and served as its "first directress" for almost thirty years, from 1821 to 1849. Women such as these would have been acutely aware of the promises and shortcomings of the Revolution, which politically bypassed them. But it is also important to remember that deference and governance were expected to go hand in hand in this "classical republic of elitist virtue." The fact that even elite white women succeeded in gaining a recognized public role without the vote, without business experience, and without direct control of property in their own right constituted a quiet revolution. And, as Graham's comments point out, it was not a battle won without sacrifices and scars.[27]

It also required some artful political maneuvering. One of the concerns that echoed through many of the first charters granted to women's groups was the fear that directors would mismanage the money, leaving their husbands legally responsible for their debts. The authors of the Widows' Society's charter felt compelled to guarantee limits on spousal responsibility by certifying that "the husband of any married woman who is or may be a Member or officer of the said Corporation, shall not be liable to the said Corporation, for any loss occasioned by the neglect or malfeasance of his wife."[28]

The charter of Philadelphia's Association for the Relief of Women and Children stipulated that the treasurer not only had to be single, but that she would have to step down from that position upon marriage. In addition, the treasurer was required to be bonded for five hundred dollars and to hand over what was in effect her security deposit to the president upon assuming office—a requirement that would have excluded all but the wealthiest candidates. Similarly, the Boston Female Asylum required its treasurer to be single and over twenty-one as a hedge against male liability.

These precautions seem all the more extraordinary when something is known of the women who initially filled these positions. The most telling example is that of the first treasurer of New York's Society for the Relief of Poor Widows with Children. Elizabeth Ann Bayley Seton was the daughter of one of the city's leading physicians and the wife of a prominent merchant. More to the point, she later founded the Sisters of Charity of St. Joseph after her husband's death and her conversion to Catholicism in 1805, which helped earn her the distinction of becoming the first American to be beatified (a preliminary step toward canonization as a saint) by the Catholic Church.

Women in Seton's position gathered and recorded dues, handed out small sums to board members for distribution to the poor, and invested the remainder in banks, stocks, land, and loans. In the case of the Female Association in Philadelphia, the treasurer was also empowered to deposit and withdraw funds from the organization's account in the Bank of the United States under the authority of her own signature. In the process, women like Seton and Graham often managed significant amounts of property, using their associations to push against the boundaries of their prescribed roles while broadening the meaning of democratic action. In a political system in which property conferred authority, these activities reinforced their political and economic standing as well.

Women Citizens, Women Entrepreneurs

As in the case of Whitefield, the women who headed the country's first female-controlled charities and asylums were quickly drawn into economic as well as quasi-governmental activities. Many became astute businesswomen, amassing funds for their endeavors from a variety of sources: subscriptions pledged over the long term in return for a voting membership in the organization, one-time donations from both women and men, state and municipal allocations (particularly in New York), investments, and income-generation projects ranging from fund-raising fairs to business ventures. By 1798, the Widows' Society counted over $1,100 from two hundred subscribers, revenues that Graham proudly attributed to a growing recognition of the organization's "usefulness" and its "respectability." A breakdown of their receipts in 1800 indicated that while the subscribers were women, male donors accounted for over half of the $1,000 in gifts, underscoring both men's superior economic power and perhaps the persuasiveness of their sisters and wives. Philadelphia's Female Association drew in double that amount, with $2,300 in memberships and another $769 in gifts from male donors.[29]

The New York Orphan Asylum was even more successful. By 1808, it had managed to pull together sufficient resources to start work on an asylum, coupling donations of land from one of its members with no-interest loans from the spouses of trustees, gleanings from charity sermons and church collections, and even a thirty-dollar donation from local schoolchildren.[30]

The directors of these organizations quickly grasped the importance of publicity for raising funds, and some of the earliest reports were clearly published with this in mind, further bolstering their credibility through institutional transparency. The officers of the Boston Female Asylum issued a separate pamphlet as well, carefully lacing their appeal with reassurances that they had been moved by charitable designs, rather than personal vanity or a desire for public recognition. Caveats such as these reveal the fine line these women had to tread, developing public programs which entailed substantial fiscal and legal responsibility while maintaining accountability and the necessary appearance of feminine modesty and diffidence to successfully carry out their initiatives.[31]

Some turned to income generation to augment their work. Joanna Bethune published a memoir of her mother's life and edited letters to raise funds for the New York Orphan Asylum in 1816, with spectacular results. Over the volume's lifetime approximately fifty thousand copies were sold domestically and abroad, figures that would constitute an outstanding run even today. Another favored fund-raising device, which may have been common in less urbanized areas, was the charity fair, where women sold homemade household goods and foodstuffs to raise funds—a form that would reach regional proportions with the abolitionist movement and the Civil War sanitary fairs. These ventures raised hundreds, and sometimes thousands, of dollars by parlaying the products of household production into hard cash, providing revenues that would assume increasing political as well as social significance over time.

Others plunged directly into business development. As noted earlier, historians have emphasized the incompatibility of liberalism's emphasis on profit making with republican injunctions against the scramble for pecuniary gain. Many women's charities in this period blended both models, pursuing profit for public ends. Two common themes that run through most if not all of these early ventures are the need for self-support, replicating a more general push to move the able-bodied poor into the wage economy that would culminate in the revised poor laws of the 1820s, and a growing concern about the need for individual independence in the new republic. Some organizations, like Philadelphia's Female Society for Assisting the Distressed, helped by giving women tools and supplies, replenishing stocks in their stores, and providing spinning wheels so they could work at home, patterns replicated by Southern women's charities as well as other areas in the North. Echoing colonial patterns, asylums put their inmates to work in the needle trades in order to provide rudimentary training in what the managers deemed marketable skills while generating institutional and charitable revenues.

The Widows' Society was concerned with problems of employment and employability from the outset, noting that landlords were "clamorous for their rent" while "complaint of the want of employment [was] universal." Faced with this dilemma, Graham, too, began to buy and distribute cloth to the society's recipients. By 1798, she reported that "above three hundred" women had been paid to make shirts from nearly three thousand yards of fabric, providing work for "widows who could not find employment elsewhere."[32]

One of the most ambitious early business ventures was started by Graham's daughter, who opened a house of industry during the economic depression that followed Jefferson's embargo and the War of 1812. New York was particularly hard hit, with food, fuel, and clothing prices nearly doubling as the hostilities increased. By 1813, the Widows' Society reported that "it is an impossibility for a widow, with the labour of her own hands," to support her family. While the society worked to "keep them from sinking," Bethune leveraged $500 ($4,550) from the municipal authorities to set up a house of industry, providing work for almost six hundred seamstresses. She also successfully competed for, and fulfilled, a contract with the government to supply a navy frigate with clothing and bedding and continued to submit bids for the production of naval uniforms at war's end. Although these numbers may seem minuscule compared to the extent of the need, it was a substantial operation, particularly when it is considered that the entire roster of federal employees in Washington (exclusive of Congress and the military but including everyone else "from President to

door-keeper") numbered only 153 in 1800, and some of the country's largest textile mills numbered less than one-third as many employees.[33]

Sometimes women's charities received municipal contracts for products. On other occasions, they were given outright donations. Municipal
grants to private charities acknowledged the role of these institutions in
lessening the burdens on public finances and in reducing almshouse populations. Although women's charities received public allocations in several
cities, including Philadelphia, Baltimore, and New Orleans, and even in
rural North Carolina, New York City was the most generous by a considerable margin. In a continuation of the liberal practices begun under Dutch
and English colonial rule, New York City and State epitomized the post-
revolutionary reliance on partnerships between government and voluntary
associations. Women's groups, ethnic groups, African Americans, mechanics, Catholics, and other religious denominations received public land,
housing, and funds for their charitable and educational work in the early
nineteenth century, giving a wide variety of constituencies a direct role in
the allocation of municipal resources and services.[34]

The year after the Widows' Society received its charter, the state authorized a $15,000 (@ $137,010 in 2000 dollars) lottery for it. Five years later,
in 1808, an outright grant of $5,000 ($45,500) was set aside for Bethune's
orphan asylum, followed by annual appropriations of $500 beginning in
1811. By 1828 the society managed to draw on the common school fund as
well for its educational work. Similarly, the Female Assistance Society began to receive donations of several hundreds of dollars for its work with
impoverished women and children in 1815, as did the Association for the
Relief of Respectable, Aged, and Indigent Females the following year.

In addition to generating revenues, women's organizations also invested them. The founders of Boston's Female Asylum clearly had this
object in mind when they stated that they sought their charter, in part,
to protect the asylum's investments. By 1810 they had amassed $10,000
($91,000) in real property—including two bequests from former mem-
bers—and another $13,000 ($118,300) in donated funds, portions of
which had been invested and were producing interest. According to one
source, by the 1830s the asylum had invested over $45,000 ($589,500) in
the Massachusetts Hospital Life Insurance Company, indirectly helping to
finance New England's nascent industrial revolution.[35]

The Widows' Society was able to save enough to have $2,500 ($22,500)
left over for investment by 1802, while the founders of Philadelphia's
Female Association vowed to set aside 20% of their annual revenues for investment in "public stock or other improvable property." Moreover, be-

cause their institutions received subscriptions and donations, they served as magnets for liquid cash in a cash-scarce economy, increasing their importance as investors. Aside from loans, most surplus funds were invested in slaves or real estate in the revolutionary era. This began to change as the growing availability of government securities and bank stocks unleashed a "rage of speculation" in the 1790s. Afterward, many nonprofit organizations—including women's groups—began to place increasing amounts of their holdings in stocks, rather than land, a practice that provided relatively safe and accessible funds to use as needed in their work. Government bonds appealed to female nonprofit managers because they were safe and they yielded high, reliable dividends, often running between 5% and 8%, providing readily available income without the problems of having to contend with defaulting tenants and building repairs. While some of the Philadelphia organizations chose to invest their funds in banks, particularly the Bank of the United States, the New Yorkers who ran the Widows' Society preferred a diversified portfolio of insurance funds, mortgage rents, and Manhattan Company stock. And some organizations, like the Widows' Society, Philadelphia's Society for the Relief and Employment of the Poor, and Charleston's Benevolent Female Society, placed a portion of their portfolios in individual loans, drawing women into an economic sphere previously reserved for male businessmen, bankers, and planters.[36]

In addition to becoming investors in their own right, the women who ran these institutions wielded an unprecedented amount of legal authority over their charges. In 1809, for example, the directors of the New York Orphan Asylum were granted the same power to apprentice children as the commissioners who ran the city's almshouse. Boston's asylum directors not only used this power themselves; they invited members from any town outside Boston with twenty or more subscribers to place children under the asylum's auspices. The directors also gained the right to sign legally binding contracts (as evidenced in their ability to sign indentures), and to obtain legal releases from parents for the guardianship of their children. For women such as these, profitability as well as property bolstered their roles as citizens in the new republic.[37]

Sympathy and Social Control

In the eyes of some contemporary scholars, ventures such as these resonated with a desire for social control. To quote John Alexander, the post-revolutionary years witnessed "the increasing effort to use privately funded

philanthropy as an instrument of social engineering." Charity, by this interpretation, was the product of "a desire to control or mold the needy in
the image of the worthy poor." Clearly, most charities made a distinction
between the "worthy" and "unworthy" poor. The Widows' Society's guidelines, for example, specifically excluded aid to women who were deemed
immoral, who sold "spirituous liquors," or who were "seen begging publicly." However, this is hardly surprising, since, to quote Linda Kerber,
"Traditional republicanism . . . had assumed that deference was the glue of
society." Indeed, by trying to discourage dissipation and begging, many of
these women doubtless felt that they were helping to secure the future
of the republic.[38]

Many of the women who participated in the Widows' Society and the
New York Orphan Asylum had experienced the precariousness of life firsthand. Within a three-year period, Seton's husband went bankrupt, her father died of yellow fever, and she was widowed, forcing her to open a
school to support her five children. Elizabeth Hamilton lost both her husband and her son to duels between 1801 and 1804. Despite his prominence,
her husband's death left her almost penniless. When her house was sold at
public auction in 1805, she was able to reclaim it only with help of friends.
Graham, too, had felt the sting of poverty and rapid downward mobility
after her husband's death, experiences that doubtless galvanized her decision to aid "any poor widows, of fair character, having two children under
ten years of age." As first directress, Graham took it upon herself to visit
each of the society's hundreds of recipients at least once a year.[39]

"WIDOW is a word of sorrow, in the best of circumstances, but a Widow
left poor, destitute, friendless, surrounded with a number of small Children . . . her situation is neither to be described nor conceived!" noted the
society's report for 1800. Was this simply boilerplate, a sentimentalized appeal to elicit public sympathy and cash? Some of the society's language
might seem to suggest this, or at least an unduly censorious attitude toward the poor, as when it announced that "almost every class of mechanics live not only plentifully, but luxuriously; an evil too general to be cured.
Our poor widows have been partners in the evil, and now sustain the whole
of the punishment. They must now learn economy from adversity, and to
their credit be it spoken they do."[40]

Some, the society's spokespersons admitted, might view this fall from
security as due punishment for their sins. "But God forgives," they continued, "and so ought we: We, who have so much to be forgiven, yet have our
necessaries, our comforts, and even our luxuries spared." Graham elabo-
rated on these themes in an address to the society. "To us, our comfortable

dwellings, cheerful fires, convivial parties, give winter its charms." But to the recently widowed, "the approach of winter is the approach of death," with no one to talk to, "every avenue of hope ... shut," and only "the wants of her children [to] urge her to exertion for their support."[41]

In later decades, descriptions such as these, like the charities they were written to support, would become formulaic. But for women like Graham, Hamilton, and Seton—the women who risked public scorn and pestilent summers for services that few even agreed was necessary or valid—some of their work must have brought a shock of recognition. Graham bitterly recalled her own sense of isolation after her husband's death, as former "intimates, some of whom had esteemed [her] friendship and honor" withdrew, and "relations, afraid of being entangled in our difficulties, kept a distance." While the desire to control their neighbor's habits may have motivated many of these women, they clearly had other reasons for their work as well, reasons that merit recognition. A desire to foster economic independence—as well as moral deference—lay at the heart of most of these endeavors, blending the older prerogatives of station and class with a new push to empower women as viable economic actors in their own right.[42]

The work of innovators like Graham and Bethune represented a feminized version of republicanism that has long been overlooked. The charities developed by white women of the upper and middling classes in the 1790s and early 1800s gave substance and form to the notions of benevolence celebrated by the statesmen of the revolutionary generation. Women's charities placed a new emphasis on female independence, fostering self-support among their clients and redefining their backers' political, legal, and economic roles in the larger society. Use of the nonprofit form ensured that even their most commercial ventures—and many were pointedly commercial from the outset—would remain aloof from the pursuit of individual gain. And the trustees' commitment to public service, even at personal risk, documented the capacity for feminine valor in the public realm. Charters made women—even wives—property holders, and with property came political visibility. Collectively, under the mantle of charity and public service, these elite white women gained the rights they lost in marriage, as well as the right to request and receive public funds. Public support brought them into the governmental sphere, providing recognition and legitimacy for their work. And the educational and charitable services that they created addressed republican concerns about popular virtue and the need for an independent, enlightened citizenry, recasting the concept of republican motherhood in tangible, institutional form.

Although religious imperatives would unleash an avalanche of women's organizational activity after the turn of the century, these first charities were secular in tenor, placing women's and children's issues on the
public agenda for the first time. They also redefined notions about the
ways in which private citizens would serve the state. Women's charities
amplified the ethos of egalitarianism, providing a stage on which women,
as well as men, might appear as collective participants in public governance. Although exiled from the rarified world of electoral office, women
like Isabella Graham nonetheless made their presence known, ushering in
a new, more inclusive definition of American democracy than the nation's
revolutionary leaders had been willing to conceive of, or concede.

3

The Legacy of Disestablishment

White women's philanthropy was born of the Revolution, but it matured in the church. Although many historians have noted the role of Protestant revivals in fostering widespread social reform in the country's youth, far less attention has been paid to Catholic and Jewish activities. While the Protestant Benevolent Empire laced the country with Bible, tract, and missionary societies, creating networks for social mobilization that reached into hundreds of communities across the republic, other religious traditions left a distinctive imprint on civil society as well. Protestantism, Judaism, and Catholicism each had a share in shaping American philanthropy and civil society over the first three decades of the nineteenth century, developments illustrated by the careers of women such as Isabella Graham, Rebecca Gratz, and Elizabeth Seton.[1]

Protestantism

Protestantism—especially evangelical Protestantism—was the single most important factor in the growth and elaboration of American philanthropy during the early national period, not only because it had the greatest number of adherents, but because of the ways in which it encouraged church members to structure their public lives. It was fueled by the Second Great Awakening, the rush of religious enthusiasm that began in the

1790s and peaked in the 1830s, and the Benevolent Empire, a cluster of national Bible, Sunday school, tract, and social reform organizations that emerged in the second decade of the nineteenth century. Together, they drew growing numbers of Americans into the associational sphere.[2]

Earlier studies of the country's first Bible, tract, and Sunday school societies have often stressed their conservatism, focusing on the wealthy, well-placed male elites who ran their national headquarters. However useful these studies may have been in "unmasking" the directors' desire for social control, they ultimately depicted only a fraction of the organizations' activities. Beyond the headquarter offices sprawled a vast and growing empire for reform, with auxiliaries that spread across the nation's cities, counties, hamlets, and towns. While some historians have painted these activities as "quintessentially bourgeois," others have argued that the phenomenal growth of evangelical sects stemmed precisely from their ability to reach the poor, the self-educated, and the marginal through revivals and publications that challenged earlier elite monopolies on information, authority, and doctrinal interpretation. And much of the backing for these proselytizing efforts came from female volunteers.[3]

Voluntarism lay at the heart of the Benevolent Empire, and female parishioners had a vital place in these activities, raising funds and often providing the services themselves. Sunday schools are a case in point. Isabella Graham and her daughter, Joanna Bethune, pioneered in transplanting the Sunday school movement from Scotland to the United States. The founder of the nation's first Sunday school remains a contested issue. The movement itself began in Edinburgh in the 1790s. Although the first American Sunday school may have actually been created by Benjamin Rush in Philadelphia based on information elicited from Divie Bethune, Joanna's husband, Graham's school was a close second, opening in New York in 1792. Beginning with informal evening classes, Graham and her daughter expanded their activities to include public asylums as well as churches and schools, teaching "reading, writing and religion" to children and adults. By the 1820s, their Female Union for the Promotion of Sunday Schools numbered almost eight thousand students.[4]

America proved a hospitable environment for these endeavors. By 1829, over 40% of all the children in New York were enrolled in Sunday schools, more than double the number that attended the city's public educational institutions. In Philadelphia the ratio was lower but still impressive, accounting for approximately one-third of the city's children at mid-decade. Nationally, estimates placed the number of students in the Sunday schools at fifty thousand in 1825; five years later that number had increased nearly sevenfold.[5]

Middle-class laywomen organized many of these classes, volunteering to teach reading, writing, and Bible studies. By the time the American Sunday School Union issued its second report in 1826, Sunday schools were operating in every state. Not surprisingly, representation from the rural cotton belt was thin in comparison to the membership in the Northeast, but still, Georgia enrolled one auxiliary and fourteen schools in the national society's first year, Alabama accounted for another four schools and an auxiliary, Mississippi and Tennessee provided three schools each, and Charleston's twenty-nine schools numbered almost two thousand students. Although the percentage of female teachers was lower in the South, as Cynthia Kierner points out, "Southern women played a crucial role" in the Sunday school movement, founding and managing schools in both urban and rural areas. Every state developed Sunday schools—even in the South—most of which dated from the second decade of the nineteenth century. Moreover, some states provided public as well as private support for these endeavors. Richmond's school commissioners allocated thirty cents per pupil in 1824, plus additional funding for books and supplies. Similarly, Delaware allocated twenty cents for each white student in 1821, accounting for one-third of the operating costs. By providing educational as well as charitable services, the women who created and staffed these institutions carried public-private collaboration into the religious realm.[6]

Their efforts fostered a notable upsurge in national literacy rates. In 1780, only about 50% of the women in New England could read and write; by 1840, almost all could. In an era when comprehensive, compulsory public education was still in the future for most states, Sunday schools fueled the democratization of basic education in tandem with several other organizations that constituted the Benevolent Empire. By 1830, the annual budget of the American Sunday School Union exceeded $70,000 ($917,000 in 2000 dollars), approximately $60,000 of which was funneled into publications. Increased literacy went hand in hand with literary production. More than a million pieces of reading material were produced during the union's first year of operation alone, ranging from primers to hymnals.[7]

At one level, these activities represented the growing financial and social power of religiously oriented associations. But these statistics hold a deeper, more profound meaning not just for women's activities, but for the growth of civil society. Religious disestablishment and the Second Great Awakening brought a new kind of Christianity to the fore. While Anglicans clung to their liturgy and rituals, and orthodox Congregationalism retained a stern emphasis on predestination, disestablishment cleared the way for more vigorous proselytizing by evangelical sects: Baptists, Methodists, Presbyterians, and non-Calvinistic Congregationalists. Unlike many of their predecessors, these sects emphasized the power of individual conversion, grace, and human perfectibility. For them, the ability to read the Bible oneself was the basis of the religious experience. In lieu of learned texts and medieval rituals, they promoted an accessible version of revealed religion. And the key to that religious experience was literacy.

Evangelicalism was the primary impetus for the rapid spread of Bible and tract societies. It was the driving force behind Sunday schools. Its popularity also provides the key to understanding the impact of Protestantism in promoting the development of civil society in the United States after 1800. The ability to read brought with it the ability to transmit ideas, to correspond with like-minded groups, to argue one's case in print as well as in person. And that ability sparked an avalanche of organizational activity that both fed and was nurtured by the spread of evangelical Christianity. White women provided the bulk of its converts and funds for its expansion, and as they were schooled in the Bible, they taught others to read as part of their religious duty.

Evangelical injunctions to go out and save the world provided another stimulus to organizational elaboration and reform. The doctrines of immediate grace and human perfectibility were deeply empowering, giving female converts as much of a stake in defining and acting upon social ills as men. Christianity became "a liberating force; [as] people were given the right to think and act for themselves rather than depending on the mediations of an educated elite," trends which increasingly led Protestant laywomen into advocacy and social reform by the 1830s.[8]

Disestablishment gave their activities an economic slant as well. During the colonial era, appointment to a ministerial post in one of the established churches was usually regarded as a sinecure. Unless the candidate subsequently exhibited some form of extremely antisocial behavior, he could expect to hold what was essentially a tenured position, supported by public funds. This situation changed dramatically when the churches were severed from public support. As ministerial appointments were transformed from public offices to professional positions, candidates became dependent on the good will of the congregations that donated their salaries. And, as women increasingly filled the pews, they also inherited much of the responsibility for raising funds, which in turn bolstered their authority.[9]

Both black and white women assumed responsibility for supporting capital improvements and church-related social services, including charitable relief. Often, these activities constituted a reciprocal relationship, an "economic bond" between female parishioners and their churches. After a lifetime spent ministering to the community's religious and social needs, elderly female volunteers could expect "rent money, food, fuel and medicine" from their fellow parishioners if needed, providing a primitive form of social security in return for good works.[10]

Fund-raising was particularly important. In addition to serving the needs of their immediate congregations, Protestant women developed a host of cent, mite, missionary, tract, and Bible societies during the first quarter of the nineteenth century. These ventures represented "a new kind of religious institution," in which private individuals voluntarily pooled their funds to promote missionary and benevolent aims, independent of direct state or ecclesiastical control. Initially, many drew their strength from lingering republican concerns about the need for a virtuous citizenry to safeguard the future of the state. Later, revivalism helped to fuel their development. The advent of these fund-raising networks marked a subtle transition from the charities founded by women like Graham in the 1790s, drawing women still further into market relations by focusing *primarily* on income generation, rather than charitable ends.[11]

By the second decade of the nineteenth century, the movement to create fund-raising auxiliaries gathered momentum, accounting for over one thousand organizations in New England alone. Nor was this solely a Northeastern phenomenon. During the early national period, Southern white women, "like their northern contemporaries, established an impressive array of prayer groups, Sabbath schools, and religious and benevolent associations." These institutions also played an important economic role. Scholars have had an ongoing fascination with the relationship among Protestantism, capitalism, and humanitarianism over the past century, an interest kindled by the work of Max Weber. Usually, their explanations hinge on values: injunctions to follow one's calling (Weber's interpretation), or to adhere to contracts and the consequences of one's actions (as Thomas Haskell has argued). The missing element in these equations is the very concrete, very direct bond between giving and economic activity. As the women of Graham's generation well knew, philanthropy, finances, and public governance were often intimately linked.[12]

This in turn had important economic consequences. A number of lively historical debates have recently flared over the timing of the nation's transition to capitalism and the epicenter of the change. Clearly, the Revolu-

tion paved the way for "the emergence of a new system of economic behavior, values and institutions." Winifred Rothenberg traces the inception
of the transition to the 1780s, while others cite varying dates between 1750
and 1820. Although the dates are imprecise, most agree that "somewhere,
somehow, something dramatic happened in the minds of many Americans: they began to seek gain through capitalistic enterprise." Analyses of
the underlying causes and consequences of this social transformation have
in turn pitted "market historians," who view this as a purely structural
process, against Marxist historians, who regard it as the product of class
struggles "fraught with conflict and violence."[13]

Few, however, have examined the role of philanthropy—including
Protestant women's philanthropy—in fostering the accumulation, investment, and liquefication of capital in a cash-scarce economy and hastening
the country's steady drift toward capitalism after the turn of the century.
Bible societies exemplify these trends. Beginning with the creation of the
country's first Bible society in 1808, associational efforts to distribute the
Scriptures proceeded on a continually widening scale. Many of these early
institutions were run by women. At least fifteen female Bible societies
emerged between 1808 and the founding of the American Bible Society
(ABS) in 1816, primarily in the Northern and Middle Atlantic states and
the upper South. Within a year, eighteen female Bible groups signed on as
ABS charter members, numbers that continued to rise. While auxiliaries
in the field raised funds and sold and donated Bibles, the national organization coordinated their efforts from its headquarters in New York under
the management of a prominent group of male political, professional, and
economic elites that included (among others) the secretary of state, John
Quincy Adams, and Governor De Witt Clinton of New York.

It was an ambitious venture, planned on national dimensions and held
together by a growing staff of full-time agents. By 1828, hundreds of auxiliaries were operating nationwide, including chapters in every state,
North and South. Although scholars such as Elizabeth Fox-Genovese have
painted the rural South as a region nearly devoid of women's voluntary associations, the records of the ABS present a different picture. Many Southern white women created auxiliaries during the society's first decade.
Nashville had a Female Bible and Charitable Society by 1817 (although
the male parishioners subsequently staged a coup, co-opting the society's
management in 1823), and Virginia also had a substantial number of female Bible, tract, and missionary societies by 1820. Women's auxiliaries
were particularly active in seaport cities such as Charleston, where a chapter was founded in 1816, but they were active in rural counties as well. Un-

like their Northern counterparts, which tended to concentrate on a single mission, many of the Southern chapters combined a variety of aims, from Bible and tract distribution to Sunday schools and visiting programs for the sick poor. The further one traveled into the hinterland, the more heterogeneous their mandates became.

A second difference was structural. While women regularly served in official capacities—particularly as the corresponding secretaries named in the ABS's annual reports—Southern women were far less likely to play a comparable role outside the major cities. Jean Friedman provides some intriguing insights into why this might have been the case. While Northern middle-class white women tended to form single-sex, or "separatist," organizations for charity and reform, their rural Southern counterparts gravitated toward mixed-sex organizations instead, a trend Friedman links to the predominant role played by kinship ties in the organization of Southern communities. Friedman argues that this factor, more than any other, may account for the lack of Southern female social reform movements in the antebellum years. As a result, women who worked through county chapters and those affiliated with rural Southern churches tended to be less independent, consigned to auxiliary roles under the patriarchal guidance of male managers and trustees, patterns that reflected the broader social arrangements of the slaveholding South. Literacy may have played a role as well. According to James Oakes, illiteracy rates were "four times as common among slaveholding women as among men of the same class," which may have further limited their capacity for independent action. These patterns also heralded growing disparities in regional philanthropy, with Southern organizations firmly implanted under the supervision of white males at a time when Northern groups were becoming increasingly independent and diverse.[14]

Like many associations, the ABS subsisted on a mixed economy of donations, investments, and earned income, in which sales revenues played a major role. In 1824, for example, sales accounted for 50% of the Society's nearly $50,000 in revenues. The scale of these operations becomes far more impressive when the current dollars of 1824 are converted into constant dollars for the year 2000, which increases the figure to approximately $550,000. Two years later, the trustees approvingly noted that almost 450,000 Bibles had been distributed over the Society's first decade. That the ABS was a relatively young organization held together by handwritten correspondence and goods delivered over transportation routes that were often primitive at best makes the scale of their operations all the more remarkable. Moreover, women were active in both gathering donations and generating sales. Many chapters regularly canvased their cities for donors and customers, and a few, such as the Boston Female Bible Society, even invested part of their earnings in "perpetual loans" to the headquarters in New York, receiving the interest in Bibles.[15]

Rather than distributing materials gratis, ABS auxiliaries were urged to sell the Scriptures at or slightly above cost, efforts that drew ABS members directly into market activities. By the 1820s, the headquarters society had hammered out a set of guidelines to regularize its distribution policies. Free Bibles were approved for the destitute, particularly in frontier regions "where their remoteness from the market renders money exceedingly scarce," but all other volumes were to be sold. Chapters were urged to become self-supporting, to avoid risky investments, and not to expect the parent society to "make gratuitous appropriations of books, however much they may be called for." Shipments were sent on credit, but auxiliaries were strongly encouraged to collect the money "as far as possible, at the time of purchase." In effect, the trustees devoted a great deal of time and effort to systematizing the society's business procedures and instructing auxiliaries in business techniques.[16]

Women, as well as men, participated in these transactions. New York's female auxiliary consistently led the list for economic returns from both donations and sales. In 1829, for example, they generated $2,584 (approximately $34,000 in 2000 dollars) in donations and $7,768 ($101,760) in receipts. Neither gender nor geography seems to have impeded the members' willingness to engage in commercial transactions. The Charleston Female Bible Society's 1829 contributions amounted to $492 ($6,445) in donations and $358 ($4,689) in revenues from sales. Surprisingly, many Southern women seem to have enthusiastically embraced the task of religious marketing.[17]

In gathering substantial amounts of cash from donations and sales, the ABS and its auxiliaries also played a role in the liquefication of capital. Auxiliaries were urged to avoid noncash transactions, a policy that sometimes seemed impossible to enforce, much to the trustees' dismay. In-kind transactions of produce were particularly annoying, since vegetables and grains had a nasty habit of rotting before they reached local markets for sale. Counterfeit bank bills were also a persistent problem, as was the worthless currency of failed banks.

By systematizing trade on a national scale, organizations like the ABS turned their auxiliaries into apostles of market values. This in turn has important implications for our understanding of the extent to which market values were resisted or welcomed as they penetrated the hinterland. Although some scholars have argued that "evangelical preachers were hardly conscious cheerleaders for a market society," the evidence from the ABS suggests that evangelical churches played a significant role in promoting market values. Rather than resisting the onset of capitalism, Bible societies encouraged parishioners to bring the market into their local communities, enlisting women and men, ministers and the laity in spreading the market revolution.[18]

White women may have had particular incentives to participate in this bloodless coup. Although the patriarchal household may have been a miniature Eden of independence for the men who headed them, it could be a Gethsemene for their wives. Young farm wives were often constantly pregnant or nursing. Even then, they were expected to care for the children, the poultry, and the dairy animals, take care of all the domestic chores, and produce textiles and other household goods. Particularly in the rural South, white men's control over the labor of their daughters and wives ensured that "nothing was purchased that could be produced at home, whatever the cost in labor and sweat." Within this setting, women and children played decidedly subordinate roles, and many may have welcomed the incursions of marketization that promised liberation from "the backbreaking toil connected with subsistence."[19]

Participation in market transactions, however modest, chipped away at patriarchal rule. Husbands who legally owned their wives' earnings lost that privilege when the funds were generated through associational activities that enabled their wives to collectively control, invest, and even loan funds themselves. Moreover, benevolent women assumed identifiable independent public personae in their communities and churches. This in turn signified a subtle shift in domestic power relationships, as female parishioners became economic actors in their own right. Although the effect may have been muffled by heterosocial organizational arrangements in the rural South, in other areas of the country laywomen headed local auxiliaries and received recognition, by name, in national publications. Given these trends, it is increasingly difficult to argue, as some have, that "Like . . . the new women's consciousness, every popular cultural or political movement in the early republic arose originally against the market."[20]

Consumers played a role in this scenario as well. As Timothy Breen points out, by the late eighteenth century, "consumer demand was the driving engine of economic change." The desire to acquire a Bible provided an incentive for even the most isolated yeoman household to engage in making at least a few marketable commodities to generate cash. Beginning in the 1750s, farm women led the movement into market relations in many areas, producing textiles, dairy products, and other household goods for cash sales. They also led the procession into the church, dominating the rosters of "virtually all known New England congregations" as early as the 1720s, a trend accelerated by antebellum revivals and echoed in the South. The spread of organizations like the ABS doubtless provided added incentives for religious laywomen to generate cash to purchase Bibles and to enhance their own status within their parishes by making donations.[21]

Building on these trends, evangelical organizations such as the ABS, the American Tract Society, and the American Sunday School Union pioneered in the development of national marketing techniques. Many businesses were beginning to develop integrated markets in the 1820s and 1830s, but for most "the ties were still fragile." Credit rather than cash transactions undergirded the movement of most commercial goods from manufacturers to far-flung stores. But the extension of credit to strangers often entailed significant risks. Organizations such as the ABS enjoyed an advantage over commercial ventures in this respect. Because the society generally worked through churches and parishioners, the problems of credit and collections could be handled through local congregations. Prompt payment was tied to individual morality and one's standing within the community, making debts easier to monitor and collect. This national religious infrastructure afforded other resources as well, including an excellent means of conducting market research. In 1825, for example, ABS auxiliaries were encouraged to do house-by-house Bible censuses in their communities, providing valuable information on consumer supplies and demand.[22]

Because its Bible empire was built on the church, the ABS was able to take a lead in forging national marketing networks and techniques, providing the template for major commercial ventures such as Lewis Tappan's Mercantile Agency, a credit-rating firm that was the precursor of Dun and Bradstreet. The son of a store owner in Northampton, Massachusetts, Tappan and his brother, Arthur, headed a lucrative silk business in New York. Early in his career, he helped to raise funds for local asylums, made donations to Massachusetts General Hospital, and helped to start the Boston Provident Association. By the 1820s, he was giving thousands of dollars to the American Tract Society, the American Bible Society, and the American Sunday School Union, and he and his brother quickly became major backers of the American Antislavery Society as well. He turned the contacts he forged in his benevolent work into financial capital with the creation of the Mercantile Agency in 1841. As one historian explains, "an economy dominated by agriculture and chronically short of capital depended upon the extension of credit," which was usually given on the basis of kinship ties or religious alliances. As trade spread beyond range of these face-to-face alliances, new ways of determining creditworthiness became vital, particularly for merchants like Tappan. His solution was to establish a Northern network of local lawyers, churchmen, and clergymen who wrote regular reports on the habits and creditworthiness of local merchants. Subscribers to the service were able to make use of these reports to determine who would—and would not—be a viable credit risk, heping to pave the way for the expansion of the market economy.[23]

Protestant parishioners also raised funds for a variety of other local and national religious endeavors. The need to generate funding was relentlessly drummed home to girls as well as women after the turn of the century. The New Hampshire Cent Institution is a case in point. Founded in 1811, it was designed to collect donations for frontier missionary work while instilling habits of giving early on. "Where is the little Female that will not join us?" it promoters unctuously oozed. Upon joining, children were asked to subscribe a penny a week, with impressive results. In 1814, these young subscribers sent $200 (@ $2,000 in 2000 dollars) into the coffers of the New Hampshire Bible Society, provided another $140 (@ $1,400) for the purchase of tracts and books, and forwarded the handsome sum of $300 (@ $3,000) for missionary endeavors. Almost $700 (@ $7,000) was contributed in all, a considerable amount for that era.[24]

Lest the key lesson be lost in all of this, the society's promoters emphasized the extent to which significant social benefits could be gleaned from "a systematic plan of charity. Let the contribution be ever so small in itself . . . when it is reduced to a system, it becomes general, and produces a very important result." Even the tiniest sums, when regularly pooled, produced sizable amounts of liquid capital for underwriting ecclesiastical ventures, providing the driving engine for American giving during the nation's youth.[25]

Some of this money helped to bolster religious revivals. While the Cent Society was acquiring its $700 nest egg in New Hampshire, fund-raising auxiliaries were spreading into upstate New York. These organizations became way stations on an evangelical highway that ultimately spanned the region, providing a "central nervous system" for the coordination of revival activities. By 1824, Oneida's auxiliaries were contributing over $1,000 per year for missionary work, including $192 (@ $2,300) for an unknown but gifted young revivalist, Charles Grandison Finney. These early religious endeavors cut across class lines (at least in the smaller towns), bringing women together from a variety of backgrounds. The Oneida Female

Missionary Society attracted a roughly equal mix of professionals', merchants', and artisans' wives. Similarly, the town's maternal association included the spouses of lawyers and artisans, merchants and printers. United by mission rather than class, these groups raised funds for both local and national initiatives.[26]

In the process, female backers financed the development of a variety of male institutions and endeavors, from seminaries and the provision of theological scholarships, to printing and publishing concerns and domestic and international missionary work. Many of the forty thousand Protestant ministers who filled the nation's pulpits in 1845 owed their positions—and their careers—to female supporters. It was a reciprocal relationship. Because laywomen played an important role in maintaining American Protestantism at both the local and national levels, their public activities as volunteers, donors, and fund-raisers held an indispensable place in fostering the growth of the church. As a result, women's participation in a wide array of church-related associational efforts was not only condoned, but actively encouraged by both the clergy and prominent laymen, helping to draw growing numbers of women into the public sphere and small-scale market activities after the beginning of the nineteenth century.

This, then, was the Protestant legacy of disestablishment: (1) women's increasing visibility, numbers, and power within a geometrically expanding array of congregations; (2) their central economic role in these developments; (3) a ministerial profession uniquely dependent on their fundraising capacities and good will; and (4) the growing predominance of a cluster of doctrines that stressed literacy, charity, and advocacy—all of which encouraged evangelical laywomen to assume enhanced public roles. In the process, American Protestantism opened expanding opportunities for service provision and social advocacy, charity, and social reform—and a steadily proliferating universe of philanthropic initiatives.

Judaism

Both Judaism and Christianity stressed the need to give and volunteer: Christianity in the form of tithing and the biblical example of the Good Samaritan; Judaism in the ancient notions of *tsdakah*, or "justice," in rendering charity and to service to others within the community, and *gemilut chasidim (or chesed)*, "loving kindness" born of compassion and voluntary contributions beyond one's normal sense of duty. Passages in the Old Testament urged the godly to give "readily and have no regrets when you do so, for in return the Lord your God will bless you in all your efforts and in

all your undertakings." But unlike evangelical Protestantism, the emphasis on communal obligations set nineteenth-century Jewish charities on a
more inward-turning path, one more focused on communal needs than on
social reform.[27]

Egalitarian notions and disestablishment had a discernible impact on
American Judaism in at least two respects. The first was to remove the constraints that historically held Jewish communities together. There were no
Jewish ghettos in antebellum America, no artificial legal boundaries to
force Jews to remain in segregated clusters, no pale to separate them from
the rest of the community. Nor did their religious institutions have the
same centrality in maintaining order and solidarity as they had had in the
Old World. In the United States, membership was voluntary and volitional. The end result, to quote sociologist Daniel Elazar, was "the breakdown of the corporate structure of Jewish life which had sustained Jewish
law for over two thousand years."[28]

Charleston, Philadelphia, and New York all had small, identifiable
Jewish communities by the 1820s. Philadelphia's Jewish population, for
example, numbered about five hundred. Jewish settlements in most other
towns remained too small to support a formal synagogue during the early
national and antebellum years. As a result, voluntary associations often
preceded—and sometimes substituted for—formal religious congregations. Burial societies were usually the first to appear. Although most, if
not all, immigrant groups developed ethnic mutual aid associations in the
colonies and the new republic, Jewish burial societies were a uniquely traditional associational form harkening back to the Old World. Initially designed to carry out prescribed ritual functions for tending the dead, they
gradually added a variety of corollary functions, such as the care and burial of strangers. Some also provided loans to Jewish businessmen, helping
to bolster the economic resources of their communities. Even in areas
without synagogues, therefore, these early associations provided a focus for
communal activity and the preservation of religious life.[29]

The first formally incorporated Jewish organization was the Hebrew
Orphan Asylum, founded in Charleston in 1801. A receiving point for
Sephardic refugees since the end of the seventeenth century, Charleston
contained the nation's largest Jewish settlement at the time of the Revolution. Following what appears to have been the prevailing pattern in that
city, the asylum was founded and managed by men, rather than women.
Like the early burial societies, it combined a variety of aims, from "reliev-
ing widows" and "educating, clothing and maintaining orphans and the
children of indigent parents," to inculcating habits of "piety, morality and

industry" among its charges. Later initiatives, such as the Society for the Education of Poor Children and the Relief of Indigent Persons of the Jewish Persuasion, founded in New York in the 1820s, echoed these agendas, mixing aid for members' widows and orphans with educational activities and charity for other indigent Jews.[30]

Philadelphia's Hebrew Society for the Visitation of the Sick sought to enforce religious conformity as well as distributing aid. Members paid an admission fee and twenty-five cents in monthly dues, which were invested to provide charitable funds and health and burial benefits for members. Like many American mutual aid groups, the Philadelphia society adopted moralistic criteria to exclude unsuitable members, adding a distinctive twist by declaring that "any member marrying contrary to the Hebrew laws, or behaving immorally shall be expelled." By shaping their programs around Jewish custom and law, these associations maintained Jewish communal practices in a secular world.[31]

Jewish elites in the seacoast cities often collaborated with Protestants in charitable endeavors as well, including Rebecca Gratz, her mother and her sisters. Although Gratz's continuing participation in the Philadelphia Orphan Asylum might be construed as a sign of her assimilation into the mainstream Protestant culture, the causes she subsequently embraced illustrate her growing interest in Jewish communalism. Nonetheless, Protestant culture left a mark on Gratz's career. A woman renowned for both her beauty and her wit (she ostensibly served as the model for the heroine of Sir Walter Scott's *Ivanhoe*), she attracted a wide circle of acquaintances and friends from among Philadelphia's elite Protestant and Jewish families, associations reinforced by her secular upbringing. According to her biographer, "Gratz knew neither Hebrew nor Yiddish which meant that she never understood the prayers of the synagogue, nor did she have access to the traditional women's devotional literature" Although she regularly attended her family's synagogue, she occasionally participated in Protestant services, underscoring a more general ethos of ecumenicalism in these years. She also attended Benjamin Rush's nondenominational female academy, founded in 1792.[32]

Reared in a predominantly Protestant culture, Gratz transposed Protestant models onto the Jewish charitable and educational activities in which she was involved. The most striking example was the nation's first Hebrew Sunday school, which she founded in Philadelphia in 1838. "We have never yet had a Sunday-School in our congregation," she explained, "and so I have induced our ladies to follow the example of other religious communities." Like its Protestant prototypes, the Hebrew school combined religious instruction with basic literacy training. Gratz's ingenuity was sorely tested in finding appropriate texts for her first crop of scholars, and family members later recalled "how they helped 'Aunt Becky' paste little slips of paper over objectionable words and sentences" in the American Sunday School Union's *Child's Scripture Question Book.*[33]

Although based on Protestant models, there were significant differences as well, some of which were designed to counter the evangelical Protestantism that permeated antebellum American culture. Although her Sunday school primer may have borrowed Christian models, it differed in content and aims, echoing other "Jewish counter-missionary activities: outwardly Jews conformed, inwardly they maintained their identity." Gratz's Sunday school was designed to teach American Jewish women about their faith, to help their children "to withstand the assaults of missionaries," and to strengthen women's networks within the Jewish community. Beginning in the second decade of the nineteenth century, Protestant efforts to convert the Jews became increasingly aggressive. Scattered efforts to bring about Jewish conversions began with the emergence of organizations such as the Female Society for Boston and the Vicinity for Promoting Christianity among the Jews, founded in 1816. These isolated initiatives eventually coalesced into the national Society for Meliorating the Condition of the Jews with powerful backing from some of the Benevolent Empire societies after Samuel Frey's autobiography, *The Converted Jew,* captured the attention of ABS president Elias Boudinot.[34]

The resulting association followed the format of other national Benevolent Empire groups, developing auxiliaries across the country to promote the conversion of the Jews. It was a surprisingly popular movement, given the limited number of Jews who resided in the United States at the time. An organizational meeting at Philadelphia's First Presbyterian Church drew a crowd of hundreds, marking widespread interest in the cause. As the movement spread, it adopted other Benevolent Empire techniques, from literature distribution to the publication of a national newspaper, *Israel's Advocate.*[35]

Some of their techniques bordered on harassment. Protestant tract distributors lined up outside Jewish Sabbath services to distribute religious tracts, and even Gratz received anonymous "gifts" of religious materials in the mail. One particularly obnoxious neighbor persisted in pressing her to read and discuss these unsolicited offerings, seeking, as Gratz put it, to "to canonize herself by my conversion."[36]

These assaults on her privacy and her faith heightened Gratz's sensitivity to the special needs of her community. As she noted in her own account of the Sunday school's history, "As Israelites in a Christian community, where our youth associate and compete with their fellow-citizens in all branches of the arts and sciences, it is essential that they should go provided with a knowledge of their own doctrines—that they should feel the requirements of their peculiar faith, and by a steadfast, unobtrusive observance of them, claim the respect of others and the approbation of their own consciences." In effect, her determination to counter the hegemonic tactics of the Benevolent Empire inspired her to help sharpen Jewish identities within her own community.[37]

Gratz was also instrumental in the creation of Philadelphia's Female Hebrew Benevolent Society in 1819, "the first Jewish non-synagogal charitable association in the U. S." In addition to the assaults of overzealous Protestant missionaries, several other factors shaped her decision to open a new chapter in American Jewish philanthropy. The lack of rabbinic leadership left a vacuum in the community, providing both needs and a "niche" for female initiatives. In Gratz's case, grief played a role as well, when the death of her sister, Sarah, in 1817 and her mother two years later spurred her to study Hebrew and Judaism. After another sister moved away, she lamented, "we have been scattering until only a small portion of the family are left." Gratz's Female Hebrew Benevolent Society created a new circle of fictive "kin," while working to build a sense of communal consciousness and cohesion at a time when their common Jewish identity and faith were under attack.[38]

There may have been other, more explicit motives as well. The evidence suggests that at least some of the Protestant missionary societies may have combined charity with moral suasion and literature distribution in their attempts to win Jewish conversions. As one Jewish leader complained, "If they give a poor Jew money—they want him to think well of the benevolence of Christians and open his heart to Christianity." These enticements held potentially dire consequences, threatening to dilute or destroy the practice of Judaism in the United States. Jewish charitable endeavors afforded a hedge against the lure of Christian largesse.[39]

Like earlier male-controlled burial and mutual aid groups, Gratz's society was funded by dues, donations, and subscriptions that were then invested to provide income for alms and services for the Jewish poor. An employment bureau for seamstresses was added in the 1830s, and the city carved into districts visited by the managers to ensure that only "Israelites . . . of good moral character" would benefit from their aid. After the society was chartered in 1838, the managers aggressively sought larger gifts, encouraging supporters to consider bequests of money and land.[40]

Gratz drew on the skills she had honed in nonsectarian charities in creating these ventures, including her ability to successfully lobby for public funds. After Philadelphia's Orphan Asylum was destroyed in 1822 in a horrifying fire in which twenty-three children perished, she petitioned for, and secured, a $5,000 ($56,500) grant to rebuild it from the Pennsylvania legislature. Three years later, she won access to the municipal funds donated by Jews for help in the Hebrew Benevolent Society's work, a pattern replicated by Jewish groups in New York and New Orleans. Like her Protestant counterparts, Gratz was able to parlay her elite status and connections into a concrete partnership with municipal officers, coupling public funds with private donations and female voluntarism in the cause of communal aid.

She also collaborated with one of the country's first national Jewish spokesmen, Isaac Leeser, in his crusade to preserve their faith. Like Samuel Frey, Leeser was an immigrant. Born in Westphalia in 1806, he emigrated to the United States in 1824 after the death of his parents. Initially, he worked in his uncle's shop in Richmond, where he published articles on Judaism in the *Richmond Whig*. He had briefly undertaken rabbinical studies in Europe, training which helped him to secure a post as a Hebrew reader in Gratz's congregation, Mikvah Israel, in 1829.

Like Gratz, Leeser was deeply disturbed by the Protestant missionary campaigns, a misgiving that inspired him to found the country's first Jewish journal, the *Occident*, and to promote the growth of Jewish communal institutions, including hers. He, too, entered an organizational void. To quote one historian, in the 1820s, "the Jewish community had no newspaper, no certified rabbi, few textbooks, and no central leader. All of this changed once the missionaries began their work." Founded in 1842 as an extension of the kind of communal activity initiated by Gratz, the *Occident* was a counterweight to Protestant organs like *Israel's Advocate*, helping to draw "disparate settlements together and ... arm Jews with the kind of information they needed to rebut missionary claims." Leeser's dread of the prospect of Jewish assimilation inspired him to found the journal and shaped its content, which featured attacks on Christian proselytizing and reports on the Jewish communal institutions that helped to resist them.[41]

He also collaborated with Gratz's Sunday school, writing materials such as his *Catechism for Younger Children* and publicizing its activities in the *Occident*. As he explained in a column published in 1847, "Though we may fail to reclaim the adults to a religious course of life, we have the fullest right to insist upon their offspring being religiously educated." He also borrowed techniques from the Benevolent Empire, including the creation of the American Jewish Publication Society in 1844, which printed its own religious literature to counter Protestant publications, and formed auxiliaries to raise funds to continue publishing the *Occident*. In effect, the missionaries' "impact was precisely the opposite of what they intended. Instead of converting the American Jewish community, they helped to transform it into a more cohesive and more secure body than it had ever been before."[42]

Leeser ultimately emerged as "the most important and most influential American Jewish leader of the antebellum period, not only of the city, but of the nation." Gratz played a key role as well, establishing "Jewish institutions that gave women independent, public, and leadership roles in philanthropy and in religious education for the first time" in the United States. By 1838, the Ladies Hebrew Sewing Society had begun operations in Philadelphia, and other Jewish women's organizations followed suit in Savannah, Baltimore, and Cleveland in the 1850s and 1860s.[43]

Although both Judaism and Protestantism encouraged philanthropy as a matter of doctrinal policy, the ways in which these policies played out were markedly different by the 1830s. While Protestant women engaged in both charitable activities and social reform in increasing numbers, spanning the country with their auxiliaries, services, and fund-raising campaigns, Jewish women focused on communal needs. Because Jewish settlements were small, their efforts were initially modestly cast and locally centered. Lacking the critical mass and the proselytizing bent of Protestant denominations, they nonetheless raised funds and created new religious resources of their own. Rather than seeking converts, they used their organizations to counter the stereotypes and Protestant proselytizing that the Benevolent Empire imposed, forwarding their own vision of their communal identity, values, and norms.

Nor did they have the same economic clout. While the women's auxiliaries of the Benevolent Empire raised hundreds of thousands of dollars—sums that would figure in the millions today—Jewish women's groups collected far smaller amounts for their smaller constituencies. In 1844, for example, Gratz's Female Hebrew Benevolent Society had a mere $259 (@ $3,400) invested in the Philadelphia Saving Fund Society, and another $1,550 invested (@ $20,000) in state and county loans and canal stock, adding their "mite" to the funding of public works, investments that nonetheless brought them into the emerging market economy. Intriguingly, they also drew down $55 (@ $700) in interest from loans, suggesting that at least some of their funds were invested in small business

development in their community. But this was a far cry from the sophisticated marketing and fund-raising infrastructure built by organizations
like the ABS.[44]

Moreover, disestablishment affected the two communities differently.
While Jefferson's separation of church and state cleared the way for competitive contests for congregants and souls among Protestants, Jews rejected proselytizing to care for their own. For them, disestablishment, and
the ethos of religious toleration it embodied, posed a different set of challenges. The charitable and educational initiatives that men and women
created in this community sought cohesion rather than expansion, fostering organizations to combat the hegemonic impulses of an overwhelmingly Protestant populace. In lieu of reforming society as a whole, they
used their groups to maintain time-honored traditions and practices for
the survival of a distinctive Jewish identity. In the process, they created a
new genre of Jewish civil society, one held together through donations and
print, rather than face-to-face interaction, persecution, and geographical
restrictions. Rather than changing the world, antebellum Jewish philanthropy sought to preserve a realm of its own.

Catholicism

Like Isabella Graham and Rebecca Gratz, Elizabeth Seton was an associational pioneer. Each of these women was reared with a republican venera-
tion for learning, and each devised ways of translating that reverence into
distinctively religious terms. Yet there were telling differences as well.
While Graham and Gratz took the initiative themselves, creating independent lay institutions, Seton's work developed within the context of a
clerical hierarchy intent upon tightening its control of Catholic properties,
Catholic policies, and Catholic charities. In the process, Catholic laywomen assumed a far different role from that of either their Protestant or
Jewish counterparts.

Republicanism and disestablishment left their mark on all three of the
country's major religious traditions. The military alliance with France
helped to soften anti-Catholic sentiments during the Revolution, introducing one of the more benign eras of religious toleration in the country's
early history. The Revolution was a time for fresh beginnings, when all
things seemed capable of being created anew, including the Catholic
Church. Like Judaism, the church had only modest numbers of adherents
at the end of the eighteenth century: estimates place the number of
Catholic churches at slightly more than fifty in 1780, a figure that had

doubled four decades later. In 1789, the year that George Washington was elected, there were fewer than thirty thousand Catholics in the United States, most of whom resided in the Middle Atlantic states. Within this milieu, churches were scattered, episcopal authority limited, and parishes often highly independent.[45]

One of the earmarks of republicanism was a deeply ingrained suspicion of centralized authority, a suspicion that played out among Catholics in a drive for local congregational autonomy that resembled that of many Protestant denominations. As in other sects, disestablishment encouraged a set of relations in which laymen had a decisive hand in controlling parish affairs. Within Catholic congregations, this translated into an emphasis on trusteeism—the right of lay trustees to own and control church properties—and autonomy over the selection and dismissal of parish priests. Just as Protestant precedents initially shaped Jewish charities, they also influenced the laity's vision of an American Catholic Church. Many of the men who spearheaded the movement toward trustee control were leaders in their communities, as well as in their congregations. As a result, they had added incentives for cultivating cordial relations with their Protestant colleagues, and during the first two decades of the nineteenth century, they often succeeded remarkably well.

While the infrastructure of Protestant evangelicalism grew dramatically during these years, Catholic congregations remained decentralized and small, hampered by the lack of priests and nuns to develop institutions. In the 1790s, when Seton and Graham were still planning their charitable ventures together, only a small number of French religious orders were in operation in North America. The Ursulines arrived in New Orleans in 1727, imported under a contract with the Company of the West Indies to promote hospital work, subsequently developing a school and an orphan asylum which received both public and private support.

American orders began to appear after the turn of the century. In addition to Seton's Sisters of Charity, new communities of nuns were established in frontier Kentucky. Founded in 1812, the Sisters of Charity of Nazareth began their operations in a log cabin. Like the Dominican nuns who joined them a decade later, the Sisters of Charity of Nazareth found themselves compelled by the rigorous demands of frontier life to roll "stumps and logs to clear the land for plowing" and to do their own construction work, as well as supporting their charitable and educational activities through cloth production and the sale of sewn goods.[46]

Perhaps the most interesting order was that of the Oblate Sisters of Providence, who founded their first convent in Baltimore in 1829. Composed primarily of refugees from Sainte Domingue, they were the country's first order of nonwhite nuns. Initially, they confined their activities to educating slaves and providing religious instruction, backed by a $1,400 ($18,340) donation from the order's leader, Elizabeth Lange. Later, they founded St. Francis's Academy for Colored Girls, a combined free school and orphanage that catered primarily to the mixed-blood daughters of plantation owners who were barred from white schools. In a pattern echoed by all the women's religious communities of this period, they supported their efforts primarily through income generation, in this instance by taking in laundry, an activity that once again underscored the ties between nonprofit organizations and the market. Although dedicated primarily to educational work, after the order was formally approved by Pope Gregory XVI in 1831, they briefly experimented in short-lived ventures to create orphanages in Philadelphia and New Orleans.[47]

When John Carroll, the country's first bishop, assumed the Baltimore episcopacy in 1789, the American church was still bereft of educational or charitable institutions. Initially, he sought to lure a group of Belgian Carmelites who had recently established a convent in Maryland to take on educational work, but they declined on the grounds that they were a cloistered order, not a charitable enterprise.

Seton was an unusual candidate to fulfill his vision of an activist order of nuns. Reared in a prominent Episcopal family in New York, she married well and was a member of the upper echelons of the city's gentry when a string of personal disasters destroyed what had seemed a secure and comfortable destiny. Her husband went bankrupt and they lost their house in 1800. Her father died the following year, and her spouse contracted tuberculosis, perishing in Italy in 1803 during an abortive journey to restore his health. Widowed at the age of twenty-eight, Seton was left with five young children to care for on her own. This in turn precipitated the crisis of faith that resulted in her conversion to Catholicism and headed her down the road to self-support. Like Graham before her she opened a school, in Baltimore, where she was befriended by Bishop Carroll.

Perhaps as a result of the severity of her recent history, as well as her growing spirituality, Seton began to gravitate toward a religious vocation, an extremely complicated proposition given her desire to keep her family intact. Initially, she considered joining an Ursuline community, but with Carroll's encouragement, she opted instead to start an order of her own. One of the incentives may have been Carroll's assurances that she would have considerable autonomy in developing the new venture, and that "no one . . . but your immediate superior . . . will have any share in the govern-

ment or concerns of the sisters," aside, of course, from "the essential su-
perintendence of the archbishop over every community in his diocese."[48]

It was an extraordinary venture. Seton established her fledgling convent in Emmitsburg, Maryland, in 1809 and ran it while supervising not
only her nuns, but her five children as well. Initially working out of a donated farmhouse, she founded a school and provided nursing services for
area residents. A year later, a day school was added in a nearby log cabin.
Moreover, she created these institutions with very little monetary assistance from the church. When the idea was first broached, she was told that
she could rent a house for $300 ($2,730) or $400 ($3,640) a year. However,
since it was likely that any support from the church would fall short of cov-
ering the rental costs, she was advised to "depend on Providence" to keep
the venture afloat.[49]

Providence did provide, in the form of a theological student who
offered the use of some of his property as a means of divesting himself of
his worldly goods. She also began to attract assistants, including close rela-
tives. By 1809, her religious community included four other women,
among them the niece of the prominent Philadelphia Catholic layman
Matthew Carey. As the order grew and became increasingly institutionalized, the women donned a distinctive religious habit and adopted a set of
rules. By 1812, single and widowed women between the ages of sixteen
and twenty-eight were being accepted, provided they were willing to take
vows of poverty, chastity, and obedience and dedicate their lives to charitable and educational work.

As the order grew, so did the level of formality. By the time of Seton's
death in 1821, a hierarchical "central government" was well in place, with
descending lines of authority from the order's spiritual adviser (an ex-offi-
cio appointment of the head of the Seminary of St. Suplicius in Baltimore); to the mother superior (who was to be at least thirty-five years old
and a veteran of a dozen or more years within the community), and on to
an assistant, a treasurer, a "procuratrix," and the superintendent of the
academy, all of whom were to be elected by the community as a whole.
The order grew as well, to more than fifty nuns by 1820.

Much of their work was educational. By 1810, the Emmitsburg school
counted thirty boarders and forty day pupils. Tuition covered some of the
costs, but Seton paid for her preferred work in educating impoverished
children through commercial activities, including the sale of cloth and
clothes, the mainstay of women's marketable goods in these years. Four
years later, her Sisters of Charity were invited to assume the management
of St. Joseph's Orphanage in Philadelphia.

The history of Seton's second convent provides a sense of some of the challenges that faced her efforts to institutionalize and extend the order. Established in 1797 by the predominantly German congregation in Trinity Parish as a means of aiding the orphans of yellow fever victims, St. Joseph's was initially supported and run by the parishioners themselves. Summoned during the War of 1812, Seton's nuns had to make the arduous journey over land, since Chesapeake Bay was blocked by British warships. When they arrived, they found the inmates in rags and the house itself mired in a $4,000 ($36,400) debt. Although the parish managers appropriated $600 ($5,460) a year for its annual upkeep, commodity prices skyrocketed during the war, leaving them perpetually short of funds.

Legend has it that the nuns and their young charges survived the first year on a diet of potatoes and coffee. The low point came when they were forced to beg for in-kind donations from local market women. Here, as in Emmitsburg, the nuns eventually managed to place the institution on a sound financial footing, coupling donations with the manufacture and sale of linens and other commodities. The situation in New York, where they assumed the management of another orphan asylum in 1817, proved much more manageable, with the finances bolstered by regular allocations of state funds, which drew the sisters into quasi-governmental activities as well as market relations.

The division of labor in the New York asylum represented the lingering decentralization of parish life. Parish trustees owned the land and controlled the asylum's financial affairs, while the nuns exercised control over the institution's management. Some additional support was provided by the Ladies Charitable Association of parish laywomen, while state and private allocations supported the physical plant, drawing the nuns into the public realm. The congregation donated $40 ($452) per annum for the nuns' personal use, including their clothing. Clearly, this was a system that depended not only on the sisters' managerial abilities, but on their vows of charity and service. Voluntarism by nuns sustained the country's first Catholic charities, coupling service with profit-making activities to support their work.

The order continued to grow after Seton's death, giving rise to a network of orphanages and schools that stretched from Baltimore to Indiana by 1835. It also ventured into hospital work, managing the infirmary at the University of Maryland at the state's request. The fact that the order survived and grew was a tribute to Seton's tenacity and skill. American convents were "expected to be self-supporting" from the outset. While European orders could afford the luxury of cloistered lives if they so chose,

since many were backed by prominent patrons and centuries of endowments, in the United States, clerics like Archbishop Carroll, who eagerly
encouraged women to start religious communities, lacked the surplus
funds to support them, forcing them to move into market activities to earn
the necessary revenues themselves. Some nuns received salaries of as little
as $25 per year ($283 in 2000 dollars) for this often arduous work, a figure
well below the poverty line.[50]

Their ability to maintain themselves at minimal cost endowed these
early orders with a substantial amount of autonomy in developing their
programs. But it also entailed substantial responsibilities and risks. Even at
this early stage in the church's development, they might see their plans
checkmated by clerical resistance, despite dire need. Seton ran into this
problem during the War of 1812, when debts incurred for capital improvements dovetailed with soaring consumer prices, placing her convent in
peril. When she mentioned her plans for an Eastern fund-raising tour to
the Bishop of Boston, he dissuaded her. Although he admitted to being
"much grieved" by her financial problems, he added somewhat callously
that he did "not see how you will be extricated from them. . . . in the present situation of affairs, very little, I am afraid, would be collected." Nevertheless, he concluded, "I am still in hope that some pious and generous
souls will give, or at least advance the money you owe."[51]

Desperate, she began to beg, imploring her patron and friend General
Robert Harper to help her salvage her vision of a "house of plain and useful education, retired from the extravagance of the world . . . providing
nurses for the rich and poor, an abode of innocence, and a refuge of afflic-
tion." Having "to discharge the endless demands of carpenters and workmen," had nearly bankrupted the institution. "The credit of twenty poor
women, who are capable only of earning their daily bread, is but a small
stock, particularly when their flour-merchant, grocer, and butcher, are
more already in advance than they are willing to afford." "What is our resource?" she queried. "If we sell our house to pay our debts, we must sev-
erally return to our separate homes." If he was unwilling to step in as their
"guardian, protector, [to] plead our cause with the rich and powerful," she
asked if his wife could be persuaded to help. Or, Seton added somewhat
ruefully, "is this an extravagant dream of female fancy?"[52]

Her desperation was compounded by the fact that her eldest daughter
was dying of tuberculosis. Both her child and her sister, another member
of the community, died that year, and another daughter later predeceased
her.

The combined burdens of building an institution and supporting and raising a family under extreme duress must have often seemed over-whelming. That women such as Seton were able to build viable institu-tions with so little assistance was a tribute to their stoicism, determination, and faith. Perhaps in a moment of envy or despair, she compared her or-der's situation to that of European convents. "We are more exposed to the world," she noted, "having in most circumstances no other monastery than the houses of the sick, or the school-room, no other cell than a rented apartment, no other chapel than the parish church, no cloister but the pub-lic street, no enclosure but obedience, no grate but the fear of God, no veil but that of modesty."[53]

Harper did eventually come to her aid, guiding her charter petition through the Maryland legislature in 1817. Shortly after the convent legally gained title to its holdings, the nuns were sued by a former owner, who sought to regain control of the Emmitsburg property by citing flaws in an earlier deed. Because they had a charter, they were able to initiate legal proceedings to keep their land. Eventually they retired their debts as well, adding a two-story brick schoolhouse shortly before Seton's death.

Unlike Protestant fund-raising efforts, appeals for support by early Catholic charities were spotty at best. Some parishes developed fraternal organizations to raise funds, and parish laywomen sometimes banded to-gether to collect the modest sums needed for the nuns' personal mainte-nance. Special collections at Easter and Christmas also provided limited amounts of cash, which were occasionally augmented by individual be-quests and donations. But unlike their Protestant counterparts, Catholic women never developed the highly organized fund-raising activities nec-essary to subsidize a concerted, national program of institutional develop-ment and elaboration. Instead, they focused their energies on parish-based altar societies, sewing societies, and short-term local fund-raising ven-tures, while the nuns themselves turned to profit-making activities or sought subsidies from the state.

Like Gratz, Seton was an experienced fund-raiser from her days as trea-surer of the Widows' Society in New York. As part of her responsibilities there, she had successfully lobbied the state legislature for permission to conduct a state-sponsored lottery in order to raise fifteen thousand dollars for the society's work. Catholic charities and schools were also granted mu-nicipal allocations in New York in this era, a policy that benefited Seton's order when it took over the management of the city's Catholic orphanage. Although public allocations for parochial education ended in the mid-1820s, when educational funding was consolidated under the Protestant-dominated Free School Society, support for the educational activities of asylums continued on a limited basis. Catholic charities also received modest but ongoing municipal allocations in New Orleans.[54]

Catholic sisterhoods managed to forge other working relationships with public bodies, especially during the cholera-ridden 1830s, when they were called upon to manage public almshouses and hospital wards. Local governments in cities such as Philadelphia and Baltimore, and smaller towns such as Augusta, Georgia, all enlisted the service of Catholic sisterhoods during these pestilent years.

Seton and her contemporaries developed their convents and charities in a unique milieu. In addition to a modicum of religious tolerance, the early national era was marked by an equally unusual—and equally transient—degree of institutional autonomy. As a result, Catholic charities attracted public funds, from outright grants to permission to hold state-sponsored lotteries. Trusteeism helped to foster this era of good feelings. Closer in form to Protestant congregationalism than to the more centralized European Church, it provided laymen in local parishes with a substantial degree of control over their religious properties and activities.

In addition, trusteeism afforded tangible evidence of the American church's independence from foreign influences, one of the bugbears of the republican ethos. Bishops who sought to centralize their control over these independent churches repeatedly had their efforts repulsed amid charges that they sought to violate parishioners' "inalienable rights as American citizens." Rather than bowing to the will of Rome, American Catholics "wanted their church identified with American republicanism, . . . popular sovereignty, religious and civil liberty, . . . and constitutionalism."[55]

While Archbishop Carroll accepted this situation out of necessity and personal inclination, his successors grew increasingly restive in the face of trustee control. Moreover, as Rome launched a concerted drive to consolidate its control over church activities in the wake of the Napoleonic Wars, the notion that clerics should confine their authority to spiritual matters while the laity held the property and hired and fired the priests became increasingly unacceptable. Some of the most vitriolic clashes occurred in Philadelphia in the 1820s, where the trustees of St. Mary's fought a pitched battle with a succession of bishops over their right to manage parish properties and affairs.

The heart of the conflict revolved around the bishops' efforts to revise the parish's charter, transferring the property to ecclesiastical control, and to curb the laity's right to appoint priests. Efforts to revise the charter were vociferously resisted amid charges of foreign conspiracies and invocations of the recent Supreme Court ruling establishing the inviolability of charters against state interference in the 1819 *Dartmouth* case. The "wall of separation" between church and state was also invoked, albeit on somewhat tenuous grounds. As one polemicist explained, Pennsylvania's constitution mandated that "no person shall be compelled to support any ministry against their own consent; which would be the case if they were compelled to . . . receive and support those whom popes and bishops might force upon them."[56]

It was a highly public conflict, waged through pamphlet wars and litigation in the courts. One priest was excommunicated (unfortunately, shortly after starting a Sunday school based on Bible readings, a dismissal that many Protestants interpreted in ominous terms); and at one point, a public riot erupted as the bishop's supporters clashed with those of the trustees. Even the pope became involved, issuing a formal reprisal against the trustees. Many of the arguments that swirled around the controversy were cast in terms that pitted American republicanism against "the arrogant and absurd pretensions of the church of Rome over the minds and judgement of her people." Americans "cannot brook the idea of fettering religion to . . . a despotic administration," concluded one polemicist. "Foreigners of every class and description" who sought "to direct and command us," must be repulsed, thundered another.[57]

The entire episode was extremely damaging, fanning Protestant suspicion of a Romish plot to undermine the republic and long-dormant prejudices against the church's adherents—sentiments that were already emerging in the evangelical press and that resurfaced more pointedly in the nativist campaigns of the 1830s. When the bishops collectively issued an edict condemning the practice of trusteeism at the Baltimore Provincial Council in 1829, it only deepened these antagonisms. Trusteeism was eventually extinguished, but at a cost.

Less visible, but no less important for the role of the Catholic laity, was the effort to consolidate episcopal control over Catholic charities, which occurred at the same time. In 1826, the bishop of Charleston issued an edict outlining this new campaign. Invoking his episcopal authority, he declared that parish vestries could no longer "buy, sell or alter Church property" without his approval. In addition, every parishioner was to be assessed an annual two-dollar fee for the church's general fund. A committee composed of the bishop, selected priests, and laymen was to handle the fund's distribution, allocating the proceeds among capital improvements, missionary campaigns, poor relief, schools, and charities as they saw fit. In the process, the clerical hierarchy began to centralize its control over Catholic philanthropy as well. The ensuing decades would be marred by continuing struggles between the bishops and trustees for control of church properties and charitable funds, a struggle in which the bishops ultimately triumphed.[58]

Later, voluntarism was reined in and made to conform to ecclesiastical standards. To quote one historian, "Bishops did not look favorably upon even limited autonomy in female activities, whether lay or religious, and the women's benevolent societies did not have even the modest legal protections enjoyed by sisterhoods." Catholic clerics also "dampened lay overtures to undertake national benevolent programs," advising their flocks to focus on their dioceses instead.[59]

In their drive to institutionalize the parish-based organization of the Tridentine church, bishops like Philadelphia's Francis Kenrick narrowed the scope of activity of the laity to their own communities. The end result was a vibrant array of parish-based institutions, from religiously oriented confraternities and sodalities to library and lecture societies, temperance groups, and fund-raising concerts and fairs. Some even offered savings and insurance services. But laywomen were accorded a minor role in these activities, aside from fund-raising. As historian Jay Dolan points out, "women were excluded from participation in church vestries and church governance," as well as work in Sunday school catechizing, a major area of activity for their Protestant counterparts. As the "monarchical form of church government" triumphed over trusteeism, parishioners were increasingly expected to "pay, pray and obey."[60]

Ironically, both republican trusteeism and the drive for episcopal consolidation ultimately limited the scope and nature of Catholic philanthropy. Prior to 1820s, churches and religious orders enjoyed a significant amount of autonomy, but because Catholics were few in number and their ranks dispersed, the system that emerged often focused on simply maintaining individual parish institutions. Subsequent episcopal policies muted both lay autonomy and the development of national organizations, aside from the religious sisterhoods. Moreover, although the boundaries separating the market, government, and associational life were blurred to a greater or lesser degree for Catholics, Protestants, and Jews alike, their efforts often differed significantly in other respects. While Protestant women embraced both charity and social reform, and Jewish women volunteered to address communal needs, Catholic laywomen served primarily as parish donors and fund-raisers for the charitable and educational activities run by nuns. Unlike their Protestant counterparts, they often had little control over the monies they raised and limited clerical encouragement to develop strong, independent organizations of their own.

The civic revolution set in motion by disestablishment achieved full flower in the growth of religious philanthropy. Spurred by a unique combination of conditions, nuns and laywomen played a significant role in building charitable and religious associations through their voluntarism and funds. In the process, they helped to create a national infrastructure for political, social, and religious mobilization. Protestant women also assumed an important, albeit unheralded, place in the front lines of the market revolution, helping to undermine the independent patriarchal yeoman household of Jeffersonian lore with every donation, every subscription, every sale. In the process, religion—and especially Protestantism—left an indelible imprint on the country's political and economic landscape, supplanting republicanism as the deus ex machina of American civil society.

4

The Geography of Generosity

Despite the growth of national initiatives like the American Bible Society (ABS), two regionally distinctive models of philanthropy and civil society had begun to emerge by the 1820s, echoing Robert Putnam's predictions. According to Putnam, regions with extensive networks of voluntary associations will be more economically developed because of the social capital—the trust—that they engender, sentiments that encourage citizens to pool their funds as well as their time in collaborative ventures. In the North, a growing number of often highly independent nonprofit associations accumulated and invested liquid capital at a time when cash was scarce and desperately needed, helping to bankroll the Northern transportation revolution, seed new businesses, provide loans, and fuel the region's fledgling industrial revolution. They also enabled growing numbers of elite white women and African Americans to become investors and "communal capitalists." Beyond simply generating trust, Northern philanthropic institutions became significant economic actors in their own right. Southern associations and nonprofit organizations, on the other hand, tended to be less likely to gather and invest sizable amounts cash, and far more subject to the supervision and control of wealthy slaveholding white male elites. As a result, philanthropy's role in spurring Southern economic diversification was more limited as well.[1]

Two types of nonprofit investors left a particular imprint on the Northern economy before 1840: philanthropically inspired mutual savings banks, and charitable and educational endowments. Here, as in so many other areas, Benjamin Franklin's career served as a harbinger of things to come.

Philanthropy and the Market: Benjamin Franklin's Will

Franklin's appreciation for the financial power of philanthropy was codified in his will. Many of his bequests were predictable: books for the American Philosophical Society and the Library Company of Philadelphia; uncollected debts left to the Pennsylvania Hospital; and £100 for the free schools of Boston. His most ingenious legacy was contained in a codicil he added on June 23, 1789, about a year before his death, bequeathing the £2,000 salary that he received for his service as president of Pennsylvania. Franklin instructed his executors to divide the money between Boston and Philadelphia, to be used for loans to apprentices. By his calculations, if the funds were loaned at 5% interest, after one hundred years each city would have £130,000, £100,000 of which was to be used for public works. The remainder was to be lent out for another century, at which time he predicted it would have grown to £4 million, which would also be allocated for public works. Franklin's intention was to test the idea that even a modest bequest, properly invested, could play a valuable role in seeding business, as well as civic ventures, underscoring the underlying ties between philanthropy and the market.[2]

Although the funds were eventually funneled into other ventures as the institution of apprenticeship declined, during the first fifty years his scheme seems to have worked much as he had anticipated. Over 270 loans were made by the Boston trustees during this period, supplying low-cost funding to housewrights, bakers, coopers, bricklayers, hatters, bookbinders, and blacksmiths. Although the grants were small, capped at sixty pounds under the terms of Franklin's will, they constituted a significant resource for men embarking on their careers, especially in the early national era immediately after Franklin's death.[3]

Franklin's choice of beneficiary was undoubtedly influenced by the lessons learned from his own career. Colonial Philadelphia was a premodern economic milieu. Because funds for investment were limited by the absence of modern financial institutions such as banks, "personal credit was usually the only source of capital for local communities." Mechanics often had difficulty securing loans from the gentry, and even when commercial banks were developed, they "seldom made direct loans to inde-

pendent artisan manufacturers." As a result, businessmen and planters—
including Franklin and Jefferson—provided personal loans, a risky proposition that could make a man's reputation or force his estate to the auction
block through bad debts. It also entangled lenders and debtors in webs of
patron-client relationships. To quote Gordon Wood, "no one in this hierarchical society could be truly independent."[4]

Nonprofits helped to undermine these hegemonies by creating independent accumulations of capital under the control of new groups such as
elite white women and African Americans—particularly in the North—
as well as prominent white male members of the elite. Although the sums
were generally small, many churches, charities, and mutual aid societies
invested part of their holdings in real estate and loans, providing funds for
mortgages and small business development for their members and within
their communities.

Franklin's decision to earmark part of his estate for loans may have also
stemmed from English precedents. The availability of philanthropic
funds provided what one historian has termed "massive accumulations of
capital" that helped to fuel "the early but rapid growth of capitalistic enterprise" in England beginning in the seventeenth century. Although one
of the strongest arguments against granting charters to charitable institutions was the fear that any resulting endowments would "undercut the liquidity of capital" by withdrawing "excessive quantities of wealth from
circulation," quite the opposite proved to be the case. Far from impeding
economic development, England's charitable endowments played a central role in helping to stimulate investments and loans.[5]

Many of these of these funds were lent to borrowers of modest means.
Generally, parish-based English charitable endowments fell into two categories. Charity loans were created "explicitly in order to supply loans to
certain classes of persons," while charity funds were "devoted to various
philanthropic ends" but could be lent at higher rates of interest. Beginning in the sixteenth and seventeenth centuries, "many successful businessmen left bequests to provide a revolving sum from which 'deserving'
young members of different guilds could borrow at low interest" rates,
usually around 5%, a significantly lower figure than that charged by
moneylenders. Thus, "the interest was devoted to charity, [and] the princi-
pal was employed as credit," helping to seed local economic development.[6]

Because the colonial economy lacked England's wealth, bequests such
as these were less common in North America, a pattern that Franklin may
have sought to change. His codicil achieved a variety of ends. At the most
basic level, it provided a source of capital for apprentices, much as his

Junto colleagues had backed his own career. It also addressed one of the central conundrums of republicanism, merging civic ends with capital gains.

Finally, it presaged the role of philanthropy in promoting capital formation and underwriting economic development in the new republic. Charities and associations stimulated economic growth in a variety of ways. Some created capital through sales, a model pioneered by the first asylums and entrepreneurs like Whitefield in the eighteenth century and amplified by institutions as diverse as Joanna Bethune's House of Industry, Mother Seton's orphanages, and the ABS, coupling donations with entrepreneurially generated revenues. These institutions created jobs for both their clients and their staffs and patronized local merchants and tradesmen, adding yet another spur to local economic growth. And, as Franklin's bequest so graphically illustrated, philanthropic ventures were potentially significant investors as well, underwriting everything from public improvement projects and business development to individual loans. During the first half of the nineteenth century, nonprofits and their endowments—including portions of the Franklin fund—would help to fund New England's industrial revolution and major public works projects such as the Erie Canal. As in the case of his charitable and educational campaigns, Franklin's bequest both anticipated and celebrated this symbiotic relationship among philanthropy, the market, and the state.[7]

The Growth of Giving

Franklin's will also presaged the slow but steady growth of individual giving. Mass-based initiatives like the Benevolent Empire societies and educational institutions accumulated and invested capital. According to Charles Sellers, thirteen of the largest Benevolent Empire societies raised an estimated $2.8 million between 1816 and 1830 (or @ $36,680,000 in 2000 dollars), a figure that compared favorably with the $3.6 million ($47,160,000) "spent by the federal government for internal improvements since its beginning." Almost all of these associations were headquartered in Northern cities, drawing Southern donations and sales revenues into Northern investments. Moreover, Northern states often provided a far more hospitable environment for philanthropic capital accumulation and investment than their counterparts in the South, patterns born of custom and law.[8]

Generally, they depended on their ability to attract substantial numbers of small gifts, rather than the massive individual donations that would become synonymous with philanthropy in John D. Rockefeller's era. The practice of small-scale, mass-based giving was assiduously cultivated by religious groups, Benevolent Empire organizations, educational institutions, and local charities, all of which helped to create a national culture of philanthropy. Religious journals were particularly aggressive in this respect. The Congregationalist *Recorder* is a case in point. Beginning with its earliest issues in 1816, the journal hammered home the notion that substantial gifts were important, but that even the smallest donation could ultimately make a difference. Thus, while one story entitled "The Will" warned that when too much money was left to heirs the end result was dissipation, sloth, and "pests of society," others traced the progress of cent and mite societies. Members of the Female Cent Society of Chillicothe, Ohio, were lauded in the journal's pages for setting aside a penny a day to aid a varied group of Princeton professors, theological seminary students, and pupils of local Sunday schools. The two hundred members of the Female Society to aid Princeton Theological Seminary were cited for contributing $700 ($6,300) through their weekly six-cent donations. The Mite Society for the Education of Heathen Children in India amassed hundreds of dollars from their "small droppings," while others donated annual sums ranging from $150 to $760.[9]

Moreover, this was an arena in which female fund-raising and giving were often accorded a central role. "It is earnestly hoped that many similar associations . . . may be formed by benevolent females," noted the editors, both for the benefit of individual causes and for the country's future. According to missionary leader Samuel Worcester, "It is a singular felicity of the times in which we live, that all persons, even those in the most humble and retired situations, can exert an active benevolence towards the most remote inhabitants of the earth. By the aid of charitable societies now in constant operation, the poor widow, who lives among the mountains of Vermont, or the waters of the St. Lawrence or Mississippi, can send her mite without the least difficulty to the spiritual relief of the Hindoo [sic], or can assist in distributing the Holy Scriptures among the benighted millions of China. Many poor widows have already contributed their mites, and many wealthy individuals have given of their abundance." For Worcester, it was essential that "persons of all classes give." As he explained, "it is necessary for a well ordered and harmonious state . . . that members should . . . act together; that they should feel their common interests, and be moved, as in a common impulse, to the promotion of a common end." Thus, the widow's mite could help to build a sense of national community, as well as a theological seminary or missionary empire.[10]

Educational ventures were also launched through subscription drives. Amherst College traced its origins to a $52,244 ($642,257) "charity fund" campaign in 1821, and Mount Holyoke Seminary and College began fifteen years later with $27,000 (@ $346,000) in subscriptions gleaned from eighteen hundred donors. Religious groups like the American Education Society (another Benevolent Empire association) played a particularly important role in raising funds for needy students. According to one estimate, the combined donations of the American Education Society, the Northern Baptist Education Society, and the Presbyterian Education Society in 1832 totaled $61,029, or $7,994,799 in current, 2000 dollars, supporting over one thousand impoverished seminarians.[11]

Collective fund-raising efforts like those of the ABS were unusually important in this era because so few large gifts were forthcoming. However, there were exceptions. Philadelphia's Girard College was one of the first institutions to receive a sizable bequest. A prominent banker, Stephen Girard was ostensibly the country's richest citizen. He was also its most generous to date. Because he had no children of his own, he bequeathed most of his estimated $6 million estate ($78 million in 2000 dollars) to charities and to the cities of Philadelphia and New Orleans for public purposes in 1831. Franklin's Pennsylvania Hospital was given a hefty $30,000 ($390,000) under his will, and Gratz's Philadelphia Orphan Asylum another $10,000 ($130,000), while Philadelphia received a $800,000 ($8,240,000) for capital improvements. But Girard's most munificent gift was his $2 million ($26 million) legacy to create the Girard College for poor white orphan boys. After years of litigation brought by Girard's surviving kin that ended in the Supreme Court, the college finally opened its doors in 1848.[12]

Five years after Girard's death, John Lowell bequeathed $250,000 ($3,250,000) for the Lowell Institute in Boston. The heir to a half-million-dollar fortune, Lowell drafted his testament in 1832, a year after tragically losing his young wife and two children, and shortly before setting out on an ill-starred journey to Asia that ended in his own death in India at the age of thirty-seven. Unlike Girard, Lowell eschewed bricks and mortar, specifying that the funds should be invested, with 10% of the earnings reinvested each year and the rest applied to free moral, intellectual, or scientific lectures for the citizens of Boston.[13]

Colleges, universities and theological seminaries generally drew the largest individual gifts given to nonprofit organizations in the early national and antebellum years. Harvard headed the list, with numerous gifts in the range of ten thousand to one hundred thousand dollars from individuals before 1840, patterns echoed on a more modest scale at Bowdoin, Oberlin, and Transylvania Colleges and Western Reserve University. Colleges in Northern states were often aided in their quest to attract sizable gifts and bequests by hospitable state laws. In Pennsylvania, for example, section 45 of the state's first constitution "encouraged the founding and guaranteed the property rights of charitable and religious organizations," legislation passed with the enthusiastic backing of the redoubtable Franklin. Massachusetts, New Hampshire, Rhode Island, and Connecticut were equally supportive, while New York legislators encouraged the creation of chartered charities but reserved the right to limit the amount of property they could hold.[14]

In the case of Harvard, the balance between public and private support was rapidly tipping during these years. According to Ronald Story, total private contributions to the university reached $182,000 in the eighteenth century, $298,000 between 1801 and 1825, and $980,000 between 1826 and 1850, while the percentage of public support fell from 55% in the eighteenth century to 33% between 1801 and 1825, and 0% between 1825 to 1850, marking a sharp contrast to patterns developing in states like Virginia and South Carolina, where many of the largest colleges and charities were public institutions—patterns epitomized by the University of Virginia.[15]

As his epitaph clearly indicated, Thomas Jefferson regarded his role in the creation of the University of Virginia as the crowning achievement of his long and distinguished career. The project was born of a republican faith in the importance of education and the former president's desire to create a comprehensive educational system for his native state. Although he failed to achieve his goal of widespread primary education, he did manage to shepherd the university through its infancy as Albemarle Academy and Central College into a university between 1814 and his death in 1826. Along the way, he recruited both James Madison and James Monroe to the boards; choreographed a major subscription drive that collected $41,248 (almost $500,000 in 2000 dollars), including $1,000 gifts from his own diminished resources and those of Madison and Monroe; seconded two parcels of former parish lands and sundry grants from the government; and played a central role in the Rockfish Gap Commission, which determined the site of the state university, writing much of the resulting report. He also essentially designed the university, from the curriculum, faculty appointments, and library holdings to the administrative structure, campus architecture, and grounds.

Eighteen nineteen was a pivotal year in these endeavors, marked by the first meeting of the new university's Board of Visitors and the Supreme Court's landmark *Dartmouth* decision. From the outset, Jefferson's university was designed as a public-private venture under state control. Despite his problems in securing support from the parsimonious Virginia legislature, Jefferson infused his efforts with a shrewd understanding of the political maneuvering needed to bring his project to fruition, including the need for private support—which is undoubtedly why he was willing to donate so large a sum when his own estate was hovering on the brink of bankruptcy. One of the criteria used in selecting the university site was the availability of local matching funds. While Washington College had $17,878 in subscriptions, noted the Rockfish Gap report, Central College had over $41,000, as well as forty-seven acres and the proceeds from the sale of two plots of public land—all of which gave it a competitive edge, as Jefferson had intended.[16]

Although Central College already held a private charter, which Jefferson had helped to secure, both he and Madison were intent on shifting the university to governmental control, as a means of both of ensuring ongoing public supervision and limiting the degree of clerical interference. Madison was particularly concerned about the "excessive wealth of ecclesiastical Corporations" and their "indefinite accumulation of property," and determined that the university not degenerate into what he termed "an Arena of theological Gladiators." One way of doing this was to place it under public, nonsectarian control, "which places all sects of religion on an equal footing" and precluded the dominance of any single denomination or creed, ensuring that the school would "in all things, at all times, be subject to the control of the Legislature."[17]

This in turn heightened the need for public support. Although the Visitors were empowered to receive "subscriptions and donations, real and personal . . . [from] persons associated, as from private individuals," the bulk of the funds were to come from the state's Literary Fund. Wresting adequate support from a "grudging legislature" proved a challenging assignment. In the early years, when the allocations were particularly miserly, Jefferson borrowed the necessary money from the government, debts that were later excused. The logjam finally broke in 1824, when the legislature appropriated $50,000 (@ $600,000), and subsequent annual appropriations became more regular, augmented by private donations, such as Madison's bequest of books and funds, and revenues generated from real estate investments and student housing. Jefferson bitterly resented the legislature's stinginess, likening his "greatest of all services" to "the odious function of a physician pouring medicine down the throat of a

patient insensible of needing it." Through his donations of cash and his
extraordinary generosity with his time, he, like Franklin, became one of
the country's greatest philanthropists in his final years, albeit with far
different results.[18]

Jefferson followed the *Dartmouth* case with interest. It began in 1816,
when the New Hampshire legislature moved to wrest control of Dartmouth College from its trustees. The former president warmly approved
of the state's position, confiding to Governor William Plumer that "the
idea that institutions established for the use of the nation cannot be
touched nor modified, even to make them answer their end . . . is most absurd. . . . Yet our lawyers and priests generally inculcate this doctrine [that]
. . . the earth belongs to the dead and not the living."[19]

In the ensuing litigation, the state supreme court ruled that legislatures
legally controlled chartered institutions, even those that had not received
public aid, a decision overturned by the United States Supreme Court. The
famed statesman and orator Daniel Webster represented the school's
trustees before Marshall's court, warning that the legislature's suit threatened to tie the country's colleges and literary institutions to "the fluctua-
tions of political opinions." Donors would have "no certainty of effecting
the object of their bounty," and colleges would "become a theater for the
contention of politics" ruled by "Party and faction." Written primarily by
Justice Story, the Court's decision held that chartered institutions were not
owned by the state; that they were private and independent; and that once
a charter was granted, governmental bodies relinquished the right to control them, whether or not they received public funds. In effect, charters
were inviolable contracts that could not be liquidated or repealed without
the corporation's consent. To quote Webster, all charitable corporations
were "private bodies." Although public in their "uses and advantages,"
they were nonetheless "private in the tenure of property and in the right
of administering the funds." The *Dartmouth* decision considerably revised
the commonwealth ideal that had cast chartered institutions not just primarily, but solely as instruments of the state, and it made it far more difficult to dissolve them on legislative impulse—a decision that Jefferson
found "repugnant."[20]

Charters were already hard to obtain in Virginia, a condition that made
it difficult for churches and charities to legally hold, sell, or inherit land or
enter into legally binding contracts and lawsuits. This also impeded their
ability to "raise funds, build churches, establish institutions, maintain
works of charity, educate their clergy and adherents, and carry out missionary activities." Shortly after the turn of the century, the Virginia legis-

lature began to refuse to incorporate "innumerable religious charities and
. . . many secular societies as well," a practice tied to concerns about religious authority and control, private corporations, and mortmain, the control of the gift from beyond the grave—misgivings later codified in what
became known as the Virginia Doctrine. This in turn limited the ability of
diverse—particularly nonelite—groups to build independent, enduring,
wealthy nonprofit institutions to the same degree as their counterparts in
the North. It also meant that the ability of Virginia's nonprofits to accumulate property for investments and their operations was diminished.[21]

Many other Southern states followed Virginia's pattern, creating some
private colleges, but consigning their major institutions to state control,
efforts that took a variety of forms. After the failure of an earlier venture
backed, in part, by a fifty-pound donation from George Washington, the
University of Maryland was grafted onto a proprietary medical school,
with a pastiche of backing that included income from state lotteries, tuition fees, and low-cost hospital service by Seton's Sisters of Charity at
forty-two dollars per annum per nun. The University of Mississippi was
initially built around a private college, although the funds were later
shifted to an independent institution after the state realized $277,332
($3,666,104) from the sale of congressionally granted public lands. South
Carolina and Alabama also created public universities. By 1829, South Carolina's system was receiving $10,500 ($137,550) per annum in public appropriations; Alabama's, $16,000 ($209,600); and Virginia's, $15,000.
Rather than collecting private donations from a multiplicity of sources,
these institutions received private gifts but subsisted primarily on annual
appropriations from the state for their operating expenses, which meant
that they had little, if any, endowment or surplus capital to invest beyond
their own campuses.[22]

Even in the North, gifts of the magnitude of the Girard and Lowell bequests were the exception rather than the rule, particularly before 1840.
Instead, many of the wealthiest organizations subsisted on subscriptions,
relatively small donations, and revenues from investments, services, and
sales—including groups such as the ABS and the Savings Bank of New
York, one of a number of mutual savings banks created in Northern cities
to foster thrift and self-support among the poor.

Mutual Savings Banks

Mutual savings banks began to appear in Philadelphia, New York, Baltimore, and Boston in the second decade of the nineteenth century. Unlike

commercial banks, these institutions sought out small depositors of modest means, investing their funds at minimal risk while providing at least a 5% return. Rather than reinvesting the profits in paid staffs, most of these early ventures were run by trustees who volunteered their time, serving without compensation. Following a Franklinesque approach to poverty, they sought to reduce public outlays for poor relief by encouraging workers to save as much as possible during their productive years.

Because mutual savings banks lay at the far end of the charitable spectrum in terms of their ability to spur large-scale capital formation, they provide useful case studies for studying the economic impact of some of the wealthiest antebellum nonprofit organizations. The most successful venture by far was the Savings Bank of New York (SBNY), which was chartered in New York in 1819. The bank was the offspring of the Society for the Prevention of Pauperism (SPP), founded in 1817 by a group of some of the most prominent members of the city's elite, including Governor De Witt Clinton and the noted Quaker philanthropist Thomas Eddy. Alarmed by growing poverty rates, the society launched a series of investigations into the underlying causes of pauperization as well as ways to encourage self-support, endorsing the creation of a mutual savings bank for the poor among its many recommendations.[23]

Like Graham's Widows' Society and Franklin's Pennsylvania Hospital, savings banks were an imported idea that had its roots in the British Isles. Some historians trace the concept of a savings bank to encourage habits of thrift and self-support among the poor to Daniel Defoe's 1705 treatise "Giving Alms, Not Charity"; others to Thomas Malthus and Jeremy Bentham. By 1815, Scotland was "covered with newly formed savings banks, except in the extreme north." England's charity banks were promoted by groups such as the Prudent Man's Friend Society and the Society for Bettering the Condition of the Poor, and publicly backed by prominent writers and reformers such as William Wilberforce, Malthus, and David Ricardo.[24]

The idea for a savings bank for New York's poor was first broached by the SPP's bluntly named Committee on Want of Economy and Extravagance and endorsed by De Witt Clinton in his 1817 gubernatorial address as a means to "prevent or alleviate the evils of pauperism." When the bank was denied a charter as a freestanding institution, Eddy drafted a report under the society's auspices, in which he presented the project as a solution to New York's endemic social and financial ills. If the poor could be taught to help themselves by providing for their own futures, Eddy argued, the city's revenues could be transferred to other, more useful ends. His ideas assumed added force during the economic downturn of 1819, as almshouse expenditures doubled to over $100,000 ($1.1 million in 2000 dollars) while the numbers of poor spiraled to over ten thousand—close to a tenth of the city's population.[25]

The goal was to "bring within the reach of every industrious person, the great advantage of public security and interest for small sums of money," in order to promote "that personal comfort of independence which arises from prudent conduct." In phrases that smacked of Franklin's reasoning, the bank's promoters vowed to encourage "habits of economy" among "tradesmen, mechanics, laborers, servants and others," by overcoming their inability to increase their savings on their own. It was designed as a philanthropic venture in its techniques, as well as its aims. Rather than hiring a full-time staff, the board members ran the bank as volunteers, with the profits reinvested in passbook dividends in lieu of being returned to the trustees. Backed by a strongly articulated rationale and influential political support, the SBNY began operations in 1819.[26]

The Philadelphia Saving Fund Society opened its mutual savings bank three years earlier. Like its New York counterpart, the society was cast as a philanthropic venture and strictly monitored to ensure that it was confining its ministrations primarily to the working class. The state legislature limited the amount of deposits to $200 ($2,400) per annum in 1828, requiring depositors who invested more than that sum to close their accounts. The Savings Bank of Baltimore was similarly designed to encourage habits of frugality and thrift in the "industrious and thrifty poor." Other prominent charitable mutual savings banks included the Provident Savings Institution in Boston and the Seamen's Bank for Savings, founded in New York in 1829 to bolster the efforts of the Society for the Promotion of the Gospel among Seamen and the Seamen's Fund and Retreat.[27]

Although fueled by small accounts, some of these institutions attracted substantial resources, surprising even their directors. One of SBNY's founders, John Pintard, optimistically predicted that the bank would accumulate $50,000 ($550,000 in 2000 dollars) worth of deposits in its first year; instead, it drew $155,000 (@ $1,705,000) in the first six months. And its resources grew exponentially thereafter. In 1825, nine thousand investors had $1.4 million ($16.8 million) on deposit; ten years later, the number of investors had risen to twenty-three thousand, with $3 million ($39 million) in funds; by 1860 over fifty thousand passbook holders had nearly $10 million ($130 million) on deposit. Similarly, the Seamen's Bank had over $8 million ($104 million) in its coffers on the eve of the Civil War, and Baltimore's bank nearly $6 million ($78 million). By 1860, "three

New York City mutuals (the Bank for Savings, the Bowery and the Seamen's) ranked among the ten largest business organizations in the country," underscoring, once again, the often indistinct lines between the market and the philanthropic sphere.[28]

Initially, at least, charitable mutual savings banks were tightly regulated, providing capital for specific types of ventures, a practice dictated, in large measure, by state legislatures. The 1820s, when many of these institutions were still in their infancy, were marked by a "severe capital scarcity," making banks' highly liquid assets particularly valuable. In the process, mutual savings banks often emerged as "the single most important sources for funds for many municipal and state governments," which had the legal authority to dictate the nature of their investments. Charity banks and companies that specialized in handling philanthropic endowments such as Massachusetts Life (discussed below) also accentuated regional disparities. By 1835, when the South had forty-three banks of all varieties, with deposits of $20,780,000, the SBNY had $3 million worth of highly liquid assets, and Massachusetts Life held another $6.1 million—or nearly half as much as all the Southern banks combined![29]

New York's Bank for Savings opened while Clinton and others were trying to raise funds for the development of the Erie Canal, which may have influenced their desire to reduce the demands of poor relief on the public treasury. Capital improvements were often funded by tax levies or foreign investments. But European investors were still recovering from the devastation of the Napoleonic Wars; few were interested in seeing their money flow into New York state. Moreover, the revenues from land sales that had initially covered New York's debts and underwritten new projects were diminishing precisely as the debts incurred in the War of 1812 came due.

Clinton and his colleagues found a new source of revenue in the savings bank, which was legally limited under the terms of its 1819 charter to investments in state and federal bonds. Because of these restrictions, the bank quickly emerged as a major force in the state's internal improvement schemes, particularly the construction of the Erie Canal. By 1821, it held $475,000 ($5,225,000) in Erie Canal debt, as opposed to the $40,000 ($440,000) held by the next largest investor. In the words of the bank's chronicler, "Within two years of its opening it had become the single most important financier of the Erie Canal and within a decade it bore a similar relationship to the internal improvement projects of Ohio and New York City," fostering the growth of transportation lines that provided the backbone for the market revolution by helping to speed the movement of money and goods across the hinterland.[30]

It was a convenient relationship for the bank's backers, several of whom sat on the Board of Canal Commissioners. Men like Thomas Eddy and De Witt Clinton were avid canal promoters, as well as charter trustees of the bank, and under their guidance the SBNY became a major financial backer of the Erie Canal, providing the necessary funds to bring the project to fruition when other financial options were lacking. It proved a crucial windfall. When New York officials were planning their $7 million ($77 million) capital improvement project, "the total amount of banking and insurance capital" in the entire state totaled less than $21 million ($231 million), including the resources of the local branch of the Bank of the United States, making the SBNY's spiraling holdings a particularly coveted resource.[31]

The popularity of institutions like the SBNY raises a number of intriguing questions about the relationships between the trustees and depositors, and why members of the elite like Clinton and Eddy were able to attract so many accounts from small investors. Mutual savings banks provide useful laboratories for testing the extent to which workers held "values and attitudes considerably different from the dominant capitalist ideology." Clearly, the rise of charity savings banks was part of the sometimes brutal effort to force the poor into the waged economy and enforce self-support that swept the United States and Western Europe beginning in the late eighteenth century—efforts reflected in Franklin's thinking and the economics of Malthus, Ricardo, and Bentham. Many urban laborers in the United States were undoubtedly angry and dazed by the social and economic changes that were engulfing them by the 1820s, including the effects of the spreading market economy, and may have mistrusted many charities and businesses that seemed to be undermining the autonomy that their fathers had enjoyed. Did these attitudes soften when they saw an opportunity to become minicapitalists themselves?[32]

The answer is necessarily complex. As Peter Way has demonstrated in his work on Irish canal workers, the antebellum era produced not one working class but many, ranging from the articulate republican idealists described by Sean Wilentz to the disorganized and disorderly laborers described by Way. Careful analyses by other scholars, such as David Zonderman, reveal the extent to which workers were divided, even in their responses to the mechanistic regimentation of the textile factories. These works, and the startling success of the mutual savings banks, suggest that far from being a self-conscious proletariat, antebellum workers fell into a variety of ideological categories that require further disaggregation by gender, religion, ethnicity, and the workers' own class orientation. More-over, the sheer numbers of laborers who invested in institutions like the SBNY hint at the possibility that even those workers who rhetorically re-jected bourgeois notions of propriety and deeply resented the social and economic upheavals that were reshaping their lives were willing to invest in their own economic advancement.[33]

In both New York and Philadelphia, a substantial number of passbook holders were skilled and unskilled laborers, patterns promoted by the trustees. Beginning in 1832, for example, the SBNY reduced its interest rates from 5% to 4% on accounts of over $500 ($6,500) to discourage in-vestments by middle-class depositors. When the bank opened in 1819, roughly 25% of its clients were unskilled workers. By 1839, that figure had risen to 51%, many of whom were female domestics. Although occupa-tional data are not available for Philadelphia's bank before 1850, by that point 38% of its accounts were held by "merchants, artisans and handy-craftsmen," 13% by porters or laborers, and 43% by domestic servants. A number of voluntary associations held passbooks as well, including Re-becca Gratz's Hebrew Ladies' Benevolent Society. Although it is unclear whether they set up their accounts at the Pennsylvania Savings Fund Soci-ety, workingmen's mutual aid groups such as the Worker's Beneficial Soci-ety and the Union Beneficial Society of Journeymen and Bricklayers also mandated that their excess funds would be deposited in area banks, a com-mon practice among antebellum charities and mutual aid societies, both large and small.[34]

The limited available data suggest that female domestics, who tended to be single, were often long-term investors, most probably saving a compe-tence for old age as a hedge against the almshouse. Men were more likely to save for the short term, withdrawing funds to buy a house or start a small business—findings that would be consistent with the patterns that Stephen Thernstrom found in Newburyport, Massachusetts, where workers often subjected themselves to "ruthless underconsumption" to save enough to buy a house. Although mutual savings banks have been criticized by some researchers as self-serving ploys of the rich to borrow from the poor, it ap-pears that many laborers were drawn by what Thernstrom termed "prop-erty mobility," seeking to become capitalistic stakeholders in pursuit of their own personal security. Just as the ABS broadened participation in the market revolution through Bible sales, mutual savings banks broadened the ranks of potential investors by catering to clients of limited means.[35]

Endowments and Investments:
The Massachusetts Hospital Life Insurance Company

While Northern mutual savings banks collected and invested hundreds of thousands of dollars from small investors each year, Boston's charities and educational institutions played a pivotal role in local economic developments by virtue of their endowments, their ties to area investors, and the unusual nature of the state's for-profit banking system. Boston's banks stood at the opposite end of the economic spectrum from mutual savings banks, serving the investment needs of the very rich and of large-scale philanthropic institutions. In most areas, bank directors were legally prohibited from self-dealing. Thus, in those states where savings banks were regulated, the trustees were expressly forbidden to profit from their position. In New England, however, banks were often treated as extensions of older, kin-based business consortia, providing financial backing for the commercial and industrial ventures of their trustees. Thus, Boston's Provident Institution for Savings, chartered in 1817, provided long-term loans for the local textile industry, a pattern repeated in other financial and philanthropic institutions as well. This was particularly true of the Massachusetts Hospital Life Insurance Company, "the largest financial institution in New England." Much as the Savings Bank of New York provided capital for the Erie Canal, Hospital Life became a major source of credit for the Massachusetts textile industry, siphoning charitable, religious, and educational endowments into regional economic development.[36]

The company was created as an extension of one of Boston's richest and most prominent charitable ventures, Massachusetts General Hospital. When the hospital received its charter in 1811, the state legislature offered it a piece of prime property, with the proviso that it raise a $100,000 (@ $1 million) matching grant by 1816. Later, it was granted an extension, owing to the lingering economic effects of the War of 1812. In 1814, the state also granted the hospital's board a monopoly over "the sale of annuities" to bolster its revenues. Chartered as a separate institution in 1818, Hospital Life paid one-third of its profits to Massachusetts General, with the freedom to invest the rest at will. Although designed as an insurance company, it made its greatest profits in the management of trusts and nonprofit endowments. In many respects, it was the antithesis of institutions like the Savings Bank of New York, eschewing deposits of less than $500 ($5,500) and accounts held on deposit for less than five years. This was an institution for the well-to-do, rather than the working poor. Created as a quasi-charitable, quasi-commercial venture, it began operations with approximately $500,000 ($5,650,000), money raised from the sale of shares. Its investors and officers brought in nonprofit accounts as well. Thus, President William Phillips secured the endowment funds of Phillips Andover Academy (which his family had helped to found), while the surplus revenues of organizations such as Harvard University, the Boston Female Asylum, the Boston Athenaeum, and even some of the more prominent Benevolent Empire societies such as the ABS also made their way into company's holdings, as did the city's share of Franklin's bequest.[37]

The trustees of many of these institutions were substantial shareholders in Massachusetts Life, and a few, like Josiah Quincy and Nathaniel Bowditch, were also on the Hospital Life board. By the 1820s, the company was managing the endowments of some of the area's richest nonprofit institutions, including Harvard's. The history of the university's endowment is a tale of increasing liquidity. Most of its holdings in the seventeenth century consisted of real estate, or revenues from real estate, including such properties as the Queen's Head Tavern in Southwark, England. It also regularly received sums from the colonial government, including the proceeds from the Boston-to-Charleston ferry. As historian Samuel Eliot Morison explains, "Most of the colonial gifts and bequests to the College were (for want of any suitable mechanism for investment) in wild land, which could seldom be rented and was often as not seized by squatters." This situation continued until the Revolution, when the university began to transfer its investments into continental loan certificates and state treasury notes paying 6% interest.[38]

In effect, the trustees set about transforming the endowment from real estate into liquid capital. By 1825, the university had about $300,000 ($3.6 million) in endowment funds, a significant amount of money at that time, and one that grew rapidly thereafter. Until the Revolution, the Board of Visitors was primarily governed by the clergy. During the war years, the mixture shifted to businessmen and lawyers, with a few clerics still in attendance. However, beginning around 1825, the Board underwent a transition in which the remaining clergymen were pushed aside by a formidable group of business entrepreneurs. Dubbed the "financial administration," these businessmen tightened the oversight of the college's finances and accounting procedures and introduced a new array of investment policies. Men like Bowditch were leaders in the region's financial and industrial revolutions, and several had direct ties to local textile mills, as well as seats on the board of the Massachusetts Hospital Life Insurance Company.[39]

In return for their support, shareholders and the fund's directors received easy access to loans. Several of these shareholders, like John Lowell, were closely associated with the textile industry, and many received sizable loans for industrial development. In the words of the company's chronicler, Hospital Life became "the most important single source of intermediate term credit for the Massachusetts textile industry during the nineteenth century," with resources that dwarfed those of all of the state's savings banks combined.[40]

Many of the trustees were also among Boston's most generous donors, collectively contributing hundreds of thousands of dollars to the city's elite charitable and educational institutions. It was a cyclical pattern of donations given for endowments that were then eventually reinvested in their mills. By the 1830s, large-scale donative philanthropy and "control over charitable and philanthropic endowments had come to represent substantial" activities in Boston. In an evolving twist to what Stephen Innes has termed "moral capitalism," donors gave the money, served on the boards, and sat on the committees that invested the endowments. In effect, "one gave money to support education or heal the sick, only to borrow it back from the Massachusetts Hospital Life and invest it in the textile industry, the very place from which the money had probably come in the first place." In Massachusetts, philanthropy and economic development were intimately linked, translating the colonial precedents pioneered by men like Franklin into capital for the region's nascent industrial revolution.[41]

Conclusion

Northern philanthropy, philanthropists, and nonprofit organizations made important contributions to economic modernization, sharpening regional differences. They also represented the growing diversity and complexity of the philanthropic sphere. During the half century between the Revolution and the Jacksonian era, the public arena had widened considerably. In Franklin's lifetime, philanthropy and social advocacy were the almost exclusive province of Protestant white male elites. By the 1820s, a lively universe of Catholics, Protestants, and Jews, laywomen and nuns, businessmen and statesmen was crafting associations, some of which were local artifacts while others circled the nation.

Several common denominators undergirded this heterogeneous universe and fostered its growth: a favorable legal environment epitomized by First Amendment guarantees, a rhetorical commitment to egalitarianism born of the Revolution, and the messianic evangelical faith in progress and perfectionism unleashed with revivalism and disestablishment. Yet beneath the surface major regional schisms had begun to appear. While Northern philanthropy was distinguished by a multiplicity of highly independent groups, each playing different political and economic roles, Southern largesse was more contained, a vibrant but fragile construct created and controlled under the vigilant watch of male slaveholding elites.[42]

This in turn has important theoretical implications for understanding the mesh between antebellum philanthropy, democracy, and the civil sphere. As previously noted, contemporary students of civil society such as Robert Putnam have emphasized the importance of associations in "making democracy work" by fostering economic development and building social capital—the shared reservoir of trust that social rules will be understood, accepted, and obeyed—that encourages citizens to pool their resources and to work together. Putnam contrasts this scenario with a different model, one weakly populated by associational networks and distinguished by hierarchical rule. "In this setting," he predicts, "we should expect . . . coercion, exploitation, and dependence to predominate." Although based on his research on Italy, in many respects Putnam's model represents the slavocracy: a society dominated by entrenched hierarchies in which behavior was coerced, whether through violence toward intransigent slaves or the threat of social ostracism in the case of wayward wives. To quote the Southern commentator, George Fitzhugh, "all government is a matter of force. . . . the white [male] citizens of the South . . . all belong to the master race, have exclusive rights and privileges of citizenship, and an interest not to see this right of citizenship extended" to "women, and negroes, and small children."[43]

Southern society bore a strong resemblance to Putnam's paradigm but with an important twist. The social geography of antebellum Southern philanthropy was distinguished not by the absence or presence of associational activities but by the amount of autonomy these institutions exercised (particularly in terms of the activities of women and free blacks), their relationship to the state, their ability to participate in social reform, and their economic roles. In each instance, Southern associations were more dependent on the supervision and control of white male elites, less active in reform, and less likely to play significant economic roles than their counterparts in the North.

One of the great ironies of American history is that Alexis de Tocqueville, who wrote his celebrated treatise on democracy against the backdrop of these emerging regional disparities, missed the implications of the competing regional visions of democratic governance that swirled about him. For Tocqueville, voluntary associations constituted one of the driving engines of American democracy, a means of empowering ordinary citizens and giving them a political voice throughout the nation as a whole. According to his reasoning, citizens in a democracy could achieve little on their own and thus were "powerless if they do not voluntarily learn to help one another." Once they coalesced, however, they were "no longer isolated men, but a power seen from afar . . . whose language is listened to," particularly if they used the power of the press to air their views. Although these activities were circumscribed in the South, for Northern groups they were indispensable tools for claiming a political voice that custom, prejudice, and law often denied—even when that voice challenged the prescriptions of some of the country's most eminent slaveholding statesmen.[44]

Race, Religion, and Reform

While white women's religious be-
nevolence led to market activities and alliances with local governments,
and Northern philanthropy was helping to underwrite regional economic
development, African American congregations became political pulpits in
national debates over slavery and the fate of free blacks, underscoring the
growing importance of social advocacy. The significance of the African
American church's capacity for political mobilization was symbolized by a
clash of patriarchs. Two former slaves, Absalom Jones and Richard Allen,
laid the groundwork for an independent black church in the 1780s, almost
a decade before Isabella Graham founded the Widows' Society. Begun as
purely religious ventures, African American religious denominations ultimately spearheaded communal opposition to the white-controlled American Colonization Society (ACS), a federally supported Benevolent Empire
enterprise to "repatriate" free blacks to the west coast of Africa. The anticolonizationist campaign pitted the country's Northern free blacks, many
of whom were recent freedmen, against a formidable array of fabled
statesmen, a contest that vividly illustrated the legacy of disestablishment
and the growing power of civil society.

In the process, Northern African American denominations provided a
resilient political voice for one of the country's most disadvantaged groups
and a means of publicly contesting the racist pronouncements of hostile
whites in much the same way that Gratz and Leeser used their charities

and publications to combat the incursions of the Benevolent Empire. Churches also served as vehicles for capital accumulation and investment within black communities. Slavery began in the colonies in 1619, was codified in law by the end of the seventeenth century, was condoned by the revolutionary generation, and expanded in the nineteenth century. By 1830, cotton constituted the country's largest export, and chattel slavery its most insidious institution. In 1790, as in 1860, the majority of African Americans were held in bondage, and the small communities of freedmen in Northern and Southern cities were held down by unremitting discrimination. Within this milieu, the success of Northern free blacks in creating a viable framework for social advocacy and community mobilization was a striking achievement. And no institution played a greater role in these developments than the black church.

Building Zion

The African Americans who created the country's first independent black organizations were heirs of the republican belief that democracy required a "spartan, self-denying virtue." Allen and Jones relentlessly publicized their belief that virtuous behavior would defuse racial prejudice and undermine negative stereotypes, a notion that infused many of their associational efforts. As they explained, "the judicious part of mankind will think it unreasonable that a superior good conduct is looked for from our race by those that stigmatize us as men." Nonetheless, virtuous behavior was imperative: "if we are lazy and idle the enemies of freedom plead it as a cause why we ought not to be free . . . by such conduct we strengthen the bonds of oppression, and keep many in bondage who are more worthy than ourselves." In effect, the ideology of racial uplift was rooted in notions of civic virtue, as well as antipathy to discrimination and slavery.[1]

For the revolutionary generation of Northern freedmen, benevolent societies and churches became instruments in "the cause of freedom" and weapons against "the enemies of our color." The Free African Society (FAS) is a case in point. One of a small but growing number of black mutual aid groups that surfaced in the wake of the Revolution, it was created in 1787 to promote charity, self-help, and individual probity among its members. Participation was based on a strict moral code that prohibited drinking, fighting, and marital infidelity. Those who violated the rules risked expulsion and loss of the dues contributed as a hedge against illness or unemployment. Begun as a mutual aid society, the FAS subsequently served as the cradle of Philadelphia's first independent black congregations, St. Thomas's Episcopal Church, headed by Jones, and Bethel Methodist Episcopal Church, directed by Allen.[2]

Both of these extraordinary men played a role in the rise of black philanthropy and social reform, succeeding against considerable odds. Absalom Jones was born into slavery on a Delaware farm in 1746. An unusual youngster, he learned to read by begging "to be taught by anybody that I found able and willing to give me the least instruction." In a phrase reminiscent of Franklin's *Autobiography*, Jones later recalled that "by this course I became singular, and escaped many evils, and saved my money." In 1760, he, his mother and five siblings were sold to a slaveowner in Philadelphia, where he worked in his master's store. During this period Jones taught himself to write and studied mathematics in night school. He wedded another slave at twenty-four with a promise to buy her freedom, raising the thirty pounds through gifts and loans from local Quakers, and working double shifts to repay the debts. Jones was ultimately manumitted in 1784, three years before the creation of the FAS.[3]

Richard Allen also began his career in bondage. A generation younger than Absalom Jones, Allen was born in 1760, the slave of a Philadelphia lawyer. He and his family were later sold to a Delaware slaveowner whom Allen considered a "humane man," although the enslavement of his youth remained "a bitter pill" throughout his life. Part of that bitterness stemmed from the sale of his family to another plantation. Allen turned to local camp meetings for consolation, where both he and his master embraced the Methodist faith.[4]

At the time of his conversion, the Methodists endorsed a sharply adversarial stance against slavery, a commitment that stemmed, in part, from the convictions of the sect's leader, John Wesley. Perhaps because of his own conversion, or possibly because of mounting personal debts, Allen's owner offered him the chance to buy his freedom in 1783. Afterwards, Allen returned to Philadelphia, where he labored at a variety of unskilled and semiskilled jobs, including preaching under the auspices of the Methodist church.

Both he and Jones used their freedom to draw Philadelphia's black community into public service. During the yellow fever epidemic of 1793, the prominent physician and reformer Benjamin Rush and Mayor Matthew Clarkson persuaded them to help in nursing the sick and burying the dead out of a mistaken belief that blacks were immune to the disease. The men agreed, enlisting volunteers through the FAS and through newspaper advertisements.

While Jones and Allen helped Rush with his patients, others tended the sick and dying, located coffins, and drove hearses to the cemetery. Tending strangers through their final agonies was a grisly task, and both blacks and whites perished in significant numbers: in less than a month over 4,000 Philadelphians died, including 240 African Americans, and Jones himself contracted the disease. When subsequent accounts accused some of the black volunteers of extortion and theft, the men responded with a detailed and remarkably temperate account of their work, backed by a testimonial from the mayor. Throughout their lives the clerics used their actions, associations, and the printed page to counter racist stereotypes and to educate an often hostile public.[5]

Although lifelong friends, the two men parted company to found separate congregations in 1794. By 1790, the FAS had assumed an increasingly religious tenor, as members pushed for the creation of a church of their own, free from white supervision and control. While both Allen and Jones were Methodists, the majority opted for an Episcopal affiliation. Unwilling to renounce his Methodist faith, Allen declined the invitation to serve as their minister, but agreed to do "nothing to retard them in building a church." As he explained, "I was confident that there was no religious sect . . . [that] would suit . . . the capability of the colored people as well as the Methodist, for the plain and simple gospel suits best for any people," a belief that galvanized his decision to found Bethel.[6]

Benjamin Rush helped to launch Absalom Jones's Episcopal church through subscription drives and donations from prominent political figures such as George Washington and Thomas Jefferson. Chartered two years later, St. Thomas's African Church quickly attracted more than four hundred parishioners, including emerging leaders like the prominent sailmaker James Forten. Jones was subsequently ordained as an Episcopal deacon in 1795, becoming the first African American Episcopal priest nine years later.

Allen's relationship with the Methodist hierarchy was far more strained. When he first broached his plan for a separate black congregation with the Methodist elders, his proposal was curtly dismissed. Allen nevertheless remained loyal to Methodism, in part because "the Methodists were the first people that brought glad tidings to the colored people." But he regarded many white clerics as "tyrants, . . . especially to the colored people," who were mistreated and often banned from congregations "for the smallest offense." Over the course of his long career, Allen experienced much of this caustic treatment firsthand.[7]

When offhand dismissals failed to deter him from building a black parish, Allen was briefly threatened with excommunication. Undeterred, he founded Bethel Church in June 1794 and was ordained as the first fully certified African American preacher in the Methodist Church five years later. Tensions continued to flare over the church's charter. Drafted with the aid of a white Methodist minister, it technically ceded the church's property and its management to the Methodist Conference, creating the conditions for escalating battles over Bethel's holdings and administration. When a recently appointed elder examined the document a decade later, he announced that he was authorized to preach at Bethel "at his convenience," and their expense. He then demanded the church's keys and books, warning Allen and his congregants that they could use the property only with his permission.[8]

After a series of increasingly acrid exchanges, the congregation hired a lawyer, who informed them that the charter could be altered by a majority vote. Casting their ballots without the permission—or knowledge—of conference authorities, the church members secured the necessary majority and revised the charter, making the congregation sole owners of Bethel's property. The "African Supplement," as it came to be known, was rejected by the Methodist hierarchy, which countered by putting Bethel up for auction. Allen managed to retain it by outbidding his highest competitor, and his congregation retained its church. The standoff finally ended when the conference's attempts to annul the revised charter were rebuffed by state supreme court in 1816.

Shortly afterward, Allen played a central role in founding the African Methodist Episcopal Church (AME), the first national, independent denomination under black control. The AME was born of two decades of white deception and dissent. It was an excruciating battle, and Allen's continuing loyalty to Methodist tenets was a tribute to the depth and tenacity of his faith, just as the rapid growth of the new denomination attested to his organizational skills. Named the AME's first bishop, he headed a flock of over ten thousand members by the mid-1820s.

Other black congregations followed in turn. John Glouster, another former slave, founded America's first black Presbyterian congregation in Philadelphia in 1807. A splinter group broke away from the Methodist conference to form the African Methodist Episcopal Zion church, a second national African American denomination, in 1821. By the 1820s, all of the major Northern cities counted one or more independent African American congregations, providing an invaluable infrastructure for grassroots mobilization, charity, and reform.

Many of the first schools in Northern black communities, aside from those created by white-controlled abolition and manumission societies, were developed in conjunction with the church. Absalom Jones initiated a variety of educational ventures at St. Thomas's, as did Richard Allen at Bethel. Some, like the African Baptist Church's school in Boston, attracted municipal support. Northern churches also collaborated with local governments in communal projects such as the creation of cemeteries, receiving grants of public money and land in at least two instances in New York. Although these alliances with public officials occurred less often than in the white community, and the amounts tended to be significantly smaller, during the early national years black-controlled educational and charitable ventures received public support in a number of cities such as Pittsburgh, New York, Boston, and—although cases were much rarer in the South—New Orleans.

Churches played economic roles as well. Like their white Protestant counterparts, the charities and benevolent societies that coalesced around Northern congregations were agents of capital formation, attracting and pooling funds for their communities. Although the amounts are hard to track owing to the paucity of surviving documents, the available data suggest that many of these groups managed to raise fairly respectable sums. The Benevolent Sons of Bethel Church, for example, had $276 (@ $3,500) in their coffers in 1827, and $431 ($5,516) two years later—amounts that in a Catholic context would have provided a year's support for ten to fifteen nuns, perhaps more. Compared to the amounts being raised by Catholic congregations, then, these were considerable holdings.[9]

Because of this ability to collect and generate income, astute students of the African American community such as W. E. B. Du Bois, maintained that any study of economic cooperation among black people must begin with the church. Organizations such as the Friendly Sons of St. Thomas, a group created at Jones's church in 1797, were keenly aware of their role in generating, collecting, and investing funds. Members sought not only to aid themselves and others, but to increase their funds through investments. Under the terms of their constitution, once the group's collective resources exceeded one hundred pounds, 50% was to be "let out [in loans] ... for no longer than twelve months," and the rest invested in real estate. In the process, they not only bolstered the available resources for members, their families, and indigents within the community; but also provided capital for small entrepreneurs. Their efforts underscored the different ways in which different groups applied their philanthropic resources to communal ends. Clearly, there were significant disparities in the amount of investment capital that white women, blacks, and Northern white businessmen and entrepreneurs commanded. But it should also be remembered that this was an era when most African Americans would have had great difficulty in securing loans from banks or wealthy white businessmen (aside from Quakers), and so philanthropic resources provided important sources of liquid capital that would not have otherwise been available for investment and reform. Northern black churches and charities also served as bases for the collection of funds for publications and pamphlets to present their issues, ideas, and causes to the broader society, providing vital resources for the growth of civil society.[10]

Southern black churches existed as well, but their independence was "always threatened by restrictions." Christianity spread to Southern blacks, in part, because many slaveowners placed a premium on Christianizing their bondsmen in order to increase their obedience and to deflect Northern criticism. But they also kept a close watch on any strains of independence. As a result, even though the region developed several of the country's first black congregations, whites tended to own church lands and oversaw African American religious activities, ensuring that "separate black churches could always be disbanded if white authorities became alarmed at their independence," a fate that befell congregations in Charleston, Virginia, and New Orleans. Whites tolerated black churches, but with misgivings. To quote Ira Berlin, many Southerners "detested the independence" these institutions offered, hemming them in with legal restrictions and the threat of mob reprisals.[11]

Nevertheless, some free blacks managed to create mutual aid associations in conjunction with their churches, such as the Brown Fellowship Society, an exclusive mulatto mutual aid association founded in Charleston in 1790. Many of these groups began as burial societies, providing cemetery plots and handling funerals for their members, and a few like the Charleston society subsidized schools as well. The amount of leeway these organizations enjoyed varied from state to state, with the greatest autonomy in the upper South.

Baltimore stood at the far end of the continuum, with a variety of educational and benevolent ventures, beginning with a Sunday school in 1809 and the Baltimore Bethel Benevolent Society of the Young Men of Color, created in 1821. A few of these initiatives even amassed a fair amount of capital: according to Christopher Phillips, the African Friendship Benevolent Society for Social Relief had $400 in the bank (or nearly $5,000 in 2000 dollars) by 1833, echoing patterns in Philadelphia. Several of the city's fraternal groups also invested in black businesses and possibly even trade with Liberia. One of the reasons why black Baltimoreans were able to build a strong institutional base doubtless was the size of the state's free black population, which was the largest in the South, and Baltimore's location on the fringes of the Southern slavocracy, where slavery and the tobacco culture that supported it were declining, at least in the city. Yet even there, many of these groups were subject to white supervision.[12]

Despite continuing discrimination, the number of African churches continued to grow in both the North and the South. In the process, they reiterated dominant Protestant patterns, creating charitable and educational resources for their communities. Although begun as exercises in religious autonomy, Northern black parishes such as Allen's and Jones's quickly evolved into tools for social protest as well, joining their parishes into an empire for reform.

Petitions and Political Participation

Richard Allen and Absalom Jones first entered the public policymaking arena in the 1790s, submitting the first petition to be sent to Congress by African Americans a decade after Franklin's volatile memorial. Although the right to petition was incorporated into the Bill of Rights and had historically been regarded as a basic English liberty, Franklin's Pennsylvania Abolition Society memorial illustrated the passionate resistance that petitions for reform could evoke. Jones and Allen's petition sparked an equally vivid response.

Both men had felt the lash of slavery as youngsters, and both remembered its sting. When the Fugitive Slave Act was passed in 1793, it quickly resulted in an escalating series of abuses, as freedmen were summarily— and illegally—returned to bondage. After sixteen freedmen who had been manumitted by Quaker slaveholders in North Carolina approached the Philadelphia clerics with their fears of being sold back into slavery, Jones and Allen drafted a congressional petition seeking governmental redress.

Representative Robert Waln of Pennsylvania, who presented the politely worded appeal to his colleagues in January 1800, cloaked his action in apologies for causing undue alarm. His caution proved well founded, as the memorial fanned an impassioned discussion of who had the right to petition and who did not. The Southerners were particularly vocal, and particularly vehement. South Carolina's Representative John Rutledge not only demanded its withdrawal, but a vote of censure as well. The country "already had too much of this new-fangled French philosophy of liberty and equality," he growled. Others noted that some of the petitioners were incapable of signing their names, attributing the document to the Quakers, "a religious body of people whose fanaticism leads them to think it a bounden duty to come to the House every year, though they now come in a different name."[13]

While some urged that the petition be rejected, others were more temperate. Representative Platt of New York suggested that "everything which was brought before the House ought to be committed, unless there was manifest indecency in the language, or it . . . [was] not consistently with[in] the power of the House." Connecticut's Representative William Edmond concurred that "no censure could be due where a petition was respectfully addressed," adding "it mattered not whether the people were black or white; the petition only was to be regarded, and not the color of the persons," concluding by asking rhetorically, is "contempt the way to recommend attachment to the Government?"[14]

Representative Samuel Dana of Connecticut noted that he, too, would object if the petition "contained nothing but a farrago of the French metaphysics of liberty and equality," in which case he would concede "that it was likely to produce some of the dreadful scenes of a St. Domingo." Similarly, "if he believed it was only the effects of a religious fanaticism . . . he might be disposed to think it quite wrong." But the petition was "decently" worded, and "expressly declared that the petitioners did not wish the House to do what was inconsistent with the Constitution, but only asked an amelioration of the severities under which people of their color labored." It therefore merited due consideration.[15]

The underlying issue, of course, was not the petition itself, but the extent of political authority that freedmen could and would enjoy. Thus, Congressman Jones of Georgia snarled, "they speak of the Federal compact, in which they consider those people as interested, in common with others, under these words: 'We the people of the United States of America,' I would ask these gentlemen whether, with all their philanthropy, they would wish to see those people sitting by their sides deliberating in the councils of the nation? He presumed not." But it was Congressman Otis who administered the coup de grâce. "To encourage a measure of [this] kind would have an irritating tendency," he noted, one that would be "mischievous" in its effect. "It would teach them the art of assembling together, debating, and the like, and would soon, if encouraged, extend from one end of the Union to the other." James Madison dismissed the issue more summarily, arguing that petitions from African Americans "had no claim on their attention," particularly when they dealt with such inflammatory issues as slavery.[16]

It was a compelling confrontation, one that presaged the ongoing struggles of men like Allen and Jones, not just to strengthen their communities, but to win a measure of political influence. Despite the egalitarian rhetoric that flowed from the pens of statesmen like Madison and Jefferson during the revolutionary years, this was an era in which white male elites jealously guarded their political monopoly. Freedmen could vote in a handful of states by 1800, but their influence was limited because their numbers were small. How, then, could they make their voices heard over the din of Southern slaveholders?

They found their answer in the church, particularly after 1816, when both the ACS and the AME were created. Just as religious bodies attracted monetary capital, they attracted human capital as well, serving as nodes for grassroots mobilization and the dissemination of ideas and communal imperatives. They also physically exemplified the growing numerical strength of African American communities. And they had financial resources which, although limited, often provided enough support for a pamphlet, a paper, and even a politically oriented crusade, capacities that would become increasingly important over time.

The petition incident brought Madison into contact with Allen and Jones for the first time. Each of these men had a proven commitment to religious libertarianism, but they had radically different ideas about slavery, liberty, and the appropriate scope of social advocacy, to the point that the clerics' petition—although fully within the bounds of the law—was ultimately brushed aside. It marked the opening round in an ongoing battle over public participation, over slavery, and over national reform that would indirectly bring these men into each others' sphere of influence for the remainder of their lives. The catalyst of that clash was the ACS.

The American Colonization Society

Colonization, rather than the constitutional right of petition, was the primary point of contention between men like Allen and Jones and prominent political leaders like Madison and Henry Clay in the 1810s and 1820s. The colonial mentality was deeply rooted in the notion of "warning out": the idea that the best way to deal with community problems was to send vagabonds and other "undesirables" somewhere else before they became a burden on the public resources or a menace to society. Where freedmen were concerned, this notion translated into a situation that equated manumission with removal. In 1691, for example, the government of Virginia legislated that manumission and deportation would go hand in hand. Manumitted slaves were expected—indeed, mandated—to leave the colony upon receiving their freedom.

Colonization schemes continued to surface from a variety of sources throughout the colonial and early national periods. Quakers in Germantown, Pennsylvania, endorsed colonization in 1713 as a panacea for racial tensions, to foster trade, and to Christianize Africa and unsettled territories in the West. Anthony Benezet, one of the leaders in the movement to promote educational opportunities for African Americans, suggested a plan for planting a colony of freedmen west of the Alleghenies, arguing that the climate would be more hospitable—and more familiar—than that of Africa. Jefferson also flirted with colonization, testing the waters in the Virginia legislature in the late 1770s with a proposal to send freedmen into the North American wilderness equipped with seeds, animals, and guarantees of military aid. Others, like Jefferson's fellow Virginian Fernando Fairfax, outlined intricate plans for federally funded colonization schemes in the wake of the Revolution, an enthusiasm shared by many prominent northerners.[17]

Some blacks endorsed the idea as well during this era, but for different reasons. The period following the Revolution witnessed the greatest upsurge of slave trading in the nation's history, with the result that approximately half of the country's slaves and free blacks were born either in Africa or of African parents between 1760 and 1810. For this brief moment, then, colonization might have constituted an exercise in genuine repatriation for some. Perhaps the most visible and articulate exponent of colonization in this period was the African American Paul Cuffe (or Cuffee), a successful Massachusetts mariner who sought to establish a colony on the West African coast for business purposes. To further his plan, he not only secured a trading license from the African Institution in London, one of the primary backers of the British colony in Sierra Leone, but developed several African Institutions among free blacks in the United States. After an abortive attempt to gain federal funding for his venture, Cuffe finally managed to make one crossing with a group of settlers in 1815, but the venture faltered with his death shortly thereafter.[18]

Newport's African Union Society planned a similarly ill-starred venture in the 1780s, ultimately abandoning the project for lack of funds. For blacks, colonization seemed to provide an antidote to the problem of racism; for whites in areas with growing numbers of freedmen, it offered a solution for dealing with a superfluous and potentially troublesome group of laborers. Many proponents (at least rhetorically) touted the dual themes of God and Mammon, arguing that the colonized freedmen would both convert the natives and promote the cause of American trade. For many, it seemed an ideal solution to a welter of problems, a means of dealing, however superficially, with the festering legacy of slavery. For many whites, blacks could live in the nation only if they were slaves.

Although endorsed by men like Jefferson and Cuffe, colonization was by no means an American invention. In 1780, British abolitionists under the leadership of prominent political figures such as William Wilberforce and William Pitt established a colony of repatriated blacks on the West Coast of Africa. Funded by private donations and treasury funds, the British colony of Sierra Leone was peopled with British blacks and repatriated slaves rescued from slavers at sea. The African Institution was created in 1788 to support the settlement by sending missionaries and explorers to map out the spiritual and geographical terrain. Begun as a quasi-philanthropic experiment, the settlement formally became a British colony in 1808.

American interest in testing a similar venture heightened after Gabriel Prosser's abortive Richmond slave revolt in 1800. The Virginia legislature responded in a secret legislative session by drafting a resolution calling for the creation of a colony outside the state where potentially troublesome blacks could be exiled, while Jefferson unsuccessfully used his presidential authority to try to place them in the British colony of Sierra Leone and Portuguese colonies in Latin America. At various times, both Jefferson and James Monroe, who was the state's governor at the time, endorsed the idea of sending disaffected blacks to colonies in other countries or the distant reaches of the Louisiana Purchase.[19]

These sentiments crystallized into a formal movement in 1816, shortly before Monroe assumed the presidency. Its originator was Robert Finley, a well-connected Presbyterian minister. Located in Washington, the ACS was designed to send freedmen to West Africa, preferably with federal funding. Participation was to be voluntary, and military protection was to be provided in tandem with efforts to intercept slave ships. Finley was remarkably adept in winning advocates for his cause. He consulted with Paul Cuffe in designing the project and lined up a stellar constellation of American statesmen to endorse his work. Chief Justice John Marshall was among the members, as were his successor, Roger Taney, future president Andrew Jackson and the famed Massachusetts orator Daniel Webster. Henry Clay chaired the organizational meeting on December 21, 1816, yielding the position to Bushrod Washington, the former president's nephew, when Washington was formally elected president on January 1, 1817.

Both Southern slaveholders from the upper South and Northern Federalists rallied to support the new organization, including James Madison and James Monroe. Despite his earlier endorsement of colonization as "the most desirable measure" for "drawing off our population," Jefferson demurred, convinced by this time, as he bluntly put it, that "we cannot get rid of them this way." Some supporters, including Finley, backed the ACS out of humanitarian leanings, including a sincere belief that American racism was so strident, and so deeply engrained, that it would never dissipate and that freedmen could only live as free men on foreign soil. Others unabashedly revealed themselves as part of the problem. Henry Clay, for example, announced at the first meeting that the organization would provide a means "to rid our country of a useless and pernicious, if not dangerous portion of its population." It would, in effect, "drain them off." Many Southerners doubtless supported the society as a hedge against future slave revolts. And others saw it as a means of strengthening slavery, by exiling the region's free blacks. To quote one historian, it reflected a bizarre "mixture of fascism and philanthropy," attracting backers with a variety of agendas, some benign, others far less so. Although regarded then, as now, as another permutation of the Benevolent Empire, the ACS was devised as a political rather than a purely religious venture from the outset.[20]

Born of a multiplicity of rationales, the ACS gained a significant amount of support from its inception (at least on paper), drawing endorsements from the clergy and from statesmen, social reformers, and business leaders, both North and South. Most of this support was rhetorical, until Reverend Ralph Gurley succeeded Finley as the director in 1825. Gurley strengthened the auxiliary system to bring the ACS more in line with other national organizations such as the American Bible Society and began to publish the *African Repository and Colonial Journal* to publicize its work.

The state and local auxiliaries were strengthened as well. John Marshall was elected to head the Richmond chapter, donating funds as well as his time. In Marshall's words, he took the assignment because he felt that colonization would save the country from "a danger whose extent can scarcely be estimated." A small number of women's auxiliaries also appeared throughout the upper South, raising funds through subscriptions and fairs. Before Gurley's advent, ACS auxiliaries generated a scant $800 ($9,040 in 2000 dollars) in 1822. By 1825, their revenues tallied over $15,000 ($180,000). The French revolutionary war hero, the Marquis de Lafayette, consented to become an honorary vice president, and clergymen across the country donated collections from their Independence Day sermons to the society. By the mid-1820s, the ACS had become a mass movement, akin to the American Sunday School Union or the American Bible Society in both structure and strength.[21]

James Madison assumed the presidency of the society in 1833, a fact that has clearly troubled his biographers. Drew McCoy, for example, describes the Virginia statesman's endorsement of the ACS as "bizarre and incongruous" adding, "The dilemma of slavery undid him." Although Madison's participation may have been rooted in an "unimpeachable" desire to eradicate slavery, "to sustain moral opposition to slavery itself, indeed to keep alive among the American people a principled commitment to the substance of their republican revolution," his support remains puzzling. Did the former president decide to assume a prominent role in the organization out of a mistaken belief that it was "the only responsible and honourable way of keeping faith with the Revolution"? Or did he regard freedmen as "generally idle" and "depraved," the very stereotypes that Richard Allen and Absalom Jones so avidly sought to dispel?[22]

Madison's correspondence reveals a certain ambivalence, admitting at times to self-indulgent "wishes and hopes" that the society would yield a "partial success" in redressing "the greatest of our calamities." In other instances, he lamented the enduring legacy of racism, arguing that "If the blacks ... be retained amid the whites, under the degrading privation of equal rights, political or social, they must always be dissatisfied with their condition as a change only from one to another species of oppression. . . . Nor is it fair, in estimating the danger of collisions with the whites to charge it wholly on the side of the blacks. There would be reciprocal antipathies doubling the danger."[23]

Madison depicted the society as meriting "encouragement from all who regard slavery as an evil, who wish to see it diminished and abolished by peaceable and just means, and who have themselves no better mode to propose." He also warmly endorsed the need for federal support. Madison's biographers often argue that he "loathed ... the 'general welfare' clause of the Constitution," and that he "vehemently" objected to the idea that this vaguely worded provision imbued Congress with "the broader power to legislate for the public good." However, when it came to the ACS, he set aside whatever misgivings he may have had, endorsing federal subsidies for the society's program through the sale of western lands.[24]

Encouraged by statesmen such as Madison, Marshall, and Monroe, the federal government established its first foreign colony under the auspices of a private voluntary association backed by state and federal funds, providing one of the more extraordinary examples of public-private collaboration. To a far greater extent than any of his predecessors, James Monroe used his presidency to expand public alliances with voluntary organizations, authorizing the use of federal funds for missionary societies, asylums, and the ACS.

The government's partnership with the ACS began in 1819, when Congressman Mercer of Virginia (another ardent backer), introduced a proposal to curb the international slave trade, which was officially outlawed by the United States in 1808. Under his plan, the president was empowered to "make such regulations and arrangements as he may deem expedient, for the safe-guarding, support, [and] removal" of captured Africans, backed by a $100,000 ($1.13 million) appropriation.[25]

Passage of the Act in Addition to Other Acts Prohibiting the Slave Trade provided the funds for an expanded U.S. presence in West Africa, while the ACS provided the means. Shortly after the measure was approved, several ACS members approached Madison with offers to help in implementing the Slave Trade Act. When Monroe polled his cabinet for their responses, John Calhoun demurred, but Treasury Secretary Richard Rush, an ACS member, enthusiastically supported the plan. Clay was cautiously supportive, while Monroe's secretary of state, John Quincy Adams, tried to dissuade the president out of an inherent dislike of the prospect of colonial entanglements, which he regarded as unconstitutional. Rush's arguments ultimately prevailed, and the ACS set about building an unofficial American colony on African soil.

The development of Liberia presents an extreme example of the ways in which the American government used private organizations to achieve objectives that fell beyond the scope of its mandated or administrative capacities. Ostensibly, the federal funds were earmarked for naval activities in policing the African coast for rogue slavers, with the ACS providing a haven for the men and women recovered from these vessels. In reality, much of the 1819 federal allocation, and the others that followed, found its way into ACS coffers. Initially, the society identified candidates to serve as federal agents, such as Samuel Bacon, an Episcopal clergyman who traded his post as an ACS agent for a federal appointment to oversee the program. Later, the ACS and federal appointments were jointly held. While the U.S. government secured the land and provided military protection and funding for salaries and supplies, the ACS transported the freedmen (under naval escort) and administered the colony's internal affairs. It also raised funds privately for the settlers' expenses and needs.[26]

It was a symbiotic relationship. As a historian of the Liberian venture explains, "American colonizationists had plans well worked out for their proposed colony, but lacked the capital resources to implement them. The federal government, on the other hand, was looking for a site on Africa's west coast to settle recaptured Africans. But possessing the financial means, policymakers were debarred constitutionally, in Adams' view, from 'the engrafting of a colonial establishment upon the Constitution of the United States.' The Antislave Trade Act of 1819 was significant in that it served as a legislative mechanism through which the United States government involved itself with the Colonization Society."[27]

Adams continued his support, despite his lingering skepticism. At one point, he likened Monroe's expansive interpretation of his constitutional authority to "an Indian cosmogomy; it was mounting the world upon an elephant, and the elephant on a tortoise, with nothing for the tortoise to stand upon." The common historical view holds that it was Whiggish New Englanders such as Adams who were the primary proponents of voluntary associations and public-private collaboration. But in this instance, republicans and Southerners were the society's strongest and most effective champions, particularly the statesmen from Virginia. Adams later recorded the reasons for his own support, which stemmed more from capitulation than conviction. "I did not feel myself at liberty to reverse the decision of Mr. Monroe," he recalled, nor of his other "secretaries, tacitly supported by Congress itself."[28]

In an even stranger twist, Maryland created its own settlement at Cape Palmas, backed by annual allocations of up to twenty thousand dollars per year from the state legislature. Funds were raised through a colonization tax, which levied an annual fee of fifteen dollars per slave for those between the ages of twelve and forty-five, and five dollars for those older or younger. Although the project was rhetorically designed "to hasten . . . the arrival of the period when slavery shall cease to exist in Maryland," the timing was revealing: it was initiated shortly after Nat Turner's slave revolt in 1831.[29]

The Liberian experiment produced a mixed legacy of successes and failures. Some slaveowners, particularly in the upper South, did free their slaves with the proviso that they relocate to Liberia. Some of the émigrés prospered, and a few managed to amass substantial fortunes through trade with the United States. They and their descendants also ruled the colony after the ACS and the government departed, a situation that continued until the 1980s. And Monrovia did provide a useful base for launching raids on French and Spanish slave-trading outposts on other parts of the coast. But Liberia was far from a hospitable setting, plagued by epidemics, tainted water, political unrest, and native attacks. Before Gurley took over in 1825 and revamped the society's auxiliaries, it was also woefully under-funded. Food and equipment were scarce in these early years, and periodic disasters, such as fires, destroyed what little the settlers had. Perhaps more important, in demographic terms, its influence was minuscule. Fewer than 1,500 new inhabitants settled there between 1822 and 1829, including approximately 140 recaptives and 350 former slaves who had been freed on condition that they emigrate.[30]

The Crusade against Colonization

One of the major reasons why so few freedmen volunteered to emigrate—aside from the significant fact that they had been born in the United States—was the vocal resistance of a number of prominent African American leaders, including Allen and Jones. The careers of these men, and influential parishioners such as James Forten, exemplified the importance of the black church in marshaling the political will of the country's African American communities, at least in Northern states. Allen was particularly active in mobilizing his parishioners to speak out on public issues. Philadelphia had a long and venerable tradition of church-sponsored political actively that dated from the 1740s. By the eve of the Revolution, all the city's "denominations and sects ... knew how to mobilize political opinion through the manipulation of ethno-religious sensibilities and networks." Although "not every clergyman or elder sought a public role, those with a taste for political action soon discovered that church networks could be used to promote both the religious and civil rights of their adherents." Allen reiterated these traditions, building a political base as he built his AME.[31]

Both the ACS and the AME were founded in 1816. Within days of the ACS's creation, Jones, Allen, Forten, and other black leaders convened a mass meeting of nearly three thousand at Allen's Bethel Church to consider the society's proposals. Forten had previously flirted with colonization ventures, helping to create a branch of Cuffe's African Institution in Philadelphia. According to some accounts, Jones and Allen were also undecided but favorably disposed to possibilities for emigration, and they and John Glouster opened the meeting with a discussion of "the advantages of colonization." But when they polled the audience for their opinions, there were no endorsements, only a thunderingly unanimous chorus of "nays." Guided by fears of deportation, Philadelphia's African American community voted to resist the society's efforts, and their views were subsequently sustained and publicized through Allen's church.[32]

Fired by communal resistance, Jones, Allen, and Forten launched a national campaign to rebuff the ACS's overtures. As they explained in their "Appeal against the Colonization Movement," they resented the "unmerited stigma . . . cast upon the reputation of the free people of color" by the society's promoters, they rejected the idea that they were "a dangerous and useless part of the community," and they refused to endorse—or cooperate in—the society's programs.[33]

Subsequent rallies repeated these themes. A second meeting produced a new set of resolutions stating that the ACS program would tear individuals from their families, homes, and communities, "where they had churches, fraternal groups, and schools, and place them in a colony that had none of these." Following Bethel's lead, African American churches in Washington, Boston, and New York vociferously condemned the society's colonization program. They declared their right to citizenship and to remain in the United States and decried the society's racist leanings. In the 1820s, Allen summarized these views in *Freedom's Journal*, arguing that "this land which we have watered with our tears and our blood, is now our mother country, and we are well satisfied to stay where wisdom abounds and the gospel is free." In the process, African American communities and congregations publicly challenged the society's ostensibly humanitarian designs.[34]

Not every group concurred. In Baltimore, although there may have been some resistance in the churches, a memorial was produced supporting emigration. As the authors explained, "Though we are not slaves, we are not free. We do not and never shall participate in the enviable privileges which we continually witness. . . . In Africa we shall be free men indeed, and republicans after the model of this republic." John Russwurm, the editor of *Freedom's Journal*, eventually migrated. And even Forten and Allen continued to explore opportunities for black-initiated projects, like the group of émigrés (including Allen's son) they sent to set up a colony in Haiti at the invitation of President Jean Pierre Boyer in 1824. The experiment was a failure, and most returned, but the issue resurfaced once again at the first national black convention movement in a plan to establish an outpost in northern Canada.[35]

It was a complicated episode, one in which the desire to escape a racist society clashed with the desire to stay and fight to win concessions, to fight discrimination, and to secure the liberties that other Americans enjoyed. The strength of the public stance assumed by the participants at these religious rallies clearly had a role in dissuading free blacks and freedmen from cooperating in the ACS's campaigns. Finley immediately recognized the challenge presented by their position and traveled to Philadelphia to try to persuade Allen, Forten, and Jones to endorse his plans. Spokesmen of the ACS particularly targeted black leaders in an effort to build a base of African American support, and some, like Russwurm, ultimately succumbed to their overtures. Daniel Coker, who helped Allen to found the AME, emigrated to do missionary work in 1820, as had one of John Glouster's sons. But most refused to publicly endorse the society's activities, or to emigrate themselves.

In 1830, the aging Allen embarked on his last political venture, helping to coordinate the country's first national African American convention in response to the recent passage of a black code and other discriminatory legislation in Ohio. The forty delegates who attended the September meeting at Bethel elected Allen the first president of the newly created American Society of Free Persons of Color, helping to set yet another national initiative in motion.

They also drafted an "Address to the Free Persons of Color of these United States." Paraphrasing Jefferson's words, it began with the belief that "all men are born free and equal, and consequently are endowed with unalienable rights, among which are . . . the enjoyments of life, liberty, and the pursuit of happiness." The document went on to castigate Ohioans for adopting "a course altogether incompatible with the principles of civil and religious liberty" and called for united political action: "Our forlorn and deplorable situation earnestly and loudly demands of us to devise and pursue all legal means for the speedy elevation of ourselves and brethren to the scale and standing of men."[36]

Moreover, they used the opportunity to reaffirm their condemnation of the ACS. "It does not meet with our approbation," the delegates noted. "We who have been born and nurtured on this soil, we, whose habits, manners, and customs are the same in common with other Americans, can never consent" to emigrate to "that much afflicted country." America, not Liberia, was their home.[37]

The convention proved to be Allen's final political act, the culmination of a long career. Born a slave, he spent a lifetime building institutional resources to combat racism and discrimination. Yet, just as he never broke faith with Methodism, he never lost faith that concerted effort, properly applied, could bring about reform. Four decades earlier, he and Absalom Jones had published a statement to slaveholders, asking "Will you, because you have reduced us to the unhappy condition our color is in, plead our incapacity for freedom and our contented condition under oppression, as a sufficient cause for keeping us under the grievous yoke?" Allen's answer in

1794, the year he founded his Bethel congregation, was the same in 1831, the year of his death. Perhaps in tribute to his convictions and contributions, the delegates to the 1831 convention declared: "This is our home, and this our country. . . . Here we were born, and here we will die."[38]

Abolitionism

The final chapter in Allen's legacy began the year of his death, when a fiery young Massachusetts abolitionist began to publish a new national newspaper, the *Liberator*, which was devoted to the twin causes of combating colonization and bringing about an immediate, uncompensated end to slavery. Like many of the men and women that he converted, William Lloyd Garrison was a former proponent of the ACS. Indeed, the list of ACS supporters who ultimately embraced abolitionism is quite extensive, including Gerrit Smith and Arthur and Lewis Tappan, two of the major financial backers of the campaign, Sarah Grimké, who later became a noted feminist and abolitionist speaker, and James G. Birney, who subsequently ran for president under the auspices of the antislavery Liberty Party in 1840.

Garrison gained backing for the abolitionist movement by touring the Northern black churches in search of support. Built on the ideas of Allen's anticolonization campaign, his presentation was eloquently calibrated to capitalize on the interests and achievements of prominent churchmen like James Forten.

"I never rise to address a colored audience, without being ashamed of my own color," Garrison began, "ashamed of being identified with a race of men who have done you so much injustice, and who yet retain so large a portion of your brethren in servile chains. To make atonement, in part, for this conduct, I have solemnly dedicated my health, and strength, and life, to your service." Branding colonization an "anti-republican crusade," he assured his audiences that "those State Laws which disfranchise and degrade you are unconstitutional," and that "The Constitution of the United States . . . has power enough to vindicate your rights. Thanks be to God that we have such a Constitution! Without it, the liberty of every man—white as well as colored—would be in jeopardy." He went on to urge them to exercise their right of petition, their right to vote (wherever possible), and their right to assemble in order to combat discrimination. Finally, he urged them to publicize their views, for "without the powerful energies of the press, every cause must languish."[39]

The last point, of course, may have masked an ulterior motive, since

Garrison was trying to marshal subscribers for his new anticolonizationist paper. But his arguments represented his own keen perception of the power of publicity and organization in shaping public opinion and political change. As he explained, the press "possesses the gift of ubiquity, it enables a man to address himself to thousands in every state at the same moment, and to throw his influence from one end of the country to the other." "The press is the citadel of liberty," he concluded, "the palladium of a free people."[40]

It was an effective argument, preached to an audience that was ready to hear Garrison's message. James Forten became one of his most generous backers, and when the first issue of the *Liberator* rolled off the press in 1831, three-quarters of its charter subscribers were African Americans. Northern freedmen also paid for Garrison's fund-raising tour of England and participated in the founding and funding of his New England Antislavery Society in 1832 and the American Antislavery Society the following year.[41]

Like the anticolonization campaigns that helped to inspire it, the abolitionist movement was born in a black church. Created in the basement of Boston's Joy Street African Church, the New England Antislavery Society was nurtured through its infancy by African American women's auxiliaries in Salem and Rochester. To quote the historian Benjamin Quarles, "Negro donations were not large, but they came during the crucial beginning years, when fewer white men of means had been converted to the cause and hence when money was scarcest." And black congregations and Sunday schools played a particularly important role in collecting these funds.[42]

Moreover, the movement coalesced around and was galvanized by the anticolonizationist crusade that men like Allen helped to set in motion. Speaking before the American Antislavery Society annual meeting in 1834, one black supporter exclaimed, "by denying even the *possibility* of our mental and moral elevation in this country," the ACS "discountenanced our efforts, misled our friends, and emboldened our enemies, an oppression which . . . sustains legislative provisions for thrusting us out of our native land."[43]

Backed by black churches, Garrison emerged as one of the ACS's most articulate foes. Denouncing the society's programs as a "conspiracy against human rights," an edifice built on "persecution, falsehood, cowardice and infidelity," he castigated it for pursuing a program that was almost unanimously opposed by free blacks and accused the ACS of seeking to make their situation so uncomfortable that they would be compelled to migrate.[44]

Garrison was especially vitriolic about the society's program in Maryland, charging that if the state's antislavery sentiment had not been chan-
neled into an unworkable plan, "it would soon seek another vent, viz.,
emancipation on the soil." Instead, state officials were determined "to get
rid of free people of color" by "restricting the power of manumission, so
that every free slave should be reduced to the alternative of perpetual
bondage, or emancipation on condition of removal." And to hasten that
removal, they had adopted increasingly discriminatory legislation, barring blacks from jobs and imposing restrictions on their movement.[45]

Garrison built the abolitionist movement on Allen's ideas, on his platform, and on his constituency. The movement echoed Allen's rhetorical
devices as well, incorporating the Declaration of Independence into the
"Declaration of Sentiments" that launched the American Antislavery Society in Philadelphia in 1833: "More than fifty-seven years have elapsed
since a band of patriots convened in this place, to devise measures for the
deliverance of this country from a foreign yoke. The corner stone upon
which they founded the temple of freedom was broadly this—'that all
men are created equal; and they are endowed by their Creator, with certain
inalienable rights; that among these are life, liberty, and the pursuit of
happiness.'"[46]

James Madison assumed the presidency of the ACS in the year these
words were penned. Three years later, he would follow Richard Allen to
the grave. The points at which their lives intersected illustrate the breadth
of the invisible revolution that men like Franklin, Madison, and Jefferson
initiated when Allen was still experiencing his first years of liberty. The
legacy of Jefferson's egalitarian rhetoric was clearly etched in the black
convention movement and the abolitionist crusade, as was the legacy of
disestablishment. To quote one historian, "At the time of the War of Independence, few blacks, slave or free, were Christians. In the next three
decades, thousands of African-Americans turned to the gospel." Absalom
Jones and Richard Allen helped to provide an independent ecclesiastical
framework for these converts, welding their individual acts of faith into a
political presence.[47]

Their efforts also highlighted the distinctions between government
and the broader practice of popular governance embedded in civil society.
The government that men like Jefferson and Madison created was fash-
ioned in their own image, providing little authority for the women, blacks,
and unpropertied males who fell outside their range of political vision.
But governance—the provision of services and the practice of advocacy
through private donations, voluntarism, and nonprofit organizations, in-

cluding churches—enabled many groups to achieve the political presence that electoral politics denied. Southern Congressmen could dismiss African American efforts to participate politically through petitions, despite First Amendment guarantees. But the public voice of the black church was more difficult to silence, or to ignore.

At least, that was true in the North. Ironically, Madison and Jefferson had championed precisely this sort of political advocacy when they castigated Washington for his attempts to muzzle the Democratic-Republican societies. And, to quote historian Joyce Appleby, "Out of the democratic societies came the political mobilization of mere voters." Advocacy provided a means of shaping national agendas for even politically disempowered groups. It afforded a hedge against discrimination, and a buffer against despotism. While white middle-class women like Isabella Graham created their political presence at the local level in collaboration with municipal governments, Northern African American religious leaders like Allen and Jones used the power of the pulpit and the press to affect national policies.[48]

In the process, they forged a template for American liberalism's commitment to promoting peaceful, gradual change. Richard Allen had a fiery temperament. He chafed at discrimination and fought repeated battles against racism for his congregation, his community, and himself. But he did so through organizations, devising institutional mechanisms for channeling communal rage and despair in public, political ways. Rather than taking up arms or gathering a mob, he built a mutual aid society, a church, a congregation, and a national convention. And in doing so, he challenged the racism of two generations of American statesmen, without elected office, and in a society in which his community was systematically being divested of even its limited right to vote.

He left a remarkable legacy, one that stretched from slavery to abolitionism. Vowing to form antislavery societies in every city, town, and village, the "Declaration of Sentiments" pledged "to break every yoke, and to let the oppressed go free." Allen's life, and that of Absalom Jones, traced the course of American philanthropy, religion, reform—and ultimately, American democracy—in the nation's youth. Writing nearly a century later, W. E. B. Du Bois deemed Allen's AME "the greatest Negro organization in the world."[49]

PART TWO

Testing the Faith

6

The Jacksonian Backlash

Northern philanthropy and Southern politics clashed head-on in the Jacksonian years, further underscoring regional differences. Three politically charged social reform movements surfaced during Andrew Jackson's presidency between 1829 and 1837: efforts to halt the Southern Indian removals, to promote Sabbatarianism, and to effect the immediate abolition of slavery. Because they sought to change political policies rather than simply bolstering government resources for service delivery, social advocacy campaigns were contested from the outset, a pattern vividly illustrated by the debates that flared around the petitions submitted by Franklin's Pennsylvania Abolition Society and by Richard Allen and Absalom Jones. These tensions emerged full-blown in the 1830s, providing an ample arena for examining the growth and politicization of antebellum philanthropy, as well as its role in fostering widespread democratic participation. The abolitionist crusade also affords a useful case study of the effects of federal efforts to silence social advocacy, issues explored in this and the following chapter.

Earlier generations of scholars often lauded Jackson's presidency as a golden age when the electorate was dramatically broadened, federal expenditures were pared to pay off the national debt, and new areas were opened for Anglo-American settlement. However, more recent work has been less celebratory. As Bertram Wyatt-Brown points out, the "substance of the Jacksonian faith" was "the fiercest possible defense of slavery," and

Jackson's Indian policies are now considered less than noble. Moreover, as Jean Baker points out, the "claim that a political system that excluded sixty percent of all adult Americans—a figure that does not include immigrants waiting for naturalization—could possibly be the 'golden age' of our democracy" is "extraordinary (and insulting)."[1]

Jackson's administrations witnessed the birth of not one, but two new political cultures, one rooted in the rapid expansion of the white male electorate, the other in the more inclusive realm of social advocacy, sparking sometimes violent clashes over how the nation should be governed and by whom. The term, "political culture" requires some explanation. In addition to the obvious trappings of elections and campaigns, it also refers to the experiences and values that lead people to make political choices—the lens that shapes their "expectations about the realities of politics and instills in them shared ideals as to what their public life might be." Popular political culture was colored by sectional considerations as well. While the Northern women and African Americans who participated in associational life built a political presence rooted in collective effort, religion, and the rights of petition, assembly, and free speech, the Southern culture that Jackson exemplified was deeply rooted in distinctions of gender and race and deeply antithetical to the lobbying efforts of independent groups beyond white male control, particularly after Nat Turner's slave uprising in 1831. In many respects, it echoed Putnam's model of the "less civic" society steeped in "vertical relations of authority and dependency."[2]

Jackson's election heralded not only the triumph of Southern values on a new scale, but also the advent of a new group of far more individualistic politicians whose careers were shaped in the vortex of mass politics and growing sectionalism. On a personal level, Jackson represented the kind of individual volatility that Southern folklore celebrated and Northern evangelicals abhorred. "Deeply committed to Southern white customs, convictions, and prejudices," he "epitomized" the sectional ethic "to perfection." Jackson had his own vision of what was good for the country, following his inner voice in military campaigns in ways that won him the censure of some of his startled superiors. As William Lloyd Garrison ominously noted, he "trifled . . . with the laws."[3]

He also had a limited appreciation for philanthropy. While all of Jackson's predecessors had been personally involved in educational projects—efforts exemplified by Jefferson's and Madison's roles in the creation of the University of Virginia—Jackson's own philanthropic record was modest at best. For example, George Washington offered to donate 150 shares of the James River and Potomac Canal stock as a corpus for a national university to be supported by both public and private donations, a project endorsed by every one of his successors through Jackson's immediate predecessor, John Quincy Adams. Washington also served as a patron and a trustee of a college that bore his name in Maryland, and he helped to create the Alexandria Academy in 1785, donating seventeen hundred pounds for its maintenance, while Madison headed a fund-raising drive for Princeton University, served on the board and in the administration of the University of Virginia, and included bequests for three colleges and the American Colonization Society in his will. Moreover, all of these men participated in learned societies, including Franklin's American Philosophical Society, and John Quincy Adams was a prominent figure in the Benevolent Empire.[4]

Jackson, on the other hand, dabbled in a few Benevolent Empire societies, but nothing more. He reputedly served as the vice president of the Nashville Bible Society, and as vice president of the American Colonization Society from 1817 to 1823, an enthusiasm that soured as his relations with Henry Clay (an ardent ACS supporter) disintegrated into political rivalry. He also used federal funding to help create an advocacy group to propagandize for his Indian policies, taking the national government into dubious ethical terrain. But these were minor detours in a life dedicated to politics and the pursuit of personal wealth and military and political glory. To a far greater extent than his predecessors, Jackson stood aloof from the philanthropic sphere.[5]

He also inherited a far more complex political arena. Within the space of his lifetime, the country had moved from a world in which *all* public activities were a white male preserve to one in which women were building institutions, selling religious materials, and claiming an increasing share of moral authority both within and outside the home—including participation in federal petition campaigns—and Northern African Americans were resisting federal policies through anticolonizationism, abolitionism, and their independent churches. At the same time, voting and all of the brouhaha that surrounded the polling process was becoming a common— and often jealously guarded—definition of white American manhood as state after state jettisoned property requirements, introducing universal white male suffrage. When Jackson was elected in 1828, 1,155,340 men cast their ballots, an increase of over 800,000 from the previous presidential election, as newly enfranchised voters flooded to the polls. The federal petition campaigns brought these two models of the public governance— one rooted in dense networks of independent associations, the other in the expanding electoral prerogatives of white men—into sharp relief, under-

scoring hardening regional imperatives and sparking bitter contests over
First Amendment guarantees.[6]

The Trail of Tears

Indian affairs was the first area to feel the force of these competing agendas. The history of Indian-white relations is one of the darker chapters in
American history. Beginning with Washington's presidency, efforts were
consistently made to clear Native Americans off their lands by a variety of
means, from persuasion and bribery, to warfare, to outright fraud. Often,
these actions were vindicated under a smoke screen of moral temporizing
and duplicitously articulated concerns for tribal welfare. Yet until Jackson
assumed office, the notion that the tribes should relinquish their eastern
lands voluntarily in return for comparable territories in the West undergirded the government's activities. Jackson—and his successor, Martin
Van Buren—opted instead for immediatism and force.[7]

Andrew Jackson had built much of his reputation as an Indian fighter,
a reputation that his "savage hatreds and readiness to violence" only
served to enhance. The Tennessean had scant sympathy for the underlying
factors that led to Indian attacks; Jackson's method was to deal with the results, exacting life for life. Thus, when 250 white settlers were massacred
at Fort Mims, Alabama, in 1813, Jackson and his troops retaliated in kind,
slaughtering approximately 200 Creek families and braves. Four months
later 900 more Creeks were killed, prompting even Jackson to admit that
"the carnage was *dreadful.*" In the aftermath, he signed a peace treaty that
resulted in "an enormous land grab" for the United States, laying the
groundwork for the destruction of the southeastern Creek nation.[8]

Two years later, he was engaged in another negotiation, this time with
the Cherokees, which resulted in their relinquishing "an enormous tract
of Cherokee land to the south of the Tennessee River" in return for the
promises of "peace and friendship between the United States and the
Cherokee Nation," an annual payment of six thousand dollars a year for
ten years, and a five-thousand-dollar bonus for signing the treaty. Between
1814 and 1825, he managed to secure vast amounts of land from Indian
tribes in Alabama, Florida, Tennessee, Mississippi, Georgia, Kentucky, and
North Carolina. An avid expansionist, Jackson had little patience with the
formality of treaties with the Indians, which he deemed an "absurdity."[9]

Having based much of his reputation on his skill in battle and in winning access to tribal lands, he made Indian removals one of his key presidential priorities, policies that quickly brought him into conflict with

Northern missionaries who were working among the tribes at federal expense. Collaboration between government agencies and voluntary associations had deep roots in the country's history, providing elected officials with information and services at minimal cost. The American Philosophical Society, for example, provided support services for the Lewis and Clark expedition in exploring the new territories acquired with the Louisiana Purchase in 1803 and for the first federal censuses. Some of these activities, such as the use of missionaries in dealing with Indian tribes, built on Revolutionary imperatives. The idea of using clerics to "civilize" the tribes dated from 1789, when Secretary of War Henry Knox suggested to Washington that "missionaries, of excellent moral character," might be encouraged to live in Indian nations as a means of binding the tribes "to the interests of the United States." Under ensuing administrations, missionaries received small federal grants for their work with various tribes, work amplified under Monroe.[10]

Negotiations for increased government support for missionary assistance began in 1816, when Monroe's secretary of war, John Calhoun, began doling out modest sums to missionary societies on an informal basis in return for assistance in building and staffing schools. Monroe authorized an annual appropriation beginning in 1819, setting aside $10,000 ($113,000 in 2000 dollars) to employ "capable persons, of good moral character . . . for teaching [Indian] children in reading, writing, and arithmetic." As he privately explained to Jackson, he had been casting about for a "compulsory process . . . to break their habits and to civilize them" by moving the Indians into agricultural pursuits, which theoretically would concentrate their settlements and free more land for white settlers.[11]

A substantial portion of the civilization fund, as it came to be known, was funneled into the coffers of the American Board of Commissioners of Foreign Missions (ABCFM), a Benevolent Empire society founded in 1810. At the time the grant was approved, the society had already invested substantial amounts of its own funds in its missionary work among the Choctaws and Cherokees, amounts second only to its allocations for mission activities in South Asia. The board continued to bolster its private donations with federal support, and by 1824 almost three hundred of its teachers were laboring in schools in Indian settlements. Calhoun worked closely with the missionaries, and Monroe even visited one of the schools as a prelude to requesting the appropriation. The administration also hired Jedediah Morse, a fiercely orthodox Calvinist divine and the founder of Andover Theological Seminary, to draft an evaluative report on the "religious, moral, and political" condition of various tribes in 1820.[12]

By the mid-1820s, political pressures to remove the Cherokees from their land holdings were mounting. Monroe favored removal but stopped short of endorsing forcible displacement, arguing that such tactics would be "unjust." At the same time, tribal officials in Georgia began to refuse to sell off any more land, increasing the possibilities of a volatile confrontation. Calhoun bluntly outlined the alternatives: "Surrounded as you are . . . you must either cease to be a distinct community, and become . . . a part of the State within whose limits you are, or remove beyond the limits of any State." In response, the Indians devised a third alternative, drafting a formal constitution in 1827 in a gesture of tribal sovereignty. The governor of Georgia responded by charging that the constitution was an illegal attempt to create a state within a state, and that the tribes were subject to Georgia legislation.[13]

Although Indian treaties fell under the jurisdiction of Congress, rather than the states, Georgia moved to extend its legal authority over the Cherokee tribal lands in the wake of Jackson's election, a decision the president backed. As Jackson explained, the "absolute independence of the Indian tribes from state authority can never bear an intelligent investigation, and [the creation of] a quasi-independent state authority when located within its Territorial limits is *absurd*." The terms of state citizenship offered by Georgia were pointedly (and doubtless intentionally) unpalatable, requiring that the tribal assemblies be disbanded, the chiefs stripped of their powers, and the Indians subjected to military conscription. They would be unable to vote but required to pay taxes. Moreover, they would be denied the right to sue or testify in court, and substantial portions of their land were to be sold at auction. The coup de grâce came in 1828, when gold was discovered on Indian lands, giving prospectors as well as slaveholders a stake in their removal.[14]

As tensions escalated in Georgia, Jackson readied his Indian removal bill for congressional approval. His Indian removal campaigns marked the first instance in which women's organizations were mobilized to engage in widespread petitioning to the federal government, moving them from proselytizing to protest. It also "arrayed [Jackson] openly against the weight of organized Christian benevolence" for the first time. Women's movement into the federal political arena was actively encouraged by Jeremiah Evarts, a Vermont-born ABCFM official with deep sympathies for the Cherokees, and by Northern women's groups enlisted through the efforts of prominent writers such as Catharine Beecher and Lydia Sigourney. When it became clear that Jackson was going to actively push for the Indian removals, Evarts began to appeal to the Northern networks of the

Benevolent Empire, mobilizing both male and female members through churches and auxiliaries to inundate legislators with petitions protesting Jackson's policies. Public meetings were convened in a number of Northeastern cities to marshal support, and Evarts drafted a series of pamphlets distilling his arguments against the removals, while a "Circular Addressed to the Ladies of the United States," was published in the *Christian Advocate and Journal* and disseminated through women's networks across the North.[15]

Hundreds of women signed and sent their protests in to Congress, missives that often reflected their own sense of the novelty of their efforts. Thus, the women of Lewis New York, admitted to being "fully aware that in proffering this petition they are departing from the usual sphere which they occupy in Society." But when "the principles of national faith and honor" were at stake, they argued that their activities were justified. Others echoed both their caution and their claims. As the women of Steubenville, Ohio, explained, while female "interference" in political matters would normally be "presumptuous" and "wholly unbecoming to the character of American females," it was warranted when "injury and oppression threaten[ed] to crush a hapless people within our borders." Their language was often strikingly deferential, casting the signatories as "supplicants in the cause of mercy and humanity," and stressing their hope that "the small voice of female sympathy will be heard." Despite their reticence, they nonetheless assumed a strong moral stance, urging Congress to "shelter the American character from lasting dishonor" by upholding its treaties with the Indians.[16]

Rebecca Gratz promoted the movement, but with an obvious sense of resignation. "Have the Ladies of Hartford requested your aid to 'supplicate justice and mercy' for the Indians?" she asked her sister-in-law. "They have sent circulars to various cities—and if their charity crosses the mountains, you have no doubt heard of them—but alas, the poor Indians have good lands—and the Georgians are savage enough to covet [them]." Although ultimately unsuccessful, the antiremoval petition campaign revealed the potential force of evangelical networks in the political mobilization of Northern laywomen, providing the model for a number of subsequent movements from moral reform to abolitionism.[17]

Jackson introduced his proposal for the Indian removals in Congress in 1829 and reiterated it in his 1830 State of the Union address. "Philanthropy could not wish to see this continent restored to the condition in which it was found by our forefathers, " he announced. "What good man would prefer a country covered with forests and ranged by a few thousand savages to our extensive Republic, studded with cities, towns, and prosperous farms, embellished with all the improvements which art can devise or industry execute . . . filled with all the blessings of liberty, civilization, and religion?" The president then went on to proffer "a fair exchange" of eastern for western lands "where their existence may be prolonged and perhaps made perpetual."[18]

Jackson underscored the theme of federal "generosity" by emphasizing that the removals would be made "at the expense of the United States." Comparing this bounty to the sacrifices of white families, he noted: "Our children by thousands yearly leave the land of their birth to seek new homes in distant regions. Does Humanity weep at these painful separations from everything . . . from which the young heart has become entwined? . . . And is it supposed that the wandering savage has a stronger attachment to his home than the settled, civilized Christian? Is it more afflicting to him to leave the graves of his fathers than it is to our brothers and children?" Given that white families endured these separations at their own expense, he deemed the government's proposal "not only liberal, but generous." In effect, Jackson presented his plan for massive Indian removals by co-opting the language of sentimentality, philanthropy, and the home. He continued to veil his Indian colonization program in the idiom of benevolence, arguing that the tribes were being moved westward for their own safety, rhetoric tragically belied by subsequent events.[19]

When Jackson's Indian removal bill was introduced in Congress on December 7, 1829, it sparked bitter, regionally based debates and a cascade of antiremoval petitions. Jackson's allies moved to table them, but the vote failed by a hair-thin margin of 91 to 92. The petition campaign pitted Jackson against the Northern benevolent community, including the Northern *female* benevolent community, in a drama played out on the very public stage of congressional hearings. Congressman Wilson Lumpkin of Georgia (who later became governor) was particularly venomous in his complaints against the missionary societies, condemning their petition drive and publications for unbecomingly political behavior. Others feigned shock at the charges the petitions contained. Citing a memorial that censured Georgia's efforts to trample "upon all laws, human and divine, under the instigation of the most foul and criminal motives," Congressman William Drayton of South Carolina urged his colleagues to reject any petition "that so grossly violates common propriety and common decency."[20]

Evarts relentlessly publicized the Indians' plight, writing under the nom de plume William Penn. He used his writings and his rallies to hammer home three themes: that Jackson's efforts were immoral and dishonorable, that the country was required to honor its treaties, and that removal was ultimately a partisan ploy. His writings were widely disseminated, appearing in religious and political papers, in the *North American Review*, and in pamphlet form. At one point, the president's supporters tried to buy Evarts' silence, offering him increased government assistance in return for endorsing the removal program. Federal inducements notwithstanding, the ABCFM continued its hard-line stance against the government's incursions. As their officers explained, whatever one's opinion, one fact was "inescapable; viz, that treaties in existence between the United States and the Cherokee nation guarantee the inviolability of the Cherokee territory and of the Cherokee government."[21]

The administration anticipated these attacks, responding with "secret agents, bribery, avarice and propaganda agencies—all [of which] reveal the weakness and uncertainty of the Jackson administration that it could effect removal on its terms, as well as the determination to do just that." The president even backed the creation of an advocacy group, the New York Indian Board, to issue publicly funded propaganda favoring the removals, and to "cooperate with the government, in inducing the Indians to acquiesce" in "their colonization." The Democratic press jumped into the fray as well, editorially railing against the "*political* philanthropists who oppose this administration!" and their "politico-ecclesiastical coalition." By 1830, the government discontinued the ABCFM's funding, with the understanding that future appropriations would be available only for Indian projects in the West.[22]

Jackson's Indian removal bill was signed into law on May 28, 1830. In one last bid for legal redress, the Cherokees filed suit against the state of Georgia, arguing that their previous treaties with the federal government had proven their sovereignty and attempting to refute Georgia's claim that they were subject to state law. Although Chief Justice Marshall was sympathetic to the Indians' plight, the court ruled that the tribe was a "domestic dependent nation" within the United States in its 1831 *Cherokee Nation v. Georgia* decision, a ruling that technically supported neither the Indians' stance nor Georgia's. While the lawsuit was still pending, Georgia passed a law barring all white settlers from entering Indian territories without state approval as of March 1st, 1831, in a ploy to oust the remaining missionaries. Samuel Worcester and Elizur Butler opted to remain and were promptly arrested and sentenced to four years of hard labor in the state penitentiary. The ABCFM responded by sending a detailed letter of grievances to Jackson, asking him to secure the missionaries' freedom.

Jackson refused, citing his inability to interfere with Georgia's legislation as a consequence of the doctrine of states' rights. The missionaries ultimately sued to regain their freedom in a case that also made its way to the Supreme Court. This time the Marshall Court ruled that the state's law was unconstitutional and ordered the missionaries to be released. Marshall found Georgia's campaign to extend its jurisdiction over the Cherokees to be "repugnant to the constitution, treaties, and the laws of the United States." Nonetheless, Jackson steadfastly refused to enforce compliance with Marshall's ruling, allowing the clerics to languish in prison until they were finally freed by Georgia's governor in January, 1833.[23]

Historians disagree about how much authority Jackson could have exercised in response to Marshall's decree. While many criticize his inaction, some argue that he had no legal reason to take action, disagreements that hinge on whether the incident is viewed as an internal Georgia issue or a diplomatic issue grounded in federal treaties. Perhaps the most convincing explanation for Jackson's inaction is Richard Ellis's. As he explains, Marshall's ruling was handed down during the nullification crisis, as South Carolinians led by John Calhoun were attempting to boycott federal tariff laws with the argument that states were entitled to declare federal legislation null and void within their borders. Governor Lumpkin, a Jackson loyalist, threatened to break ranks with the party if he were barred from enforcing his own version of states' rights by handling the missionaries according to Georgia's laws rather than the Supreme Court's ruling. In effect, by this interpretation, Jackson refused to intervene at a time when such interference might have shattered the Democratic Party and worsened the Southern nullification crisis and threats of secession.[24]

After years of legal wrangling, the Cherokee removals took place in 1838 under the supervision of General Winfield Scott. Although they were carried out under Van Buren's administration, Jackson was a major catalyst, persistently "badger[ing]" his successor to enforce the treaty. He was, to quote his biographer, Robert Remini, "obsessed about removal." The end result was that an estimated eighteen thousand Cherokees were rounded up by the army troops, with many forced to stand by as white settlers pillaged their houses and possessions. Before the journey, they were herded into "a concentration camp"of prison stockades. In the course of their eight-hundred-mile western trek the Indians were "boxed like animals" in cramped and poorly ventilated railroad cars and overcrowded stockades, denied adequate food, and continually cheated. In the process, over four thousand (and perhaps twice that number) men, women, and children died, and Georgia came into possession of a vast tract of new land for the expansion of slavery.[25]

Sabbatarianism and Abolitionism

A second contest arose over control of the mails. The Post Office was a vitally important antebellum institution, for several reasons. At one level, organizations like the American Bible Society held their networks of auxiliaries together primarily through the mails. Although railroads began to appear in the 1830s, and telegraphs a decade later, in the 1820s the postal service lay at the heart of any national enterprise. It was also a prime source of political patronage. In 1816, the 3,341 employees who manned the nation's post offices accounted for 69.1% of all federal employees. During Jackson's first term, in 1831, that figure rose to 8,764, accounting for 76.3 % of the available governmental positions, and 79.2% in the following decade. This was larger than the federal army, larger than all of the assembled bureaucrats in Washington, and most assuredly larger than the number of jobs controlled by any nascent political machine. Moreover, because it reached into local communities, the postal service provided immediate access to grassroots constituencies on a daily basis—including Sundays.[26]

The Sabbatarian petition campaign evolved through two phases, providing a dress rehearsal for the more hotly contested abolitionist crusades of the mid-1830s. The first, from 1809 to 1817, consisted of a relatively modest federal petition drive born of the enthusiasms of the Second Great Awakening and federal legislation passed in 1810 requiring post offices to deliver mail "on demand," even if those demands were made on Sunday. In response, Presbyterian and Congregationalist leaders circulated blank petitions to their parishioners nationwide, urging them to protest. It was an unprecedented maneuver, mobilizing a mass-based federal petition drive under nonprofit sponsorship on a national scale. It also marked a new relationship between the citizenry and the national government. As Richard John explains, "Before 1809, the federal government had seemed . . . removed from the day-to-day activities of ordinary Americans" most of whom had "assumed it lacked the power to regulate personal behavior." Passage of the 1810 postal law brought this assumption "under close scrutiny for perhaps the first time in the history of the republic."[27]

This fledgling protest produced few results. Post offices stayed open on the Sabbath, and the mail coaches continued to run seven days a week. The second phase was far more organized. Spearheaded by the General Union for the Promotion of the Christian Sabbath, a Benevolent Empire offshoot created in 1826, it inspired prominent clerics such as Lyman Beecher and the burgeoning religious press to recruit new advocates and mobilize a fresh wave of petition campaigns. Sabbatarian reformers also skillfully exploited the mails, sending blank petitions to local postmasters to distribute among their clientele. Evarts played a central role in choreographing this campaign as well, casting the pleas "in terms derived from republican theory and constitutional law," in addition to religious beliefs. "Driven by the need to appeal to an ever-widening audience," notes John, "Sabbatarians found themselves projecting the moral authority of the Ten Commandments onto the Bill of Rights" by arguing for "the postmasters' constitutionally guaranteed right to the free exercise of religion."[28]

By May of 1831, over nine hundred petitions had been sent, anticipating the abolitionist tidal waves that would spill into Congressional mail sacks by mid-decade—with two major exceptions. First, this was the only one of the three Jacksonian petition drives to have substantial Southern representation, with 11% of the petitions drawn from the South Atlantic States, and 5% from the Southwest. Second, although it overlapped the Indian removal protests—which were also coordinated by Evarts—no women seem to have signed the Sabbatarian petitions. Both patterns would change dramatically with the advent of abolitionism.[29]

Unlike Sabbatarianism, abolitionism was a volatile crusade, tempered in persecution. The abolitionist movement grew to national dimensions during Jackson's second administration, structured along the lines of the Benevolent Empire auxiliaries and nurtured by the collective financial support of African Americans, female fund-raising, and a few larger donations from prosperous white businessmen such as Gerrit Smith and Arthur and Lewis Tappan. Its goal was the immediate, uncompensated eradication of slavery. As the members of the New England Antislavery Society explained, their demands were rooted in the belief (1) that no one had the right to buy and sell other human beings like "cattle"; (2) that husbands and wives should be legally married, and their unions "placed under the protection of law"; (3) "that parents shall have the control and government of their own children"; (4) that the ability of slaveowners "to punish [their] slaves without trial, and to a savage extent" should be "taken away"; (5) "that all those laws which now prohibit the instruction of the slaves," should "instantly be repealed"; (6) that planters should "employ their slaves as free laborers, and pay them just wages"; and (7) that slaves should "be encouraged to toil for the mutual profit of themselves and their employers." "Is this unreasonable?" the movement's spokesmen rhetorically queried. "Is this diabolical?" Many antebellum Americans felt it was. Yet despite a controversial agenda, approximately 200 American Antislavery Society (AAS) auxiliaries were operating by 1835; over 1,000 by 1837; and 1350 the following year, accounting for an estimated 250,000 members. When one considers that John Quincy Adams was elected President by a scant 109,000 votes in 1824, the scope of this rapid mobilization is striking.[30]

If these statistics are correct, they represent a stunning level of recruitment, accounting for almost 2% of the national population within the scant space of five years in an era of primitive communications. To place these numbers in a contemporary frame, this is a higher percentage of the citizenry than the combined 1999 membership of the National Rifle Association (3.3 million members), the National Organization of Women (500,000), Amnesty International (300,000), and the Chamber of Commerce (200,000), which together account for 4.3 million members out of a national population of approximately 273 million. It is larger than the membership of Mothers Against Drunk Driving (3 million members and supporters), the Boy Scouts (4.8 million), the National Wildlife Federation (4 million), or the American Legion (1 million). It had more chapters than the March of Dimes (104) or the National Urban League (115). Only a few organizations currently have memberships representing a higher percentage of the population or more expansive operations, including (among others) the American Association of Retired Persons (AARP, 33 million), the PTA (6.5 million), and the Red Cross (1,650 auxiliaries). Moreover, unlike members of contemporary groups like the AARP, abolitionists tended to be very active, personally risking the abuse and scorn of their neighbors by signing and circulating petitions to free Southern slaves.[31]

Southern antiabolitionists and their Northern political allies vehemently denounced AAS members, accusing them of fanaticism, a desire to overthrow the union, and endangering Southern property and lives. These fears were heightened by events such as Nat Turner's bloody slave rebellion in Virginia in 1831, in which dozens of whites were massacred by enraged bondsmen. And it was against this backdrop that the AAS launched its national mail campaign against the sins of the slavocracy. Beginning in 1835, the AAS flooded the country, North and South, with antislavery publications, mailing its papers and tracts to ministers, legislators, and other white figures of property and influence. Backed by an estimated $30,000 (@ $385,000 in 2000 dollars) in subscriptions, this campaign built on earlier precedents established by the Benevolent Empire and the national religious press, which capitalized on printing innovations such as steam presses to spread the gospels of temperance, Sabbatarianism, and personal piety to national audiences. Aided by old ideas and new technologies, Lewis Tappan's publications committee mailed almost two hundred thousand items by July of 1835, and over a million by the end of the following year.[32]

Despite charges to the contrary, the society was careful to ensure that none of these materials were sent to slaves or Southern freedmen, for several reasons: "First.—They are not addressed nor adapted to the slaves, but to their masters. Secondly.—If sent, they probably would never reach the slaves, so vigilant is the espionage of their oppressors. Thirdly.—If they should get safely to their hands, they could not read them. Fourthly.—We fear, if any of our publications should be found in their hands, they would be as fuel added to their afflictions." Instead, the mailings were carefully aimed at local leaders: ministers, members of Congress and state legislatures, justices of the peace, "and other men of standing in the community." Abolitionist spokesmen also claimed that none were sent to persons who expressly notified the New York office that "they wished not to receive them," following "the well known course of the publishers of moral or religious periodicals." Nor were they inflammatory, as critics claimed, containing primarily sermons, verbatim reports of congressional speeches, information from AAS auxiliaries, editorials, and literary reviews—material designed to instruct and sway, rather than to incite.[33]

Jackson immediately responded by defending his slaveholding compatriots, calling for a national censorship law to prohibit the circulation of "incendiary" writings in his annual message to Congress in 1835. Efforts were also made to cast Vice President Van Buren as an "emphatically firm friend of the South" despite his New York origins. Privately, Jackson seethed that the abolitionists were "monsters" bent on fomenting slave revolts. "Could they be reached," he told his newly appointed postmaster general, Amos Kendall (a fellow slaveowner), "they ought to be made to atone for this wicked attempt, with their lives." Yet he sought to at least remain within the letter of the law, if not its full intent. "We have no power to prohibit anything from being transported in the mail that is authorized by law," he complained to Kendall. "The only thing that can be done is . . . *to deliver to no person these inflammatory papers*, but those who are really subscribers." He also suggested that postal officers be encouraged to publish the names of anyone requesting the abolitionist literature, exposing them to the fury of their peers. The sharp-eyed observer of American manners, Harriet Martineau, was among a growing number of commentators who marveled at the irony of "General Jackson, the people's man, who talked of liberty daily, with energetic oaths and flourishes" lobbying the Congress for censorship laws.[34]

Taking his cue from Jackson, Kendall informed Charleston's postmaster that he was duty bound to deliver the materials but bore no responsibility for their local distribution. Besides Jackson's backing, Kendall had an additional incentive to placate the South, since he had been appointed but not yet confirmed and needed the Southern votes to secure his position. And so, to quote a contemporary observer, he "truckled to the domineering pretensions of the slaveholders." The end result was that the abolitionist pamphlets were seized and torched in tandem with effigies of Arthur Tappan and Garrison. Shortly thereafter, citizen committees were appointed to "sort" the mails and dispense with abolitionist documents. Kendall was warmly supportive of these proceedings. "I cannot sanction, and will not condemn, the steps you have taken," he wrote to Postmaster Huger. "We owe an obligation to the laws, but a higher one to the communities in which we live." Not everyone agreed. Years later, John Quincy Adams continued to deride Kendall's actions as "a violation of the freedom of the press . . . of the sacred character of the post office, and of the rights and liberties of all the free people of the United States."[35]

Freedom of the press became an increasingly contested issue in the South following the publication of David Walker's *Appeal to the Colored Citizens of the World* in 1829, which openly issued a clarion call for slave revolts, and the appearance of Garrison's antislavery journal, the *Liberator*, in 1831. Some connected Turner's rebellion directly to these publications, and this was used to justify substantial incursions against civil liberties throughout the region. Laws limiting the rights of free speech and of the press were passed in every state but Kentucky, sometimes with heavy criminal penalties. Georgia, for example, mandated the death penalty for circulating incendiary materials in 1835, an offense that carried a ten- to twenty-year prison sentence even in more moderate slaveholding states such as Maryland. Postmasters in the South, and even in New York, intercepted abolitionist tracts with Kendall's blessing. Southern legislators even sought to impose a "gag law" on abolitionist activities in the North. In 1836, for example, lawmakers from several Southern states unsuccessfully petitioned the Massachusetts General Court to make it illegal to form abolitionist societies, or to publish or speak on abolitionism. Vigilantism also held sway. Georgians offered a $5,000 bounty for Garrison's extradition and trial, and a hefty $10,000 for Amos A. Phelps, while other leading antislavers, like Arthur Tappan, were increasingly hounded by death threats.[36]

Martyrs build constituencies, and the ranks of the antislavery movement grew precipitously as evidence of governmentally sanctioned civil rights violations mounted. As Russell Nye explains, "The restrictive laws of the South, and the almost universal failure of Southern newspapers to continue publication if they were critical of domestic institutions, showed that a powerful minority of vested interests could . . . effectively nullify Federal and state constitutional guarantees of free speech and press." The abolitionists concurred. Pointing an accusing finger at Jackson, they complained that "the Executive Magistrate of the American Union . . . has sanctioned a censorship of the press, by which papers . . . are excluded from the southern mails, and he has officially advised Congress to do by law, *although in violation of the Constitution,* what he had himself virtually done already in despite of both."[37]

The postal campaign set the stage for yet another brush between Southern policymakers and Northern abolitionists, this time focusing on the right of petition rather than freedom of the press. The politicization of Northern female reformers that began with the Cherokee campaigns accelerated with the antislavery petition drives. Earlier antislavery efforts had been run almost entirely by men, in part because this was viewed as a political issue, and therefore not an appropriate arena for women. The American Colonization Society listed only one female auxiliary, in Wilmington, Delaware, out of the almost eighty affiliated groups listed in its tenth annual report in 1827 (the number increased slightly thereafter), and none of the six manumission and antislavery societies that sent delegates to their annual convention in 1829 included women. Like the Indian campaigns that preceded them, the antislavery drives of the mid-1830s were a new phenomenon, marking a shift from women's class-based to mass-based petitioning, from charity to politics, and from the state to the federal level.[38]

Prominent abolitionists such as Angelina Grimké underscored the importance of these activities, reminding her female audiences that "men may settle this and other questions at the ballot box, but you have no such right. It is only through petitions that you can reach the Legislature." Female antislavery societies echoed her theme, underscoring their right to exercise their First Amendment guarantees: "We are bound to the constant exercise of the only right we ourselves enjoy," noted the members of the Boston Female Antislavery Society in 1836. "By a provision in the Constitution; and by an *act* of the *first Congress,* the right of petition was secured to us." "If we have no right to act," Grimké argued, "then may we well be termed the 'white slaves of the North'—for, like our brethren in bonds, we must seal our lips in silence and despair."[39]

Adams, ever ready to stir "the bubbling cauldron of religion and politics" in the name of civil liberties, delivered many of these petitions to the House of Representatives. As the opposition to the antislavery campaign mounted, even he began to tally the personal costs of defending so unpopular a cause. "The voice of Freedom has not yet been heard," he confided to his son, "and I am earnestly urged to speak in her name. She will be trampled underfoot if I do not, and I shall be trampled underfoot if I do. . . . What can I do?" He persisted, actions which won him the censure of many his congressional colleagues, and accusations of treason.[40]

As the antislavery petitions continued to pour in, opponents moved to have them tabled with neither review nor debate, a proposal that immediately struck Adams as a violation of First Amendment guarantees. By 1836, it was becoming increasingly clear that a formal gag rule might be imposed, sparking debates about the scope and meaning of the right to petition. As Congressman William Slade reminded his colleagues, efforts to "suppress the utterance of hostility to slavery," could easily provide enduring precedents for suppressing "the popular voice on other subjects . . . until at last it shall sweep away . . . all the guarantees of popular rights." Congressman John Pinckney of South Carolina led the movement to have the petitions set aside without printing or discussing their contents.[41]

Pinckney's proposal to table all petitions and memorials on slavery "without being printed or referred," was presented in the House of Representatives on May 18th, 1836. Democratic stalwart Martin Van Buren helped pass the gag rule in the House and steered the proposal through the often acrimonious debates, energetically backing the measure in an effort to cement his alliances with Southern Democrats and to ensure the party's future as a cohesive, national institution. When the resolution passed six days later, Adams rose to denounce it as "a violation of the Constitution of the United States, of the rules of the House, and the rights of my constituents." Despite his protests, and the constitutional issues embodied in the House's action, the gag rule remained in effect until 1844. True to his prediction, Adams's courage won him the censure of his peers, and a lifetime of anonymous threats and abuse.[42]

And yet, the Northern public response indicated that his valor was not entirely misplaced. The number of signatures immediately rose, exceeding 2 million between 1838 and 1839, many of them from women. Estimates place the total percentage of female signatures as high as 70% in 1837, while women accounted for 59% of the signatories on petitions to abolish slavery in the nation's capital. The tenor of female petitioning immediately became more radical in the wake of the gag rule, shedding the rhetorical vestiges of female deference that infused the Cherokee petitions. Labeling the resolution "a violation of the Constitution[al] . . . right of the people of the United States to petition—and of the right of their representatives to freedom of speech," the female petitioners from Brookline, Massachusetts, castigated it as "dangerous and destructive to the fundamental principles of the representative government," urging the House "to immediately rescind it." Others were still more pointed, more acrid, and more visibly discontented with women's impotence within the political arena. Aiming a slap at senatorial criticism that "countrywomen" who sought "to interfere with public affairs " were "out of [their] appropriate arena," they demanded the "bare right of petition, especially when we have to be governed by laws in which we have *no* voice in making."[43]

As James Forten, Jr., exclaimed to the members of the Philadelphia Female Anti-slavery Society, "the recent scenes in Congress" had "immolated" the Constitution on "the altar of expediency . . . the right to petition, the right of free discussion, the freedom of speech, the freedom of the press" had been "trampled under foot." Members of the AAS further underscored the connection among Southern opposition, civil rights, and First Amendment guarantees: "The right of petition and the freedom of debate are . . . sacred. . . . Can the Constitution at the same time secure liberty to you, and expose us to oppression—give you freedom of speech, and lock our lips—respect your right of petition and treat ours to contempt? No, fellow-countrymen!—we must all be free, or all slaves together." With the gag rule, noted the members of the Boston Female Antislavery Society, "the whole nation is made to feel the slaveholder's scourge." New York Antislavery Society president William Jay captured the developments most succinctly. "We commenced the present struggle to obtain the freedom of the slave," he noted, but "we are compelled to continue it to preserve our own."[44]

The federal campaign to silence antislavery dissent ultimately heightened many Northerners' awareness of their own entitlements, beyond the realm of Indian policy and abolitionism—efforts to aid constituencies that many citizens personally disdained. In the process, it offered a stunning example of the ability of philanthropy and nonprofits to shape the social construction of reality, as well as the extent of the growing rift between Northern and Southern notions of civil society and the public sphere. Although abolitionism was far from a popular cause in and of itself, and was continually embattled at both the local and the federal level, it grew to significant proportions in a strikingly short space of time by linking the plight of the slave to the preservation of individual liberties. It also raised the political consciousness of a broad swath of Northern women, heightening their appreciation of the limited constitutional guarantees that surrounded their own public roles.

Historians have often attributed the political contests to emerging partisan differences between Democrats and nascent Whigs. Thus, in the words of one writer, "the Sabbatarian controversy of the late eighteen-twenties revived the religious community as a national political-pressure group," casting the Jackson administration as "the culmination of organized irreligion" and the Whigs as the champions of "national religion." Similarly, Elizabeth Varon notes that "scholars have long identified the Whig party with benevolent reform. . . . All around the country, Whigs were leaders in reform movements." Or, to quote another historian, the "separation of church and state and hostility to clerical meddling in politics became part of the Democrats' founding creed, shaping their opposition to the sabbatarian crusade, to missionary intercessions for Indian tribes, and finally to abolitionism."[45]

And yet, this much-vaunted partisan split was consistently evidenced neither in the major political papers that backed Jackson and Van Buren, such as the Albany *Argus* and the Washington *Globe*, nor on the pages of national religious journals such as the Congregationalist's *Boston Recorder*. Even prominent abolitionists such as Garrison ultimately dismissed proslavery Democrats and Whigs with equal disdain. Instead, the fault lines of the 1830s were regional, pitting the Northern evangelical culture of reform against the Southern political culture in which Jackson was born and bred.

By vesting all policymaking authority in the narrow arena of partisan politics and shunting the petitions aside without a hearing, nationally elected Southern apologists abrogated the constitutional entitlements that many Northern Americans regarded as the basis of American liberty. In the process, they helped to forge a new genre of American liberalism grounded in the sanctity of First Amendment guarantees, even as they stoked the fires of reprisal and reform.

The Jacksonian Legacy

The Jacksonian geography of philanthropy produced two markedly different renditions of civil society by the 1830s: one rooted in Southern political imperatives and a growing white male electorate; the other in a sprawling array of highly autonomous charitable, educational, and social reform movements. Jackson's efforts to quash dissent underscored the tension between the Southern slavocracy and Northern philanthropy during the antebellum years. The indefatigable Adams captured the essence of these disparities in a speech in 1842. He began with a litany of abuses, focusing on the way in which slavery undermined freedom of speech, of the mails, of the press, and of the right to petition. He then "contrasted the schools, internal improvements, and general prosperity of New York State with the tumbled-down buildings, wretched roads, and cultural stagnation of Virginia."[46]

Yet even the canny Adams missed the main point of the drama in which he had played so central a role. One of the fundamental differences between the societies he contrasted, beyond slavery, was that they represented two very different notions of governance, philanthropy, and political culture. Virginians kept the leavening potential of civil society in check, granting charters sparingly, and watchfully curbing any trend which might contribute to the development of alternative, independent power bases beyond the control of the white male slaveholding elites who monopolized the state's economy, its government, its educational system, its press, and even (to an unusual degree) its religious institutions. Virginia's civic arena was carefully circumscribed. White women formed voluntary associations, but they controlled them, as Suzannne Lebsock has noted, only when "the stakes were small." Most blacks were subordinated in slavery, and those who were free commanded only limited rights. This was a world where white males reigned supreme, and this was the world that Jackson emulated, supported and esteemed.[47]

Democracy in New York was a far more sprawling affair. Although barred from the polling place, elite white women had successfully contended for public funding since the beginning of the nineteenth century, creating expanded resources for other women and children. New York's women also ran the country's most active Bible auxiliary, and they played a major role in abolitionist petitioning and the Burned Over District revivals in upstate New York, where the waves of religious enthusiasm were most intense. Blacks, too, had independent churches from which they pronounced their views on national issues such as colonization and slavery. And New York was en route to becoming the nation's economic hub, a trend bolstered by nonprofit institutions that provided the funding for large-scale capital improvements and models for the systematization of national marketing techniques—patterns of associationalism and development that, once again, echo Putnam's paradigm.

One man's paradise is another man's hell, and much of Jackson's political popularity undoubtedly stemmed from the fact that he challenged the Northern evangelical model through his persona, his temperament, and his convictions. For white men who were losing status as independent farmers and laborers, Jackson's election must have seemed like a heaven-sent opportunity to turn back the clock, to return to an era of independence and unquestioned patriarchal authority. It was a losing battle. The contagion of liberty and republican legitimacy unleashed by the Revolution spurred a second revolution in its wake, spawning a growing associational infrastructure, and a new emphasis on social advocacy in which even voteless groups demanded the right to be heard. Jackson learned to his chagrin that narrowing public culture to regional prerogatives could be achieved, but at a cost. His was a mottled legacy. The 1830s and 1840s were among the most violent decades in the nation's history, as groups increasingly jostled for power through both legal and illegal means. And where the rule of law faltered, mob rule began.

Civil Society / Civil Disorder

In the 1830s, the contests ignited in Congress spilled over into city streets. African Americans and abolitionists bore the brunt of this animosity, repeatedly forced to defend their property, as well as their political rights, from public assault. Many of these confrontations centered, quite literally, on the church, as exemplified by the riot that raged through New York City over three sultry summer nights in 1834. The violence began in the Chatham Street Chapel when the members of the Sacred Music Society disrupted a small meeting of African Americans, ordering them to vacate the premises so that they could have it for their rehearsal. Racism permeated American society during these years, North and South, which helps to explain the vehemence of the singers' response when the blacks refused to disband, sparking a small riot.

News of the encounter reached the newspapers, including James Watson Webb's *Courier and Enquirer.* No friend of the Tappan brothers or their abolitionist campaigns, Webb editorially fanned a second night of rioting through his columns, efforts bolstered by an incendiary meeting convened by Webb and Democratic leaders such as James Gordon Bennett at the party's stronghold, Tammany Hall. Galvanized by print and rousing speeches, the crowd marched on Chatham Chapel, where an abolitionist meeting was in session, and from which Arthur Tappan barely escaped being knifed. Later that evening, Lewis Tappan's home was sacked by a crowd of "butcherboys and day laborers" who pulled his possessions into the street and torched them as local men of property and standing hovered approvingly at the sidelines. By the time the city's Democratic mayor, Cornelius Lawrence, called in the troops to enforce martial law, a lifetime of Tappan's family possessions lay in cinders, and a terrified Arthur Tappan had barricaded himself, his employees, and his friends in an impromptu arsenal at the family store. A pacifist by nature, Arthur reportedly instructed his homespun militia to "Fire low . . . [so] they can't run."[1]

The crowd also demolished St. Philip's African Episcopal Church, and later inquiries revealed that they had planned to level not only Finney's chapel, but the offices of the reformist *McDowalls' Journal* and the Tappans' store as well. The encounter left Lewis Tappan disillusioned and dazed, but even more determined to lobby for social reform. As he explained in a letter to fellow abolitionist Theodore Dwight Weld shortly afterward, "It is true I have advocated Anti-slavery principles, [but I] have done nothing contrary to law or to propriety. . . . exercising the privileges of an American citizen I have contended earnestly for the doctrines of Immediate Emancipation." Despite the obvious dangers to his "person [and] property," Tappan was doggedly undeterred.[2]

Interestingly, historians writing during the reformist 1960s often portrayed men like Tappan as fanatics bent on pursuing a destructive and unpopular cause. But the point these scholars missed by focusing on the abolitionists' extraordinary capacity for martyrdom was that these men and women were defending all the civil liberties that Northern philanthropy required and that Southern slaveholders and their Northern allies denied: the right of all citizens to gather, to speak, to publicize, and to petition, even in the name of an unpopular cause and on behalf of groups that were marginalized and publicly disdained. The clashes that reddened New York's skies on those violent summer nights in 1834 represented in far more graphic terms than the congressional debates the fierce rivalries that flared in the antebellum era over who would govern, and whose voice would be legitimately heard.[3]

Race, Rioting, and Abolitionism

For the men who read Webb's inflammatory columns and crowded in the firelight before Tammany Hall, the answer was unequivocal and clear. Those who could not be silenced by political action would be constrained by the club. The decades following the Revolution had been relatively peaceful, although not entirely free of popular protests. Seven riots occurred in American cities in the second decade of the nineteenth century, and 21 over the ensuing decade. In the 1830s, the number rose dramatically, totaling 115 incidents, falling to 64 a decade later. Fifty-three confrontations were reported in 1835 alone, in which dozens of citizens were killed. In the 1830s, a significant number of these incidents were either aimed at abolitionists, or were racist in intent. Abolitionist journals placed the percentage of racial and antiabolitionist riots as high as 60% between 1833 and 1838, some of which were exceedingly violent, causing even Jackson to express concern. "This spirit of mob-law is becoming too common and must be checked," he remarked (perhaps somewhat disingenuously) to Amos Kendall in the aftermath of the Charleston riot that destroyed the abolitionist mails. If not, "ere long, it will become as great an evil as a servile war, and . . . we will soon have no safety under our happy Government of laws."[4]

Research by scholars such as Leonard Richards indicates that many prominent men, including political figures like Bennett, not only endorsed these activities, but often led them. The history of the disturbances they helped to create in the mid-1830s reads like a litany of atrocities. Garrison was captured by a mob at a meeting of the Boston Female Antislavery Society and summarily dragged through the city's streets. A New York Antislavery Society convention was attacked. The newly constructed Pennsylvania Hall was sacked and torched during a meeting of the Anti-slavery Convention of Women. And a publisher and abolitionist sympathizer, Elijah Lovejoy, was killed in Alton, Illinois, in 1837 as an enraged mob sought to dismantle his press. His body still slumped in the doorway, the building was burned, and the press hammered into pieces and thrown into a river. John Quincy Adams likened Lovejoy's death to "an earthquake." Yet Lovejoy was clearly aware of the risks he was taking, publicly vowing "never, while life lasts, to yield to this new system of attempting to destroy, by means of mob-violence, the right of conscience, the freedom of opinion, and of the press." For Ralph Waldo Emerson, as for many others, the Illinois publisher was a martyr for civil liberties, as well as his antislavery beliefs.[5]

The men who participated in these vicious escapades sometimes sought to justify their atrocities in patriotic terms, as efforts to redress social ills and remove public perils. Some likened their activities to those of the Revolutionary Sons of Liberty: colonial mobs marshaled by local elites to protest governmental abuses. Astonishingly, the attorney general of Massachusetts went so far as to compare Lovejoy's murderers to Samuel Adams and James Otis, men who had fomented revolutionary popular protests in the name of liberty.[6]

Jackson's policies indirectly helped to legitimize these assaults. When his calls for a national censorship law failed to produce results, Southern slaveholders and officials created vigilante committees to seize and burn the mails and to prevent other abolitionist incursions through force and intimidation. Others raised funds in their communities to offer bounties for prominent abolitionists. Savannah's leaders offered ten thousand dollars for Amos Phelps, while their counterparts in East Feliciana, Louisiana, offered a stunning $50,000 to silence Arthur Tappan. Although the violence receded in the North after Lovejoy's murder, Southern vigilante committees remained in place throughout the antebellum period, providing models for secret societies like the Ku Klux Klan after the Civil War.

Given the violence of these activities, the prominence of the men who led them is somewhat puzzling. Historians such as Leonard Richards tie their efforts, in part, to Democratic policies, particularly some of the statements in the president's annual messages to Congress. In 1835, for example, Jackson called for "severe penalties" to suppress the "unconstitutional and wicked" efforts of abolitionist societies. Jackson's successor, Martin Van Buren, publicly vowed to oppose efforts to eradicate slavery in the District of Columbia in a bow to Southern Democrats. New York's Democratic governor William Marcy also issued antiabolitionist statements at Van Buren's behest, and Samuel Beardsley, another prominent Van Burenite, led the mob that disrupted the abolitionist meeting in Utica. The Democrats' *Albany Argus* kept up a barrage of criticism during the presidential campaign of 1836, railing against "Abolitionist Fanaticism" and its "merciless warfare" against the "property and the lives of the people of the southern states." "It is with difficulty that the popular feeling against the incendiaries can be restrained from again breaking out in acts of violence," the editor suggestively concluded.[7]

However, mob activities cascaded over party lines. Richards's careful analysis of the backgrounds of the antiabolitionist rioters revealed that while 60% of the participants in the Utica disturbance were Jacksonian Democrats, a comparable percentage of anti-Jacksonians rioted in Cincinnati. For Democrats, as well as Whigs, the key to partisan survival was the ability to weld their Northern and Southern constituencies together, which meant placating Southern voters. Whigs were more divided than the Democrats, split between what Emerson termed their "cotton" and "conscience" wings, but leaders in both parties were keenly aware of the need for political expediency.[8]

The era was marked by efforts to limit black suffrage as well, counterpointing the growth of the white electorate. The 1820s and 1830s witnessed a series of efforts to dissolve the limited political rights of free blacks, as state after state redrafted their constitutions and enforced new laws. Although African American men continued to exercise the right to vote in Massachusetts, Rhode Island, Vermont, New Hampshire, and Maine, they were disfranchised in New Jersey, Connecticut, and Pennsylvania and briefly threatened with forced expulsion from Ohio. In New York, property requirements for suffrage were lifted for white males but retained for African Americans in 1821. By 1860, only four thousand African Americans were entitled to vote, a figure that underscores the importance of the philanthropically based political culture that they developed through their publications and their churches.[9]

Economic considerations also undoubtedly figured into the decision to promote public disorder. Although some scholars argue that abolitionism ultimately helped to promote capitalism by extolling the virtues of free labor over slavery, this interpretation would have been lost on many antebellum Americans. The cotton trade lay at the heart of the American economy during these years, accounting for 50% of all of the country's exports and a sizable portion of its textile industry. Because of that, anything that threatened slavery would have directly threatened the livelihoods of some of the country's wealthiest men, endangering North-South economic as well as political alliances. Abolitionism also posed a direct challenge to the right of Southern white males to engage in the unbridled pursuit of individual gain, which went to the heart of the slaveholding ethos, as well as the profit margins of many Northern manufacturers and merchants.[10]

If the expansion of the white male electorate signaled a new chapter in men's political history, the mob violence of the 1830s and 1840s backed their authority with brute force. As Richards points out, antiabolitionists realized that voluntary associations had become a permanent fixture on the civic landscape but felt that they should be "restrictive," that "organizers should follow the example of the colonizationists and seek out only prudent, judicious 'gentlemen of property and standing' as members." By this thinking, abolitionists were attempting to subvert democratic processes by "molding large segments of the Northern population—primarily women . . . into helpless puppets responding to every beck and call of a highly organized, centralized bureaucracy." The fact that women figured prominently in abolitionist campaigns was particularly galling. Editorials described the appropriate borders of political behavior. The *Boston Commercial Gazette*, for example, denounced the "petticoat politicians" of the Boston Female Antislavery Society as "simpletons" whose primary object was "to lead captive, silly women, who would be much more usefully and profitably employed at home attending to their household affairs, [into] prowling about stirring up discord and dissension, preaching about that which they know no more than the man in the moon." The ne plus ultra of these unfeminine activities, according to this author, was their "impudence" in equating antislavery with "*Christian charity*, as if it were an act of Christian charity to *stir up sedition and rebellion, and urge blacks to commit murder, by cutting their master's throats*, and to solicit signatures to a foolish petition to Congress."[11]

Comments such as these suggest the depths of popular misgivings about women's public aspirations and changing gender roles. Periods of intense social and economic flux, particularly those in which gender roles are redefined, often catalyze a quest for new criteria for measuring masculine and feminine behavior. In the 1830s, middle-class white women appropriated the high road to maternal moral authority. Disinterested precisely because it was, at least rhetorically, removed from the rough-and-tumble world of partisanship and the scramble for commercial gain, the doctrine of female moral superiority enabled some middle-class white women to create more public roles. Female abolitionists and Indian advocates transferred this newly minted authority into federal petition drives, casting their "pleas" in increasingly insistent tones.

For many Americans, the Grimké sisters stood at the far end of the radical continuum. The daughters of a prominent South Carolina slaveholding family, Angelina and Sarah Grimké joined the American Antislavery Society (AAS) after moving north and converting to Quakerism. Angelina was also one of the first American women to publicly address "promiscuous" audiences of women and men. As Kathryn Kish Sklar points out, public oratory was a valued form of male political performance in the 1830s. Thus, the General Association of Massachusetts Clergy censured women like the Grimkés for what they deemed their "unnatural" behavior in assuming "the tone of a man as a public reformer." To this the members of the Boston Female Antislavery Society tartly responded that it was woman's duty and province "to plead the cause of the oppressed, in our land, and to do all that she can by her voice, and her pen, and her purse, and the influence of her example, to overthrow the horrible system of American slavery." Angelina Grimké gave her final speech in Philadelphia's Pennsylvania Hall during the 1838 women's antislavery convention, mounting the podium as a crowd of ten thousand sullenly loitered outside. Bricks were hurled through the windows as she was introduced to the audience, accompanying her talk with a rain of shattering glass. Grimké held her ground and was followed by Abby Kelley before the hall was cleared. By the next day Pennsylvania Hall lay in cinders, yet another casualty of Jacksonian unrest.[12]

Racial animosities also helped to fuel the public disorder that was emerging from the volatile brew of Jacksonian politics and philanthropy. African American populations were growing in many Northern cities, raising the specter of competition for jobs. Many laborers—both black and white—lived close to the margins of poverty. Estimates hold that a family of five needed $330 ($4,290) per annum, or $8 per week for forty weeks, to stay above the poverty line in the 1820s. For unskilled and semi-skilled workers in an economy marked by intermittent opportunities for employment and frequent layoffs, even this modest amount was often hard to earn. In 1850, the threshold of the poverty line was $500 ($7,000), and $600 ($8,400) in more expensive cities like New York. Journeymen's salaries, however, tended to hover around half that sum. Employment opportunities were often scarce, especially in winter, and every job was precious and necessary. Blacks who threatened to compete for those jobs were seethingly resented, and blocked at every turn by white artisans who refused to work with them or train them in their skills and trades.[13]

Political leaders often fanned these resentments as a means of building solidarity and winning partisan allies. Thus, slaves were depicted as the pampered minions of their owners, fed, clothed and employed at the slave-owners' expense while white laborers could barely keep their families fed and housed. As David Roediger has argued, racism was part of the social glue that bound many white laborers together, just as it helped unite the parties that acknowledged and promised to remedy their grievances. Honest laborers, rather than pampered slaves, were rhetorically designated the truest citizens and the most honorable heirs of the Revolution, rhetoric that initially made white workers' weakened economic position all the harder to explain or endure. The end result was a "desire to punish anyone transgressing their notions of the rightful order of things," including abolitionists and African Americans.[14]

The drama of events such as Elijah Lovejoy's death and Garrison's brush with lynch law often obscured the extent to which blacks bore the brunt of Northern mob attacks in the antebellum years. One of James Forten's sons was brutally attacked by a mob of whites in 1834, Frederick Douglass was beaten by an Indiana mob, and white rioters habitually descended on black neighborhoods when they wearied of other targets, destroying houses and churches. Black churches had been at the heart of African American communal efforts for self-help since they first appeared in Northern cities at the turn of the century. They served as incubators for a growing array of mutual aid societies, educational activities, and politically oriented social advocacy campaigns, including abolitionism. They also served economic functions, providing loans and support for parishioners as they slowly ascended the social ladder. Although most blacks were poor, held down by racism and discriminatory hiring practices, a few like Philadelphia's Fortens were relatively wealthy by any standards. In the 1830s, Philadelphia's black community of fifteen thousand accounted for only 10% of the city's population, but collectively they owned almost $1 million ($13 million in 2000 dollars) in property, 70% of which was held by one thousand families. Seven years later, survey data revealed that six of those families were among the wealthiest in Philadelphia—a status that must have irked white workingmen whose own economic fortunes were more precarious. In attacking churches, rioters destroyed not only potent community symbols, but also key centers of black political culture and influence. In effect, rioters sought to physically dismantle the tangible evidence of black economic and political authority in Jacksonian society.[15]

Just as the gag rule exemplified a fundamental clash between two competing systems of governance, one participatory, the other rooted in paternalism and partisanship, so too did the mob activity that flared across American cities in the years when the Indian removals and the mail and petition campaigns were unfolding in Washington. Many of the meagerly propertied men who joined the ranks of new voters in the 1820s fiercely defended their hegemony over the vote and public affairs, vigilantly patrolling the borders of the political arena. They attacked the institutions that symbolized the political and economic achievements of radical reformers and traditionally subordinate groups, violating the churches and homes of African Americans, rich and poor, as well as those of prominent white reformers such as Tappan. The competing political cultures of the 1830s—one rooted in white male solidarity around the vote and the other in the more encompassing frame of philanthropy and civil society—played out their struggle in volatile conflicts throughout the decade. In the process, the public sphere was convulsively redefined at both the local and federal levels as men and women, black and white, jousted for public authority in new ways.

Black Philanthropy

Northern African American leaders initially responded to mob attacks and growing political repression by developing an impressive array of secular institutions for education, moral reform, and political protest within their own communities—a pattern that echoed the growth of the abolitionist movement in the wake of the gag rule. Efforts to abolish slavery and reduce prejudice resonated through all of these activities. Gradually, however, more radical initiatives were added, linking civil disobedience with efforts to raise funds, mount petition campaigns, and promote moral and educational reform.

African Americans were active in the abolitionist movement from the outset. Strengthened by martyrdom and repression, the movement grew steadily over the course of the 1830s. Although many auxiliaries remained racially segregated, some of the most visible chapters, such as the Philadelphia Female Anti-slavery Society, were racially mixed. Women's auxiliaries choreographed petition drives, raised funds, hosted increasingly elaborate antislavery fairs, and distributed information on slavery and the problems of Northern racism. In the process, abolitionism politicized traditional female fund-raising activities, shifting the focus from charity and the church to matters of state while drawing growing numbers of Northern women into political contests through nonprofit entrepreneurship and their gifts of money and time.[16]

By the 1840s, the movement began to splinter along both ideological and racial lines. A major schism occurred in 1840 when Abby Kelley was elected to the executive committee of the AAS. Conservatives led by the Tappans and Gerrit Smith protested, forming the politically oriented American and Foreign Antislavery Society (AFASS) as an alternative to the more inclusive Garrisonian wing. While AFASS members campaigned for candidates of the Liberty, Free Soil, and Republican Parties, the AAS clung instead to moral suasion in lieu of electioneering. They also accorded women like Kelley full parity as agents and trustees. And while Garrisonians increasingly called for secession under the rubric of "No Union with Slaveholders!" AFASS representatives worked within the framework of partisan politics and federal elections.[17]

Abolitionists also divided over racial issues. While the majority of whites focused primarily on eradicating slavery, blacks were equally interested in eradicating the pervasive racism that blighted their communities and their lives. Moreover, despite the fact that Garrison had launched his movement from the black church, and on the bedrock of the black anticolonizationist crusade, and blacks continued to provide about one-seventh of the AAS's funding, African Americans remained markedly underrepresented among the leadership of both the parent society and its auxiliaries. Racism within the ranks remained a constant problem. Although some

leaders, like Lewis Tappan, were relatively free of prejudice and actively
worked to end segregation both within and outside the society, many white
abolitionists pitied the Southern slaves but forgot their Northern counterparts. By the 1840s, many blacks had become increasingly aware of the
taint of racism within the movement, diverting their energies to black-
controlled organizations instead.[18]

Some of these differences surfaced in the society's own materials. Much
of the movement's imagery centered on victimization, featuring popular
illustrations that showed supplicating bondsmen kneeling in chains.
While black oratory as well as white antislavery tracts stressed the brutal-
ity of slavery, Northern blacks sought to popularize a second image, one
that highlighted the achievements of African Americans, as well as their
degradation.[19]

Organizations such as the AAS, the black church, and the black moral
reform movement played pivotal roles in what might be termed the
social construction of reality, providing mechanisms through which their
members presented and challenged public images of their causes and
themselves. As Edward Said explains, one group will seek to justify its
domination—or persecution—of another by "making statements about
it, authorizing views of it, describing it, teaching it, ruling over it . . . re-
structuring and having authority over" it. This was the aim of the racist
apologists who justified enslavement and discrimination on the basis of
blacks' presumed "childlike" qualities, lack of intellect and ability, licen-
tiousness, and incapacity for self-governance. Combating these stereotypes
was a major preoccupation of black philanthropy during the 1830s and
1840s, but of only marginal interest to many antislavery whites. As a result, the two groups often harbored different aspirations for the kind of political culture they sought to create.[20]

While national antislavery journals devoted themselves to publicizing
the degradations of slavery and the threat to Northern civil liberties posed
by mobs and political repression, African Americans created institutions to
promote and publicize black virtue and success. This was the aim of early
African American leaders such as Richard Allen and Absalom Jones, and it
remained an important goal throughout the early national and antebellum years. The black convention movement that Allen helped to set in motion provided an important vehicle for identifying issues and mobilizing
resources in black communities throughout the North. The conventions
joined African American churches in combating repressive legislation and
racist practices through their publications and petitions. As the delegates
of the 1834 convention defiantly noted, this was "a revolution where the

contest is not for landed territory, but for freedom, the weapons not carnal, but spiritual; where the struggle is not for blood, but for right, and one in which our . . . only hope is in God." Local petitioning had a long and venerable history in the black community dating back to the 1780s. By 1830, the Association for the Political Improvement of People of Color was supplementing the AAS antislavery petition drives with campaigns of its own. African American suffrage associations also organized statewide petition drives, lobbying legislators through printed materials, meetings, and legislative testimony in areas where their rights were imperiled or denied.[21]

Several of these statewide campaigns began to yield results by the 1840s, vividly counterpointing the political stalemate at the federal level. By 1841, Connecticut, New York, and Vermont had granted jury trials to blacks arrested as fugitives, and the Massachusetts school system was desegregated a decade later. Black petition campaigns also won the right of African Americans to testify against whites in legal actions in Ohio in 1849 and in California in 1855. Ohio repealed its black laws in 1843, and several Northern states passed personal liberty laws between 1843 and 1849, absolving citizens and public officials of the duty to assist in the enforcement of federal fugitive slave laws. Although racism remained undiminished and blacks were regularly harassed by mobs and aggressively pushed to the sidelines in congressional deliberations, a growing number of political gains were secured at the state and local level through the fragile right of supplication, a trend assiduously tracked by abolitionist groups.[22]

This raises an important point. Historians sometimes portray Garrisonian abolitionists as anti-institutionalists who indulged in wholesale rejections of both church and state. To quote Kenneth Stampp, they "opposed all political action." However, this interpretation overlooks some significant distinctions. Garrisonians rejected electoral activity because they felt that both of the major parties were corrupt, and that the number of antislavery voters was too small to influence federal policymaking, providing a canny assessment of the ballot power of both the Liberty and Free Soil parties. As the members of the Massachusetts Antislavery Society explained, "A *third* party, of any kind, in a land of majorities, is an absurdity in terms . . . attempting to accomplish with the few what can only be done by the many." As such, it was a "waste of time, means and energy, in a struggle which must of necessity be fruitless." But they never rejected the right of petition, which is also a political act (indeed, the only form of political action that was open to the women and most of the free blacks who joined their ranks), and the Massachusetts society religiously tracked state policymaking and petitioning in their annual reports. This split between federal and local action became still more pronounced in the 1850s, as even Garrisonians endorsed resistance to federal policies while lobbying for increased liberties within their states.[23]

They also continued to join with blacks in their opposition to the American Colonization Society (ACS). Despite the small number of blacks who ultimately emigrated—totaling fewer than twenty thousand even during the turbulent period between 1824 and 1862—the ACS continued to receive substantial backing from individuals, the federal government, and selected states. Moral reform leaders explicitly underscored the links between ACS propaganda and their own efforts to promote temperance, frugality, and education. As they bitterly explained, the society "represents us as the most corrupt, vicious and abandoned of any class of men in the community. . . . Here we are ignorant, idle, a nuisance and a drawback on the resources of the country. But abandoned as we are, in Africa we shall civilize and Christianize all that heathen country [sic]." Moral reform provided an antidote to these stereotypes, as well as a spur to black philanthropy.[24]

As the spokesmen for the American Moral Reform Society explained, "we see two *rival* institutions invoking the benevolence . . . to aid in changing our condition. The former proposes an indirect action on the sin of slavery, by removing the free to the land of their fathers. The latter a direct action on the subject of slavery, by denouncing its guilt, while it pleads for the elevation of the free coloured man in the land of his nativity." It was precisely this political object—the urge to counteract and contain the incursions of the ACS—that initially politicized the black church and stimulated the abolitionist movement, both black and white. And it was the urgency of *this* political objective that white abolitionists failed to sufficiently address in their single-minded crusade to eradicate Southern slaveholding.[25]

Black leaders continually pointed to the growing number of black-initiated churches, charities, and educational ventures as tangible proof of African American virtue and achievement. To an extraordinary degree, philanthropy marked the yardstick by which African American leaders measured their communities among themselves, and among white allies and foes. This was the arena in which African Americans challenged the stereotypes created by endemic racism, partisan politics, the colonization society, and the Southern slavocracy. By this measure, blacks were neither victims nor moral reprobates; they were men and women of limited means who had created an impressive array of charitable and educational endeavors for their own, on their own.

In addition to moral reform, a variety of literary, library, educational, and temperance societies were created by African American women and men in the 1830s, promoting "mutual aid, hard work, thrift, learning, piety and sobriety as the keys to social advancement and emancipation." Like white women's organizations, the first black female mutual aid societies dated from the 1790s. Sunday schools appeared in the second decade of the nineteenth century, charities in the 1820s, and antislavery and literary societies in the 1830s. Most of these ventures had an antislavery tinge, combining self-help, charity, and mutual aid with an awareness of the continuing plight of Southern slaves. Groups like the Afric-American Female Intelligence Society in Boston pooled their resources (in this case, a 25¢ initiation fee and 12½¢ dues) to create small libraries for their communities, as well as themselves, reiterating the themes of Franklin's Junto.[26]

African American women also created a significant number of self-help groups, beyond literary societies. According to an 1838 survey of almost one hundred black mutual aid groups in Philadelphia conducted by the Pennsylvania Abolition Society, two-thirds of these associations were run by women, numbering almost seventy-six hundred members among the city's nearly eighteen thousand black residents—a significant figure, even allowing for overlapping memberships that would have skewed the final tally.[27]

Temperance activities had similarly deep roots in the black community, dating from efforts by the first mutual aid societies to bar tipplers from their rosters in the 1780s. By 1834 the Colored American Temperance Society had twenty-three branches in eighteen cities, and the Daughters of Temperance accounted for another fourteen auxiliaries with fifteen hundred members in Pennsylvania alone in the 1840s. Part of the movement's appeal stemmed from the skill with which its spokesmen linked intemperance to prejudice, and to lost opportunities for communal self-help. Thus, a protemperance article entitled "Prostitution of our Means" complained that thousands of dollars were wasted each year on gambling and drink, money that could have funded schools, literary societies, libraries, and reading and lecture rooms where African Americans could "acquire useful, scientific and practical knowledge, such as would qualify them to be respectable, efficient freemen and citizens. Brethren," the editorial asked rhetorically in conclusion, "when shall the state of things be changed—if you say never, we will answer then *we never* shall be a respected or happy people." National leaders like Frederick Douglass echoed these themes, admonishing audiences to "save your money—live economically," while hailing philanthropy as a key to communal independence.[28]

The pervasiveness of these activities calls into question some well-worn analytical chestnuts, particularly the notion of American individualism. Although the careers of many white businessmen and slaveowners like Andrew Jackson certainly epitomized the notion of male individualism, this concept was far less relevant for either antebellum African Americans or middle-class white women. These citizens made their greatest public impact through collective rather than individualistic acts, a pattern that reflected African, as well as American traditions. Although the Northern black community produced many notable leaders during these years, including outstanding figures like Frederick Douglass and Sojourner Truth, impressive numbers of black Americans were deeply enmeshed in webs of philanthropy, mutuality, and communal self-help, and it was these activities rather than untempered individualism that accorded their most potent social and political roles. True to Tocqueville's dictum that individuals were powerless in a democracy on their own, but powerful and authoritative in groups, much of the public history of antebellum African Americans can only be understood in communal terms.

The other striking feature is their generosity. Although poor in comparison to whites, African American communities managed to support a large and increasingly sophisticated universe of voluntary associations both within and outside the black church. Even the literary firebrand David Walker saw this ethos of mutuality as his race's greatest strength in an intensely racist society, in part because associational networks were instruments for social mobilization. They also helped to accumulate capital, providing a hedge against destitution and funds for the development of business ventures, including the black press. The number of black benevolent societies grew markedly in the 1820s and 1830s, increasing from twenty-four to sixty in Philadelphia alone, each with between seventy-five and two hundred members. In part, this reflected their exclusion from white institutions, as well as a "bunker mentality" born of physical and political reprisals. But it also reflects an emphasis on collective effort which, given the numbers, suggests that a significant segment of the community, both well-to-do and poor, was involved, providing an interesting window onto issues of class. While some of Philadelphia's black parishes, particularly St. Thomas's, were economically exclusive, others like Mother Bethel were extraordinarily mixed, encompassing some of the city's wealthiest African Americans as well as the very poor.[29]

Many of these institutions—including churches—played important economic roles in their communities by providing benefits and loans for their members, patterns that harkened back to the eighteenth century. A

Philadelphia survey conducted in 1853 found 108 incorporated mutual benefit societies with a collective annual income of $29,600 ($420,320 in 2000 dollars) and $28,266 ($401,377) in permanent investment funds. They also listed 9,762 members, out of a potential population of 30,000. These figures were exclusive of the city's twenty-seven churches, which claimed another 8,000 members, its Sunday schools, fifteen temperance societies, three libraries, five literary associations, and twenty-seven schools supported by the black community and run by black teachers. Statistics such as these were often used as indices of communal achievement, underscoring the social and economic results of decades of self-denial and community service by Northern blacks.[30]

Clearly, philanthropy played an important role in defining and maintaining Northern free black communities, generosity that was often extended to other groups as well. African American subscribers and donors helped to bankroll Garrison's *Liberator* during its early years, and they provided most of the funds for his first trip abroad. Other whites were aided as well, as when New York's First Colored Presbyterian Church raised $60 ($780) for Elijah Lovejoy's widow shortly after the editor's murder in 1837. Black churches and literary societies also held fund-raising benefits for the Africans captured on the *Amistad*, providing money for their defense and to send them back to Africa after they were freed by the Supreme Court in 1841.[31]

They also subsidized the rise of the black press. Maintaining a specialized newspaper solely on a commercial basis was a difficult and often unsuccessful task. African American generosity helped to underwrite a number of independent black journals, including Frederick Douglass's influential *North Star*. Samuel Cornish and John Russwurm underscored their desire to present their community's point of view in the first issue of *Freedom's Journal*, noting that they sought to plead their own cause. Douglass was more blunt, arguing that "it has long been our anxious wish to see, in this slave-holding, slave trading, Negro hating land," a paper under black control to "put to silence and to shame, our oppressors." Publications such as these addressed both black and white audiences, presenting an African American perspective on slavery, antislavery, and racist stereotypes in tandem with definitions of their own strengths and weaknesses, achievements, and needs. In publicizing these views, black writers, editors, and orators exercised their rights and performed their roles as legitimate political actors, beyond their limited right to vote. Philanthropy played an important role in supporting these activities. Juvenile antislavery societies gave contributions and raised funds for their publications through the sale of hand-sewn items made by young girls, while women's groups hosted benefits and bazaars and collected individual donations. The Female Unification Publication Society was even created at Philadelphia's Bethel AME Church explicitly to raise funds for black publications, efforts that wedded commercial practices—the creation and sale of marketable goods—with communal ends, once again underscoring the relationship among philanthropy, the market, and the public sphere.[32]

Philanthropy and Civil Disobedience

The 1840s marked the emergence of a new genre of black philanthropy, one that increasingly blended benevolence with civil disobedience. It also brought a group of powerful new black leaders to the fore, many of whom—like the charismatic Frederick Douglass—were former slaves. Conditions had changed within Northern free black communities since Jones and Allen's generations held sway, beyond the growth of a critical mass of gifted new leaders. There was now a substantial mass of African Americans who had been born into freedom after the importation of slaves was barred in 1808 and the gradual abolition of slavery unfolded in the North. Literacy rates among Northern freemen and women had increased markedly due to the growing number of educational and literary societies and Sunday schools. Moreover, the members of this generation were far more politicized than their parents had been. Schooled in the harsh milieu of antiabolitionism and urban riots, they were well versed in the acrid debates surrounding the perpetuation of slavery. Despite abolitionist resistance, they had seen Southern slavery spread and grow. While there were fewer than 2 million blacks held in bondage in 1820, by 1860 that figure had more than doubled, underscoring the need for stronger measures.

This generation also evinced a growing willingness to rely on civil disobedience to achieve what could not be accomplished through legal means, particularly by harboring, protecting, and aiding fugitive slaves. And, with the emergence of vigilance societies, cross-class alliances were strengthened, as manual laborers collaborated with black elites in identifying slave catchers before they reached their prey, building social capital and communal cohesion within black communities on a new scale.

Vigilance societies emerged as important African American organizations of the late 1830s and 1840s. Although some were racially mixed, many were not. Like earlier black initiatives, these associations tended to have heterogeneous agendas, mixing charitable and educational ends with lobbying, petition drives, and efforts to publicize communal attitudes, aspirations, and needs. But their most distinctive feature was the extent to which they openly embraced civil disobedience, bringing men and women together in the pursuit of both legal and illegal agendas. Although some white antislavery groups helped fugitive slaves, few were as open or as adamant about their activities as the Northern African American vigilance societies before the 1850s. And although many black women's voluntary associations resembled those of their white counterparts, coupling charity with commercial activities in the name of benevolence, their growing willingness to break the law in the name of social justice set them apart from most of their white peers.[33]

The basis of the moral authority that justified women's public roles differed as well. Although both black and white women's organizations drew much of their strength and their capacity to mobilize from the Protestant church, black women did not automatically win the level of public deference accorded middle-class white "ladies," particularly when they ventured outside their own communities. Nor did most white women bring the same acute sense of discrimination to their work. The end result was that Northern black women tended to be more willing to experiment with different organizational models, sometimes working in segregated separatist groups, sometimes in tandem with black men, and sometimes with their white counterparts in female antislavery auxiliaries. Because their resources were limited, their organizations often pursued a variety of ends, blending charity with education and mutual aid, as well as efforts to undermine slavery and to promote the development of a black political culture to challenge racism and redefine the African American community on their own terms. When the underground railroad developed, it was added to women's portfolio as well. Thus, while white women promoted a variety of single-purpose charitable, benevolent, and ultraist organizations that often separated them by interest and class, black women adopted a more flexible, more eclectic approach, incorporating whatever resources were at hand in their pursuit of communal aspirations and goals.[34]

Vigilance committees both reflected and reinforced this heterogeneity. The first black vigilance committee was founded by David Ruggles in New York in 1835. Although designed primarily to aid fleeing slaves, Ruggles's group embraced a variety of activities. Members raised money to provide runaway slaves with food, clothes, and legal services. They gathered and distributed information on kidnappings and slave catchers. They inspected incoming ships to check for fugitives and captives illegally smuggled from Africa. And the committee "exposed official connivance with kidnaping rings by compiling a *Slaveholder's Directory*, giving the names and addresses of police, judges and city officials who aided in the seizure of fugitives." Although the New York committee withered after Ruggles resigned in 1839, comparable ventures later surfaced in Philadelphia, Boston, and Detroit.[35]

Some secured legislative gains. Ruggles's group successfully petitioned to allow fugitives captured in New York the right to jury trials in 1841, only to see the ruling overturned at the federal level by the Supreme Court's *Prigg v. Pennsylvania* decision the following year. Other vigilance committee campaigns yielded more enduring results, including a petition drive that culminated in the Massachusetts Personal Liberty Act of 1843. The vigilance committees illustrate the capacity for mobilization embodied in the dense network of black communal organizations—sometimes working in tandem with whites—that developed in the antebellum years. Women's groups and church auxiliaries helped them to raise funds, run programs, and aid escaping slaves. Information about kidnappings was disseminated through communal institutions as well, including female literary societies, underscoring the changing nature of African American philanthropy. In the process, vigilance committees politicized the agendas of many groups that had initially been created for other purposes, drawing them into social advocacy, legislative lobbying, and civil disobedience.[36]

Revolt

Passage of the Fugitive Slave Act in 1850, the Kansas-Nebraska Act of 1854, and the Supreme Court's *Dred Scott* decision three years later hastened the drift from vigilance to violence for many abolitionists, both black and white. Included in the Compromise of 1850 to offset Southern concessions, the Fugitive Slave Act denied alleged runaways the right to trial by jury and the ability to testify on their own behalf and enabled them to be remanded into slavery on the flimsiest of evidence: an alleged owner's affidavit certifying his ownership. Moreover, the court-appointed commissioners who tried the cases were awarded ten dollars if they ruled in the slaveowner's favor, but only five dollars if they set the defendant free. Physical resistance to the abduction of slaves, previously muted, now flared into armed confrontations as African Americans moved to block the enforcement of a law that jeopardized the safety of any black, slave or free.

Veteran abolitionists like the indefatigable Tappans immediately denounced the law as "iniquitous and unconstitutional," arguing that it left the Northern freedman with no alternative but to open his house to the

"panting fugitive. . . . *he must disobey the law.* . . . This covenant with death
. . . must be trampled underfoot, resisted, disobeyed, and violated at all
hazards." Douglass's faith in the federal government had soured in the
1840s. "I have no love for America," he confessed in 1847. "I have no patriotism, I have no country. . . . I desire to see it overthrown as speedily as
possible, and its Constitution shivered in a thousand fragments." His sentiments were shared by growing numbers of black and white leaders in
the 1850s. Although Northern abolitionists continued to stage formal
protests through petition and political and legislative campaigns throughout the decade, they also evinced a greater willingness to take up arms to
achieve their aims, hastening the transition from philanthropy to open insurrection.[37]

For example, shortly after the Fugitive Slave Act was passed, Chicago
blacks met in churches to set up vigilante committees to forcibly resist the
law, while others rhetorically endorsed the overthrow of the American
government and the creation of organized militias. A crowd of fifteen
hundred attended a meeting at New York's African Methodist Episcopal
Zion church to hear speakers "brush aside Garrisonian pleas for nonresis-
tance and invoke the right of self-defense," while speakers at a similar
gathering at Boston's First Baptist Church brandished weapons "to demon-
strate the proper greeting for slavecatchers." Black leaders throughout the
North urged the creation of quasi-military groups, petitioning their state
governments to rescind legislation barring blacks from service in state
militias. When approval was not given, they launched subscription drives
to buy the arms themselves. Suddenly, Northern churches were being used
as venues for arming their communities, as well as promoting philanthropy and political mobilization.[38]

Efforts to aid fugitives also became more coordinated and more public,
including actions in a number of celebrated cases in Boston. One of the
most successful was the rescue of a coffee house waiter named Shadrach in
February 1851. As he was being brought into the courthouse for trial, the
waiter was surrounded by a crowd of African Americans who quickly spirited him into the street and on to freedom in Canada. For many Bostonians, the confrontation "established the positive value of a clear-cut and
deliberate confrontation with the government." While the Massachusetts
Antislavery Society glowingly compared it to the Boston Tea Party, reporting that "an enterprise better contrived and conducted was never
known," Secretary of State Daniel Webster pronounced it treason, and
helped to draft a presidential proclamation condemning the act and de-
manding prosecution. Presidential intervention notwithstanding, only

eight of the participants were tried, and none convicted, reflecting a hardening line against local enforcement of the detested law.[39]

Other confrontations were more violent. One of the bloodiest flared over efforts to recapture fugitives in Christiana, Pennsylvania, where a slaveowner was killed and several others wounded by a group of about forty African Americans in a clash incited, in part, by antislavery groups and vigilance societies. Douglass lauded the fugitives who sparked the Christiana confrontation and aided their escape. "I do not look upon them as murderers," he noted. "To me they were heroic defenders of the just rights of men."[40]

Several abolitionists went further, openly embracing insurrection by sending guns to antislavery settlers in Kansas and bankrolling John Brown's raid on Harpers Ferry. Sectional politics assumed a new level of ferocity with the passage of the Kansas-Nebraska Act of 1854, which repealed the prohibition on the expansion of slavery in new territories above the 36°30′ line, turning the decision over to the popular sovereignty of local voters. Although the assumption was that Nebraska would be added as a free state and Kansas opened to slavery, both slaveowners and free-soil advocates flooded into the territory to determine its fate in increasingly violent clashes. Abuses were rampant. Ignoring local election returns, the territorial government at Lecompton drafted a constitution featuring "a series of incredible laws that stripped antislavery men of basic constitutional rights," limiting office to those who swore an oath to uphold slavery, criminalizing assertions that slavery was illegal, and making the circulation of abolitionist literature punishable by death. An antislavery settlement at Lawrence, Kansas, was "sacked" by a proslavery posse the following year, and the presses of the *Herald of Freedom* and the *Kansas Free State* smashed and hurled into the river, echoing the events of Elijah Lovejoy's death but with far higher political stakes. Shortly afterwards, on May 24, 1856, the abolitionist zealot John Brown led a retaliatory attack on proslavery settlers at Pottawatomie Creek, brutally murdering—and in some cases, dismembering—five men within sight of their horrified families and friends.[41]

Historians concur that Brown's role in the Pottawatomie massacre was not well known, which helps to explain the level support he garnered both before and after his abortive 1859 raid on the federal arsenal at Harpers Ferry, Virginia, to spark a major slave revolt. Although Lewis Tappan and Garrison refused to aid him, a surprising number of antislavery advocates rallied to Brown's cause, including Gerrit Smith, Frederick Douglass, the transcendentalist luminary Ralph Waldo Emerson, and Henry Ward

Beecher, who raised funds from his Brooklyn pulpit for what became known as "Beecher's Bibles": the Sharp's rifles favored by antislavery guerillas. Even Garrison retrospectively lauded Brown's Harpers Ferry raid in an uncharacteristic breach of his enduring pacifism. "We are growing more and more warlike," he confessed, and yet even he conceded that in moving from moral suasion to force abolitionists were merely "taking the American people on their own ground, and judging them by their own standard."[42]

It was a bitter climax to years of striving. Jacksonian efforts to disempower African Americans reached their final permutation in 1850s, with the Fugitive Slave Act and the 1857 *Dred Scott* decision handed down by Jackson's Supreme Court appointee Roger Taney, formally denying citizenship to African Americans under federal law. Taney's ruling was the culmination of a long and twisted process that began with the gag rule and Jackson's call for federal censorship of the press. The government's tampering with First Amendment guarantees unleashed a Pandora's box of evils, from Southern vigilantism, to mob reprisals against Northern abolitionists and blacks, to insurrection. Charles Remond captured his community's anger and despair over the court's decision. "The time has gone by for the colored people to talk of patriotism," he thundered. "We owe no allegiance to a country which grinds us under its iron heel and treats us like dogs." For many, the choice was now between "dying freemen, or living slaves."[43]

The years of repression and persecution initially bred Northern resistance through the elaboration of associational networks. Thus, the number of antislavery auxiliaries grew and their petitions lengthened in the wake of the gag rule, and Northern African American leaders created increasingly intricate labyrinths of organizational resources within their communities. In the process, Northern free blacks forged a vibrant civil society and a distinctive political culture of their own, one that counterpointed the distortions of both sympathetic whites and racist partisans, challenging the popular stereotypes of an overwhelmingly racist society. Although they won a number of political concessions at the state level, in the end African Americans were collectively and violently stripped of their citizenship by a stroke of Taney's pen. Unable to ensure justice through the instruments of civil society, many abolitionists—both black and white—lost faith in the American creed, endorsing armed resistance against the federal government in lieu of exercising civil liberties. While antislavery advocates moved from voluntarism to violence, middle-class white women waged their own quiet war against discrimination.

The Politics of Chivalry

Abolitionism constituted one strain of antebellum philanthropy—but only one. Far less volatile were the growing array of female-controlled charities and reform movements that ran the gamut from humanitarianism to labor reform. Many of these women's groups pursued politically oriented agendas, whether through petition drives or ongoing requests for state and municipal appropriations. The common denominator that united them was their dependence on what might be termed "the politics of chivalry"—their shared reliance on the patronage and good will of male politicians. And, as the infamous Eaton affair so aptly demonstrated, politics and chivalry could sometimes be a combustible mix.

The incident arose when John Eaton, one of the members of Jackson's inner circle of advisers, his Kitchen Cabinet, brought his wife into the president's circle. A lively woman of dubious reputation, Peggy Timberlake married Eaton shortly after her first husband's death. Some whispered that Timberlake committed suicide in a fit of despair over his wife's liaisons; others alluded to Mrs. Eaton's easy ways with customers at her father's tavern. But most of her detractors concurred that Mrs. Eaton was not respectable and should not be received by honorable matrons intent on protecting their own reputations and upholding the standards of virtue in Washington society. Unwilling to be cowed by female moral authority, Jackson insisted on presenting her in public and ensuring that she was publicly, if not graciously, received. Jackson split the cabinet, but with his backing Mrs. Eaton prevailed.[1]

For men like Jackson and John Eaton, women were to be protected, guided, perhaps even privately revered. But they were not to be tolerated as political actors, whether in the cloistered setting of the drawing room or on the national stage. The chivalry these men demonstrated in rallying to Mrs. Eaton's defense was considered by many of their contemporaries an earmark of male gallantry, a prize to be accorded to those women whom they themselves deemed virtuous and who remained within their appointed sphere. But virtue, as this episode so clearly illustrated, was in the eye of the beholder. Chivalry, graciously extended, could be just as quickly withdrawn. Antebellum women constructed their claims to political authority on moral suasion and the expectation that their voices would be heeded because they were presumably disinterested, aloof from direct political or economic gain. This was the philosophy that legitimized their entrance into the federal petition campaigns, their work in developing charities and asylums, and their success in winning charters and state and local funding. Like the redoubtable matrons who shunned the unfortunate Mrs. Eaton, many of these women would see their efforts to assert their authority contested by policymakers offering protection, but not parity, in the public sphere.

The Rhetoric and Reality of Retrenchment

These trends played out in several ways. While female abolitionists were being publicly castigated for their political aspirations and agendas, many of their more conservative "benevolent" sisters were losing ground well. During the 1820s and 1830s, public funding for women's charities in Northern cities such as New York and Philadelphia often dwindled to a trickle, particularly in comparison to the substantial sums that flowed into the coffers of charities and asylums headed by politically well-connected men. While white male political fortunes burgeoned, white women— even among elites—remained mired in the politics of deference, constrained by their ability to implore but not demand.

Beginning with the depression of 1819, as the electorate was just expanding, major cities like Boston, New York, and Philadelphia launched a concerted effort to trim their welfare budgets and consolidate municipal charities under the control of white male elites. As the electorate expanded, so did municipal campaigns to reduce taxes by lowering local poor relief, much of which was increasingly centered in male-controlled asylums rather than "outdoor" grants of money or alms. In the process, women's charities were distanced from the public treasury in cities such as Philadelphia and New York where they had historically been funded, providing an interesting case study for the "golden age" hypothesis of public and private funding. Although, as we have seen, the notion that the nation's charities were historically devoid of public funding is a myth—at least for those controlled by whites—Jacksonian retrenchment produced nearly that result for many Northern women's groups. What were the implications of these policies? Who benefited most and who the least?

Attitudes toward the poor considerably harshened in the wake of the panic of 1819, particularly among male policymakers, both Democrats and nascent Whigs, who guarded the public purse strings. In part, these patterns reflected a transatlantic reversal in attitudes toward the poor, as increasingly Draconian legislation was introduced in England, Scotland, Germany, and the United States. Beginning at the end of the eighteenth century, leading British economic theorists such as Adam Smith, David Ricardo, and Thomas Malthus—many of the same men who pioneered in the development of Britain's charity banks—recontextualized the practice of poor relief within the framework of capitalism and laissez-faire economics. Rather than "indiscriminate" charity, they sought to reduce the level of aid in order to force the destitute into the waged economy—no matter how low the wages. Toward that end, poverty was deemed an individual vice, undue aid immoral, and harsh discipline and self-support the only appropriate anodyne for public want. Increasingly, the poor were blamed for their own destitution, an attitude reinforced by the findings of public commissions. Within this milieu, public reports continually compared urban poor relief expenditures, pitting city administrators in a Dickensian contest to see who could lower their relief rolls most dramatically. One thousand Philadelphians received outdoor aid in 1826. Two years later, following a comparative report on urban poor relief systems, the state redrafted its poor laws, built a new almshouse, abolished outdoor payments, and lowered the number of recipients of outdoor relief to 250, marking a striking decline from the 5,500 citizens aided in 1819. Humanitarianism fell by the wayside as city fathers vowed to cut local budgets in austerity drives that paralleled Jackson's parsimonious campaign to trim the federal budget and extinguish the national debt.[2]

Philadelphia's poor relief study was echoed in New York's Yates Report of 1823 and the Quincy and Tuckerman inquiries in Boston in the mid-1820s and 1830s. Each stressed the need to cut expenditures, centralize and institutionalize relief, and reduce fraud by wily paupers. And each implicated private charities in rising poor rates, charging that indiscriminate charity was the breeding ground of pauperism. In the process, policies toward "sturdy beggars" became increasingly harsh, as the able-bodied poor were auctioned to farmers in New England and New York to keep them off the welfare rolls. In addition to farming out the poor, several reports advocated the construction of public workhouses replete with "stepping mills," where beggars, vagrants, and potential criminals could be disciplined and subjected to hard labor in return for public support. Jacksonian editorials lauded these endeavors, charging that charities promoted "erroneous principles, and do infinitely more harm than good."[3]

Women's charities bore the brunt of much of this opprobrium, as their revenues dwindled in the face of mounting public antipathy toward the poor. Philadelphia's Female Hospitable Society recorded a sevenfold drop in its subscribers over the course of the 1820s. The city's St. Joseph's Orphanage, run by Seton's nuns, marked a similar decline, as its subscribers plummeted from over three hundred to only seven by 1828, and the Widows' Society in New York suffered similar problems.[4]

State and municipal funding also became more difficult for charities to obtain—especially women's charities. As Anne Boylan explains, elected officials in New York "urged [the] reduction of the city's support for all charitable societies, arguing that they promoted a 'lamentable dependency' on the part of the poor." Several historians, including Christine Stansell, have remarked on the efforts of women's charities to keep humanitarian ideals alive in the 1820s. It was a challenging assignment. As the belief that philanthropy bred poverty was invoked to justify cutbacks in municipal aid, "Jacksonian era . . . politicians redefined most women's charities as . . . undeserving of public funds."[5]

Rebecca Gratz's Philadelphia Orphan Asylum and Joanna Bethune's Orphan Society in New York both experienced a dearth of public funding. Although Jacksonian policymakers "discovered" the asylum in the 1820s and 1830s, there was a sharp distinction between the economic fortunes of the ostensibly private "homes" headed by women and men. Philadelphia's orphanage is a case in point. Although it had previously received municipal allocations and the state legislature granted Gratz's Philadelphia orphanage a $5,000 ($55,000 in 2000 dollars) emergency appropriation after a tragic fire that killed twenty-three children and leveled the asylum in 1822, within two years both its public and private donations were vanishing. By 1827, the asylum's annual subscriptions had fallen to $549 (@ $6,600). One year later, subscriptions dropped still further, to a scant $359, and by 1836 they had plummeted to $294. Moreover, no public donations were recorded between 1823 and 1840. As early as 1824, the board was beginning to note that the subscriptions were "so far insufficient for the support of the family" that they were obliged to divert two legacies to cover daily expenses that otherwise would have gone into the asylum's endowment fund. By decade's end, they were indulging in veiled criticisms deriding the public almshouse as the wellspring of pauperism while admitting that their orphanage was falling into arrears and increasingly unable to "meet *all* their expenses" despite " the most vigilant economy."[6]

Joanna Bethune's orphanage in New York also felt the sting of public cutbacks, as city officials "refused to give help or recognition of any kind to the Asylum" between 1817 and 1836, a pattern repeated in charities like the Widows' Society and the city's Association for the Relief of Aged and Indigent Females. The orphanage's official history read like a litany of woes. Donations fell noticeably by 1821. To compensate, the trustees were empowered to draw the necessary funds from their bank account and dip into their endowment funds to expand the building. Over the next ten years, the asylum was repeatedly scourged by epidemics, from yellow fever to whooping cough and cholera. The board also became embroiled in costly litigation over a five-thousand-dollar bequest from Phillip Jacobs, one of several such suits that "left the Society burdened with debt." By the early 1830s, it was faced with a choice between selling more property or applying "the whole income for some years to come to . . . discharge the debts."[7]

The directresses of Philadelphia's Female Hospitable Society were unusually outspoken about the growing distress caused by municipal policies that "cut off any allowance to *out-door applicants.*" "This breaks up many a decent poor family," they noted caustically, "demoralizing . . . many a poor widow, with helpless children, sometimes grandchildren, [who] could get along with the help of thirty-seven and a half or fifty cents a week from the Guardians." But for lack of this inconsequential sum, impoverished families were "compelled either to *suffer* or go into the Almshouse" where they were "subjected to the lowest moral contamination, and . . . amalgamated with every grade of vice." In the process, their "independence . . . is lost." Had "a *little* timely assistance been given them," the directors snapped, "they would soon have been able to *help themselves.*" Far from saving money, they sullenly noted, it cost ninety four cents per week to confine a family to the public almshouse—almost twice the cost of keeping them in their own homes.[8]

Beyond a dimming appreciation for the virtues and the needs of the poor, there were undoubtedly political motivations for the cutbacks as well. Allocations for private charities, particularly those headed by women like the directors of the Female Hospitable Society, produced few, if any, direct political gains. Although elite women exercised influence in terms of their family ties and their ability to broker contacts for aspiring politicians, this was an era when the prerogatives of the deferential political system that produced the first women's charities were being swept away on a tidal wave of newly enfranchised male voters. The rules of the political game were changing. Neither the directresses nor their clients voted, and because benevolent women couched their claims to public authority in terms of their ethical purity, they were unlikely to tarnish their personal reputations by dabbling in the murky practice of handing out contracts for political gain.[9]

Public almshouses and asylums, on the other hand, promised partisan windfalls, from building contracts to custodial jobs. Philadelphia's poor relief system was rife with corruption after it was reorganized in 1828, as politically appointed board members speculated for personal gain with the taxpayers' money and handed out lucrative contracts to their supporters. By 1850 the abuses had become so flagrant that the board of guardians was popularly rechristened the "board of buzzards." The history of Chicago's almshouse was similarly troubled, marred by decades of corruption and mismanagement. From Boston to Savannah, municipal administrators "discovered" the virtues of the asylum, often infusing plans for institutional relief with partisan fervor.[10]

Despite the rhetoric of austerity, several male-controlled charities and societies did very well indeed during these years, receiving sizable public allocations under both Whiggish and Democratic administrations. New York's House of Refuge was one of them. Founded by the Society for the Prevention of Pauperism in 1824, the asylum was created by many of the same members of the business and political elite who backed the American Bible Society and the Savings Bank of New York, including Thomas Eddy and John Pintard. Designed to house and discipline the city's juvenile delinquents, the refuge was planned as a public-private venture from the outset, blending $16,000 (@ $200,000 in 2000 dollars) in private donations with land from the city, a former arsenal acquired from the federal government, and a pledge of $2,000 (@ $ 24,000) per annum from New York State, a figure augmented by $6,000 (@ $90,000) in appropriations from the Marine Hospital Fund in 1831. Stephen Allen, a close associate of Martin Van Buren and one-time mayor of New York, also joined the board, sharpening the asylum's competitive edge for continued state and city funding through his ties to Tammany Hall. Indeed, Van Buren publicly endorsed the venture in his first and only gubernatorial message to the state legislature, in 1828.[11]

Many of these trustees also sat on the board of the Public School Society, a private voluntary association that consolidated its control over the city's school system in 1825. Like the House of Industry, the society received generous amounts of public funding, which topped the $40,000 (@ $480,000) mark by 1824. Philadelphia's House of Refuge evinced a similar pattern, founded with $10,750 (@ $129,000) in private donations and $7,500 (@ $90,000) in ongoing state and city funds in 1825, which was bolstered a $20,000 allocation from the county commissioners ($262,000) in 1832. The privately initiated New York Dispensary also received significant amounts of public funding during the period of austerity that spanned the Jackson years. By 1837, New York's House of Refuge recorded $21,000 ($264,600) in revenues, $14,000 ($176,400) of which was derived from public outlays, almost $5,000 ($63,000) from the sale of goods produced by the inmates, ranging from clothing to cabinets and chairs, and a scant $1,500 ($18,000) from private donations—figures that once again reveal the blend of government, commercial, and donated revenues that historically supported ostensibly private charities.[12]

Nor were these institutions necessarily less costly to run than women's asylums. While the Philadelphia orphanage housed an average of 100 children at an annual cost of $3,500—or $35 per annum, per child—the House of Refuge managed approximately 125 inmates at a cost of $165 per inmate in 1835. Similarly, outlays at the New York orphanage ran about $41 per child, or 11¢ per day, a figure far below the costs of the male-controlled delinquent's asylum. Part of these cost differentials stemmed from the level of organization. Philadelphia's House of Refuge, for example, featured bells, locked cells, and heavy discipline, as well as a grinding regimen of twelve-hour days (four in school, eight "at some mechanical or other labor") every day but Sunday and Christmas. Asylum directresses were more humane, and more solicitous of their charges' welfare. Explaining their reasons for pulling children from bad indentures, Philadelphia's directresses emphasized that although wayward "children may frequently require discipline and habitual strictness," this "can afford no apology for cruelty or total neglect," admonishing masters to treat their charges "mercifully and justly."[13]

While asylums like the New York House of Refuge increasingly benefited from public appropriations, women's charities and asylums relied instead on their investment skills to keep their institutions afloat. Many of their investments were fueled by bequests. The New York Orphan Asylum received $2,500 ($32,500) from a Miss Ludlow in 1837, and the Colored Orphan Asylum received $1,000 ($13,000) from the estate of Lindley Murray a year later. Similarly, the Philadelphia orphanage received an unusually large gift from Stephen Girard's estate in the 1830s, which was used for expenses and building repairs. Others compensated for the cutbacks by plunging more fully into market activities, including fee-based services such as weekly charges for boarding children. Thus, Philadelphia's Female Society augmented the $101 (@ $1,300) in donations it received in 1835 with $702 (@ $9,000) in sales and $774 (@ $10,000) in investment income. That same year, the city's orphan asylum received $1,424 (@ $18,000) in subscriptions and bequests but derived the bulk of its operating funds—$3,377 (@ $43,000)—from stock dividends and rental fees. Some institutions even cut into their investment capital or took out loans from other charitable institutions to cover their costs and debts when government support was not available, despite the fact that investments, rather than donations or public outlays, were often the lifeblood of their institutions during the heyday of Jacksonian retrenchment.[14]

Beneficiaries

Charities benefited a dual constituency: the trustees who managed them and the people they aided. The long-standing quasi-governmental roles of the middle-class white women who headed urban charities and asylums were curtailed in the Jackson and Van Buren years by public cutbacks. But what about their constituencies? What impact did the cutbacks have on the impoverished women and children that these institutions were designed to help?

One of the interpretive threads that has woven through the literature on social welfare since the 1960s is the theme of social control. According to this line of argument, the men and women who created urban charities were often motivated by a desire to coerce moral behavior among their recipients, instilling lifelong habits of industry, self-control, piety, and thrift as an antidote to urban unrest and as a means of enhancing their own authority. More recently, scholars have begun to document the resilience of the poor in drawing on charitable resources to further their own ends by combining often limited earnings and mutual aid from neighbors and kin with public and private charitable support. Rather than allowing themselves to be the victims of an omniscient middle class, they turned the system to their own ends. How did the social geography of Jacksonian charity affect their lives?[15]

Social control had many meanings in Jacksonian America and took many forms. There is a vast difference between an effort to change another's behavior by selling a Bible and exercising authority by applying manacles and chains. Some of the male-controlled, publicly supported asylums like the New York House of Refuge fell at one end of the institutional spectrum, isolating inmates and applying physical force when it was deemed necessary; while female-headed asylums that provided short-term housing for children fell at the other. Both were utilized by the poor.

Most of the youngsters who went into the House of Refuge came in after being arrested and went out as newly indentured servants and apprentices. Petty theft most commonly led them into the asylum, rather than more serious crimes. Although initially placed primarily by the police, by the late 1830s, many of the children were being committed by their parents as well. Parental commitments were often used for uncontrollable or habitually disobedient children. In effect, these harried mothers and fathers turned to the asylum as a means of disciplining their youngsters and reinforcing their own parental authority. In 1835, almost half of the refuge's inmates were admitted by their parents rather than the police, with the majority of these placements made by men. In effect, fathers were using the asylum as an extension of the home, relying on the state to bolster patriarchal authority in working-class households.[16]

In an earlier era, paternal authority had been undergirded by men's control over the family business or farm. By the 1820s and 1830s, many male laborers no longer enjoyed this sort of monopoly over coveted resources, which made their authority more difficult to establish and maintain. "As the economic basis of patriarchal and familial control diminished," notes Stansell, "parents lost the ability to limit their children's social adventures—where they went, what they did with their money, how they earned a living and who they courted." Daughters who flirted with promiscuity were particularly problematic, since their behavior could result in unwanted pregnancies. The asylum disciplined them, trained them, and bound them into trades. In 1831, for example, the majority of boys were sent to sea or were placed on farmsteads, while others were apprenticed to shoemakers, blacksmiths, and tailors. Girls were funneled primarily into domestic service. Punishments meted out to those who rebelled against the asylum's regimens and programs ranged from mild to the macabre. While small offenses might result in the loss of play or exercise time, or a meal, serious offenses could result in confinement in solitary cells, corporal punishment, and fetters and handcuffs. This, unquestionably, was social control. But it was also a program that obviously

met with the approval of a significant portion of the inmates it was designed to serve—or, at least, the inmates' parents.[17]

The fact that so many men committed their own children may have
also enhanced the asylum's ability to attract funds. Even poor men voted.
By providing institutional support for the maintenance of paternal dominance within working-class households, institutions like the House of
Refuge, however oppressive their programs might seem to the modern
reader, may have had a solid base of support among the working poor.

Some charities, like the New York Children's Aid Society founded in
the 1850s, expressed an open disdain for the poor. Organizations like the
Children's Aid Society tried to frighten potential donors into parting with
their money with lurid depictions of "an ignorant, debased, permanent
poor class" imbued with "the lowest passions" and "thriftless habits" supplying ready audiences for demagogues. They were a seething mass, ready
to "burst forth into Rapine. Neither liberty nor property would be safe" in
their unchecked presence. Although this was undoubtedly a useful fund-
raising device (most of the donations were used to purchase one-way tick-
ets to send street children to western farms), many earlier Jacksonian
charities evinced somewhat more respect for their potential beneficiaries,
at least rhetorically.[18]

Asylum programs, like charities, often differed dramatically in their
approaches. While the New York Orphan Asylum's literature suggests that
the trustees pursued the permanent removal of youngsters from their
widowed or impoverished parents, others offered short-term boarding
facilities as well as long-term care. The Boston Female Asylum, for example, enabled mothers to board their children during periods of economic
duress, providing an alternative to the almshouse. The Society for the Relief of Poor Widows with Small Children also helped by boarding youngsters, as well as distributing alms, money, and medical supplies to needy
women. The Colored Orphan Asylum founded in 1833 provided short-
term boarding facilities, and at least initially seems to have worked closely
with neighbors and parents to make its programs both accessible and re-
sponsive to its clients' needs. Many children were committed and boarded
by their parents. With typical generosity, black newspapers such as the
Colored American solicited funds for the asylum's support, despite the fact
that it was controlled by whites. Special collections were also taken up in
African American churches, and a charity fair held by black women raised
$761 (@ $10,300) in 1856. Tragically, this institution was leveled in the
draft riot of 1863, yet another victim of a racist mob assault.[19]

As these examples suggest, many charities provided useful resources for

their clients, however demeaning their literary descriptions of their programs, or however condescending their staffs or trustees might have been
in their personal encounters with the poor. As Christine Stansell points
out, "both the local and the migratory poor incorporated relief into their
survival patterns; poor relief was, for many, not simply a recourse in a ca-
tastrophe, but a structural element of subsistence." These resources were
often particularly important for women because of the widespread feminization of poverty and because they provided a refuge both from and for
the working-class home. For example, Protestant and Catholic homes for
the friendless and refuges for battered women afforded a haven from domestic violence, while outdoor relief provided a margin of subsistence
during periods of unemployment. Industrious women often turned to a
variety of public and private agencies, gathering "rent money, food, wood,
clothing, medicines, and jobs" in the course of their rounds.[20]

Public cutbacks jeopardized this "mixed economy of welfare" by significantly reducing outdoor relief and investing the majority of governmental resources in specialized asylums. This in turn made it harder to
"manipulate the system," particularly for working-class widows and wives
intent on holding their families together. Private charity was limited and
never sufficient to meet all of the needs of the poor. But each decentralized
source of money, alms, and medicine provided one more resource in a
piecemeal system. And women, especially those supporting small children, were generally the poorest of the poor. In 1853, when a male laborer
required approximately $600 ($8,520) per annum to keep a family of four
above the poverty line in New York, a fully employed needlewoman could
expect to earn approximately $91 ($1,292). Stansell's research on two New
York census districts in 1855 revealed that over half of the wage-earning
women (355 out of 599) were supporting families. In this setting, women
suffered disproportionately from any reduction in charitable funding. According to Priscilla Clement, "By 1850, fewer women per thousand in
Philadelphia obtained any form of aid than . . . in 1810 or 1830." Moreover,
as public attitudes about poor relief soured, women often received the
greatest censure, criticized for their consistently high levels of need and
for running up the public tab by bearing illegitimate children.[21]

Women and children generally accounted for the majority of almshouse inmates, drawing some public support, but these were truly institutions of last resort. Perhaps as a hedge against future need, many people of
relatively limited means supported charities themselves. Although we
have no data on native-born working-class white women, blacks extended
their circle of communal generosity to include institutions like the Col-

ored Orphan Asylum, and Irish working women supported Catholic charities, as well as constituting a disproportionate share of charity clients in
cities like Boston and New York. Although middle-class female trustees
may not have enveloped their clients in webs of "sisterhood" and mutual
respect, the evidence suggests that they were nonetheless bound in a symbiotic relationship. While middle-class women created public roles for
themselves and enlarged their legal rights by building charitable institutions, their clients gained an expanded selection of resources. And both
these roles were jeopardized by the cutbacks of the Jacksonian era.[22]

State and local policymaking echoed national patterns during the Jacksonian years. Under a rhetorical mantle of austerity, public funds for
women's charities were cut while men's were increased, changes that had
the greatest impact in Northeastern states but that also produced a decidedly inequitable social geography of charity and public aid in the newer
states of the Midwest. While asylums such as New York's House of Refuge
drew at least some of their authority through their ability to supplement
the paternal discipline of the working-class home, women's charities pulled
together whatever resources they could through donations, investments,
and efforts to generate additional income. Two groups suffered most in
this scenario: middle-class female trustees who saw their public influence
undermined and their institutions fiscally threatened, and the women and
children they aided, who constituted a disproportionate share of the urban
poor. Charity, as well as abolitionism, became a highly contested arena in
the 1820s and 1830s, one in which women and children were consistently
shortchanged.

The Geography of Governance

Nor were these isolated events, confined to a single city or state. Antebellum voluntary associations are often depicted as regional phenomena, institutions that had the greatest relevance for New England and New York.
As previously noted, generalizations such as these obscure as much as they
reveal. Charities appeared in cities and at the county level throughout both
the North and the South. What distinguished the activities of voluntary
associations in different regions was not their presence, but their relationship to the state.[23]

By the end of the 1830s, three distinctive patterns were beginning to
emerge. Northern groups were distinguished by the decentralized nature
of their decision making and economic authority. Although the era between 1825 and the 1840s marked a trough in public allocations for insti-

tutions not controlled by politically connected white male elites, associations in states like New York and Pennsylvania had a long history of receiving public funding, funds they coupled with private donations, volunteer time, investment income, and quasi-commercial revenues, enabling them to deliver services at reduced cost. Access to public funding was moderately democratic before the 1820s, as ventures headed by white women, black males, some immigrant groups, and both Catholic and Protestant charities received at least limited amounts of public largesse.

Sanctions against public support for women's charities in these areas began to weaken in the 1840s, a pattern that paralleled white women's changing political fortunes (and to a lesser extent, those of free blacks in several Northern states). Beginning with the presidential election of 1840, first the Whigs and then the Democrats began to court female participation in national electoral campaigns, which strengthened women's political authority. A few scattered grants began to be made to women's groups in the mid-1830s, like the $500 ($6,500) the Widows' Society received from New York City in 1834. Although a pittance in comparison to the funding accorded the House of Refuge or the Public School Society, it was an important windfall, accounting for a tenth of the society's revenues that year. The society received a second, $400 municipal allocation in 1839, during the national economic depression, despite the city council's resolution to completely cut off public funding for private charities.[24]

The Home for Colored Orphans signed a contract with the city in 1845, providing an alternative to the almshouse for black children at public expense. They also received a plot of what would later become some of the most valuable real estate in New York, fronting on Fifth Avenue between Forty-second and Forty-third Streets, in 1842. Founded in 1844, the American Female Guardian Society's Home for the Friendless received its first $500 ($7,000) municipal allocation in 1849, revenues subsidized by receipts from sales of its journal, the *Advocate and Guardian*, which reached eleven thousand subscribers. Philadelphia loosened its purse strings in the late 1840s, eventually increasing municipal funding for poor relief in tandem with growing state appropriations for asylums like the Rosine Association's home for former prostitutes.[25]

In the South, the most heavily capitalized charitable and educational institutions were often created under public charters such as those of the University of Virginia or the Charleston Orphan House, which ensured their continuing control by the region's white male slaveholding elite. White women's charities existed but were less likely to receive public backing than their Northern counterparts and tended to command smaller budgets than comparable charities controlled by men. Barbara Bellows notes women's "receding . . . roles of influence as the male-dominated public institutions assumed greater responsibility" for Charleston's poor in the antebellum era, echoing trends in Philadelphia and New York. As a result, "many small independent women's groups fell victim to the Depression of 1840."[26]

Nat Turner's 1831 slave uprising and the advent of the American Antislavery Society in 1833 marked a crucial turning point in the history of Southern civil society, as controls were tightened over the black population and the philanthropic activities of white women. This was particularly evident in the realm of reform, which was closely regulated, with activities like abolitionism proscribed by custom and law, and women's associations carefully reined in by kinship networks, mixed boards, and the weighty authority of the Southern churches. Historians disagree about the extent of female reform in the antebellum South. Cynthia Kierner suggests that "men scrutinized the conduct of women's organizations, especially those with reformist objectives" throughout the region, particularly concerning "radical" causes such as temperance campaigns to curb male drinking. Conversely, Elizabeth Varon's study of antebellum Virginia points out that almost half of that state's thirty-five thousand temperance society members were women by 1835, and that a few women even submitted antislavery petitions to the state legislature in the aftermath of the Turner debacle. All of this, however, had declined by the late 1830s, tarred by the association with abolitionism—and later, feminism—in the North.[27]

Conventional interpretations traditionally suggested that Southern associational activity was limited by the lack of urbanization. However, as previously noted, recent research has revealed an extensive array of charitable and religious associations throughout the region—including at the county level—while underscoring the dearth of social reform movements. Part of what fueled the Southern aversion to abolitionism—beyond the implied civil and economic threat and the prospect of racial equality—was the way in which the Northern antislavery movement politically emboldened women and blacks, subordinates "who knew their place" in the South. To quote Stephanie McCurry, "the yeomanry's passionate commitment to independence and equality betrayed an equally passionate commitment to dependence and desperate inequality." White men's belief in their common right to exercise "paternal" dominance over all subordinate groups both within and outside their individual households and the promise of rapid social mobility through the acquisition of slaves were the ingredients that cemented Southern yeomen's allegiance to the expansion of slavery. The growth of a healthy and decentralized civil society threatened to subvert these prerogatives by creating a more diverse array of groups capable of independent action, thereby undermining the common bond of white patriarchal liberty and the ability to coerce subordination on which the slaveowning system relied.[28]

Added to this was the implied threat that undergirded the politics of chivalry. As an outspoken champion of the Southern slavocracy, George Fitzhugh, explained, "the right to protection involves the obligation to obey. . . . If [a woman is] obedient, she is in little danger of maltreatment; if she stands upon her rights, is coarse and masculine, a man loathes and despises her, and ends by abusing her." Backed by a system of restrictive legislation and implied threats, Southern slaveowners developed their own distinctive version of the civil sphere.[29]

Virginia stood at one extreme of the Southern philanthropic spectrum, with even churches often serving at the pleasure of the state owing to the difficulty in obtaining charters. Similarly, South Carolina's largest charities were firmly implanted under public control. In a reversal of Northern patterns, Charleston's wealthiest citizens left their charitable bequests to the city and municipally controlled institutions like the Charleston Orphan House, rather than to private charities. Although a third of those who left bequests of one hundred dollars or more to the orphanage were female donors, and one woman bequeathed seven thousand dollars for the city's homeless children, none served on the board, a situation echoed in Georgia as well. Once again, Northern and Southern charities were distinguished not by their prevalence, but by their control. Even during the bleakest years of the Jacksonian austerity crusade, female-headed asylums managed substantial investment holdings in the North, affording autonomous institutional bases to a degree unmatched even in wealthy Southern cities like Charleston by the 1840s. Ironically, because Southern charities were already under patriarchal rule, the Jacksonian austerity drives may have been less keenly felt in the South. Having few resources of their own, and still less access to public finances, women's charities in these areas had less to lose.[30]

The associations founded in Midwestern states like Illinois tended to be either public or private, unlike the hybrid arrangements found in older, Eastern states—a pattern that persisted well past the Jacksonian years. Private charities received little or no public funding either in cash donations or grants of land in towns like Chicago before 1860, and public relief outside asylums tended to be limited and grudgingly rendered. In part, this may have stemmed from their youth. Unlike the older, Eastern settlements, states like Illinois had never had a state church, they had no tradition of supplying public charity through parish vestries, and they had little firsthand experience with the older commonwealth ideal that regarded charitable charters as an extension of the state. By the time that cities like Chicago were founded, Jacksonianism was in ascendance and public and private responsibilities were more neatly delineated.

Within this milieu, charities and private educational ventures were often small, and always vulnerable, while public institutions could be quite generously funded. Throughout the antebellum era, towns like Jacksonville, Illinois, aggressively competed for public asylums for the mentally ill and the deaf and dumb (to use the terminology of the time). As Don Doyle points out, these bids tended to be motivated more by partisan and economic considerations than humanitarianism per se. Democrats were particularly adept at milking these projects as a source of patronage. As Doyle explains, a state asylum could bring in as much as $75,000 ($975,000) in annual operating funds, as well as "several hundred thousand dollars in construction costs over the years. This money fell largely to local contractors, laborers, merchants and farmers," fueling local economic growth as well as partisan alliances. Beyond their value as symbols of progress and successful boosterism, these institutions meant "brick and mortar manufactured by local firms, buildings constructed by local contractors, wages spent in local stores, and markets for food and clothing." In dozens of other ways these charitable institutions were seen as rich fountains of public largesse flowing into the local economy.[31]

At the same time that the Illinois legislature was pouring hundreds of thousands of dollars into state asylums, it retained its commitment to Jacksonian parsimony toward the poor. Cook County resolutely refused to provide outdoor relief, even during the disastrous cholera epidemic that swept Chicago in 1849. Within this context, private charities emerged in a vacuum, creating resources where nothing else existed rather than serving as collaborators or creatures of the state. Public monies flowed into the politically well-connected asylums controlled by local, white male elites, while the charities created by women were run on modest donations and heavy infusions of volunteer time. The Chicago Orphan Asylum is a case in point. Set up by an interdenominational coalition of local women at the height of the epidemic of 1849, it subsisted on donated funds, furniture, clothing, and food, coupled with substantial amounts of volunteer work by the trustees. No public support was received despite their repeated requests. Unlike publicly funded male-controlled asylums, the orphanage lived a peripatetic existence during its first five years, moving from one rented house to another. Unable to fund a full-time matron, the trustees did the cooking and housework themselves and furnished their "home" with cast-off furniture, patterns repeated in the female-controlled Home for the Friendless.[32]

Only one asylum received adequate support before the Civil War, the Chicago Reform School. Devised by a group of public-spirited male business and professional leaders, the reformatory received substantial municipal backing from its inception in 1854. While the women's asylums lived a hand-to-mouth existence by cobbling together volunteer service and donated goods, the reform school flourished on its well-appointed grounds. Adequate funding enabled the trustees to craft an elaborate system in which boys with differing levels of antisocial behavior were divided into color-coded "families," each with its own cottage, disciplinary routines, uniforms, and staff. Casting a covetous eye on its operations, a spokeswoman for the Home for the Friendless complained that "one institution . . . I *could* name, has the advantage of us in the systematic training it affords its inmates," training funded from the public treasury. While criminals, delinquents, and the physically and mentally handicapped received ample attention, women, dependent children, and law-abiding immigrants and blacks had recourse only to the almshouse, or to the very limited resources that private charities were able to provide. In the process, the most vulnerable citizens were generally those who suffered most and gained the least.[33]

Thus, local charities, as well as national legislative campaigns, yielded distinctive regional patterns of American governance. The end result was that support for female-controlled charities dwindled during the austerity drives of the 1820s and 1830s in Northern states, where women's charities were initially launched with public backing, even as institutions headed by prominent politicians and businessmen prospered on public funding. In these areas, the rhetoric of retrenchment was used to disempower conservative middle-class white women while bolstering the projects, lining the pockets, and advancing the political fortunes of white male elites. The impact of public downsizing was less keenly felt in many Southern states, where the largest charities were already firmly under patriarchal rule by custom and law. Distinctions between public and private responsibilities were most sharply drawn in the Midwest, where public charities prospered and grew rich, building partisan alliances by aiding the deviant and the disabled, while women's "private" charities maintained a precarious existence, backed by small donations, voluntarism, and in-kind gifts. Despite their public mission, these fragile institutions played a clearly subordinate role in the state's universe of charities, overshadowed by the institutions and initiatives of male elites.

Social Reform

Although both African Americans and white women were pushed to the political sidelines in the Jacksonian era through public cutbacks and antiabolitionist tactics such as the gag rule, afterward their paths diverged. During the 1840s, while Northern black philanthropy was repeatedly mobilized through the churches, fairs, institutional fund-raising drives, and appeals in the black press, white women's organizations slowly recovered their lost capacity for courting local governments, as public contracts, in-kind donations, and grants once again began to subsidize their endeavors. While African American leaders, particularly men, became increasingly active in marshaling votes for the antislavery Liberty Party, many white women began to participate in Whig electioneering, and as their political currency rose, so too, did their ability to garner public charitable support.[34]

By the 1840s and 1850s, as the economic fortunes of white women's charities improved with accelerating state and local appropriations, a portion of the black community embraced civil disobedience instead, in a desperate attempt to cope with increasingly discriminatory federal legislation that denied their right to freedom in their communities, and to personal safety on their streets and in their homes. While the black community's faith in the federal government soured, Northern white women launched a series of reforms to widen their authority in the political, as well as the charitable, sphere.

Forged in the evangelical webs of the Benevolent Empire, politicized and tempered by the Jacksonian petition campaigns, and fired to new levels of individual authority and zeal by revivalists' injunctions to save the world by eradicating sin in all its guises, white women's reform movements aggressively pushed the prerogatives of female moral authority into a variety of political realms. Here, too, geography left an imprint. While Southern white women were barred from aggressive social reform activities by custom and patriarchal control, many of their Northern counterparts increasingly lobbied for social change. Some also began to break away from the sponsorship of the male-dominated structures that consigned them to auxiliary, fund-raising roles for groups such as the agencies of the Benevolent Empire, creating independent, separatist reform movements of their own. The American Female Moral Reform Society (AFMRS) exemplifies this new independence. Founded as a local organization to combat prostitution in 1834, the AFMRS began in response to the publication of Reverend John McDowell's controversial exposé, "Magdalen Facts," in which the cleric charged that New York was overrun with thousands of streetwalkers and bordellos, making the city a citadel of sin. Initially devised as a local initiative to distribute McDowell's antivice manifesto, the society was headed by the wife of the prominent evangelist Charles Grandison Finney. By 1839 the movement had spread across the nation, with almost 450 auxiliaries and its own journal, the *Advocate for Moral Reform*, edited by Mrs. S. R. Ingraham.[35]

Just as African American newspapers helped to shape the contours of black political culture, so the *Advocate* sought to mold a common female political agenda around moral reform. By 1838, the journal was reaching 16,500 regular subscribers, and the New York chapter was engaged in coordinating a massive statewide petition campaign for the criminalization of seduction and abduction. In the process, the *Advocate for Moral Reform* became a primer in the rudiments of public lobbying and the labyrinthine ways of political maneuvering. In addition to its columns on moral concerns, information was published on petitions and pending antivice bills. By 1843, "legislative action" columns provided updates on bills submitted in Pennsylvania, Ohio, and New York, including the names of their sponsors and the committees in which the proposed legislation was lodged.[36]

Other essays provided progress reports on a three-thousand-signature petition sponsored by Ohio women and the deliberations of the select committee to which it was submitted. The Ohio bill illustrates the radicalism of the society's agenda. Under the bill's provisions, those convicted of luring a woman into prostitution would spend one to five years in prison, and male seducers could expect to remain in jail for six months to three years for each offense. Adulterers would be punished with twenty to ninety days "in the cell or dungeon" of the county jail, to which an additional $100 ($1,300) fine was added for male offenders. Presiding over a brothel was punishable by one hundred days in jail and a $100–$500 ($1,300–$6,500) fine, while signing a lease for the purpose of setting up a house of ill repute incurred a $50–$300 penalty. If miscreants were not deterred by the prospect of incarceration, the sponsors obviously reasoned, they would at least feel some economic pain.[37]

After a decade of seeing their political efforts stalemated and trivialized, women's petition initiatives began to yield some solid gains in the Northern states in the more liberal 1840s. The society's bill to criminalize seduction passed into New York law in 1848, approved in tandem with the state's first Married Women's Property Act. Female reformers also waged a successful municipal crusade that secured a matron for women prisoners at Bellevue Hospital in 1845 and brought about the appointment of a public truant officer in 1853. Moreover, a four-year campaign to legally remove children from parents who allowed their youngsters to wander New York streets unattended resulted in a law passed in 1853, legislation replicated in Massachusetts. As in the case of public funding for women's charities, white women's petition drives became increasingly influential at the state level in the 1840s and 1850s.

Working women also began to lobby for reform. Female labor protests were a new phenomenon, as factory life brought together a critical mass of women workers who in earlier generations would have been sequestered in the home. One of the interesting questions surrounding the appearance of the Lowell Female Labor Reform Association (LFLRA) in 1844 is the extent to which it heralded the birth of a distinctively working-class female consciousness. Writing on English workers, E. P. Thompson noted that by the 1830s, "everything, from their schools to their shops, their chapels to their amusements, was turned into a battle-ground of class." Did the Lowell association fit this description as well?[38]

The answer is fairly complex. Class considerations clearly figured into the association's call to "see the virtuous poor protected and their rights maintained, against the purse-proud aristocrats and the growing evils of the systems of labor which are filling the coffers of the rich and making the real producers poorer." Yet the tone of many of their publications was far less militant than that of their male counterparts. Moreover, the Lowell women readily adopted the idiom of benevolence, presenting themselves as "philanthropists and lovers of equal rights" and urging "the daughters of New England [to] kindle the spark of philanthropy in every heart till its brightness shall *fill* the whole earth." Rather than simply helping their colleagues in the Lowell textile mills, association leaders sought to "elevate humanity [and] to assert and maintain the rights of a republican people."[39]

They also "evinced a pervasive and powerful strain of piety and Christian mission," to quote Jama Lazerow, as well as an unusual degree of sympathy with other groups, collecting garments for Irish famine victims and participating in antislavery meetings. Some female labor reformers cast their grievances in unmistakably feminist terms, noting that "woman is wronged in every occupation and condition of life." On the other hand, they raised funds for other strikers, as well as for a press for themselves, adapting a traditional array of female fund-raising events to the cause of labor reform. And, like the AFMRS, they developed a distinctive political culture, grafting religion, charity, the language of benevolence, and market techniques onto the cause of workers' rights.[40]

They also launched petition campaigns, moving into the political arena. Like their middle-class counterparts in the moral reform society, LFLRA members tracked the legislative progress of labor petitions in the columns of the *Voice of Industry*, naming elected allies and adversaries. They also actively promoted labor reform legislation for female operatives, which won them an invitation to present their case to Massachusetts legislators in 1845, an opportunity rarely accorded to women. Sarah Bagley, one of the LFLRA's leaders, was keenly aware of the offer's significance. As she explained: "for the last half century, it has been deemed a violation of woman's sphere to appear before the public as a speaker; but when our rights are trampled upon . . . shall not our voice be heard?"[41]

Bagley was one of several LFLRA representatives who testified before the Massachusetts legislature on February 13, 1845. Their depositions were part of the state's first investigation into labor conditions—an inquiry spurred, in large measure, by their petitions. The women gave firsthand testimony about the ailments caused by working twelve- to fourteen-hour days, often for minuscule wages. Despite compelling evidence, their request for a legally mandated ten-hour day was rejected. Legislators explained that such a law would have to be enforced across the board, imposing unfair requirements on small businesses, and urged the women to use arbitration to achieve their ends instead. As Bagley curtly noted, their next petition drive should ask the legislature "to extend to the operatives the same protection they have given to animals, and our condition will be greatly improved." Although the legislative campaign was unsuccessful, the publicity that surrounded the petition drives and the legislative inquiry ultimately forced at least a few mill owners into negotiations, reducing factory workdays from thirteen hours to eleven. The LFLRA collapsed shortly after the legislative hearings. But their success in spurring a public investigation into labor conditions constituted a significant achievement in the wake of the recalcitrant Jacksonian years.[42]

Three models of Northern female political action emerged in the 1840s. The AFMRS and the Lowell association represented one model. Built on older precedents, these groups drew growing numbers of white women into petition drives for causes they defined themselves, blending moral and religious imperatives with a determination to effect social change. These groups turned the traditional tools of female organizing—auxiliaries, fund-raising events, petitions, and independent, separatist organizations—to new ends, with some success at the state and local level.

The women's rights movement and abolitionism constituted a second model. Although the political fortunes of conservative Northern white women began to improve in the 1840s, ultraist campaigns that sought to fundamentally reorder American society by granting women full citizenship or overturning slavery remained far more controversial than more traditional charitable activities. Women who sought the franchise sought political parity, the right not merely to request by petition, but to compel via the vote. Their egalitarianism threatened not only to co-opt a common emblem of male identity, but also to sweep away the prerogatives of male chivalry: the power to protect or attack, to admit or deny at will. However effectively female reformers presented their cases and pursued their campaigns, in the final analysis it was men, rather than women, who were the ultimate arbiters of morality and efficacy. Male legislators, rather than female reformers, determined whose causes were legitimate, and whose should be denied.

Elizabeth Cady Stanton, one of the pivotal figures in the early women's rights movement, was the heir to a long political tradition, the granddaughter of a state legislator, and the daughter of a congressman and judge. Her cousin, Gerrit Smith, was a prominent abolitionist, as was her husband, Henry Stanton. Stanton took her to the World Antislavery Convention in London on their honeymoon. According to conventional lore, her feminist conversion occurred in the balcony, where she and Lucretia Mott were sequestered with other female delegates who had been barred from the convention floor. Eight years later, she drew on her abolitionist contacts to convene the first women's rights convention in Seneca Falls, New York.[43]

Held over two days in July, the Seneca Falls meeting ranged widely over the social and civil landscape, from property rights to wives' ability to retain their own earnings. Over three hundred people attended, including the black abolitionist leader Frederick Douglass. Stanton coordinated the meeting just months after the state's first Married Women's Property Act was passed into law after a campaign spearheaded by women's petitions but also backed by wealthy men who were concerned, in part, about the fate of their own estates as they passed into the hands of married daughters. The culmination of twelve years of legislative lobbying, the law strengthened women's economic status and raised new questions about the scope and nature of their role as citizens. In overturning the doctrine of *femme coverte*, the legislature also undermined the rationale for denying women the franchise, weakening "the whole legal and philosophical scaffolding of resistance to women's political power."[44]

Casting their claims as a paraphrase of Jefferson's declaration—"We hold these truths to be self-evident, that all men *and women* are created equal"—the conference participants moved one small segment of the emerging empire of female social reform squarely into suffragism and the electoral arena. And they did so at a time when the right to vote was bitterly contested, even among white males. By the 1840s, partisan rivalries had begun to feed upon themselves, as different groups of white male voters sought to bar competitors from the polling booth. Nativist Protestants contested the right of Catholics and recent immigrants to vote. Irish Democrats blocked the prerogatives of free blacks. Southerners not only denied blacks, both slave and free, the right to vote, but whittled away their remaining entitlements as well. And partisan policymakers, both North and South, avidly worked to contain the political incursions of abolitionism.[45]

The rough-and-tumble partisanship unleashed with Jackson's election continued to resonate in often raucous and illiberal ways throughout the antebellum arena. Although Stanton clearly saw the value of the vote as a means of bolstering women's charities and reforms, as well as their rights, she initially made few converts: female suffrage remained a poorly populated crusade. Stanton's failure to gain widespread backing for women's suffrage before the Civil War may have been due, in part, to the fact that full equality would have jeopardized the rationale on which the majority of middle-class white women based their claims to public participation, and given the blood sport of partisan politics, many doubtless opted for the safety of the moral high ground. But the post-Jacksonian "thaw" would have played a role as well. After more than a decade of seeing their efforts blocked and publicly derided, the logjam began to loosen and then broke after 1840, allowing at least some middle-class white women to fund their charities with state and local appropriations and to successfully push for legislative reforms. The resurgence and expansion of female governance may have made Stanton's claims seem superfluous to many, a crusade of dubious merit and great peril in which they stood to lose the limited rights they had so recently regained.[46]

Dorothea Dix may have played a role as well. Dix represented the third model of female reformism that emerged in the late antebellum era. Unlike the abolitionists and female moral and labor advocates, Dix worked alone, relying on her writing ability and her finely honed political instincts to win support for improved mental health facilities. Unlike Stanton, she had a marked aversion to the thought of women engaging in electoral politics. More than any other antebellum figure, Dorothea Dix personified the dictum of female self-sacrifice.

Feminist scholars have tended to give Dix a wide berth, with good reason. In many respects, she epitomized the worst elements of female moral superiority. She was self-righteous, self-absorbed, and self-sufficient to the point of veering toward antifeminism. In many ways, she was sui generis, a law unto herself, an individualist in an era accustomed to female collectivism. Dix was one of several prominent antebellum women, including Catharine Beecher and Sarah Josepha Hale, who created highly influential careers for themselves by promoting the doctrine of female self-sacrifice. Briefly stated, this was the idea that women's power was rooted in their selfless "devotion and service to others." Charities, teaching, and humanitarianism (excluding the politically charged realm of abolitionism) spread this influence onto the larger society. Dix had little patience with women who transgressed the dictates of ladylike demeanor by publicly challenging the rulings of elected political leaders, dismissing the actions of abolitionist women as the misguided products of "unfeminine and mischievous conduct."[47]

Born in Massachusetts in 1802, she inherited a small but comfortable fortune, which gave her the necessary economic independence to pursue a lifestyle of her own making. She found her métier in midlife, launching her successful career as an advocate for the insane at the age of forty-one. From the time she submitted her first memorial detailing the horrors of mental health care to the Massachusetts legislature in 1843 until her fall from grace with the wartime nursing corps in the 1860s, Dix secured one legislative victory after another. She was a force of nature, acting on her own in the name of the dispossessed.

Her first brush with public asylums came through fairly traditional means, via her work in teaching Sunday school classes at the Charlestown State Prison. Samuel Gridley Howe, another prominent Boston reformer, encouraged her interest in the insane, and the use of "moral treatment" to instill self-control as an alternative to punishment and coercion. Encouraged by Howe, Dix began to investigate the care of mental patients in almshouses, insane asylums, and jails across Massachusetts. Her 1842 report was replete with vignettes of naked, beaten, and filthy inmates consigned to prison-like cages and cellars. Wardens rebutted her charges, legislators pondered them, and their constituents debated them, vaulting the needs of a previously neglected constituency into the public limelight. To quote one biographer, Dix's report was "an unforgettable kaleidoscope of horror."[48]

"If my pictures are displeasing, coarse and severe," she noted, it was because "the condition of human beings, reduced to the extremest states of degradation and misery, cannot be exhibited in softened language, or adorn a polished page." She capped her lurid exposé with an appropriately feminine supplication: "Men of Massachusetts," Dix concluded, "I beg, I implore, I demand, pity and protection for these of my suffering and outraged sex!" Dix's campaign brilliantly manipulated public opinion, coupling it with female deference. Unlike Stanton, she demanded chivalry rather than parity, and unlike Sarah Bagley, Dix absented herself from the ensuing legislative deliberations, relying on her male supporters to present her case. Her strategy was highly effective, yielding a $25,000 ($325,000) appropriation and access to a $40,000 ($520,000) bequest to build a new wing on the Worcester Asylum so that the inmates could be more humanely housed.[49]

The Massachusetts campaign was the first of an almost unbroken string of legislative coups, as Dix conducted investigations and disseminated her recommendations in state after state. In each instance, she pursued a threefold strategy, (1) marshaling public opinion through exposés, (2) submitting petitions for reform, and (3) personally lobbying influential leaders. Despite her professed aversion to female politicking, she was instinctively a political animal, a woman with a gift for identifying influential politicians and wooing their support. Dix crafted bipartisan alliances in an era riven by partisan animosities, and gathered hundreds of thousands of dollars in public and private support for a relatively invisible and politically impotent constituency as legislators in Massachusetts, Maryland, and even Mississippi succumbed to her entreaties.

One biographer attributes her success to her persistence, as "politicians who lacked the slightest interest in the lunacy question became convinced that nothing short of a new law would stop Dix's agitation" and "daily badgering." Beyond this, she had a genius for exploiting the politics of chivalry. In a time when the borders of feminine and masculine behavior were being aggressively reconfigured, with Northern middle-class white women claiming new political ground only to be repulsed by policymakers and politicians, she was viewed as "a woman's rights woman worth having, going in for their rights in the right way." In a period when women's organizations were increasingly visible, vocal, and politically aggressive, Dix worked alone, pleading for hapless victims who had failed through no fault of their own, and from whom she had nothing to gain. In effect, she was nonthreatening, cloaking her campaigns in rhetoric and techniques that superficially condoned the status quo even as her success ostensibly recast the parameters of female political influence.[50]

Perhaps more important, her cause dovetailed neatly with partisan

agendas. At a time when the poor, especially women, were publicly criticized, blamed for their own poverty, and often despised, Dix's constituency
elicited public sympathy. They also resided in male-controlled asylums
that could be expanded and improved at public expense, providing contracts and jobs for their backers to distribute. By directing funds to local
economies in the name of humanitarianism, the men who advocated Dix's
reforms created patronage windfalls for their parties and themselves. Unlike the earnest matrons who lobbied for "private" charities for women
and the poor, Dix discovered a political gold mine, embracing a cause that
enabled legislators to appear both gallant and politically astute. By helping
Dix they helped their parties and themselves, while striking a blow for the
sexual status quo. In the process, she achieved stunning political success.

It lasted until she reached the federal level. Dix launched her assault on
federal policymakers in 1848, requesting 10 million acres of federal land to
be sold to upgrade state facilities for the insane. Later, another 2.5 million
acres were added for the aid of the deaf, dumb, and blind. She based the
idea on previous, smaller federal grants that had been made to two state
asylums for the deaf and dumb in 1819 and 1826, and the "general welfare" clause of the Constitution, a vaguely worded proviso under section 8
concerning the appropriate uses of public funds. Over the course of six
years of intensive lobbying, Dix built a bipartisan coalition of supporters
who successfully shepherded the bill through both the Senate and the
House, only to have it killed by presidential veto in 1854.

Franklin Pierce was a weak man despised for his political ineptitude
and personal failings, and his veto constituted one small and thoroughly
atypical spark of political will in an otherwise undistinguished presidency.
Pierce argued that he lacked the constitutional authority to make "the
Federal government the great almoner of public charity throughout the
United States," depicting his decision as a bulwark against a swelling tide
of humanitarian sympathies and human needs. If Congress could aid the
insane, he reasoned, it could be called upon to help others as well, an approach that threatened to make the federal government responsible for
"all the poor in all the States" and "every species of human infirmity." In
the process, the federal government—rather than the states and private
philanthropy—would be forced to care for "the dependent, the orphan,
the sick, or the needy." Pierce also predicted that public support would dry
up the wellspring of local charity and communal self-help, skipping
lightly over decades of collaborative precedents between private citizens
and the states. Like Roger Taney, Pierce was a dedicated Jacksonian De-
mocrat, and like Taney, he inscribed a Jacksonian signature on the federal

policymaking of the 1850s. In the process, he overrode Dix's years of humanitarian pleading and politicking at a single stroke.[51]

Dix's career helps to illustrate ways in which "gender became a prism through which the political tensions of the 1850s were filtered." Women like Stanton and Dix stood at the far ends of the reformist continuum, the one espousing parity, the other self-sacrifice as the key to female authority in the public realm. Most Northern white women occupied more of a middle ground, working collectively to promote their charities and reforms in ways that increasingly intersected with their state and local governments. While Northern black women immersed themselves in expanding circles of communal self-help, philanthropy, and legislative and civil protest, whites pursued a number of discrete causes at the state level with increasing success.[52]

Most engaged in a delicate balancing act, seeking public power while straddling an invisible line between "acceptable" behavior that accorded authority, and ostensibly immoral or unwomanly efforts that invited public censure and, occasionally, physical reprisals such as the mobbing of female antislavery societies. For many women, the final decades before the Civil War were a time of achievement, when the boundaries of female governance were expanded to include social advocacy by and for Northern women, for causes and constituencies that they themselves defined. During the Civil War, many achieved the federal authority that had consistently eluded even seasoned reformers such as Dix.

Civil Society and the Civil War

The politics of chivalry symbolized the clash of two competing political cultures, one dominated by the partisan imperatives of white male political elites, the other predicated on a sprawling patchwork of associations. These competing visions of public governance, one hierarchical, the other decentralized, formed a subtext for the Civil War, both in its origins and in its execution, pitting these differing philosophies against each other in a struggle to define the appropriate parameters of civil society. During the hostilities, the Northern model of associational culture that was challenged under Jackson was amplified and incorporated into governmental initiatives on a new scale, drawing Northern white women and African Americans into federal programs for education and military support, and Southern white women into state-sponsored relief work for the first time. In the process, female deference and the mask of feminine subordination that Dix so artfully manipulated were cast aside in the name of efficiency, as both men and women dealt with state and federal officials in more direct, more straightforward terms.

Their efforts underscored the historical tendency of American governmental officials to forge partnerships with voluntary associations when they lacked the resources, the expertise, or the will to execute public programs themselves, a tendency that dated from the colonial era and that some scholars have recently dubbed "third party government." By this interpretation, local, state, and federal government officials have historically brokered partnerships with nonprofit organizations for the provision of charitable, health, and educational services, a practice that obviated the need for permanent bureaucracies, lowered costs, and allowed substantial flexibility in public policymaking. Pioneered by male elites in Franklin's era and women like Isabella Graham, then shunned by tight-fisted municipal authorities in the 1820s and 1830s—at least for women's charities—these practices resurfaced on a new scale during the 1860s.[1]

The Civil War underscored the extent to which the country's ethos of limited government was predicated, in part, on the ability of private citizens to subsidize the government with their money, their time, and their expertise, an ability that enabled them to create alternative power bases outside elected office. Students of women's political culture such as Kathryn Kish Sklar have emphasized the role of disestablishment and limited government in opening a policymaking vacuum that was filled by America's educated female middle class, which pursued activities monopolized by male civil servants and public bureaucracies in European nations. Equally important was the extent to which the government's circumscribed role was reinforced by its lack of adequate funding to maintain extensive public services. Quite simply, strong governments and the elaborate bureaucratic infrastructures that support them cost money. And the American government did not have a great deal of surplus cash at its disposal until the twentieth century. Because of this, even disfranchised groups were able to play important political roles by virtue of their ability to subsidize the state through their donations, their voluntarism, and their skill in generating capital for communal ends, patterns vividly illustrated during the war.[2]

Northern White Women and the Sanitary Commission

Northern white women played their most significant federal roles under the auspices of the United States Sanitary Commission (USSC). Authorized by Abraham Lincoln on June 9, 1861, the Sanitary Commission provided advice and support services for the Union troops, including medical aid, funding, and assistance in systematizing the collection of donated supplies. The men who headed it used their authority to apply the lessons from the Crimean War, where the introduction of new scientific techniques and Florence Nightingale's nursing corps significantly lowered mortality rates. Middle- and upper-class white women, on the other hand, contributed their administrative and fund-raising skills, with impressive results. Over seven thousand soldier's aid auxiliaries eventually joined the commission's networks, helping to gather and distribute more than $15 million (or almost $200 million in 2000 dollars) in supplies for the Union troops.[3]

It was a contested ascent. In the North, encounters between the military and private associations, and between male and female policymakers and volunteers, often produced spirited contests for authority, reconfiguring the boundaries of gender and class. The war also brought a variety of contenders together in an ongoing battle for control of the soldiers' welfare, pitting an entrenched and often incompetent masculinist military culture against the scientific pretensions of elite male volunteers and the familial and racial imperatives of women and blacks.

Women, rather than men, mobilized the first citizen efforts to aid the troops, as hundreds of soldier's aid societies surfaced in cities and towns shortly after the first volleys ignited the war at Fort Sumter. Many worked independently, sending books and supplies directly to individual soldiers in the camps. Plans for the coordinated Woman's Central Relief Association were introduced at a meeting of prominent New York matrons on April 25, 1861, and adopted four days later at a mass meeting at Cooper Union, centralizing efforts to distribute accurate information on military needs, enlist and train nurses, and introduce insights gained from Nightingale's celebrated work into American military practices. A few doctors and ministers were also invited to attend the meeting, including the Reverend Henry W. Bellows, who subsequently headed the new commission.

The takeover by a small group of prominent men like Bellows and Charles Stillé, the commission's chronicler, raises intriguing questions, particularly given the wealth of women's organizational experience and the scope of their charities and reforms. Some of the answers doubtless stem from class-related issues. The women who coordinated the Cooper Union meeting—prominent matrons like Mrs. Hamilton Fish, Mrs. W. B. Astor, Jr., and Mrs. J. Auchincloss—were not necessarily antebellum reformers or asylum officers. Encouraged to defer to the men in their families and social circles, they keenly felt a need for guidance on "the work to be done." Many undoubtedly also felt that they lacked the courage—and the clout—to deal with the military establishment themselves.[4]

The commission's struggle to win the cooperation of the military medical corps was hard fought, and hard won. Many officers dismissed the Sanitary Commission as "superfluous, obtrusive," and potentially "troublesome" in a bid to protect their own terrain. They were particularly leery of women's involvement, arguing that it could have "no practical value whatever to the army." Many mistakenly felt that the conflict would be of short duration, and that volunteer efforts would only get in the way. Even Lincoln initially had misgivings, labeling the venture "a fifth wheel to the coach" of army operations. As Stillé acridly recalled, government officials finally capitulated in the belief that "it could do no great harm" and would quickly be abandoned as a "worthless ... monument of the folly of weak enthusiasts, and of well-meaning but silly women."[5]

The commission returned these aspersions tenfold. Doctors and volunteers of the USSC unearthed and publicized a host of "frightful evils" born of "bad military organization and defective administration" during their camp inspections, exposing the profound "self-complacency" of the officers. As Stillé candidly admitted, the commission was "far too inquisitive, earnest and persistent to invite the sympathy of those who had so long borne rule in the offices at Washington." Their exposés culminated in a national petition campaign waged by medical luminaries across the nation to oust the surgeon general. The USSC's efforts to generate data and to document and quantify the abuses they found in the camps increasingly formed the basis of their claims to a voice in military policymaking, providing a new tenor for male philanthropy. After the war, their faith in science and "disinterested expertise" would become the leitmotiv of a new generation of extraordinarily wealthy male donors who invested unprecedented sums in institutions to promote the twin gospels of professionalism and scientific reform.[6]

Female Sanitarians were quickly embroiled in contests of their own. One of the sharpest rivalries flared over the nursing corps. Dr. Elizabeth Blackwell was the Woman's Central Relief Association's candidate to head the nurses' training program, an assignment she lost after Bellows's coup. Army officers balked at the prospect of female nurses, preferring to bar women from the camps entirely. Although the commission ultimately trained some nurses, Dorothea Dix used her political connections to secure an appointment as the army's superintendent of women nurses just days after the Sanitary Commission was approved by Lincoln. It was an odd choice, one that was destined for disaster from the outset, enlisting a woman with virtually no organizational or medical experience and an ill-concealed dislike for women's groups to recruit and train a bureaucracy of nurses. The fact that Dix was an icon of politically crafted female deference undoubtedly sealed her appointment, but it also sealed the end of her public career. Her imperiousness and her insistence on placing moral imperatives over medical priorities undercut her ability to create a viable program, leading detractors to dismiss her as a "philanthropic lunatic."[7]

Conversely, women's efforts in systematizing the distribution of donated supplies and raising funds for the troops were widely lauded. Under the able management of women like Chicago's Mary Livermore, USSC offices collected and systematically distributed a virtual tidal wave of donated clothing, foodstuffs, reading materials, and medical supplies. Within four months of the commission's creation, over sixty thousand articles had been received. Depots were set up in New York, Boston, Chicago, Philadelphia, Washington, Cincinnati, and Wheeling, West Virginia, and a circular entitled "To The Loyal Women of America" sent out, urging them to form auxiliaries. Some solicited funds; others made uniforms, all of which were distributed via the commission, creating an immense shipping business akin to "the best business houses" under the rubric of humanitarianism.[8]

They also coordinated a series of highly successful Sanitary Fairs in major cities between 1863 and 1865. Women's organizations had participated in quasi-commercial ventures since their inception in the 1790s. The Sanitary Fairs amplified this work tenfold, with often stunning results. The idea originated with Livermore and Jane Hoge, both of whom were alumnae of Chicago's antebellum charities. Livermore's position as head of the commission's Northwestern regional office provided access to almost three thousand soldier's aid auxiliaries throughout the Midwest, a network she combed for supplies and goods to sell at the Northwestern Sanitary Fair.[9]

The fair was a marked success, raising between $80,000 and $100,000 (or between @ $1 million and $1.3 million in 2000 dollars) in less than a month for the troops and for battlefront hospitals, and was subsequently replicated in Cleveland, Cincinnati, Pittsburgh, Philadelphia, Albany, Brooklyn, and New York City. Each fair patched together a veritable department store for humanitarianism, providing booths and displays for books, jewelry, sewn goods, and decorative arts, art galleries, hat and dress boutiques, antique stalls, and large-scale commercial ventures such as restaurants and skating rinks. Men as well as women were asked for contributions as sponsors reached out to "every loyal and patriotic workingman, mechanic or farmer, who can make a pair of shoes or raise a barrel of apples . . . to contribute something that can be turned into money, and again from money into the means of ensuring the health and life of our national soldiers." Some groups, like the one in Chicago, spent the money on their own operations, while the coordinators of New York's Metropolitan Fair donated their revenues to the commission. According to Stillé's tally, the Sanitary Fairs raised $2.7 million, or over half the commission's total revenues of @ $5 million (or @ $65 million in constant dollars), with the rest donated by public and private donors in the United States, Central and Latin America, and Hawaii. The Sanitary Fairs showcased and exploited women's commercial skills on a new level, providing tangible, fiscal evidence of their contributions to the war. Market activities, as well as administrative skills, formed the basis of Northern white women's first successful partnerships with the federal government in the Civil War.[10]

African Americans, Soldier's Relief, and Southern Education

Fund-raising also provided an entrée into national policymaking for African Americans. Although elite white women may have been better positioned to coordinate large-scale projects like the Northwestern Sanitary Fair, African Americans drew on a long tradition of communal generosity. Black women created a variety of soldier's aid societies when the war began, some of which were subsumed into the Sanitary Commission's organizational networks while others remained independent. As in the case of their earlier charities, many of these groups focused primarily on the needs of African Americans, particularly recently liberated slaves and black soldiers, who (in yet another manifestation of discrimination) were paid less than their white counterparts. In effect, African American women's groups subsidized the Union military service of black men.

They were especially active in raising funds for slaves freed during the war. Thus, the Louisville Colored Ladies Society solicited donations to build a hospital and school for recently liberated Southern bondsmen, and the Philadelphia's Women's Freedmen's Relief Association was created in 1865 with an ambitious pledge to support teachers and schools, send clothing and medical supplies to Southern blacks, and establish asylums for dependent children and the elderly. Toward that end, they solicited donations from local congregations, set up sewing circles, sponsored fairs, and even established children's fund-raising groups. Washington's Contraband Relief Association was headed by Elizabeth Keckly, Mary Lincoln's dressmaker, who used her contacts to collect and distribute supplies and other contributions from African American women's groups. Black abolitionist societies and churches also collected and distributed donations, activities in which women played a prominent role. Many of these organizations later collaborated with the federal Freedmen's Bureau, drawing this previously disaffected community into joint ventures with federal policymakers at the war's end.

Nor was giving confined to Northern communities. Commentators were struck by the extent to which former slaves invested their time and meager earnings in the creation and incorporation of churches and schools, establishing permanent, legal institutional bases for black communal life. Despite the opposition of local whites who feared that "the black school was as potent a force for social change as black suffrage," freedmen often donated "truly amazing" amounts—W. E. B. Du Bois placed the final tally at $786,000 (a staggering $10 million in 2000 dollars) between 1866 and 1870—revenues painstakingly raised through fairs, subscription drives, and charity events.[11]

By 1865, over fourteen hundred Northern teachers, both black and white, were active in Southern freedmen's schools. Many endured considerable harassment from local whites, ranging from threats and verbal abuse to physical attacks. The women who participated in these programs were particularly potent symbols of the changes wrought by war, as the traditional prerogatives of white males were overturned by Northern women intent on empowering former slaves.[12]

These activities brought free and freed blacks into alliances with government officials through the Freedmen's Bureau, which was created by Congress in 1865 to provide relief for refugees and to resettle former slaves on abandoned lands. Despite a troubled history, the bureau made a lasting contribution by bolstering Southern and Northern contributions to an enduring array of black schools, funneling over $1 million of federal funds into collaborative alliances with organizations like the American Missionary Association, Northern black donors, and Southern freedmen. It also built and repaired hundreds of schoolhouses and provided protection to ensure the schools' survival. Thirty-one Northern societies added another $15 million (or over $200 million in 2000 dollars) in donations between 1865 and 1870, affording instruction for almost 150,000 students in twenty-seven hundred schools taught by thirty-seven hundred white and black teachers, many of whom were supported by African Americans.[13]

Postwar philanthropy—both black and white—also established a string of black colleges across the Southern states, including Fisk University in Tennessee and Hampton Institute in Virginia, providing valuable training grounds for African American leaders. The impetus for public education in the South was born of the black community, as well as the impetus for African American civil rights. Without the postwar schools and colleges created through the coupling of Reconstruction era philanthropy and federal intervention, to quote W. E. B. Du Bois, "the Negro would, to all intents and purposes, have been driven back to slavery."[14]

Southern White Women and Soldier's Aid

The war produced comparable, albeit smaller and far less coordinated, initiatives in the South. The Southern pattern, in which the wealthiest private charities and donations coalesced around municipal bodies rather than developing independently, had a number of consequences during the war. First, many of these institutions lost their endowments when city fathers unwisely invested them in Confederate bonds, which became worthless. Many Southern charities were crippled by the war, leading to bread riots in Richmond and Savannah. The dearth of independent Southern women's organizations outside the major cities also meant that the majority of Southern women lacked the organizational skills that enabled their Northern counterparts to assume the helms of massive regional networks and fairs. Nor did they have the dense networks of female-run auxiliaries that connected Northern women's empire of charity, religion, and reform. As a result, the sudden emergence of Southern women's soldier's aid societies produced piecemeal, often limited results.

Their zeal was unquestionable. Despite the lack of widespread precedents, Southern white women's organizations surfaced with impressive speed at the beginning of the war. Anne Firor Scott estimates that 150 appeared in South Carolina alone during the first three months, and Drew Gilpin Faust places the total regional tally as high as 1,000. Most devoted themselves to fund-raising and to sewing goods for the troops, but a few took a more direct hand in shaping Confederate policies by subsidizing the purchase of gunboats to patrol coastal waters.[15]

Several factors distinguished the Confederate situation. As the portfolios of older charities crumbled, the edifice of male-controlled philanthropy was weakened as well, opening a new venue for women's initiatives in the postwar years. But the older patterns endured in one important respect: government, rather than the volunteers themselves, often served as the rallying point for the recruitment and coordination of women's soldier's aid societies, in a marked reversal of Northern patterns. For example, women were absent from organizational life in frontier cities like Dallas before they were conscripted and their participation legitimized by the governor's wartime call for service and aid. While government gave rise to many Texas women's organizations, Alabama women formed fragile statewide alliances at the behest of the governor's office, which distributed raw materials for them to sew into garments and tents, goods collected and distributed by county officials. Rather than forging their own networks, many Southern women continued to focus their charitable activities according to the dictates of office-holding male elites.[16]

They would be far less dependent in the future. Anne Firor Scott's pioneering work highlighted the expansion of Southern women's philanthropy in the postwar years, a theme echoed in the small but growing array of books on Gilded Age Southern women's associations. Interpretations about the nature and extent of wartime transformations vary. Although George Rable depicts the war's legacy as one of "change without change," yielding "modest and limited improvements in an atmosphere of ideological reaction," others such as Scott see the war as a major catalyst to white women's increased associationalism, laying the groundwork for the rise of Southern feminism. As Elizabeth Varon explains, "the number of politically active women and of female associations—particularly those dedicated to missionary work and temperance—increased markedly in the postwar decades." In effect, wartime mobilization "strengthened their claim to a role in politics." Building on these interpretations, historians of Southern women's progressivism emphasize the extent to which white women worked with their governments to create services and wield policymaking authority, heralding the expansion of Southern governance.[17]

Conclusions

Wartime initiatives helped to build new forms of social capital, fostering the spread of independent, separatist organizations among Southern women and drawing former slaves into new types of communal activity. Their efforts deepened and extended existing associational networks for charity, social mobilization, and reform through the development and coordination of relief activities, and through the creation of independent, chartered charities, churches, and educational institutions throughout the South. Although many wartime gains were subsequently lost, these networks endured, providing the framework for more than a century of civil rights and social welfare activism. In the process, wartime philanthropy helped to forge a more comprehensive version of civil society—and citizenship—than earlier generations of Southern Americans had imagined or designed. The war also swept away many of the vestiges of patriarchal philanthropy, opening expanded opportunities for independent social action both by white women and African Americans. Although the "prerogatives of race" would continue to undermine "the commonalities of gender," the scope of Southern civil society significantly expanded over the course of the Civil War.[18]

Alumnae of the Northern Sanitary Commission and Northern soldier's aid societies also forged a vital universe of new institutions. Examples abound. Annie Wittenmyer, a local leader in Iowa women's wartime relief groups, founded an orphan asylum with state funds in an old cavalry barracks donated by the federal government, backed by $6,000 ($90,000 in 2000 dollars) in hospital supplies donated by Congress. She also introduced a diet kitchen program in military hospitals and later served as the first president of the national Women's Christian Temperance Union. Mary Livermore became a prominent figure in the suffrage movement, serving as vice president of the American Women's Suffrage Association, and editor of the *Woman's Journal*, the association's newspaper. Louisa Lee Schuyler became a leading advocate for the feminization and professionalization of nursing and a prominent participant in New York's State Charities Aid Association, a watchdog group that monitored the operations of public asylums, while Josephine Shaw Lowell emerged as one of the era's most prominent welfare authorities under the auspices of the Charity Organization Society.[19]

Scholars such as Lori Ginzberg have depicted the war as a watershed that separated the older, gender-based alliances of the antebellum era from more class-based associational networks in the Gilded Age. Certainly, this was the pattern followed by many of the elite women who headed the Sanitary Commission's efforts in cities like New York, a trend presaged by their passive acceptance of the male takeover of the commission's management and design. But Livermore's and Wittenmyer's careers suggest that these patterns may have differed in Midwestern states, where many of the middle-class women who headed regional relief efforts subsequently moved into key positions in national women's organizations such as the WCTU and feminist campaigns. Perhaps the more telling transition among Northern women was that cited by Paula Baker: that many female reformers shifted the rationale for their public participation and policymaking from moral authority to social science research. In the process, they undercut the prerogatives of the politics of chivalry as well. Although American women still lacked the vote, and would continue to do so for another half century, the postwar glorification of science, research, and "disinterested expertise" provided a more solid base on which to stake their claims to public authority. After the turn of the century, middle-class white women's associational networks used their research findings to spur a host of Progressive reforms, entering into an array of collaborative ventures with elected officials in the design and implementation of local, state, and federal public welfare programs.[20]

   Their activities marked the culmination of a long and turbulent evolution. The framework for philanthropy embedded in Jefferson's epitaph had served the country well. Three factors, in particular, undergirded the growth of giving, voluntarism, and civil society in the new republic: the egalitarian ideals embodied in the Revolution, the legacy of religious disestablishment, and First Amendment guarantees of freedom of religion, speech, assembly, and the ability to petition the government for a redress of grievances. Together, they formed an American creed that held that every citizen had an implicit right to create organizations, lobby for change, and participate in political and economic developments through the voluntary sphere.

   The teeming organizational universe that surfaced between the Revolution and the Civil War served a variety of aims. Despite the idea that the United States was a nation of unvarnished individualists, the early history of American philanthropy was written in collective terms, echoing Tocqueville's dictum that the citizen who stands alone stands powerless, while those who unite attain a public presence and voice. The practice of philanthropy—that segment of social activity that encompasses the giving of time and money for public benefit—was pervasive, encompassing citizens of different economic strata, racial backgrounds, and religious beliefs. Collectivism, rather than individualism, was the leitmotiv of early American philanthropy—and democracy—particularly for politically disadvantaged women and blacks.[21]

   By creating churches, charities, and reform movements, some defined "the other," some themselves. For colonial elites like Franklin, philanthropy provided a means of linking masculinity to republican virtue in highly visible, public ways. The advent of women's organizations in the 1790s added a feminine twist, providing tangible evidence of female virtue, valor, self-sacrifice and public service that cast the republican ethos in a feminine frame. More than the nebulous doctrine of republican motherhood, these activities afforded concrete examples of women's capacity for governance and citizenship in the immediate postrevolutionary years. Similarly, men like Absalom Jones and Richard Allen used their associations to co-opt the notion of republican virtue by crafting republicanism into an enduring ethos of racial uplift through their associational work. For them, philanthropy had a twofold aim: helping others while helping themselves to combat racial stereotypes in terms that they themselves defined.

   Some used their service and their associations to push against the barriers of prejudice, discrimination, or misogyny; others defined "the poor."

Middle-class white women's efforts did both, earning a niche for women's and children's issues on public policymaking agendas while collectively enlarging an array of legal, political, and economic rights and roles for female trustees. In the process, they provided resources for the impoverished women who constituted the bulk of the urban poor, casting their beneficiaries (sometimes misguidedly) as the mirror image of themselves. Each group used its associations and its funds to counter and to create stereotypes, to amass capital and to set communal and public agendas. Rather than bowing pliantly to the hegemonic pronouncements of others, they sparked a spirited dialectic, producing a vibrant, highly contentious public sphere in which only those who failed to organize were left voiceless and unheard.

These efforts had significant political implications as well. Discussions of "political culture" have broadened our understanding of the practice of American governance in recent years, highlighting the activities of a new cast of public actors. Women's political participation, for example, has been traced through everything from the ideology of republican motherhood to handkerchiefs waved at political rallies. Most of these discussions, however, overlooked the far more substantial roles afforded by public-private alliances and public support for nonprofit organizations.[22]

Collaborative ventures between nonprofits and governments took a variety of forms. Some involved the simple sharing of resources, an arrangement exemplified by the role of Pennsylvania's colonial government when it provided housing for Franklin's fledgling Library Company. Sometimes expertise was shared, as when Catholic nuns were called to manage public hospital wards and pesthouses during epidemics. Often, the exchange entailed a trade of rights for service—a practice embodied in the granting of charters to female-run charities and asylums, instruments that significantly enhanced the legal prerogatives of their trustees. Governmental funding was given as well, a practice encouraged by an economy of scarcity in which citizen groups were regularly prevailed upon to supplement governmental resources in meeting public needs. This was the pattern that inspired the pooling of public and private resources in the provision of colonial welfare services and that undergirded the work of the USSC during the Civil War. It was the rationale behind the federal government's Civilization Fund, which siphoned public dollars to missionary groups for work with Indians, and for public subsidies to the American Colonization Society, which enabled the United States to establish its first colony through private means.

Charities and educational ventures that won public appropriations gave their backers a hand in the allocation of public resources, even as they acknowledged the political contributions of citizens who supplemented the services of the state, a sharing of power that was embodied in the commonwealth ideal. Measured in these terms, politics and political culture take on a new slant, enabling us to trace the civic status of groups both within and outside the formal electorate while providing a yardstick for measuring fluctuating levels of democratic participation in public policy-making and service provision.

Viewed from this perspective, the Jacksonian era policies that financially "disfranchised" Northern women's charities take on a new cast. By providing a rationale for the consolidation of public funding in politically oriented asylums under white male control, the language of retrenchment became a smoke screen for disempowering those who already had most to lose, and loosening their fragile place in the political arena to further consolidate the entitlements of white male elites.

Social advocacy was similarly contested. Between the Revolution and the 1830s, the scope of American advocacy continually widened, democratizing American governance. Beginning with the Democratic-Republican societies in the wake of the Revolution, religious groups, African Americans, and middle-class white women all made a bid to monitor governmental performance, contest federal policies, and effect legislative change. The confrontation between Northern black churches and the federally funded American Colonization Society exemplified both the strengths and the limits of social reform. Although Absalom Jones, Richard Allen, and their peers lacked the electoral clout to hobble the ACS politically, they were able to mobilize resistance to its aims, helping to stalemate the political agendas of a stellar array of white statesmen.

Jacksonian politicians led the drive to narrow the policymaking sphere, endorsing policies of sometimes dubious legality to undercut free speech, petitioning, and protests when they impeded their political designs. The record of the Jacksonian years raises a number of interesting questions. Although the right of average citizens to monitor the government, protest abuses, and pursue legislative reform was hardly a given at the time of the Revolution, as evidenced by the contention over the Democratic-Republican societies, these practices ultimately provided a balance wheel for democracy, enabling groups with often widely varying agendas to air their concerns and lobby for a redress of grievances. The pervasiveness of factions was something that men like Madison clearly predicted. Madison's genius lay in his understanding of their role in democratic societies. The right to plead, to persuade, to lobby, and to resist the aggressions of other groups afforded an important "safety valve" for communal antipathies, allowing them to be played out in the press and in public meetings rather than through physical violence among competing groups. In effect, voluntary associations provided mechanisms for ritualized combat by airing and addressing collective complaints.

They also served as lightning rods for popular misgivings about the fluctuating boundaries of gender, class, and race. The country experienced several "identity crises" over the course of its history. Often, the eras in which the lines of normative behavior for men and women were radically recast coincided with major periods of rapid socioeconomic change and social reform. This was the case in the 1830s, when the effects of the market revolution dovetailed with the growing politicization of women and blacks, as well as during the Progressive Era and the 1960s. Voluntary associations and charitable, religious, and educational institutions often served as flash points for communal anxieties in this setting owing to their ability to foment and symbolize change.

The history of antebellum America suggests that two things happen when rights are suppressed. Initially, repression breeds social action, a pattern demonstrated by the rapid growth of abolitionism in the 1830s. However, if the government remains unresponsive, or continues to turn a blind eye to acts of violence, or succumbs to ongoing repression, at some point civic activism will sour into civil disobedience, a trajectory followed by disenchanted antislavery advocates in the tumultuous period between Jackson's election and the Civil War. As in the case of government support for nonprofit organizations, democracy works best when the boundaries between "public" and "private" activities are permeable and blurred, when even disadvantaged groups are engaged in formal political processes through advocacy and public support. Elected officials who sunder these relationships do so at their peril, pushing disaffected citizens to seek other, more violent means to achieve their ends.

In addition to their political and propagandistic functions, U.S. nonprofit organizations historically played a variety of economic roles. Philanthropy and nonprofits were bound to the market in a variety of ways. At one level, they served as important mechanisms for the accumulation and liquification of capital in a cash-scarce economy; the extraordinary success of antebellum mutual savings banks graphically illustrated the economic power of the nonprofit sphere. Most nonprofits operated on a less ambitious scale, generating income through a mixed portfolio of donations, charitable events, sales, royalties, and fairs. Far from subsisting solely on individual *or* public generosity, nonprofits engaged in commercial activities from their inception. They also served as employers, and as engines for economic development, particularly in the more democratic milieu of the North, helping to finance the region's increasingly diversified economy.

Scholarly debates over the past two decades have amply illustrated the products and pitfalls of American capitalism. Far less attention has been paid to the impact of what might be termed "communal" or philanthropic capital: the ways in which different groups generated and invested funds in pursuit of their collective aims through nonprofit organizations. During the years between the Revolution and the Civil War, most chartered voluntary associations invested their surplus funds, backing everything from banks and immense capital improvement programs, such as the Erie Canal, to loans for businesses, charities, and homes in local communities. Some of these efforts may have had a negative (and sometimes profoundly negative) impact on other groups, as evidenced by George Whitefield's misguided endorsement of slavery to support his Bethesda Orphanage. But others were deeply empowering. Because of their generosity and their ability to raise funds, African American communities helped to launch the abolitionist movement as well as black churches and newspapers, creating a unique political culture of their own. Groups of women, from middle-class charity trustees to female labor reformers, also raised, generated, pooled, and invested their funds in pamphlets, publications, and programs. And many parlayed their generosity and their entrepreneurial skills into expanded public roles during the Civil War.

The ability of private citizens to forge partnerships with the state casts American governance—and American democracy—in a new light. Far from a narrow forum for consensual discourse and the crafting of collective "trust," the public sphere provides a prism for studying the ways in which ordinary men and women shaped their society and their lives in tandem and tension with elected officials. Their donations of time and money, much of which was generated through what we would now term "nonprofit entrepreneurship," ultimately underwrote the nation's commitment to limited government, making it a viable proposition by subsidizing the state with private resources. Seen from this perspective, the interstices between philanthropy, the government, and the market—once viewed as separate and unique—become the place where the day-to-day pursuit of democracy was often played out and defined.

The interrelationships among these spheres created a vibrant arena in which the borders between citizen associations, the government, and the market were continually renegotiated and recast. Rooted in colonialism, tempered by revolution, spread by faith, and galvanized by repression, civil society was transformed once again on the shoals of the shattered Union. Each generation imposed its own interpretation on this sprawling universe to fight new contests and to achieve differing ends. What *has* endured is the faith that all citizens have a right to gather, to speak, and to lobby for reform, reiterating the American creed in an idiom uniquely their own.

Notes

Introduction

1. Thomas Jefferson, *Public and Private Papers* (New York: Vintage Books, Library of America, 1990), 380. Despite Jefferson's claims to authorship, John Adams and Benjamin Franklin also sat on the committee that shaped the final draft of the declaration. For an interesting discussion of their role in drafting the document, see Robert M. S. McDonald, "Thomas Jefferson's Changing Reputation as Author of the Declaration of Independence: The First Fifty Years," *Journal of the Early Republic* 19, no. 2 (summer, 1999): 169–96.

2. The notion of an "American creed" based on a shared set of political beliefs was developed by Gunnar Myrdal in his landmark study, *An American Dilemma: The Negro Problem and Modern Democracy* (New York: Harper and Row, 1944). As he explained, "Americans of all national origins, classes, regions, creeds, and colors have something in common: a social *ethos,* a political creed" rooted in "the belief in equality and in the right to liberty" (1:8). Interpretations of civil society abound. Useful overviews of the vast literature on civil society are Jean L. Cohen and Andrew Arato, *Civil Society and Political Theory* (Cambridge, Mass.: MIT Press, 1994); John Keane, ed., *Civil Society and the State: New European Perspectives* (London: University of Westminster Press, 1988); John Keane, *Democracy and Civil Society* (London: University of Westminster Press, 1988); and Adam B. Seligman, *The Idea of Civil Society* (Princeton: Princeton University Press, 1992). Questions concerning the relation of civil society and civic participation to the practice of democracy have generated a good deal of interest in recent years, including the creation of a National Commission on Civic Renewal. For scholarly perspectives concerning these issues, see Robert Fullinwider, ed., *Civil Society, Democracy and Civic Renewal* (New York: Rowman and Littlefield, 1999), which contains essays by members of the commission's task force on civil society. I was interested to hear Daniel Walker Howe's engaging presidential address at the annual meeting of the Society for Historians of the Early American

Republic in Baltimore, in July 2001, which also dealt in part with the issues raised by Jefferson's epitaph. His paper is scheduled to be published in the *Journal of the Early Republic*.

3. For fuller definitions of philanthropy, nonprofit organizations, and the "third sector," see Lester M. Salamon, *America's Nonprofit Sector: A Primer* (New York: Foundation Center, 1999), chap. 2. A great deal of definitional research has been done by researchers both within and outside the United States over the past fifteen years, efforts that have infused the literature of the emerging field of nonprofit and voluntary studies, as well as sparked reclassifications of nonprofit activities by the U.S. Internal Revenue Service and the United Nations' system of national income accounts. Research on the nonprofit sector based on these definitions is currently underway in over thirty countries worldwide. For international trends, see Lester M. Salamon and Helmut Anheier, *The Emerging Sector: An Overview* (Baltimore: Institute for Policy Studies, Johns Hopkins University, 1994), as well as their working papers on trends in individual countries. All of this work points toward long-established practices of giving, voluntarism, and nonprofit development in other countries, many of which significantly antedate efforts in the United States. See, for example, Kathleen D. McCarthy, ed., Special Issue on Women and Philanthropy, *Voluntas* 7, no. 4 (December 1996), and Kathleen D. McCarthy, ed., *Women, Philanthropy and Civil Society* (Bloomington: Indiana University Press, 2001).

4. For an interesting and nuanced discussion of the concept of democracy, see Robert H. Wiebe, *Self-Rule: A Cultural History of American Democracy* (Chicago: University of Chicago Press, 1995).

5. Although most studies do not concentrate on philanthropy per se, the secondary literature on the institutions and social reform movements discussed in this study is immense. A selection of some of these books includes the following: On philanthropy and charities generally: Robert H. Bremner, *American Philanthropy* (Chicago: University of Chicago Press, 1988), and his *From the Depths: The Discovery of Poverty in the United States* (New York: New York University Press, 1956); Peter Dobkin Hall, *The Organization of American Culture, 1700–1900: Private Institutions, Elites, and the Origins of American Nationality* (New York: New York University Press, 1982), and his *Inventing the Nonprofit Sector and Other Essays on Philanthropy, Voluntarism and Nonprofit Organizations* (Baltimore: Johns Hopkins University Press, 1992); Conrad Edick Wright, *The Transformation of Charity in Postrevolutionary New England* (Boston: Northeastern University Press, 1992); Merle Curti and Roderick Nash, *Philanthropy in the Shaping of American Higher Education* (New Brunswick: Rutgers University Press, 1965); Howard Miller, *The Legal Foundations of American Philanthropy, 1776–1844* (Madison: State Historical Society of Wisconsin, 1961); Barbara L. Bellows, *Benevolence among Slaveholders: Assisting the Poor in Charleston, 1670–1860* (Baton Rouge: Louisiana State University Press, 1993); Raymond A. Mohl, *Poverty in New York: 1783–1825* (New York: Oxford University Press, 1971); John K. Alexander, *Render Them Submissive: Responses to Poverty in Philadelphia, 1760–1800* (Amherst: University of Massachusetts Press, 1980); Robert E. Cray, Jr., *Paupers and Poor Relief in New York City and Its Rural Environs, 1700–1830* (Philadelphia: Temple University Press, 1988); David Rothman, *The Discovery of the Asylum: Social Order and Disorder in the New Republic* (Boston: Little, Brown and Co., 1971); John S. Whitehead, *The Separation of College and State: Columbia, Dartmouth, Harvard and Yale, 1776–1876* (New Haven: Yale University Press, 1973); Ronald Story, *Harvard and the Boston Upper Class: The Forging of an Aristocracy, 1800–1870* (Middletown, Conn.: Wesleyan University Press, 1980); Kathleen D. McCarthy, *Noblesse Oblige: Charity and Cultural Philanthropy in Chicago, 1849–1929* (Chicago: University of Chicago Press, 1982), and *Women's Culture: American Philanthropy and Art, 1830–1930* (Chicago: University of Chicago Press, 1991). On social reform: Robert H. Abzug, *Cosmos Crum-*

bling: American Reform and the Religious Imagination (New York: Oxford University Press, 1994); Ronald G. Walters, *American Reformers, 1815–1860* (New York: Hill and Wang, 1978); Stephen Mintz, *Moralists and Modernizers* (Baltimore: Johns Hopkins University Press, 1995); Whitney Cross, *The Burned Over District: A Social and Intellectual History of Enthusiastic Religion in Western New York, 1800–1850* (Ithaca: Cornell University Press, 1950); Alice Felt Tyler, *Freedom's Ferment: Phases of American Social History from the Colonial Period to the Outbreak of the Civil War* (New York: Harper Torchbooks, 1944). For the Benevolent Empire: Clifford Griffin, *Their Brothers' Keepers: Moral Stewardship in the United States: 1800–1860* (New York: H. Wolff, 1960); John Bodo, *The Protestant Clergy and Public Issues, 1812–1848* (Princeton: Princeton University Press, 1954); Charles I. Foster, *Errand of Mercy: The Evangelical United Front* (Chapel Hill: University of North Carolina Press, 1960); Carroll Smith-Rosenberg, *Religion and the Rise of the American City: The New York City Mission Movement, 1812–1870* (Ithaca: Cornell University Press, 1971); John W. Kuykendall, *Southern Enterprize: The Work of National Evangelical Societies in the Antebellum South* (Westport.: Greenwood Press, 1982); Peter Wosh, *Spreading the Word: The Bible Business in Nineteenth Century America* (Ithaca: Cornell University Press, 1994); Ann Boylan, *Sunday School: The Formation of an American Institution, 1790–1880* (New Haven: Yale University Press, 1988); John W. Quist, *Restless Visionaries: The Social Roots of Antebellum Reform in Alabama and Michigan* (Baton Rouge: Louisiana State University Press, 1998). For general histories of black organizations, see Ira Berlin, *Slaves without Masters: The Free Negro in the Antebellum South* (New York: Oxford University Press, 1974); Leon Litwack, *North of Slavery: The Negro in the Free States, 1790–1860* (Chicago: University of Chicago Press, 1961); Christopher Phillips, *Freedom's Port: The African American Community of Baltimore, 1790–1860* (Urbana: University of Illinois Press, 1997); Gary B.Nash, *Forging Freedom: The Formation of Philadelphia's Black Community: 1720–1840* (Cambridge, Mass.: Harvard University Press, 1988); Jane H. Pease and William H. Pease, *They Who Would Be Free: Blacks' Search for Freedom, 1830–1861* (New York: Atheneum, 1974); James Oliver Horton and Lois E. Horton, *Black Bostonians: Family Life and Community Struggle in the Antebellum North* (1979; reprint, New York: Holmes and Maier, 1999), and *In Hope of Liberty: Culture, Community and Protest among Northern Free Blacks, 1700–1860* (New York: Oxford University Press, 1997); Benjamin Quarles, *Black Abolitionists* (New York: Oxford University Press, 1969); Julie Winch, *Philadelphia's Black Elite: Activism, Accommodation, and the Struggle for Autonomy* (Philadelphia: Temple University Press, 1988). On the American Colonization Society: P. J. Staudenraus, *The African Colonization Movement, 1816–1865* (1961; reprint, New York: Octagon Books, 1980). On the Indian removals: Robert V. Remini, *Andrew Jackson and His Indian Wars* (New York: Viking, 2001); William G. McLoughlin *Cherokees and Missionaries, 1789–1839* (New Haven: Yale University Press, 1984); Ronald Satz, *American Indian Policy in the Jacksonian Era* (Lincoln: University of Nebraska Press, 1975); Francis Paul Prucha, *The Great Father: The United States and the American Indians* (Lincoln: University of Nebraska Press, 1984); Michael Paul Rogin, *Fathers and Children: Andrew Jackson and the Subjugation of the American Indian* (New York: Vintage Books, 1976); John A. Andrew III, *From Revivals to Removal: Jeremiah Evarts, the Cherokee Nation, and the Search for the Soul of America* (Athens: University of Georgia Press, 1992). On abolitionism: Ronald G. Walters, *The Antislavery Appeal: American Abolitionism after 1830* (Baltimore: Johns Hopkins University Press, 1976); Lewis Perry, *Radical Abolitionism: Anarchy and the Government of God in Antislavery Thought* (Ithaca: Cornell University Press, 1973); James Brewer Stewart, *Holy Warriors: The Abolitionists and American Slavery* (New York: Hill and Wang, 1976); Aileen S. Kraditor, *Means and Ends in American Abolitionism: Garrison and His Critics on Strategy and Tactics, 1834–1850* (New

York: Pantheon, 1969); Russel B. Nye, *Fettered Freedom: Civil Liberties and the Slavery Contro-versy* (East Lansing: Michigan State College Press, 1949); Lawrence Friedman, *Gregarious Saints: Self and Community in American Abolitionism, 1830–1870* (New York: Cambridge University Press, 1982); Louis Filler, *The Crusade against Slavery, 1830–1860* (New York: Harper and Brothers, 1960); Paul Goodman, *Of One Blood: Abolitionism and the Origins of Racial Equality* (Berkeley: University of California Press, 1998); Shirley J. Yee, *Black Women Abolitionists: A Study in Activism, 1828–1860* (Knoxville: University of Tennessee Press, 1992); Julie Roy Jeffrey, *The Great Silent Army of Abolitionism: Ordinary Women in the Antislavery Move-ment* (Chapel Hill: University of North Carolina Press, 1998); Jean Fagan Yellin and John C. Van Horne, eds., *The Abolitionist Sisterhood: Women's Political Culture in Antebellum America* (Ithaca: Cornell University Press, 1994); Deborah Gold Hansen, *Strained Sisterhood: Gender and Class in the Boston Female Antislavery Society* (Amherst: University of Massachusetts Press, 1993). On women's nonprofit organizations: Lori Ginzberg, *Women and the Work of Benevolence: Morality, Politics, and Class in the Nineteenth-Century United States* (New Haven: Yale University Press, 1990), and her *Women in Antebellum Reform* (Wheeling, Ill.: Harlan Davidson Co., 2000); Kathryn Kish Sklar, *Women's Rights Emerges within the Antislavery Move-ment, 1830–1870: A Brief History with Documents* (New York: Bedford/St. Martins, 2000); Nancy A. Hewitt, *Women's Activism and Social Change: Rochester, New York, 1822–1872* (Ithaca: Cornell University Press, 1984); Anne Firor Scott, *Natural Allies: Women's Associations in Amer-ican Society* (Urbana: University of Illinois Press, 1991); Kathleen D, McCarthy, ed., *Lady Boun-tiful Revisited: Women, Philanthropy and Power* (New Brunswick: Rutgers University Press, 1990); Christine Stansell, *City of Women: Sex and Class in New York, 1789–1860* (New York: Al-fred A. Knopf, 1986); Barbara J. Berg, *The Remembered Gate: Origins of American Feminism: The Woman and the City, 1800–1860* (New York: Oxford University Press, 1978); Nancy F. Cott, *The Bonds of Womanhood: "Woman's Sphere" in New England, 1780–1835* (New Haven: Yale University Press, 1977); Cynthia Kierner, *Beyond the Household: Women's Place in the Early South, 1700–1835* (Ithaca: Cornell University Press, 1998); Elizabeth R. Varon, *We Mean to Be Counted: White Women and Politics in Antebellum Virginia* (Chapel Hill: University of North Carolina Press, 1998); Suzanne Lebsock, *The Free Women of Petersburg: Status and Culture in a Southern Town, 1784–1860* (New York: W. W. Norton and Company, 1984); Jane H. Pease and William H. Pease, *Ladies, Women and Wenches: Choice and Constraint in Antebellum Charleston and Boston* (Chapel Hill: University of North Carolina Press, 1991); Darlene Clark Hine and Kathleen Thompson, *A Shining Thread of Hope: The History of Black Women in America* (New York: Broadway Books, 1998); Ellen Carol DuBois, *Feminism and Suffrage: The Emergence of an Independent Women's Movement in America, 1848–1869* (Ithaca: Cornell University Press, 1978); Thomas Dublin, *Women at Work: The Transformation of Work and Community in Low-ell, Massachusetts, 1826–1860* (New York: Columbia University Press, 1979). On the Civil War and the United States Sanitary Commission: Jeanie Attie, *Patriotic Toil: Northern Women and the American Civil War* (Ithaca: Cornell University Press, 1998); Judith Ann Giesberg, *Civil War Sisterhood: The U.S. Sanitary Commission and Women's Politics in Transition* (Boston: North-eastern University Press, 2000); Drew Gilpin Faust, *Mothers of Invention: Women of the Slave-holding South in the American Civil War* (Chapel Hill: University of North Carolina Press, 1996); Robert Bremner, *The Public Good: Philanthropy and Welfare in the Civil War Era* (New York: Alfred A. Knopf, 1980); Elizabeth D. Leonard, *Yankee Women: Gender Battles in the Civil War* (New York: W. W. Norton and Co. 1994); Catherine Clinton and Nina Silber, eds. *Divided Houses: Gender and the Civil War* (New York: Oxford University Press, 1992). See also individual bi-ographies of donors and social reformers, cited elsewhere in the text and in the bibliography.

6. Lowell Female Labor Reform Association, "Factory Tract #1: Factory Life as It Is," and "Preamble and Constitution of the Lowell Female Labor Reform Association," in *The Factory Girls*, edited by Philip S. Foner (Urbana: University of Illinois Press, 1977), 132. Other examples ranged from colonization (see, for example, the American Colonization Society, First Annual Report [1818], 7) to manumission societies (American Convention for Promoting the Abolition of Slavery, and Improving the Condition of the African Race, Minutes of the Twenty-first Biennial Convention [1829], 38, 39; "Address of the Manumission Society of North Carolina," ibid., appendix, 65). The first reference equating philanthropy with monetary donations rather than a general benevolence toward and willingness to benefit others in the 1909 edition of the Oxford English Dictionary is an 1875 quotation to the effect that "a great philanthropist has astonished the world by giving it large sums of money during his lifetime." James A. H. Murray, ed., *A New English Dictionary on Historical Principles* (Oxford: Clarendon Press, 1909), s.v. "philanthropist." Nor was the widespread use of the term a uniquely American phenomenon. Even England's Friendly Societies, institutions that social historians such as E. P. Thompson regarded as indices of nascent working-class consciousness, cloaked their efforts in the idiom of philanthropy, coupling "the language of Christian charity" with "the slumbering image of 'brotherhood.'" E. P. Thompson, *The Making of the English Working Class* (1963; reprint, New York: Vintage Books, 1966): 422. Interestingly, Robert Bremner included both giving and voluntarism in his classic history, *American Philanthropy*.

7. In response to Reaganomics, a few researchers began to probe more deeply into these relationships in the mid-1980s and found that government was often the major source of funding for ostensibly private nonprofit organizations, followed by fees for service and *then* private donations, patterns that accelerated with the Great Society programs of the 1960s. Most of these works focused on contemporary health, education, and welfare institutions, providing valuable perspectives for thinking about the mesh between "public" and "private" services, while overlooking the social, political, and economic impact of philanthropy within a highly heterogeneous, multicultural population. See, for example, Lester M. Salamon, *Partners in Public Service: Government-Nonprofit Relations in the Modern Welfare State* (Baltimore: Johns Hopkins University Press, 1995), and his book *America's Nonprofit Sector*.

8. Robert D. Putnam, *Making Democracy Work: Civic Traditions in Modern Italy* (Princeton University Press, 1993), and *Bowling Alone: The Collapse and Revival of American Community* (New York: Simon and Schuster, 2000).

9. Martin Heidegger quoted in Thomas Bender, "Wholes and Parts: The Need for Synthesis in American History," *Journal of American History* 73 (June, 1986): 135. The literature on cultural hegemony and the social construction of reality is immense. Perhaps the best introduction is Edward W. Said, *Orientalism* (New York: Vintage Books, 1979). For an introduction to the use of the concept in an American setting, see T. J. Jackson Lears, "The Concept of Cultural Hegemony: Problems and Possibilities," *American Historical Review* 90, no. 3 (June 1985): 567–93. For a discussion of social capital, see Robert D. Putnam, "The Prosperous Community: Social Capital and Public Life," *American Prospect* 13 (Spring, 1993): 35–42, *Making Democracy Work*, and *Bowling Alone*; and Francis Fukuyama, *Trust: The Social Virtues and the Creation of Prosperity* (New York: Free Press, 1995).

10. Cohen and Arato, *Civil Society and Political Theory*, 7. For an excellent introduction to the contemporary implications of public-private partnerships, see Salamon's *America's Nonprofit Sector* and his *Partners in Public Service*. For the notion of political culture, see Lucien Pye and Sidney Verba, *Political Culture and Political Development* (Princeton: Princeton University Press, 1965); Daniel Walker Howe, *The Political Culture of the American Whigs* (Chicago: Uni-

versity of Chicago Press, 1979); Kathryn Kish Sklar, *Florence Kelley and the Nation's Work: The Rise of Women's Political Culture, 1830–1900* (New Haven: Yale University Press, 1995); and Yellin and Van Horne, *The Abolitionist Sisterhood.*

11. The role of nineteenth-century charities in market activities is just beginning to be explored. See, for example, McCarthy, *Women's Culture*, chap. 3; Ginzberg, *Women and the Work of Benevolence;* and Kathleen Waters Sander, *The Business of Charity: The Woman's Exchange Movement, 1832–1900* (Urbana: University of Illinois Press, 1998). The term "communal capitalism" is drawn from Stephen Innes, *Creating the Commonwealth: The Economic Culture of Puritan New England* (New York: W. W. Norton, 1995). Conversely, the literature on the market revolution and the transition to capitalism is extensive. See, among others, Charles Sellers, *The Market Revolution: Jacksonian America, 1815–1846* (New York: Oxford University Press, 1991); Christopher Clark, *The Roots of Rural Capitalism: Western Massachusetts, 1780–1860* (Ithaca: Cornell University Press, 1990); Howard Bodenhorn, "Capital Mobility and Financial Integration in Antebellum America," *Journal of Economic History* 52, no. 3 (September 1992): 585–603; Paul A. Gilje, "The Rise of Capitalism in the Early Republic," *Journal of the Early Republic* 16 (summer 1996): 159–81; Alan Kulikoff, "The Transition to Capitalism in Rural America," *William and Mary Quarterly* 46 (1989): 120–44, and *The Agrarian Origins of American Capitalism* (Charlottesville: University Press of Virginia, 1992); Paul Johnson, *A Shopkeeper's Millennium: Society and Revivals in Rochester, New York, 1815–1837* (New York: Hill and Wang, 1978); Winifred Rothenberg, "The Emergence of a Capital Market in Rural Massachusetts, 1730–1830," *Journal of Economic History* 45, n. 4 (December 1985): 781–808. Throughout the text, I have tried to convert nineteenth-century "current" dollars into "constant" 2000 dollars to indicate the approximate value of these sums today. These figures should be used with care but have been added to give a reasonable sense of the present value for purposes of comparison. I am deeply indebted to the chairman of the Economics Department of the Graduate Center, City University of New York, Professor Thom Thurston, for his help in determining the formula for changing current to constant dollars. The multipliers are 9.1 for 1810, 11.3 for 1820, 13.1 for 1830, 12.6 for 1840, 14.2 for 1850, and 12.8 for 1860. For dates that fall at mid-decade, I have averaged the decennial markers, indicating this by the use of the @ sign before the parenthetically noted amounts. However, these estimates are conservative, since there are a variety of ways in which to calculate the value of constant dollars. Samuel H. Williamson provides a range of potential yardsticks. According to his estimates, the multiplier used to determine the value of a 2002 dollar in 1830 could range from 19 for the consumer price index to 436 for gross domestic product per capita. "What Is the Relative Value?" Economic History Services, April 23, 2002. http//www.eh.net/hmit/compare/.

12. For a recent discussion of the notion of Jacksonian democracy, see Glenn C. Altschuler and Stuart M. Blumin, "Limits of Political Engagement in Antebellum America: A New Look at the Golden Age of Participatory Democracy," *Journal of American History* 84, no. 3 (December, 1997): 855–85.

Chapter One

1. Joseph J. Ellis, *American Sphinx: The Character of Thomas Jefferson* (New York: Vintage Books, 1998), 63. For interesting commentaries on the declaration, see Gary Wills, *Inventing America: Jefferson's Declaration of Independence* (New York: Vintage Books, 1979); and Pauline Maier, *American Scripture: Making the Declaration of Independence* (New York: Alfred A. Knopf, 1997).

2. W. K. Jordan, *Philanthropy in England, 1480–1660: A Study of the Changing Pattern of English Social Aspirations* (London: George Allen and Unwin, 1959); David Owen, *English Philanthropy, 1660–1960* (Cambridge, Mass.: Harvard University Press, Belknap Press, 1964).

3. Cotton Mather, *Bonifacious: An Essay upon the Good* (1710; reprint, Cambridge, Mass.: Harvard University Press, Belknap Press, 1955), 13, 17, 25, 23.

4. John C. Van Horne, "Collective Benevolence and the Common Good in Franklin's Philanthropy," in *Reappraising Benjamin Franklin: A Bicentennial Perspective,* ed. J. A. Leo Lemay (Newark: University of Delaware Press, 1993), 425; Esmond Wright, *Franklin of Philadelphia* (Cambridge, Mass.: Harvard University Press, Belknap Press, 1986), 6. See also Carl Van Doren, *Benjamin Franklin* (New York: Viking Press, 1938); and H. W. Brands, *The First American: The Life and Times of Benjamin Franklin* (New York: Doubleday, 2000).

5. Mather, *Bonifacious,* 25; Daniel Defoe, "An Essay upon Projects," in *Selected Poetry and Prose of Daniel Defoe,* ed. Michael F. Shugrue (1697; reprint, New York: Holt, Rinehart and Winston, 1968), 6.

6. The literature on republicanism is immense. For an overview of the historiographical nuances of the concept of republicanism, see Daniel T. Rodgers, "Republicanism: The Career of a Concept," *Journal of American History* 79, no. 1 (June 1992): 11–38. Rodgers divides the interpretations of eighteenth-century republicanism into two camps. Gordon S. Wood, in *The Creation of the American Republic: 1776–1787* (New York: W. W. Norton and Co., 1969), defines republicanism as "the sacrifice of individual interests to the greater good of the whole." Rodgers contrasts Wood's interpretation with the one that J. G. A. Pocock puts forward in his essays and in *The Machiavellian Moment* (Princeton: Princeton University Press, 1975). As Rodgers explains, "The heart of Wood's republicanism was the preeminence of the public good; not *public,* but *civic* was the key term in Pocock's construct. It was on the field of civic action, if anywhere, that corruption might be withstood. 'Virtue,' which Wood read as self-denial, Pockock read as public self-activity—in which 'personality,' undergirded by sufficient property to give it independence, threw itself (for its own 'perfection' and the survival of the republic) into citizenship, patriotism, and civic life" (18, 19). Both interpretations, however, stressed simplicity, patriotism, integrity, valor, and a love of justice and liberty. See also Bernard Bailyn, *The Ideological Origins of the American Revolution* (Cambridge, Mass.: Harvard University Press, 1967); J. G. A. Pocock, "Virtue and Commerce in the Eighteenth Century," *Journal of Interdisciplinary History* 3 (summer 1972): 119–34; Joyce Appleby, *Capitalism and a New Social Order: The Republican Vision of the 1790s* (New York: New York University Press, 1984), "Republicanism and Ideology," *American Quarterly* 37 (1985): 461–73, and "Republicanism in Old and New Contexts," *William and Mary Quarterly* 43 (1986): 20–34; Robert E. Shalhope, "Republicanism and Early American Historiography," *William and Mary Quarterly* 39, no. 2 (1982): 334–56; and Drew R. McCoy, *The Elusive Republic: A Political Economy in Jeffersonian America* (Chapel Hill: University of North Carolina Press, 1980). For a discussion of changing notions of manhood, see Anthony E. Rotundo, *American Manhood: Transformations in Masculinity from the Revolution to the Modern Era* (New York: Basic Books, 1993).

7. Gordon S. Wood, *The Radicalism of the American Revolution* (1991; reprint, New York: Vintage Books, 1993), 107. There may have been a few charity schools as well. See Christine Leigh Heyrman, "The Fashion among More Superior People: Charity and Social Change in Provincial New England," *American Quarterly* 34, no. 2 (summer 1982): 107–24, and her dissertation, "A Model of Christian Charity: The Rich and Poor in New England, 1630–1730" (Ph.D. diss., Yale University, 1977).

8. Van Doren, *Benjamin Franklin*, 20. For the "Silence Do-Good Letters," see *Benjamin Franklin: Writings*, ed. J. A. Leo Lemay (New York: Library of America, 1987), 5–44.

9. *The Papers of Benjamin Franklin*, ed. Leonard W. Labaree and Whitfield Bell, Jr. (New Haven: Yale University Press, 1959), 1:257; Van Doren, *Benjamin Franklin*, 78. See also Benjamin Franklin, *The Autobiography of Benjamin Franklin* (1793; reprint, New Haven: Yale University Press, 1964).

10. Michael Zuckerman, "The Selling of the Self: from Franklin to Barnum," in *Benjamin Franklin, Jonathan Edwards and the Representation of American Culture*, ed. Barbara Oberg and Harry S. Stout (New York: Oxford University Press, 1993), 157. For a discussion of social capital, see Robert D. Putnam, "The Prosperous Community: Social Capital and Public Life," *American Prospect* 13 (spring 1993): 35–42; Robert D. Putnam, *Making Democracy Work: Civic Traditions in Modern Italy* (Princeton: Princeton University Press, 1993); Francis Fukuyama, *Trust: The Social Virtues and the Creation of Prosperity* (New York: Free Press, 1995); and Robert D. Putnam, *Bowling Alone: The Collapse and Revival of American Community* (New York: Simon and Schuster, 2000). For Franklin's description of the Junto's role in reorganizing the night watch and the creation of the fire brigade, see his *Autobiography* in *Benjamin Franklin: Writings*, 1404–5.

11. Benjamin Franklin, "Arator" (November 29, 1766), in *The Papers of Franklin*, ed. Leonard Labaree, Helen Boatfield, and James Houston (New Haven: Yale University Press, 1969), 13:515; Gary B. Nash, "Poverty and Poor Relief in Pre-revolutionary Philadelphia," *William and Mary Quarterly* 33 (1976):18; Howell W. Williams, "Benjamin Franklin and the Poor Laws," *Social Service Review* 18 (1944): 11. Franklin's attitudes can also be traced in his essay "On the Laboring Poor," written in 1768. The poor laws of the 1820s and 1830s are discussed more fully in chapter 8. The Philadelphia statesman has been roundly criticized by some scholars for his insensitivity to the plight of the city's poor, depicting his sponsorship of the Pennsylvania Hospital as little more than a ploy to curb rising poor rates. Although his attitudes may strike the modern reader as unduly callous, many thinkers depicted the poor and property-less as ready tinder for demagogues—potentially destructive forces that could ultimately undermine society if left unchecked. Throughout his long career, Franklin remained an unwavering apostle of the gospel of self-help.

12. *The Papers of Benjamin Franklin*, 5:287; Van Doren, *Benjamin Franklin*, 195. See also William Williams, "The 'Industrious Poor' and the Founding of the Pennsylvania Hospital," *Pennsylvania Magazine of History and Biography* 97, no. 4 (October 1973): 431–43.

13. Franklin, *Autobiography*, in *Benjamin Franklin: Writings*, 1420; John S. Whitehead, *The Separation of College and State: Columbia, Dartmouth, Harvard and Yale, 1776–1876* (New Haven: Yale University Press, 1973), 11–14.

14. Howard Miller, *The Legal Foundations of American Philanthropy, 1776–1844* (Madison: State Historical Society of Wisconsin, 1961), xi; Nash, "Poverty and Poor Relief," 13, 16. Private asylums also relied on income generation to reduce the costs of care. For example, Philadelphia's Quakers built an almshouse for the Quaker poor. Here, too, the emphasis was on self-support, with inmates expected to teach school or make salable items in return for their care. Recent scholarship suggests that these practices may have been viewed as a reciprocal relationship between the inmates and the asylums, rather than a form of exploitation. For a fuller discussion of this idea, see Peregrine Horden and Richard Smith, eds., *The Locus of Care: Families, Communities, Institutions and the Provision of Welfare since Antiquity* (London: Routledge, 1998). Quaker philanthropy is discussed in Sidney V. James, *A People among Peoples: Quaker Benevolence in Eighteenth Century America* (Cambridge, Mass.: Harvard University Press,

1963). For a fuller discussion of colonial poor relief practices, see Carl Bridenbaugh, *Cities in the Wilderness, 1652–1742* (New York: Ronald Press Co., 1938), and *Cities in Revolt: Urban Life in America, 1743–1776* (New York: Alfred A. Knopf, 1955); Gary B. Nash, *The Urban Crucible: Social Change, Political Consciousness and the Origins of the American Revolution* (Cambridge, Mass.: Harvard University Press, 1979); John K. Alexander, *Render Them Submissive: Responses to Poverty in Philadelphia, 1760–1800* (Amherst: University of Massachusetts Press, 1980); Robert E. Cray, Jr., *Paupers and Poor Relief in New York City and Its Rural Environs, 1700–1830* (Philadelphia: Temple University Press, 1988); and Stephen Wiberly, "Four Cities: Public Poor Relief in Urban America, 1700–1775" (Ph.D. diss., Yale University, 1975).

15. Pauline Maier, "The Revolutionary Origins of the American Corporation," *William and Mary Quarterly*, 3d ser., 50, no. 1 (January 1993): 55; Oscar and Mary Flug Handlin, *Commonwealth: A Study of the Role of the Government in the American Economy: Massachusetts, 1774–1861* (1947; reprint, Cambridge, Mass.: Harvard University Press, 1969), 98.

16. Frank Lambert, *"Pedlar in Divinity": George Whitefield and the Transatlantic Revivals, 1737–1745* (Princeton University Press, 1994), 13, 128, and "'Pedlar in Divinity': George Whitefield and the Great Awakening, 1737–1745," *Journal of American History* 77, no. 3 (December 1990): 834, 836. This section draws heavily on Lambert's essays, including his "Subscribing for Profits and Piety: The Friendship of Benjamin Franklin and George Whitefield," *William and Mary Quarterly* 3d ser., 50, no. 3 (July 1993): 529–54.

17. Lambert, *Pedlar*, 112.

18. For the history of Bethesda and Whitefield's attitudes about slavery, see Lambert, *Pedlar*, 60, 204, and passim. According to Lambert, the introduction of slavery into Georgia was Whitefield's "long held dream" (198). See also Neil J. O'Connell, "George Whitefield and Bethesda Orphan-House," *Georgia Historical Quarterly* 54 (1970): 41–62; Boyd Stanley Schlenther, "'To Convert the Poor People in America': Bethesda Orphanage and the Thwarted Zeal of the Countess of Huntingdon," *Georgia Historical Quarterly* 77, no. 2 (summer 1994): 225–56; Winthrop D. Jordan, *White over Black: American Attitudes toward the Negro, 1550–1812* (1968; reprint, New York: W. W. Norton, 1977), 214. Blacks were banned from Georgia until 1750. See Winthrop D. Jordan, White over Black, 262–65. For Franklin's description of Whitefield's fundraising skills, see his *Autobiography* in Benjamin Franklin: Writings, 1407–8.

19. Louis P. Masur, " Age of the First Person Singular: The Vocabulary of the Self in New England, 1780–1850," *Journal of American Studies* 25 (1991): 197; Kimberly K. Smith, *The Dominion of Voice: Riot, Reason, and Romance in Antebellum Politics* (Lawrence: University Press of Kansas, 1999), 39.

20. Thomas Jefferson, "A Bill Establishing Religious Freedom," in *Public and Private Papers* (New York: Vintage Books, Library of America,1990), 20, 21. For an interesting discussion of the immediate impact of Jefferson's legislation, see Thomas E. Buckley, "Evangelicals Triumphant: The Baptists' Assault on the Virginia Glebes, 1786–1801," *William and Mary Quarterly*, 3d ser., 45, no. 1 (January 1988): 33–69. For Jefferson's religious views, see Charles B. Sanford, *The Religious Life of Thomas Jefferson* (Charlottesville: University Press of Virginia, 1984); and Edwin S. Gaustad, *Sworn on the Altar of God: A Religious Biography of Thomas Jefferson* (Grand Rapids: William B. Eerdmans Publishing Company, 1996). The phrase "wall of separation" is Jefferson's. See his message to "Mssrs Nehemiah Dodge and Others, a Committee of the Danbury Baptist Association in the State of Connecticut" (January 1, 1802), in his *Public and Private Papers*, 184.

21. Alexander Hamilton, James Madison, and John Jay, *The Federalist Papers* (1787–88; reprint, New York: New American Library), 78. As David Hammack points out, "Madison did

not use the term voluntary association, but his argument that many small interests would check one another provided the basis for a political theory that makes voluntary associations central to American politics." *Making the Nonprofit Sector in the United States: A Reader* (Bloomington: Indiana University Press, 1998), 88.

22. James Madison, speech in the Virginia Convention (June 12, 1788), in *The Writings of James Madison,* ed. Gaillard Hunt (G. P. Putnam's Sons, 1904), 5:176. Irving Brant, "Madison: On the Separation of Church and State," *William and Mary Quarterly* 3d ser., 8, no. 1 (January 1951): 12. See also Robert S. Alley, ed., *James Madison on Religious Liberty* (Buffalo: Prometheus Books, 1985).

23. T. H. Breen, "Narrative of Commercial Life: Consumption, Ideology and Community on the Eve of the American Revolution," *William and Mary Quarterly,* 3d ser., 50, no. 3 (July 1993): 501. For the early history of American mobs, see Pauline Maier, *From Resistance to Revolution: Colonial Radicals and the Development of American Opposition to Britain, 1765–1776* (New York: Alfred A. Knopf, 1972).

24. "Constitution of the Democratic Society in the County of Addison [Vermont]" (September 9, 1794), in *The Democratic-Republican Societies, 1790–1800: A Documentary Sourcebook of Constitutions, Declarations, Addresses, Resolutions and Toasts,* ed. Philip S. Foner (Westport: Greenwood Press, 1976), 276–77. Members defended their activities as the bedrock of democracy. For interesting discussions of these organizations and of the backgrounds of the participants, see Matthew Schoenbachler, "Republicanism in the Age of Democratic Revolution: The Democratic-Republican Societies of the 1790s," *Journal of the Early Republic* 18 (spring 1998): 237–61; Eugene Perry Link, *Democratic-Republican Societies, 1790–1800* (New York: Columbia University Press, 1942); and Saul Cornell, *The Other Founders: Anti-Federalism and the Dissenting Tradition in America, 1788–1828* (Chapel Hill: University of North Carolina Press, 1999), 195–99.

25. Thomas Slaughter, *The Whiskey Rebellion: Frontier Epilogue to the American Revolution* (New York: Oxford University Press, 1986).

26. George Washington, letter to the secretary of state (October 16, 1794), and sixth annual address to Congress (October 19, 1794), in *The Writings of George Washington from the Original Manuscript Sources,* ed. John C. Fitzpatrick (Washington, D.C.: United States Government Printing Office, 1940), 34:2, 29; Stanley Elkins and Eric McKitrick, *The Age of Federalism: The Early American Republic, 1788–1800* (New York: Oxford University Press, 1993), 484; Slaughter, *The Whiskey Rebellion,* 221; Thomas Jefferson, letter to James Madison (December 28, 1794), in *The Portable Thomas Jefferson,* ed. Merrill D. Peterson (New York: Penguin Books, 1975), 467–68. It should also be noted that Jefferson and Madison also defended these organizations because they sympathized with their political views.

27. Masur, "Age of First Person Singular," 197, 196; Madison quoted in Foner, *The Democratic-Republican Societies,* 32.

28. Franklin, "Plan for Improving the Condition of Free Blacks," in *Benjamin Franklin: Writings,* 1156–57. For a highly critical view of post-Revolutionary white-controlled manumission and abolition societies, see John L. Rury, "Philanthropy, Self-Help, and Social Control: The New York Manumission Society," *Phylon* 46, no. 3 (1985): 231–41.

29. "Petition to End the Slave Trade," February 12, 1790, *Annals of Congress* (Washington, D.C.: United States Government) 2:1198. See also Richard S. Newman, "Prelude to the Gag Rule: Southern Reaction to Antislavery Petitions in the First Federal Congress," *Journal of the Early Republic* 16 (winter 1996): 571–99.

30. *Annals of Congress,* 2:1187, 1188; William C. di Giacomantonio, " 'For the Gratification

of a Volunteering Society': Antislavery and Pressure Group Politics in the First Federal Congress," *Journal of the Early Republic* 15 (summer 1995): 183.

31. Benjamin Franklin, "Sidi Mehemet Ibrahim on the Slave Trade," *Federal Gazette*, March 25, 1790, reprinted in *Benjamin Franklin: Writings*, 1160. Franklin penned his satire in an era when American ships in the Mediterranean were plagued by North African Barbary pirates, including Algerians.

Chapter Two

1. "Republican motherhood" is discussed in Linda K. Kerber, *Women of the Republic: Intellect and Ideology in Revolutionary America* (Chapel Hill: University of North Carolina Press, 1980). See also Mary Beth Norton, *Liberty's Daughters: The Revolutionary Experience of American Women, 1750–1800* (Boston: Little, Brown and Co., 1980); Rosemarie Zagarri, "Morals, Manners, and the Republican Mother," *American Quarterly* 44, no. 2 (June 1992):192–215; and Linda K. Kerber, "The Republican Mother: Women and the Enlightenment—an Historical Perspective," *American Quarterly* 28 (summer 1976): 187–205.

2. For a fuller discussion of the "ladies associations," see Norton, *Liberty's Daughters.*

3. Parrish quoted in Bruce Allen Dorsey, "City of Brotherly Love: Religion, Benevolence, Gender and Reform in Philadelphia, 1780–1844" (Ph.D. diss., Brown University, 1993), 69, 135; Female Hospitable Society, "Reports . . . since Its Commencement in 1808" (Philadelphia, Lydia R. Bailey, 1831), 2; Christine Stansell, *City of Women: Sex and Class in New York, 1789–1860* (New York: Alfred A. Knopf, 1986). For the history of white women's charities in this era, see Lori Ginzberg, *Women and the Work of Benevolence: Morality, Politics, and Class in the Nineteenth Century United States* (New Haven: Yale University Press, 1990); Stansell, *City of Women*; Barbara J. Berg, *The Remembered Gate: Origins of American Feminism: The Woman and the City, 1800–1860* (New York: Oxford University Press, 1978); Anne Boylan, "Timid Girls, Venerable Widows and Dignified Matrons: Life Cycle Patterns among Organized Women in New York and Boston, 1797–1840," *American Quarterly* 38 (winter 1986): 779–97, and "Women in Groups: An Analysis of Women's Benevolent Organizations in New York and Boston, 1797–1840," *Journal of American History* 71, no. 3 (December 1984): 497–515; Susan Porter Benson, "Business Heads and Sympathizing Hearts: Women and the Providence Employment Society," *Journal of Social History* 71 (1984): 497–524; Dorothy G. Becker, "Isabella Graham and Joanna Bethune: Trailblazers of Organized Women's Benevolence," *Social Service Review* 61, no. 2 (June 1987): 319–33; Rosemary Abend, "Constant Samaritans: Quaker Philanthropy in Philadelphia, 1680–1799" (Ph.D. diss., University of California, Los Angeles, 1988); Susan Lynne Porter, "The Benevolent Asylum—Image and Reality: The Care and Training of Female Orphans in Boston, 1800–1840" (Ph.D. diss., Boston University, 1984); Dorsey, "City of Brotherly Love"; Priscilla Ferguson Clement, "The Response to Need, Welfare and Poverty in Philadelphia" (Ph.D. diss., University of Pennsylvania, 1977), and "Nineteenth Century Welfare Policy, Programs, and Poor Women: Philadelphia as a Case Study," *Feminist Studies* 18, no. 1 (spring 1992): 35–58, and *Welfare and the Poor in the Nineteenth Century City: Philadelphia, 1800–1854* (Rutherford, N.J.: Fairleigh Dickinson University Press, 1985); Vincent Francis Bonelli, "The Response of Public and Private Philanthropy to the Panic of 1819 in New York City" (Ph.D. diss., Fordham University, 1976); Margaret Morris Haviland, "Beyond Women's Sphere: Young Quaker Women and the Veil of Charity in Philadelphia, 1790–1810," *William and Mary Quarterly*, 3d ser., 51, no. 3 (July 1994): 419–46; Anne Firor Scott, *Natural Allies: Women's Associations in American Society* (Urbana: University of Illinois Press, 1991); Cynthia

Kierner, *Beyond the Household: Women's Place in the Early South, 1700–1835* (Ithaca: Cornell University Press, 1998); Elizabeth R. Varon, *We Mean to Be Counted: White Women and Politics in Antebellum Virginia* (Chapel Hill: University of North Carolina Press, 1998); and Suzanne Lebsock, *The Free Women of Petersburg: Status and Culture in a Southern Town, 1784–1860* (New York: W. W. Norton and Co., 1984).

4. Mary Ryan, *Cradle of the Middle Class: The Family in Oneida County, New York, 1790–1865* (New York: Cambridge University Press, 1981), 77; Nancy F. Cott, *The Bonds of Womanhood: "Woman's Sphere" in New England, 1780–1835* (New Haven: Yale University Press, 1977). Between 1792 and 1845, the percentage of female congregants in Philadelphia's Protestant churches ranged between 64.5% and 81.3%. Dorsey, "City of Brotherly Love," 209. Donald G. Mathews also estimates that "southern women outnumbered men in the churches (65:35), though men outnumbered women in the general population (51.5:48.5)" by 1792. During the antebellum era as well, "women comprised a majority of church members" in Southern congregations, although "they were not equal to men in terms of power, even though they provided indispensable support to the clergy." *Religion in the Old South* (Chicago: University of Chicago Press, 1977), 47, 102.

5. Rebecca Larson, *Daughters of Light: Quaker Women Preaching and Prophesying in the Colonies and Abroad, 1700–1775* (New York: Alfred A. Knopf, 1999), 19. For Quaker philanthropy more generally, see Sidney V. James, *A People among Peoples: Quaker Benevolence in Eighteenth Century America* (Cambridge: Harvard University Press, 1963); Abend, "Constant Samaritans"; and Haviland, "Beyond Women's Sphere."

6. For the notion of female philanthropy as parallel to that of men, see Kathleen D. McCarthy, "Parallel Power Structures: Women and the Voluntary Sphere," in *Lady Bountiful Revisited: Women, Philanthropy and Power*, ed. Kathleen D. McCarthy (New Brunswick: Rutgers University Press, 1990), 1–31. Initially, charitable and philanthropic models were spread primarily through emigration and correspondence, as well as some publications. By the second decade of the nineteenth century, the religious press was beginning to play an active role as well, reporting on charitable and reform activities around the world. For example, the Congregationalists' *Recorder* regularly reported on international activities, beginning with some of the issues in its first year, 1816. Some of the ventures covered included the London Society for Promoting Christianity among the Jews, which was founded in 1808 under the patronage of the Duke of Kent, the Royal Danish Missionary College, and Bible societies in St. Petersburg (founded under the patronage of Prince Galitzen, with additional auxiliaries in Moscow and Riga), the Netherlands, Copenhagen, and England, among others. See, for example, the journal's second edition, published on January 10, 1816.

7. Society for the Relief of Poor Widows with Small Children (hereafter cited as SRPW), Annual Report (New York, 1800), 12; Isabella Graham, letter to Mrs. Walker, 1798, in *The Power of Faith: Exemplified in the Life and Writings of Mrs. Isabella Graham of New York*, by Joanna Bethune (New York: J. Seymour, 1816), 234. The Widows' Society is discussed briefly in Berg, *The Remembered Gate*; and Becker, "Isabella Graham and Joanna Bethune." See also Boylan, "Timid Girls, Venerable Widows and Dignified Matrons," and "Women in Groups."

8. Barbara L. Bellows, *Benevolence among Slaveholders: Assisting the Poor in Charleston, 1670–1860* (Baton Rouge: Louisiana State University Press, 1993), 121; Jane H. Pease and William H. Pease, *Ladies, Women and Wenches: Choice and Constraint in Antebellum Charleston and Boston* (Chapel Hill: University of North Carolina Press, 1991), 124. Although Elizabeth Fox-Genovese argues in *Within the Plantation Household: Black and White Women of the Old South* (Chapel Hill: University of North Carolina Press, 1988) that voluntary associations were

primarily the work of Northern women, there is a fair amount of evidence to challenge this idea. See, for example, Lebsock, *The Free Women of Petersburg;* Varon, *We Mean to Be Counted;* and Kierner's excellent book *Beyond the Household,* particularly chap. 6.

9. Graham, letter to Mrs. Walker, 1798, 224.

10. Clement, "Nineteenth Century Welfare Policy," 36; Clement, "The Response to Need, Welfare and Poverty in Philadelphia," 64. See also Clement's *Welfare and the Poor in the Nineteenth Century City.*

11. Female Association of Philadelphia for the Relief of Women and Children in Reduced Circumstances (hereafter cited as FAPRWC), Annual Report (Philadelphia, 1803), 13.

12. Female Hospitable Society, "The Nature and Design of the Hospitable Society" (Philadelphia, 1803), 13. Working-class organizations also imposed moral requirements for membership and aid, patterns which are discussed in n. 42 below.

13. Joyce Appleby, "Republicanism in Old and New Contexts," *William and Mary Quarterly* 43 (1986): 20; Rogers M. Smith, *Civic Ideals: Conflicting Visions of Citizenship in U.S. History* (New Haven: Yale University Press, 1997), 112. "As to your extraordinary Code of Laws, I cannot but laugh," John Adams wrote to Abigail. "Depend upon it, We know better than to repeal our Masculine systems," since to do so "would compleatly subject Us to the Despotism of the Petticoat." John Adams, letter to Abigail Adams, April 14, 1776, in *The Adams Family Papers,* ed. L. H. Butterfield, Wendell Garrtt, and Marjorie Sprague (Cambridge, Mass.: Harvard University Press, Belknap Press, 1963), 1:382.

14. Abigail Adams, letter to John Adams, May 7, 1776, in *The Adams Family Papers,* 1:402.

15. Linda Kerber, "The Republican Ideology of the Revolutionary Generation," *American Quarterly* 37, no. 4 (fall 1985): 484.

16. Abigail Adams, quoted in Joan Hoff, *Law, Gender and Injustice: A Legal History of U.S. Women* (New York: New York University Press, 1991), 63; SRPW, Annual Report (New York, 1800), 15, 14, 19. For a graphic description of the yellow fever epidemic in Philadelphia, see Thomas Slaughter, *The Whiskey Rebellion: Frontier Epilogue to the American Revolution* (New York: Oxford University Press, 1986), 143–44; and John Harvey Powell, *Bring Out Your Dead: The Great Plague of Yellow Fever in Philadelphia in 1793* (Philadelphia: University of Pennsylvania Press, 1949). The issue of female valor would continue to surface in discussions of citizenship over the first half of the nineteenth century. See Nancy Isenberg, *Sex and Citizenship in Antebellum America* (Chapel Hill: University of North Carolina Press, 1998), chap. 5.

17. Gordon S. Wood, *The Radicalism of the American Revolution* (New York: Vintage Books, 1993), 104. Wood is referring to men, rather than women, in this passage because, as he explains, "To be completely virtuous citizens men—never women, because it was assumed they were never independent—had to be free from dependence and from the petty interests of the market." The term "moral capitalism" is derived from Stephen Innes, *Creating the Commonwealth: The Economic Culture of Puritan New England* (New York: W. W. Norton, 1995).

18. Joyce Appleby, "Republicanism and Ideology," *American Quarterly* 37, no. 4 (fall 1985): 465; Pauline Maier, "The Revolutionary Origins of the American Corporation," *William and Mary Quarterly,* 3d ser., 50, no. 1 (January 1993): 83. As Eric Foner explains, "To John Adams, this egalitarian upheaval, including his wife's claim to political freedom, was an affront to the natural order of things. . . . Property, and property alone, meant independence; those without it had 'no judgment of their own.'" *The Story of American Freedom* (New York: W. W. Norton and Co., 1998), 17–18.

19. Maier, "The Revolutionary Origins," 54–55; Kerber, *Women of the Republic,* 287. See also Ruth Bogin, "Petitioning and the New Moral Economy of Post-revolutionary America,"

American Quarterly, 3d ser., 45, no. 3 (July 1988): 391–425. Lori Ginzberg also discusses the importance of charters for women's groups in *Women and the Work of Benevolence*, 48–53.

20. Kerber, *Women of the Republic*, 41.

21. Thomas Jefferson, "Opinion on the Constitutionality of a National Bank," February 15, 1791, in *Public and Private Papers* (New York: Vintage Books, Library of America, 1990), 90.

22. Isabella Graham, "Address on Opening a Charity School for Poor Children" (for SRPW), in Bethune, *The Power of Faith* (1817 edition), 382.

23. Lebsock, *The Free Women of Petersburg*, 200; Boston Female Asylum, Annual Report (Boston, 1810), 9. For the history of the Boston Asylum, see Porter, "The Benevolent Asylum."

24. Curtius quoted in Conrad Edick Wright, *The Transformation of Charity in Postrevolutionary New England* (Boston: Northeastern University Press, 1992), 113–14; Hannah Kinney quoted Ginzberg, *Women and the Work of Benevolence*, 53.

25. Wood, *The Radicalism of the American Revolution*, provides many interesting insights into the social reorganization of American society in the aftermath of the Revolution.

26. Wright, *The Transformation of Charity*, 218, 220. For a general discussion of the impact of the Revolution on poverty in Philadelphia, see John K. Alexander, *Render Them Submissive: Responses to Poverty in Philadelphia, 1760–1800* (Amherst: University of Massachusetts Press, 1980); and Billy G. Smith, "Inequality in Late Colonial Philadelphia: A Note on Its Nature and Growth," *William and Mary Quarterly*, 3d ser., 41, no. 4 (October 1984): 629–45, and *The "Lower Sort": Philadelphia's Laboring People, 1750–1800* (Ithaca: Cornell University Press, 1990). For New York, see Raymond A. Mohl, *Poverty in New York: 1783–1825* (New York: Oxford University Press, 1971). The multipliers for changing current to constant dollars are 9.1 for 1810, 11.3 for 1820, 13.1 for 1830, 12.6 for 1840, 14.2 for 1850, 12.8 for 1860.

27. Wood, *The Radicalism of the American Revolution*, 369.

28. SRPW, Annual Report (New York, 1802), 7–8.

29. SRPW, Annual Report (New York, 1800), 11, 19; FAPRWC, Annual Report (Philadelphia, 1803), 12.

30. Joanna H. Mathews, *A Short History of the Orphan Asylum Society in the City of New York, Founded 1806* (New York: Anson D. F. Randolph and Co., 1893), 19–21.

31. Boston Female Asylum, *An Account of the Rise, Progress, and Present State of the Boston Female Asylum* (Boston: Russell and Cutler, 1810). The early and enduring emphasis on publications, including annual reports with detailed financial data, is striking, constituting one of the earmarks of American philanthropy since at least the 1780s. This in turn would have helped to build public trust in these ventures, encouraging people to donate even if they were not directly involved in the operations themselves.

32. SRPW, Annual Report (New York, 1800), 12, 13. For a description of similar efforts in Charleston, see Kierner, *Beyond the Household*, 191. Some groups used their entrepreneurial activities to promote economic reforms, as well as institutional sustainability and public charity. The Seaman's Friend Society in Boston, headed by the celebrated publisher of *Godey's Lady's Book*, Sarah Josepha Hale, managed its own store, selling clothing made under its auspices by impoverished sailors' wives and paying the women who sewed for them up to 50% more than commercial manufacturers. Seaman's Friend Society, Annual Report (Boston, 1835).

33. SRPW, Annual Report (New York, 1813), 21; Bethune, *The Power of Faith*, 121–22; Charles Sellers, *The Market Revolution: Jacksonian America, 1815–1846* (New York: Oxford University Press, 1991), 37. According to Christopher Clark, the Northampton Cotton and Woolen Manufacturing Company, which was founded in 1809 "with capital of $100,000 and as many as fifty employees . . . was for a while one of the largest woollen mills in America," figures that

point out both the scale of Bethune's operation, as well as its relative efficiency, given the modest level of her capitalization. *The Roots of Rural Capitalism: Western Massachusetts, 1780–1860* (Ithaca: Cornell University Press, 1990), 112.

34. Lori Ginzberg, in *Women and the Work of Benevolence,* also notes the role of women's organizations in securing public funding and profits via their nonprofit organizations in chap. 2, "The Business of Benevolence," and chap. 3, "Hot Conflict with the Political Demon." For a discussion of the role of female nonprofit entrepreneurship in creating a national "subterranean economy for the production and sale of goods produced by and for women, see Kathleen D. McCarthy, *Women's Culture: American Philanthropy and Art, 1830–1930* (Chicago: University of Chicago Press, 1991), chap. 3.

35. Boston Female Asylum, Annual Report (Boston, 1810), 26; Ginzberg, *Women and the Work of Benevolence,* 62. For a fuller discussion of the Massachusetts Hospital Life Insurance Company, see chap. 4 as well as Peter Dobkin Hall, "The Model of Boston Charity: A Theory of Charitable Benevolence and Class Development," *Science and Society* 38, no. 4 (1974): 465–77; and Gerald T. White, *A History of the Massachusetts Hospital Life Insurance Company* (Cambridge, Mass.: Harvard University Press, 1955).

36. FAPRWC, Constitution (Philadelphia, 1803), 7; Nathan Miller, *The Enterprise of a Free People: Aspects of Economic Development in New York State during the Canal Period, 1792–1838* (Ithaca: Cornell University Press, 1962), 78; Haviland, "Beyond Women's Sphere," 439; Kierner, *Beyond the Household,* 192. For a discussion of government bonds, see Peter L. Payne and Lance Edwin Davis, *The Savings Bank of Baltimore, 1818–1866: A Historical and Analytical Study* (Baltimore: Johns Hopkins University Press, 1956), 101–5. For a fuller discussion of early female charities in Philadelphia, see Haviland, "Beyond Women's Sphere." Kierner notes that approximately 10% of the Charleston society's holdings were invested in private loans by 1820. The bulk of their funds were invested in state and federal bank stocks.

37. Boston Female Asylum, Annual Report (Boston, 1810), 19.

38. Alexander, *Render Them Submissive,* 133, 122; SRPW, Annual Report (New York, 1812), 8; Kerber, "The Republican Ideology of the Revolutionary Generation," 486. One of the most interesting and nuanced elaborations of the social control argument is Stansell, *City of Women.*

39. SRPW, Annual Report (New York, 1812), 6.

40. SRPW, Annual Report (New York, 1800), 16, 18.

41. Isabella Graham, "Address to Society for the Relief of Poor Widows with Small Children," April 1800, in Bethune, *The Power of Faith* (1817 edition), 373, 374.

42. Isabella Graham, letter, May 3, 1785, in Bethune, *The Power of Faith,* 30. The emphasis on morality was not solely an upper-class concern. Working-class women's mutual aid societies also began to appear in this period, providing a different perspective on female organizational imperatives. The Female Friendly Institution founded in Philadelphia in 1819 offered its members health and burial benefits in return for their dues. Membership was limited to women between eighteen and forty-five, and dues set at 25c per annum in addition to a $1 initiation fee. Members were guaranteed $3 per week for up to five weeks if they were sick, $1 per week for the aged, and $20 to provide a decent burial for their husbands or themselves. Any remaining funds above $150 were to be invested at interest, in an intriguing, but not unique, indicator of working-class concern with capital formation. Like the charities created by middle- and upper-class women, they had guidelines for aid that were strict and clearly etched. Any member accused of immorality would be given an opportunity to confront her accuser, but if deemed guilty she faced expulsion from the society. Similarly, any attempt to defraud the society by feigning sickness would result in termination of membership, and the sick benefits were given only with the

proviso that the member's "incapacity did not proceed from indecent or improper conduct." Applications for aid had to be verified by two witnesses before the money would be released, and funding for the funerals of applicants' husbands was also to be given only if the men had been "of good morals." Female Friendly Institution of the City and Liberties of Philadelphia, Constitution and By-Laws (Philadelphia, 1830), 8. Similarly, the New York Journeyman's Society decreed that "none but persons of good character shall be admitted." Clearly, issues of morality and moralism transcended class lines when material benefits were at stake. New York Journeyman's Shipwright's Society, 1804 Constitution, in *Keepers of the Revolution: New Yorkers at Work in the Early Republic,* ed. Paul A. Gilje and Howard B. Rock (Ithaca: Cornell University Press, 1992), 89. For a discussion of these practices among later working-class temperance advocates, see Ruth M. Alexander, " 'We Are Engaged as a Band of Sisters': Class and Domesticity in the Washingtonian Temperance Movement," *Journal of American History* 75, no. 3 (December 1988): 763–85.

Chapter Three

1. Research on women's philanthropy and the rise of civil society in other countries also underscores the primacy of religion in the eighteenth and nineteenth centuries. For an introduction to this topic, see Kathleen D. McCarthy, ed., *Women, Philanthropy and Civil Society* (Bloomington: Indiana University Press, 2001).

2. Examples of the literature linking Protestant revivals to the rise of social reform include Whitney Cross, *The Burned Over District: A Social and Intellectual History of Enthusiastic Religion in Western New York, 1800–1850* (Ithaca: Cornell University Press, 1950); Paul E. Johnson, *A Shopkeeper's Millennium: Society and Revivals in Rochester, New York, 1815–1837* (New York: Hill and Wang, 1978); Sydney E. Ahlstrom, *A Religious History of the American People* (New Haven: Yale University Press, 1972); and Leo P. Hirrell, *Children of Wrath: New School Calvinism and Antebellum Reform* (Lexington: University of Kentucky Press, 1998). Nathan O. Hatch explored the rise of religious populism and Protestant denominationalism in *The Democratization of American Christianity* (New Haven: Yale University Press, 1989); and Robert H. Abzug examined the impact of religious cosmography on social reform in the second decade of the nineteenth century in *Cosmos Crumbling: American Reform and the Religious Imagination* (New York: Oxford University Press, 1994). Women's historians have also contributed significant works on the relationship of religious revivalism to female reform. See, for example, Nancy A. Hewitt, *Women's Activism and Social Change: Rochester, New York, 1822–1872* (Ithaca: Cornell University Press, 1984); and Mary Ryan, *Cradle of the Middle Class: The Family in Oneida County, New York, 1790–1865* (New York: Cambridge University Press, 1981). None, however, deals with the comparative roles of Protestantism, Judaism, and Catholicism in drawing women into the philanthropic arena and shaping the nature of their participation. An accessible introduction to the history of Protestant philanthropy is Angelo Angelis, "Anglo-American Protestant Philanthropy, 1600 to the Present" (New York: Center for the Study of Philanthropy, Graduate Center, City University of New York, 1997).

3. Johnson, *Shopkeeper's Millennium,* 9, 136–41, cited in Hatch, *The Democratization of American Christianity,* 224–25; Clifford Griffin, *Their Brothers' Keepers: Moral Stewardship in the United States, 1800–1860* (New York: H. Wolff, 1960); John Bodo, *The Protestant Clergy and Public Issues, 1812–1848* (Princeton: Princeton University Press, 1954); Charles I. Foster, *Errand of Mercy: The Evangelical United Front, 1790–1837* (Chapel Hill: University of North Carolina Press, 1960). For an early critique of this approach, see Lois W. Banner, "Religious Benevolence

as Social Control: A Critique of an Interpretation," *Journal of American History* 60 (June 1973): 23–41.

4. Joanna Bethune, *The Power of Faith: Exemplified in the Life and Writings of Mrs. Isabella Graham of New York* (New York: J. Seymour, 1816), 121.

5. Paul Boyer, *Urban Masses and Moral Order in America, 1820–1920* (Cambridge Mass.: Harvard University Press, 1978), 34, 41. Black Sunday schools may have also emerged before the 1830s in the South. According to Elizabeth R. Varon, "During the 1810s and 1820s, the evidence suggests, the Commonwealth [of Virginia] contained scores of Sunday schools for blacks, some run by blacks and others by whites." *We Mean to Be Counted: White Women and Politics in Antebellum Virginia* (Chapel Hill: University of North Carolina Press, 1998), 27. For a detailed discussion of the Sunday school movement, see Anne M. Boylan, *Sunday School: The Formation of an American Institution, 1790–1880* (New Haven: Yale University Press, 1988). Boylan explores the differences between Sunday schools, some of which focused on basic literacy skills, some on catechizing, and some on a mixture of both. She also details the tensions that emerged between the auxiliaries and the American Sunday School Union, including struggles for authority and autonomy between female-headed auxiliaries and classes, and male directors and superintendents. In effect, Sunday schools provided one of many associational venues where contests over the parameters of gender were tested, contested, and refined. I have used the generic term "women" in discussing Sunday school activities because we lack definitive data on the racial and class backgrounds of the women who conducted these classes. The majority of volunteers were doubtless white women of the middling ranks. However, black churches also had Sunday schools, some of which were taught by women, and there is some evidence that working-class women may have given instruction as well. For an interesting discussion of working-class religion that goes against the grain of "the neo-Marxist preoccupation with the formation of social classes and . . . the assumption that religion is generally a conservative and pernicious force" (Hatch, *The Democratization of American Christianity*, 224), see Jama Lazerow, "Rethinking Religion and the Working Class in Antebellum America," *Mid-America* 75, no. 1 (January 1993): 85–104, "Religion and the New England Mill Girl: A New Perspective on an Old Theme," *New England Quarterly* 60 (1987): 429–53, and her book *Religion and the Working Class in Antebellum America* (Washington, D.C.: Smithsonian Institution Press, 1995).

6. Cynthia Kierner, *Beyond the Household: Women's Place in the Early South, 1700–1835* (Ithaca: Cornell University Press, 1998), 184; American Sunday School Union, Annual Report (1826), xii—xiii.

7. Nancy F. Cott, *The Bonds of Womanhood: "Woman's Sphere" in New England, 1780–1835* (New Haven: Yale University Press, 1977), 15; American Sunday School Union, Annual Report (Philadelphia, 1830), 12, and Annual Report (Philadelphia, 1825), 6.

8. Hatch, *The Democratization of American Christianity*, 11.

9. For changing ministerial fortunes, see Donald M. Scott, *From Office to Profession: The New England Ministry, 1750–1850* (Philadelphia: University of Pennsylvania Press, 1978).

10. Suzanne Lebsock, *The Free Women of Petersburg: Status and Culture in a Southern Town, 1784–1860* (New York: W. W. Norton and Co., 1984), 216.

11. Ahlstrom, *A Religious History of the American People*, 422.

12. Kierner, *Beyond the Household*, 6; Max Weber, *The Protestant Ethic and the Spirit of Capitalism* (1920), trans. Talcott Parsons (New York: Charles Scribner's Sons, 1958); Thomas L. Haskell, "Capitalism and the Origins of the Humanitarian Sensibility," parts 1 and 2, *American Historical Review*, 90, no. 2 (April 1985): 339–61; no. 3 (June 1985): 547–66; Thomas Bender, ed., *The Antislavery Debate: Capitalism and Abolitionism as a Problem in Historical Interpreta-*

tion (Berkeley: University of California Press, 1992). According to Kierner, Bible and tract societies were "probably the most widespread form of women's organization in the antebellum south" (194). The ties among philanthropy, the market, and economic development are discussed more fully in chap. 4.

13. James A. Henretta, *The Origins of American Capitalism: Collected Essays* (Boston: Northeastern University Press, 1991), xxxiv; Winifred Rothenberg; "The Emergence of a Capital Market in Rural Massachusetts, 1730–1830," *Journal of Economic History* 45, no. 4 (December 1985): 781–808; Paul A. Gilje, "The Rise of Capitalism in the Early Republic," *Journal of the Early Republic* 16 (summer 1996): 159-81; Alan Kulikoff, "The Transition to Capitalism in Rural America," *William and Mary Quarterly* 46 (1989): 123. In fact, the very concept of capitalism is contested terrain, with neo-Marxists equating it with proletarianization and the commodification of labor, as opposed to others who cast it in terms of efforts to "maximize profits [by] accumulating wealth for investment." In the process, they often run the risk of romanticizing a "noncommercial world we have lost," one in which women, children, slaves, and apprentices were sequestered and often victimized. Alan Kulikoff, *The Agrarian Origins of American Capitalism* (Charlottesville: University Press of Virginia, 1992), 5; Charles Sellers, *The Market Revolution: Jacksonian America, 1815–1846* (New York: Oxford University Press, 1991). See also Christopher Clark, *The Roots of Rural Capitalism: Western Massachusetts, 1780–1860* (Ithaca: Cornell University Press, 1990); Joyce Appleby, "The Popular Sources of American Capitalism," *Studies in American Political Development* 9 (fall 1995): 432–57; and Stephen Innes's excellent discussion of trends in seventeenth-century Massachusetts in *Creating the Commonwealth: The Economic Culture of Puritan New England* (New York: W. W. Norton, 1995).

14. Elizabeth Fox-Genovese, *Within the Plantation Household: Black and White Women of the Old South* (Chapel Hill: University of North Carolina Press, 1988); Jean Friedman, *The Enclosed Garden: Women and Community in the Evangelical South, 1830–1900* (Chapel Hill: University of North Carolina Press, 1985); James Oakes, *The Ruling Race: A History of American Slaveholders* (New York: Vintage Books, 1983), 50. Regional patterns are discussed more fully in chap. 5. Kierner concurs with Friedman's contention about the role of mixed-sex organizations in curbing women's associational autonomy in some areas of the South (*Beyond the Household*, 215). See also Douglas W. Carlson, " 'Drinks He to His Own Undoing': Temperance Ideology in the Deep South," *Journal of the Early Republic* 18 (winter 1998): 682. According to Carlson, although "significant numbers of southern women participated in the temperance movement," they generally did so "as members of mixed societies rather than in separate women's organizations." For example, women constituted 43% of the members of Georgia's 123 temperance groups in 1844 (ibid.). Conversely, the notion that women's voluntary associations were a sectional—and particularly, a Northeastern—phenomenon in the early national and antebellum years has increasingly come under attack. See, for example, Kierner's *Beyond the Household;* and Varon's *We Mean to Be Counted.* Although Stephanie McCurry suggests that few women were active in associations in her book *Masters of Small Worlds: Yeoman Households, Gender Relations, and the Political Culture of the Antebellum South Carolina Low Country* (New York: Oxford University Press, 1995), Kierner dismisses her contention, arguing that "McCurry minimizes both the numbers and the diversity of women's organizations" (*Beyond the Household,* 277). Most students of Southern religion agree that white women often constituted the majority of the congregants but had little, if any, role in church governance. See, for example, Christine L. Heyrman, *Southern Cross: The Beginnings of the Bible Belt* (Chapel Hill: University of North Carolina Press, 1997), 167–69.

15. American Bible Society, Annual Report (1825), 6, and Annual Report (1826), 3.

16. American Bible Society, *Annual Report* (1827), 11, and *Annual Report* (1829), 7.

17. American Bible Society, *Annual Report* (1830), 122–24. For Southern resistance to Benevolent Empire activities, see John W. Kuykendall, *Southern Enterprize: The Work of National Evangelical Societies in the Antebellum South* (Westport: Greenwood Press, 1982). Resistance was particularly strong among antimission Baptists.

18. Eric Foner *The Story of American Freedom* (New York: W. W. Norton and Co., 1998), 57. Southern complaints concerning what some perceived as "a spirit of commercial, Northern imperialism" are examined in Bertram Wyatt-Brown, "Paradox, Shame and Grace in the Back Country," in *The Shaping of Southern Culture: Honor, Grace, and War, 1760s–1880s* (Chapel Hill: University of North Carolina Press, 2001), 122.

19. Stephanie McCurry, "The Politics of Yeoman Households in South Carolina," in *Divided Households: Gender and the Civil War,* ed. Catherine Clinton and Nina Silber (New York: Oxford University Press, 1992), 29.

20. Sellers, *The Market Revolution*, 208.

21. T. H. Breen, "An Empire of Goods: The Anglicization of Colonial America, 1690–1776," *Journal of British Studies* 25 (October 1986): 476; Jon Butler, *Awash in a Sea of Faith: Christianizing the American People* (Cambridge, Mass.: Harvard University Press, 1990), 170. For the role of farm women in fostering marketization, see Jean Boydston, "The Woman Who Wasn't There: Women's Market Labor and the Transition to Capitalism in the United States," *Journal of the Early Republic* 16 (summer 1996): 183–206. For the importance of Bibles in working-class culture, see Lazerow, *Religion and the Working Class.* According to Donald G. Mathews, women outnumbered men sixty-five to thirty-five in antebellum Southern churches. *Religion in the Old South* (Chicago: University of Chicago Press, 1977), 47.

22. Howard Bodenhorn, "Capital Mobility and Financial Integration in Antebellum America," *Journal of Economic History* 52, no. 3 (September 1992): 589.

23. James D. Norris, *R. G. Dun and Company, 1841–1900: The Development of Credit-Reporting in the Nineteenth Century* (Westport: Greenwood Press, 1978), 18. In addition to fees, Tappan sent his reporters subscriptions to the *Columbian Lady's and Gentleman's Magazine.* When several complained that the magazine was "flighty," he sent them the *Christian Parlor Magazine* instead. Historians such as Christopher Clark emphasize the extent to which the Mercantile Association blended business and moral agendas, focusing on personal habits. Thus, "because the reports . . . influence[d] wholesalers' decisions to advance or deny credit, men of poor character would be excluded from trade." *The Roots of Rural Capitalism*, 216. To this Ronald G. Walters adds that it gave "economic preference to virtue," aiming at "security and predictability and also profit." *The Antislavery Appeal: American Abolitionism after 1830* (Baltimore: Johns Hopkins University Press, 1976), 127. The ties among philanthropy and business and economic development merit a good deal more examination. Taken together, asylums, hospitals, colleges, universities, and comparable nonprofit organizations would have been major employers in their communities. The Bible and tract societies, for example, hired large numbers of printers and binders for their work, as well as contracting out for suppliers of paper and binding materials. It would be very interesting to learn what percentage of the economy these activities represented in different periods. For technical definitions of the types of organizations that would fall within this universe, and contemporary figures on their aggregate roles as employers in the national economy, see Lester M. Salamon, *America's Nonprofit Sector: A Primer* (New York: Foundation Center, 1999). For international comparisons, see Lester M. Salamon and Helmut Anheier, *The Emerging Sector: An Overview* (Baltimore: Institute for Policy Studies, Johns Hopkins University, 1994). A number of prominent churchmen and abolitionists were part of

Tappan's network of reporters, including Liberty Party presidential candidate James G. Birney, Salmon P. Chase of Ohio, and a young Illinois attorney, Abraham Lincoln. Ironically, Tappan's leadership of the company ultimately foundered on his inability to line up subscribers or reporters in the South, where his reputation as a skilled businessman was offset by his abolitionism. Afterward, the company was sold to other managers, who eventually turned it into Dun and Bradstreet. But Tappan made a major contribution to the development of the Northern market economy by grafting a viable region-wide credit-rating system onto the infrastructure of the Benevolent Empire and the antislavery movements in which he played so prominent a role.

24. New Hampshire Cent Institution, Report (Concord, N.H., 1814), 13, 1.

25. Ibid., 12.

26. Ryan, *Cradle of the Middle Class*, 61, 84, 60.

27. Terry K. Fisher, "Lending as Philanthropy: The Philadelphia Jewish Experience, 1847–1954." (Ph.D. diss., Bryn Mawr College, 1967): 6; Susan Chambré, "Philanthropy," in *Jewish Women in America: An Historical Encyclopedia*, ed. Paula E. Hyman and Deborah Dash Moore (New York: Routledge, 1997): 2:1049–55; Deuteronomy 15:7–11.

28. Daniel J. Elazar, *Community and Polity: The Organizational Dynamics of American Jewry* (Philadelphia: Jewish Publication Society of America, 1976), 15.

29. Fisher, "Lending as Philanthropy," 33. For the history of American Judaism in this period, see Eli Faber, *A Time for Planting: The First Migration, 1654–1820* (Baltimore: Johns Hopkins University Press, 1992); and Hasia R. Diner, *A Time for Gathering: The Second Migration, 1820–1880* (Baltimore: Johns Hopkins University Press, 1992).

30. Thomas J. Tobias, *The Hebrew Orphan Society of Charleston, South Carolina* (Charleston, S.C.: Hebrew Orphan Society, 1957), 2.

31. Hebrew Society for the Visitation of the Sick and Mutual Assistance, Constitution and By Laws (Philadelphia, 1824), 9.

32. Dianne C. Ashton, "Rebecca Gratz and the Domestication of American Judaism" (Ph.D. diss., Temple University, 1986), xvi.

33. Rebecca Gratz, letter to her sister-in-law, February 25, 1838, in "Rebecca Gratz," by Miriam Mordecai, in *Celebration of the Seventy-fifth Anniversary*, by Hebrew Sunday School Society (Philadelphia: Hebrew Sunday School Society, 1913), 6–7. Gratz was Mordecai's great-aunt.

34. Jonathan Sarna, "The American Jewish Response to Mid–Nineteenth Century Christian Missions," *Journal of American History* 68, no. 1 (June 1981): 49; Ashton, "Rebecca Gratz," xviii.

35. American Society for Meliorating the Condition of the Jews, Annual Report (1823), passim.

36. Gratz quoted in Marion L. Bell, *Crusade in the City: Revivalism in Nineteenth Century Philadelphia* (Lewisburg: Bucknell University Press, 1977), 155.

37. Rebecca Gratz, "Report on Hebrew Sunday School" (February 25, 1838), reprinted in *Four Centuries of Jewish Women's Spirituality*, ed. Ellen M. Umansky and Dianne Ashton (Boston: Beacon Press, 1992), 85.

38. Ashton, "Rebecca Gratz," ix, 200.

39. Bell, *Crusade in the City*, 156.

40. Female Hebrew Benevolent Society, Constitution (Philadelphia, 1825), 6, and Constitution (1858).

41. Sarna, "The American Jewish Response," 49.

42. *Occident,* December 1847, p. 427, quoted in Fisher, "Lending as Philanthropy," 43; *Occident,* 1844, 628; Sarna, "The American Jewish Response," 51.

43. Bell, *Crusade in the City,* 155; Ashton, "Rebecca Gratz," viii–ix.

44. *Occident,* 1844, 459.

45. Patrick W. Carey, *People, Priests and Prelates: Ecclesiastical Democracy and the Tensions of Trusteeism* (Notre Dame: University of Notre Dame Press, 1987), 107. By 1815 that number of Catholic churches had almost doubled, to approximately one hundred.

46. For Southern orders, see Sister Frances Jerome Woods, "Congregations of Religious Women in the Old South," in *Catholics in the Old South: Essays on Church and Culture,* ed. Randall M. Miller and Jon L. Wakelyn (Macon: Mercer University Press, 1983), 107.

47. Mary J. Oates, *The Catholic Philanthropic Tradition in America* (Indianapolis: Indiana University Press, 1995), 59. The Oblates are briefly discussed in Mary Carroll Johansen, "'Intelligence, Though Overlooked': Education for Black Women in the Upper South, 1800–1840," *Maryland Historical Magazine* 93, no. 4 (winter 1998): 443–65.

48. John Carroll, letter to Elizabeth Seton, September 11, 1811, in *Life of Mrs. Eliza A. Seton,* by Reverend Charles I. White, 3d ed. (New York: Kelly Publishing Co., 1879), 292.

49. Mr. Dubourg, letter to Elizabeth Seton, May 27, 1808, in *Life of Mrs. Eliza A. Seton,* by Reverend Charles I. White, 1st ed. (New York: Edward Dunigan and Brother, 1852), 223.

50. Woods, "Congregations of Religious Women in the Old South," 106.

51. Quoted in White, *Life of Mrs. Eliza A. Seton* (1852), 292.

52. Elizabeth Seton, letter to General Robert G. Harper, December 28, 1811, in White, *Life of Mrs. Eliza A. Seton* (1879), 280.

53. White, *Life of Mrs. Eliza A. Seton* (1852), 305.

54. By the 1850s, Catholic institutions were also receiving public allocations in California.

55. Carey, *People, Priests and Prelates,* 171, 159. For an excellent summary of the trustee issue, see Dale Light, "The Reformation of Philadelphia Catholicism, 1830–1860," *Pennsylvania Magazine of History and Biography* 112, no. 3 (July 1988): 375–405. Protestant reactions to the trustee conflicts, and the growth of nativism, are detailed in Ray Allen Billington, *The Protestant Crusade: 1800–1860: A Study of the Origins of American Nativism* (New York: Macmillian Co., 1938).

56. "A View of the Application for an Amendment of the Charter of Incorporation of St. Mary's Church" (Harrisburg: William White, 1823), 7. The Dartmouth case is discussed in chap. 4.

57. "An Observer," "The Battle of St. Mary's" (Philadelphia: n.p., 1822), 1; "A Layman of the Congregation," "An Inquiry into the Causes Which Led to the Dissensions Actually Existing in the Congregation of St. Mary's" (Philadelphia, n.p., 1821); John Leamy et. al., "Address of the Committee of St. Mary's Church of Philadelphia to Their Brethren of the Roman Catholic Faith" (New York: J. Kingsland and Co., 1821), 9.

58. Roman Catholic Church, "The Constitution of the Roman Catholic Churches of the States of North Carolina, South Carolina, and Georgia, Which Are Comprised in the Diocese of Charleston and Province of Baltimore" (Charleston, S.C.: Office of the Seminary, 1826).

59. Oates, *The Catholic Philanthropic Tradition,* 28, 27. See also Mary Oates, "Catholic Philanthropy in America" (New York: Center for the Study of Philanthropy, Graduate Center, City University of New York, 1997).

60. Jay Dolan, *The American Catholic Experience: A History from Colonial Times to the Present* (Garden City, N.Y.: Doubleday and Co., 1985), 167.

Chapter Four

1. Robert D. Putnam, *Making Democracy Work: Civic Traditions in Modern Italy* (Princeton: Princeton University Press, 1993). However, there were exceptions. For example, Charleston's Ladies Benevolent Society had $858 ($8,000 in 2000 dollars) in bank stock by 1814 and $9,200 ($104,000) worth of investments a decade later (as opposed to the $45,000 the Boston Female Asylum had invested in Hospital Life by the 1830s). At least one African American association in Baltimore also had a $400 bank account by the 1830s, and members of Charleston's elite mulatto Brown Fellowship Society undoubtedly had substantial investments as well. Cynthia Kierner, *Beyond the Household: Women's Place in the Early South, 1700–1835* (Ithaca: Cornell University Press, 1998), 192; Lori Ginzberg, *Women and the Work of Benevolence: Morality, Politics, and Class in the Nineteenth Century United States* (New Haven: Yale University Press, 1990), 62; Christopher Phillips, *Freedom's Port: The African American Community of Baltimore, 1790–1860* (Urbana: University of Illinois Press, 1997), 171. Putnam defines social capital as the "features of social organization, such as networks, norms, and trust, that facilitate coordination and cooperation for mutual benefit. Social capital enhances the benefits of investment in physical and human capital," which he defines as the "tools and training that enhance individual productivity," respectively. Robert D. Putnam, "The Prosperous Community: Social Capital and Public Life," *American Prospect* 13 (spring 1993): 35–36.

2. "Benjamin Franklin's Last Will and Testament," in *The Writings of Benjamin Franklin*, ed. Albert Henry Smyth (New York: Haskell House Publishers, 1970), 10:493–510. Franklin was elected to the Supreme Executive Council of Pennsylvania, which he chaired as "president," in 1785.

3. Bruce Harley Yenawine, "Benjamin Franklin's Legacy of Virtue: The Franklin Trusts of Boston and Philadelphia" (Ph.D. diss., Syracuse University, 1995), 63–64.

4. Gordon S. Wood, *The Radicalism of the American Revolution* (1991; reprint, New York: Vintage Books, 1993), 69, 57; Howard B. Rock, *Artisans of the New Republic: Tradesmen of New York City in the Age of Jefferson* (New York: New York University Press, 1984), 165.

5. W. K. Jordan, *Philanthropy in England, 1480–1660: A Study of the Changing Pattern of English Social Aspirations* (London: G. Allen and Unwin, 1959),7–8; Pauline Maier, "The Revolutionary Origins of the American Corporation," *William and Mary Quarterly*, 3d ser., 50, no. 1 (January 1993): 71; Howard Miller, *The Legal Foundations of American Philanthropy, 1776–1844* (Madison: State Historical Society of Wisconsin, 1961), xiiii.

6. Frances Godwin James, "Charity Endowments as Sources of Local Credit in Seventeenth and Eighteenth Century England," *Journal of Economic History* 8 (1948): 157–58, 160.

7. Franklin made his bequest in an unusually generous city. For statistics on Philadelphia bequests, see Rosemary Abend, "Constant Samaritans: Quaker Philanthropy in Philadelphia, 1680–1799" (Ph.D. diss., University of California, Los Angeles, 1988), 48, 58, 70, 156, 243. While Philadelphians made hundreds of bequests during the eighteenth century, a random sample of New York testaments indicates that the number of bequests made in the 1790s was extremely limited. I would like to thank Shawn Savage for his work in gathering these data. The Boston fund did better than its counterpart in Philadelphia. In 1894, the Boston fund amounted to $427,544; while Philadelphia recorded only $89,000 three years earlier. Gerald T. White, *A History of the Massachusetts Hospital Life Insurance Company* (Cambridge, Mass.: Harvard University Press, 1955), 40. The role of nonprofits as contractors and consumers is discussed more fully in chap. 8. For example, the ABS had hundreds of employees at its "Bible House" in New York by the 1850s, including 250 female bookbinders. Peter J. Wosh, *Spreading the Word: The Bible Business in Nineteenth Century America* (Ithaca: Cornell University Press, 1994), 18.

8. Charles Sellers, *The Market Revolution: Jacksonian America, 1815–1846* (New York: Oxford University Press, 1991), 217. Interestingly, all of these associations were headquartered in cities in the Northeast, causing concern among at least some Southerners that too much Southern capital was flowing to the North. See Wosh, *Spreading the Word.*

9. *Recorder,* May 29, 1816, p. 1; June 19, 1816, p. 1; April 10, 1816, p. 3; January 31, 1816, p. 2; July 24, 1816, p. 118.

10. *Recorder,* January 31, 1816, p. 3.

11. Jesse Brundage Sears, *Philanthropy in the History of American Higher Education* (1922; reprint, New Brunswick: Transaction Publishers, 1990), 35, 45, 50.

12. Harry Emerson Wildes, *Lonely Midas: The Story of Stephen Girard* (New York: Farrar and Rinehart, 1943), 294, 299; Sarah Knowles Bolton, *Famous Givers and Their Gifts* (1896; reprint, Freeport, N.Y.: Books for Libraries Press, 1971), 51. Howard Miller places the amount of Girard's estate at $7 million. *Legal Foundations,* 36.

13. Bolton, Famous Givers and Their Gifts, 6. Robert H. Bremner also has a brief but interesting description of the Lowell Institute in *American Philanthropy* (Chicago: University of Chicago Press, 1960; 1988),51–52; as does Ronald Story, *Harvard and the Boston Upper Class: The Forging of an Aristocracy, 1800–1870* (Middletown, Conn..: Wesleyan University Press, 1980).

14. Howard Miller, *Legal Foundations,* 15. The endowment gifts to Harvard included (among others) $95,000 ($1,140,000) from Christopher Gore in 1826; $20,000 ($260,000) from John McLean in 1834; and $40,000 ($504,000) from Henry W. Thompson in 1838. Other large donations included $20,000 from Samuel Eliot, Abiel Smith, and Benjamin Thompson in 1814, 1815, and 1816, respectively; $20,552 from John McLean in 1821; $20,000 from James Perkins in 1822; $10,000 from Nathan Dane in 1826; $20,000 from Joshua Fisher in 1834; and $10,000 from Sarah Jackson in 1835. Harvard University, *Endowment Funds at Harvard University* (Cambridge, Mass.: Harvard University, 1948), passim; Story, *Harvard,* p. 28. Bowdoin received $33,000 ($300,300) in an 1811 bequest from the founder's son; Oberlin and Western Reserve University raised donations of $17,000 ($222,700) and $10,000 ($131,000), respectively, from Arthur Tappan in the 1830s; and Transylvania College in Lexington, Kentucky, received a $50,000 ($565,000) bequest from Colonel James Morrison in 1823. Merle Curti and Roderick Nash, *Philanthropy in the Shaping of American Higher Education* (New Brunswick: Rutgers University Press, 1965), 46, 51, 55. See also Samuel Eliot Morison, *Three Centuries of Harvard: 1636–1936* (Cambridge, Mass.: Harvard University Press, 1936). According to statistics gathered by Jesse Brundage Sears, educational institutions in Massachusetts and Connecticut attracted far larger donations than similar institutions in other states. Between 1800 and 1859, Harvard received over $1.3 million in private donations, Yale over $800,000, Princeton @ $250,000, and Columbia a mere $22,000. Sears, *Philanthropy,* 23–26. For an interesting discussion of antebellum elite philanthropy in the Northeast, see Edward Pessen, *Riches, Class and Power before the Civil War* (New York: D. C. Heath, 1973). Howard Miller notes that Joseph Burr of Vermont bequeathed "nearly $96,000 to religious and charitable societies throughout the United States" in the 1830s. *Legal Foundations,* 36.

15. Story, *Harvard,* 25.

16. Thomas Jefferson, "Report of the Commissioners for the University of Virginia," August 4, 1818, in Thomas Jefferson, *Public and Private Papers* (New York: Vintage Books, Library of America, 1990), 146. Less than a year after Jefferson's pledge was signed, his finances had deteriorated to the point that he had to borrow one hundred dollars from a local merchant to participate on the Rockfish Gap Commission. Jefferson's role in creating the university is discussed in Dumas Malone, *Jefferson: The Sage of Monticello* (Boston: Little, Brown and Co.,

232   NOTES TO PAGES 85–87

1977). On Jefferson's indebtedness toward the end of his life, see also Merrill D. Peterson, *Thomas Jefferson and the New Nation: A Biography* (New York: Oxford University Press, 1970), 988ff.

17. James Madison quoted in Ralph Ketcham, *James Madison: A Biography* (1971; reprint, Charlottesville: University Press of Virginia, 1990), 652; and Thomas E. Buckley, "After Disestablishment: Thomas Jefferson's Wall of Separation in Antebellum Virginia," *Journal of Southern History* 41, no. 3 (August 1995), 469; Jefferson, "Report," 145. For Jefferson's views on religion, see Edwin S. Gaustad, *Sworn on the Altar of God: A Religious Biography of Thomas Jefferson* (Grand Rapids: William B. Eerdmans Publishing Co., 1996).

18. Jefferson, "Report," 145; Merrill D. Peterson, *Thomas Jefferson*, 980, 982, 988; Thomas Jefferson Papers, series 1, General Correspondence, 1651–1827, John Hartwell Cocke and Alexander Garrett, May 31, 1826, University of Virginia Financial Statement, image 1108, Library of Congress, American Memory website.

19. Thomas Jefferson, letter to Governor William Plumer of New Hampshire, July 21, 1816, in *The Writings of Thomas Jefferson*, ed. Albert Ellery Bergh (Washington, D.C.: Thomas Jefferson Memorial Association, 1907), 15:46. The Dartmouth and Hart cases are also discussed in Irwin G. Wyllie, "The Search for an American Law of Charity," *Mississippi Valley Historical Review* 46 (1959): 203–21; and Howard Miller, *Legal Foundations*.

20. Webster quoted in Peter Dobkin Hall, *"Inventing the Nonprofit Sector" and Other Essays on Philanthropy, Voluntarism and Nonprofit Organizations* (Baltimore: Johns Hopkins University Press, 1992), 29; and Timothy Farrar, *Report on the Case of the Trustees of Dartmouth College against William Woodward* (Portsmouth, N.H.: John W. Foster, 1819), 256. The Dartmouth case is discussed more fully in John S. Whitehead, *The Separation of College and State: Columbia, Dartmouth, Harvard and Yale, 1776–1876* (New Haven: Yale University Press, 1973), chap. 2, and "How to Think about the Dartmouth College Case," *History of Education Quarterly* 26, no. 3 (fall 1986): 333–49; Wyllie, "Search"; and Howard Miller, *Legal Foundations*.

21. Buckley, "After Disestablishment," 479–80; Howard Miller, *Legal Foundations*, 20, 21, 50. Interestingly, part of the Virginia lawmakers' objection hinged on the notion that "all charities withdrew from general circulation wealth that should be re-allocated in every generation." According to John Taylor of Caroline, the power this bestowed "begat enormous oppression." As a result, Henry St.-George Tucker, president of the Virginia Supreme Court, felt that "Unless Virginia acted quickly to curb bequests to religious organizations, the 'whole property of society' would be 'swallowed up in the insatiable gulph [sic]' of public charities." Howard Miller, *Legal Foundations*, 46, 25.

22. *Historical Catalogue of the University of Mississippi, 1849–1909* (Nashville: Marshall and Bruce Co., 1910), 4; George H. Callcott, *A History of the University of Maryland* (Baltimore: Maryland Historical Society, 1966), 44; E. Merton Coulter, *College Life in the Old South* (New York: Macmillan Co., 1928), 225; E. Merton Coulter, "Benjamin Braswell: Georgia Pioneer Philanthropist," *Georgia Historical Quarterly* 65, no. 2 (summer 1981): 67–81. Conversely, although Indiana, Michigan, Missouri, and Wisconsin founded their state universities in 1820, 1837, 1839, and 1848, respectively, none received state appropriations before 1867, underscoring the uniqueness of the antebellum Southern system. Whitehead, *Separation*, 133–34. The University of Virginia's investments were tied up in land and a hotel at the time of Jefferson's death, rather than more liquid holdings such as bank accounts or stocks. William W. Freehling provides some interesting insights into the history of South Carolina College, as well as the state's "spotty economy," in *Prelude to Civil War: The Nullification Controversy in South Carolina, 1816–1836* (New York: Oxford University Press, 1966), 20–21, chap. 2. Although the South was

the country's richest section, many ostensibly wealthy slaveholders would have been land poor. As Douglas R. Egerton explains, "By the election of Andrew Jackson, slaveholders had invested nearly $30,000,000 in human property; a figure almost as vast as had been sunk into land. . . . but unless a planter wished to liquidate his entire labor supply, neither his investment in land nor slaves could be reclaimed for industrial ventures." Thus, although rich in real property, they would have had less liquid cash than many Northern nonprofits. "Markets without a Market Revolution: Southern Planters and Capitalism," *Journal of the Early Republic* 16 (summer 1996): 214–15.

23. For the SPP, see Raymond A. Mohl, "Humanitarianism in the Preindustrial City: The New York Society for the Prevention of Pauperism, 1817–1823," *Journal of American History* 57, no. 3 (December 1970): 576–99; and Vincent Francis Bonelli, "The Response of Public and Private Philanthropy to the Panic of 1819 in New York City" (Ph.D. diss., Fordham University, 1976).

24. H. Oliver Horne, *A History of Savings Banks* (London: Oxford University Press, 1947), 52.

25. Alan L. Olmstead, *New York City Mutual Savings Banks, 1819–1861* (Chapel Hill: University of North Carolina Press, 1976), 10; *Commercial Advertiser*, October 16, 1819. The SPP took a dim view of pauperism and poverty, recommending incarceration in jail or the workhouse as an antidote to street begging. Their committee structure provides a window into their own view of the pathologies of the poor, with committees on idleness and lack of employment, want of economy and extravagance, intemperance, lotteries, pawnbrokers, houses of prostitution, charitable institutions and poor laws, ignorance and lack of religious values, and hasty marriages. SPP, Annual Report (1819), 3–9.

26. SPP, "Documents Relative to Savings Banks, Intemperance and Lotteries" (New York, 1819), 3, quoted in Bonelli, "Public and Private Philanthropy," 79.

27. James M. Willcox, *A History of the Philadelphia Saving Fund Society, 1816–1916* (Philadelphia: J. B. Lippincott, 1916), 144; Peter L. Payne and Lance Edwin Davis, *The Savings Bank of Baltimore, 1818–1866: A Historical and Analytical Study* (Baltimore: Johns Hopkins University Press, 1956), 24. The consensus among all of the authors who have written on these banks is that they were initially philanthropic, rather than commercial ventures.

28. Olmstead, *New York City Mutual Savings Banks*, 11, 157–58, 4.

29. Ibid., 77, 4. Larry Schweikart, "Southern Banks and Economic Growth in the Antebellum Period: A Reassessment," *Journal of Southern History* 53, no. 1 (February 1987): 26; White, *Massachusetts Hospital Life*, appendix 3, 190.

30. Olmstead, *New York City Mutual Savings Banks*, 82–83, 4. The SBNY continued to play an important role in New York finances and capital improvements. By 1833, the "the trustees still held almost $600,000 of the state's debt," about two-thirds of which was in Erie Canal stock, and three years later they held about half of the city's total outstanding debt as well. They also invested $400,000 in the city's $1 million campaign to build the Croton Reservoir as a means of providing clean water during the cholera years of the 1830s. Olmstead, New York City Mutual Savings Banks, 85–86. The bank also held "about half of the city's outstanding total debt" by 1836. Alan L. Olmstead, "Investment Constraints and New York City Mutual Savings Bank Financing of Antebellum Development," *Journal of Economic History* 32, no. 3 (1972): 827. According to Nathan Miller, by December, 1821, the Savings Bank of New York "held almost 30 per cent of the outstanding [Erie] canal stock . . . a total investment of more than half a million dollars of the depositors' savings." *The Enterprise of a Free People: Aspects of Economic Development in New York State during the Canal Period, 1792–1838* (Ithaca: Cornell University

Press, 1962), 89. By 1833, it held "almost $1,000,000 of Erie and Champlain Canal Stock," making it "the largest single investor in this type of stock" (ibid., 90). Savings banks played a pivotal and often little understood role in stimulating America's transportation revolution. For example, according to Charles Sellers, De Witt Clinton persuaded the "New York legislature to finance the Erie Canal itself," which it had initially not done. *The Market Revolution*, 43. For a fuller discussion of the role of savings banks, see George Alter, Claudia Goldin, and Elyce Rotella, "The Savings of Ordinary Americans: The Philadelphia Saving Fund Society in the Mid–Nineteenth Century," *Journal of Economic History* 54, no. 4 (December 1994): 735–67. Mutuals in other states invested their holdings differently. Baltimore's savings bank put most of its funds into commerce, rather than capital improvements. By 1832, 92% of the bank's assets were invested in loans. Some were small, like the two thousand dollars they lent to a local carpenter to start a box-manufacturing business. But most were large mercantile loans, in accordance with policies that helped to consolidate the city's role as a leading Southern commercial entrepôt. The bank also "played a significant, if minor, role in providing capital for the early industrial development of Baltimore," allocating between 5% and 7% of its holdings for iron foundries and midsized firms run by skilled artisans. Payne and Davis, *The Savings Bank of Baltimore*, 99, 134, 125, 137. I have not found any references to other slave state mutuals.

31. Nathan Miller, *Enterprise*, 85.

32. John Patrick Diggins, "Comrades and Citizens: New Mythologies in American Historiography, *American Historical Review* 90, no. 3 (1985): 626. Scholars such as Ann Fabian have suggested that savings banks exploited the poor, rather than aiding them. *Card Sharps, Dream Books, and Bucket Shops: Gambling in Nineteenth Century America* (Ithaca: Cornell University Press, 1990). The impact of the new poor laws on Jacksonian charities is discussed in chap. 8.

33. Peter J. Way, *Common Labour: Workers and the Digging of North American Canals, 1780–1860* (Cambridge: Cambridge University Press, 1993), and "Evil Humors and Ardent Spirits: The Rough Culture of Canal Construction Laborers," *Journal of American History* 79, no. 4 (March 1993): 1397–1428; Sean Wilentz, *Chants Democratic: New York and the Rise of the American Working Class, 1788–1850* (New York: Oxford University Press, 1984); David A. Zonderman, *Aspirations and Anxieties: New England Factory Workers and the Mechanized Factory System, 1815–1850* (New York: Oxford University Press, 1992). Bruce Laurie also points out that "There was not one but several worker cultures with distinctive politics at any point in time." *Artisans into Workers: Labor in Nineteenth Century America* (1989; reprint, Urbana: University of Illinois Press, 1997), 10. An interesting question is where workingmen's organizations invested their funds. One example is the Massachusetts Charitable Mechanic Association, a group of skilled tradesmen which was founded in 1795. The members valued safe investments over small loans to their colleagues, placing most of their funds in bank and government stocks. Only six hundred of the nearly twenty-five hundred dollars they invested in 1804 was given out in loans. Massachusetts Charitable Mechanic Association, Constitution (1806) (Boston, 1855), 8; Joseph T. Buckingham, *Annals of the Massachusetts Charitable Mechanic Association* (Boston: Crocker and Brewster, 1853), 81.

34. Olmstead, *New York City Mutual Savings Banks*, 35, 50–51; Alter, Goldin, and Rotella, "The Savings of Ordinary Americans," 742; Workingmen's Beneficial Society, Annual Report (1836), 5–6; Union Beneficial Society of Journeymen and Bricklayers, Constitution and By-Laws (1836), 7. Mutual savings banks may have been particularly important for African Americans, who would have had a difficult time gaining access to most of the standard sources of credit and loans. The Philadelphia Saving Fund Society, which invested heavily in home mortgages, "mostly in the working-class communities of Philadelphia," attracted a high ratio of

black depositors. Approximately 15% of the bank's depositors were African Americans, although they only accounted for 8% of the city's overall population. Michael Nash, "Research Note: Searching for Working Class Philadelphia in the Records of the Philadelphia Saving Fund Society," *Journal of Social History* 29, no. 3 (spring 1996): 683, 685. Patronizing these institutions was hardly designed to be a pleasant experience, if the SBNY is an accurate index. A fictionalized account conveyed some of the flavor of the encounter. The protagonist enters, "trembling from head to foot . . . taking my place among the files of chambermaids, cooks, waiters, carmen, mechanics, young and old, fat and thin, clean and dirty." After waiting for a small eternity he finally makes his way to the window, where the trustee-cum-teller's reception "made me so nervous that I nearly fainted," capped with "a look of perfect contempt . . . over his specks, that haunted me for years afterwards." If this description has any degree of accuracy, one can only conclude that the men and women who used these institutions had to really want to patronize them. Their behavior was hardly coerced. Stephen C. Massett, "Drifting About," 29–32, quoted in Olmstead, *New York City Mutual Savings Banks*, 24–25.

35. Stephen Thernstrom, *Progress and Poverty: Social Mobility in a Nineteenth Century City* (Cambridge, Mass.: Harvard University Press, 1964), 136, 115; Ann Fabian, *Card Sharps*, 52.

36. White, Massachusetts Hospital Life, 3. For earlier interpretations of the significance of Hospital Life for Boston philanthropy, see Peter Dobkin Hall, "The Model of Boston Charity: A Theory of Charitable Benevolence and Class Development," *Science and Society* 38, no. 4 (1974): 464–77; and Story, *Harvard*. Boston's banking practices are discussed in Naomi R. Lamoreaux, "Banks, Kinship and Economic Development: The New England Case," *Journal of Economic History* 66, no. 3 (1986): 647–67. The Franklin Trust began investing in Hospital Life in 1827 "and remained heavily invested in that company for over 100 years." By 1852, its loan program had been scrapped entirely, and the funds shifted into Hospital Life and its investments. Yenawine, "Benjamin Franklin's Legacy of Virtue," 80.

37. White, Massachusetts Hospital Life, 7, 9, appendix 3, 190.

38. Samuel Eliot Morison, *Three Centuries of Harvard, 1636–1936* (Cambridge, Mass.: Harvard University Press, 1936), 16.

39. Story, Harvard, 25, 41–42; Robert F. Dalzell, Jr., *Enterprising Elite: The Boston Associates and the World They Made* (Cambridge, Mass.: Harvard University Press, 1987), 133–37.

40. White, Massachusetts Hospital Life, 5.

41. Dalzell, *Enterprising Elite*, 160, 136. See also Story, *Harvard;* Peter Dobkin Hall, "What the Merchants Did with Their Money: Charity and Testamentary Trusts in Massachusetts, 1800–1880," working paper 214, Program on Nonprofit Organizations, Yale University, New Haven, 1995.

42. While Northern philanthropy helped to supply significant amounts of liquid capital for major public works and economic diversification, the Southern economic system, with its heavy investment in slavery and land, remained less liquid and more deeply mired in patron-client relationships that helped to maintain the social and political hegemony of the planter elite. As Eugene Genovese explains, "Southern banking tied . . . bankers to the plantations," via their boards and ongoing supervision by "the planter-dominated state legislatures," making them "their auxiliaries." As a result, it "guaranteed the extension and consolidation of the plantation system" in lieu of stimulating a more diversified economy. Eugene D. Genovese, *The Political Economy of Slavery: Studies in the Economy and Society of the Slave South* (New York: Vintage Books, 1967), 22. This had political implications as well. To quote Bertram Wyatt-Brown, "As late as the 1850s . . . the [Southern] yeomanry often sought help, in cash or in kind, from wealthy landowners with an unspoken understanding about who should receive the farmer's vote when

the squire's name appeared on the ballot." Bertram Wyatt-Brown, "Andrew Jackson's Honor," in *The Shaping of Southern Culture: Honor, Grace, and War, 1760s–1880s* (Chapel Hill: University of North Carolina Press, 2001), 65. See also Egerton, "Markets without a Market Revolution." However, the South was not entirely monolithic. For example, free blacks created a number of charitable and educational institutions in antebellum Maryland, and modest manufacturing ventures sporadically appeared, suggesting movement toward a more diversified economy.

43. Putnam, *Making Democracy Work*, 177; George Fitzhugh, *Cannibals All! Slaves without Masters* (Richmond, Va.: A. Morris, 1857), 153, 152.

44. Alexis de Tocqueville, *Democracy in America* (1835, 1841; Reprint, New York: Modern Library, 1981), 405, 407.

Chapter Five

1. Bernard Bailyn, *The Ideological Origins of the American Revolution* (Cambridge, Mass.: Harvard University Press, 1967), 65; Absalom Jones and Richard Allen, "To the Free People of Color," (Philadelphia, 1794), 23, 26. For a discussion of free black communities before and after the Revolution, see James Oliver Horton and Lois E. Horton, *In Hope of Liberty: Culture, Community and Protest among Northern Free Blacks, 1700–1860* (New York: Oxford University Press, 1997).

2. Jones and Allen, "To the Free People of Color," 26. For a discussion of Philadelphia's free black community, see Gary B. Nash, *Forging Freedom: The Formation of Philadelphia's Black Community: 1720–1840* (Cambridge, Mass.: Harvard University Press, 1988); and Julie Winch, *Philadelphia's Black Elite: Activism, Accommodation, and the Struggle for Autonomy* (Philadelphia: Temple University Press, 1988). In addition to the FAS, mutual aid groups quickly developed at both churches. See, for example, Friendly Society of St. Thomas's African Church of Philadelphia, Constitution and Rules (Philadelphia, 1797). See also Robert L. Harris, Jr., "Early Black Benevolent Societies, 1780–1830," *Massachusetts Review* 20, no. 3 (1979): 603–25; and Leon Litwack, *North of Slavery: The Negro in the Free States, 1790–1860* (Chicago: University of Chicago Press, 1961). The rise of the black church is briefly discussed in Winthrop D. Jordan, *White over Black: American Attitudes toward the Negro, 1550–1812* (1968; reprint, New York: W. W. Norton, 1977), chap. 11. For an overview of African American philanthropy, see Colin Palmer, "Topics in Black American Philanthropy since 1785" (New York: Center for the Study of Philanthropy, Graduate Center, City University of New York, 1997).

3. Absalom Jones, "Memoir," in *Annals of the First African Church in the United States of America, Now Styled the African Episcopal Church of St. Thomas* (Philadelphia: King and Baird, 1862), 119, 120. By the 1830s, estimates place the percentage of black Philadelphians who belonged to churches, mutual aid societies, or other voluntary associations as high as 80%. Nash, *Forging Freedom*, 273. Nash also estimates that nearly "half of all [black] adults" in Philadelphia belonged to the five largest black congregations in 1813 (260). Although St. Thomas's parish was fairly elitist, Mother Bethel attracted a strikingly mixed congregation that included both extremely wealthy and extremely poor blacks. In 1837, 14.8% of the congregation reported holdings of $0–$20, and another 30% had estates valued under $50, while 14.7% had estates of $251–$1,000, and 3.2% had over $1,000 in property. Nash, *Forging Freedom*, 266.

4. Richard Allen, *The Life, Experience, and Gospel Labours of the Rt. Rev. Richard Allen* (Philadelphia: Martin and Boden, 1833), 6, 7. For some interesting insights into Allen's character, see Gary B. Nash, "New Light on Richard Allen: The Early Years of Freedom," *William and Mary Quarterly*, 3d ser., 46, no. 2 (1989): 332–40.

5. For Jones and Allen's account, see "A Narrative of the Proceedings of the Black People during the Late Awful Calamity in Philadelphia in the Year 1793: And a Refutation of Some Censures Thrown upon Them, in Some Late Publications" (Philadelphia, 1794). For a more detailed discussion of their activities, see John Harvey Powell, *Bring Out Your Dead: The Great Plague of Yellow Fever in Philadelphia in 1793* (Philadelphia: University of Pennsylvania Press, 1949).

6. Allen, *Life, Experience*, 17, 16.

7. Ibid., 17, 16.

8. For additional information on Allen and Jones, see Winch, *Philadelphia's Black Elite;* Carol V. R. George, *Segregated Sabbaths: Richard Allen and the Emergence of Independent Black Churches, 1760–1840* (New York: Oxford University Press, 1973); and Nash, *Forging Freedom.*

9. Benevolent Sons of Bethel Church (later renamed Union Benevolent Society), Minutes, 1826–1844, entries for February 7, 1827, and October 14, 1829, Mother Bethel African Methodist Episcopal Church Manuscripts, reel 504.8, Historical Society of Pennsylvania, Philadelphia.

10. W. E. B. Du Bois quoted in George, *Segregated Sabbaths*, 103; Friendly Society of St. Thomas's African Church of Philadelphia, Constitution and Rules, 3, 5. Although most of these ventures were modestly conceived, backed by subscriptions, endowment income and small donations, African Americans occasionally did give larger sums. One of the largest bequests was from Mrs. Bernard Couvent. Willed to the diocese of New Orleans in 1837, the money was used to found the Catholic School for the Instruction of Indigent Orphans a decade later.

11. Albert J. Raboteau, *Slave Religion: The "Invisible Institution" in the Antebellum South* (New York: Oxford University Press, 1978) 143; Donald G. Mathews, *Religion in the Old South* (Chicago: University of Chicago Press, 1977), 200; Ira Berlin, *Slaves without Masters: The Free Negro in the Antebellum South* (New York: Oxford University Press, 1974), 285. Historians have traced the creation of the nation's first black churches to a short-lived venture in Silver Bluff, North Carolina, between 1773 and 1775. A second congregation was launched in Savannah, Georgia, shortly thereafter, antedating the FAS by several years. According to Berlin, white mobs "disbanded many of the most promising black institutions" in the antebellum years (ibid.). For the history of Southern plantation missions, see Raboteau, *Slave Religion*, chap. 4; and John W. Quist, *Restless Visionaries: The Social Roots of Antebellum Reform in Alabama and Michigan* (Baton Rouge: Louisiana State University Press, 1998), chap. 5.

12. Christopher Phillips, *Freedom's Port: The African American Community in Baltimore, 1790–1860* (Urbana: University of Illinois Press, 1997), 171; Berlin, *Slaves without Masters*, 310–11, 288. Berlin notes that "many associations agreed to lend money to members and became an important source of capital for black businessmen" in selected Southern cities, citing the situation in Baltimore, the work of the Brown Fellowship Society in Charleston, and the African Benevolent Society in Wilmington, which "could draw on the treasury whenever it held more than two hundred dollars" (310).

13. *Annals of Congress*, January 2, 1800 (Washington, D.C.: United States Government, 1803), 1:230, 234.

14. Ibid., 236, 237.

15. Ibid., 234.

16. Ibid., 235, 231. Madison quoted in Nash, *Forging Freedom*, 187.

17. According to Douglas Egerton, Jefferson went so far as to ask Rufus King, the American minister to London, to contact William Wilberforce about possibilities of sending Virginia's free blacks to Sierra Leone in the wake of Gabriel's rebellion in 1800. "'Its Origin Is Not a Little Cu-

rious': A New Look at the American Colonization Society," *Journal of the Early Republic* 5 (winter 1985): 466–67.

18. Contemporaries spelled Cuffe's name both ways. See, for example, American Colonization Society, Annual Report (1818), 11, 27.

19. For Gabriel's rebellion, see James Sidbury, *Ploughshares into Swords: Race, Rebellion, and Identity in Gabriel's Virginia, 1730–1810* (New York: Cambridge University Press, 1997).

20. Thomas Jefferson, letter to John Lynd, January 21, 1811, reprinted in American Colonization Society, Annual Report (1818), 13–24; quoted in John Chester Miller, *The Wolf by the Ears: Thomas Jefferson and Slavery* (Charlottesville: University Press of Virginia, 1991), 266; Henry Clay quoted in P. J. Staudenraus, *The African Colonization Movement, 1816–1865* (1961; reprint, New York: Octagon Books, 1980), 28; Katherine Harris, "The United States, Liberia and Their Foreign Relations to 1847" (Ph.D. diss., Cornell University, 1982), 129. For Clay's role in the American Colonization Society, see also Merrill D. Peterson, *The Great Triumvirate: Webster, Clay and Calhoun* (New York: Oxford University Press, 1987). See also Amos J. Beyan, *The American Colonization Society and the Creation of the Liberian State: A Historical Perspective, 1822–1900* (Lanham: University Press of America, 1991).

21. Staudenraus, *The African Colonization Movement*, 107, 116. For the role of Southern white women in supporting the ACS, see Elizabeth R. Varon, *We Mean to Be Counted: White Women and Politics in Antebellum Virginia* (Chapel Hill: University of North Carolina Press, 1998), chap. 2. Varon portrays the ACS as a vehicle for Southern female antislavery activities in the years before the Turner Rebellion of 1831. Some scholars have raised questions about whether the ACS was actually racist in intent. However, the first annual report, which includes a lengthy missive from Robert G. Harper arguing that free blacks were "idle and useless, and too often vicious and mischievous" people "condemned to a state of hopeless inferiority and degradation by their colour" suggests that it was. Letter, August 20, 1817, in American Colonization Society, Annual Report (1818), 29.

22. Drew R. McCoy, *The Last of the Fathers: James Madison and the Republican Legacy* (New York: Cambridge University Press, 1989), 252, 284, 303, 285. Madison accepted the presidency on February 25, 1833. American Colonization Society, Series V:9, Minutes, p. 347, Business Papers, Manuscript Collections, Library of Congress.

23. McCoy, *The Last of the Fathers*, 303, 279. According to Clay, America's freedmen lived "in the lowest state of social gradation . . . political—moral—social aliens, strangers, though natives." In Africa, "they would be in the midst of their friends and their kindred, at home, though born in a foreign land, and elevated above the natives of the country, as much as they are degraded here below the other classes of the community." American Society for Colonizing the Free People of Colour of the United States (American Colonization Society), Tenth Annual Report (Washington, 1827), 15.

24. McCoy, *The Last of the Fathers*, 280, 77; Ralph Ketcham, *James Madison: A Biography* (1971; reprint, Charlottesville: University Press of Virginia, 1990), 625.

25. *Annals of Congress*, 15th Cong., 1st sess., 1771–74; 2d sess., 2544–46; Katherine Harris, "The United States, Liberia and Their Foreign Relations to 1847," 87.

26. According to his biographer, Monroe was "deeply sympathetic with the aims of the Colonization Society." Nonetheless, "he did not think that he had power under the Constitution to acquire territory in Africa, nor did he feel that the loosely worded bill gave him authority to resettle free Negroes in Africa. . . . During Monroe's administration the agents appointed to resettle captured Africans were invariably chosen from candidates named by the Colonization Society. With the indirect help of the administration the Colonization Society acquired title to

Liberia from its own funds and then permitted the federal government to use the colony as a base for resettling captured Africans. In its early years the colony was largely sustained from funds allocated to the federal agents resident in Liberia. It was in gratitude to the President that the directors of the Society named the first settlement Monrovia." Harry Ammon, *James Monroe: The Quest for National Identity* (Charlottesville: University Press of Virginia, 1990), 522–23.For the role of the navy, see Judd Scott Harmon, "Marriage of Convenience: The United States Navy in Africa, 1820–1843," *American Neptune* 32, no. 3 (July 1972): 264–76.

27. Katherine Harris, "The United States, Liberia and Their Foreign Relations to 1847," 93.

28. *Memoirs of John Quincy Adams, Comprising Portions of His Diary from 1795 to 1848*, ed. Charles Francis Adams (Philadelphia: J. B. Lippincott, 1871), 293–94, 309; Katherine Harris, "The United States, Liberia and Their Foreign Relations to 1847," 117, 118. For a discussion of Whig philosophies, see Daniel Walker Howe, *The Political Culture of the American Whigs* (Chicago: University of Chicago Press, 1979).

29. Katherine Harris, "The United States, Liberia and Their Foreign Relations to 1847," 165. An 1831 appropriation in Maryland raised $200,000 ($2.62 million) with the aim of deporting all of the state's free blacks within a generation. The law also forbade manumission unless the freedmen were sent outside the state. Two days later, legislation was passed providing that any free black who left the state for more than a month would be sold into slavery upon his or her return, and that any free blacks moving into the state would be required to pay $50 per week for the duration of their stay. The rulings were subsequently praised in an ACS resolution that deemed them a "patriotic and *benevolent* system in regard to [the state's] colored population." Similarly, the Virginia legislature began appropriating $50,000 ($710,000) per annum in 1850 to deport free blacks. Giles Badger Stebbins, *Facts and Opinions Touching the Real Origin, Character and Influence of the American Colonization Society* (New York: Negro Universities Press, 1961), 107. See also William D. Hoyt, Jr., "The Papers of the Maryland State Colonization Society," *Maryland Historical Magazine* 32 (September 1937): 247–71.

30. Katherine Harris, "The United States, Liberia and Their Foreign Relations to 1847," 110. For the number of emigrants sent to Liberia, see Frankie Hutton, "Economic Considerations in the American Colonization Society's Early Effort to Emigrate Free Blacks to Liberia, 1816–1836," *Journal of Negro History* 68, no. 4 (fall 1983): 386, table 1.

31. Patricia U. Bonomi, *Under the Cope of Heaven: Religion, Society, and Politics in Colonial America* (New York: Oxford University Press, 1986), 181, 168.

32. Nash, *Forging Freedom*, 238. Officials of the ACS noted African resistance with some alarm, attributing it to "ignorance and misapprehension." Annual Report (1818), 10. Ironically, earlier histories such as George M. Frederickson, *The Black Image in the White Mind: The Debate on Afro-American Character and Destiny, 1817–1914* (Middletown, Conn.: Wesleyan University Press, 1987), overlooked the role of African Americans in opposing the society's plan. According to Fredrickson, "The first intense opposition to colonization came in the 1820s from the slaveholding states of the deep South" (25).

33. William Lloyd Garrison, "Sentiments of the People of Color," in *Thoughts on African Colonization*, pt. 2 (Boston: Garrison and Knapp, 1832), 9.

34. George, *Segregated Sabbaths*, 153, 154; *Freedom's Journal*, November 2, 1827. See also Ella Forbes, "African-American Resistance to Colonization," *Journal of Black Studies* 21, no. 2 (December 1990): 210–23.

35. Katherine Harris, "The United States, Liberia and Their Foreign Relations to 1847," 126. A fairly substantial number of free blacks also emigrated from Richmond. See Marie Tyler McGraw, "Richmond Free Blacks and African Colonization, 1816–1832," *Journal of*

American Studies 21 (1987): 2, 207–24. Baltimore is discussed in Phillips, *Freedom's Port,* chap. 7.

36. American Society of Free Persons of Color, *Constitution and Proceedings of the Convention* (Philadelphia, 1831), 9.

37. Ibid., 10.

38. Absalom Jones and Richard Allen, "An Address to Those Who Keep Slaves, and Approve the Practice," (Philadelphia, 1794), 25; Staudenraus, *The African Colonization Movement,* 193.

39. William Lloyd Garrison, "An Address Delivered before the Free People of Color in Philadelphia and New York" (Boston: Stephen Foster, 1831), 1, 18, 16, 15, 9. He also proffered some interesting economic advice: "support each other—I mean, sell to each other, and buy of each other, in preference of the whites. . . . the whites do not trade with you—why should you give them your patronage?" (14).

40. Ibid., 10.

41. Although Benjamin Quarles and Paul Goodman tie the origins of abolitionism to the black community, many excellent histories of the movement and its leaders, such as Henry Mayer's highly readable biography of William Lloyd Garrison, have tended to minimize or overlook this connection. I have emphasized it here because Garrison so clearly co-opted the black anticolonizationist campaigns as the basis of the abolitionist movement, and because much of his earliest support came from African Americans. Benjamin Quarles, *Black Abolitionists* (New York: Oxford University Press, 1969); Paul Goodman, *Of One Blood: Abolitionism and the Origins of Racial Equality* (Berkeley: University of California Press, 1998); Henry Mayer, *All on Fire: William Lloyd Garrison and the Abolition of Slavery* (New York: St. Martin's Press, 1998).

42. Quarles, *Black Abolitionists,* 32.

43. American Antislavery Society, Annual Report (New York, 1834), 26.

44. William Lloyd Garrison, *Thoughts on African Colonization* (Boston: Garrison and Knapp, 1832),10, 11, from an editorial in the *Liberator.*

45. William Lloyd Garrison, "The Maryland Scheme of Expatriation Examined" (Boston: Garrison and Knapp, 1834), 6. See also Phillips, *Freedom's Port,* chap. 7.

46. American Antislavery Society, "Declaration of Sentiments" (New York: American Antislavery Society, 1833), 1.

47. Nathan O. Hatch, *The Democratization of American Christianity* (New Haven: Yale University Press, 1989), 102.

48. Joyce Appleby, *Capitalism and a New Social Order: The Republican Vision of the 1790s* (New York: New York University Press, 1984), 56.

49. American Antislavery Society, "Declaration of Sentiments," 2; Du Bois quoted in George, *Segregated Sabbaths,* vii.

Chapter Six

1. Bertram Wyatt-Brown, *The Shaping of Southern Culture: Honor, Grace, and War, 1760s–1890s* (Chapel Hill: University of North Carolina Press, 2001), 65; Jean Harvey Baker, "Politics, Paradigms and Public Culture," *Journal of American History* 84, no. 3 (December 1997): 897; Robert V. Remini, *Andrew Jackson and His Indian Wars* (New York: Viking, 2001). For Richard Hofstadter, Jackson was a champion of economic reform: "When Jackson left office he was the hero of the lower and middling elements of American society who believed in expanding opportunity through equal rights." *The American Political Tradition and the Men Who Made It* (New York: Vintage Books, 1948), 67. According to Daniel Feller, he led a "war against privi-

lege." *The Jacksonian Promise: America, 1815–1840* (Baltimore: Johns Hopkins University Press, 1995), 172. See also Harry Watson, *Liberty and Power: The Politics of Jacksonian America* (New York: Hill and Wang, 1990). Edward Pessen is more critical of Jackson's record, as is Donald Cole. Pessen concurs with the idea that Jackson's was a laissez-faire presidency but makes the surprising assertion that his administration had "little effect on the social, economic, religious, and intellectual developments that were shaping American civilization." *Jacksonian America: Society, Personality, and Politics* (Urbana: University of Illinois Press, 1985), 2. See also Marvin Myers, *The Jacksonian Persuasion: Politics and Belief* (Palo Alto: Stanford University Press, 1957); Donald B. Cole, *The Presidency of Andrew Jackson* (Lawrence: University Press of Kansas, 1993); Arthur Schlesinger, *The Age of Jackson* (Boston: Little, Brown and Co., 1945); Daniel Feller, "Politics and Society: Toward a Jacksonian Synthesis," *Journal of the Early Republic* 10 (summer 1990): 135–61; and Donald B. Cole, "The Age of Jackson: After Forty Years," *Reviews in American History* 14 (March 1986): 149–59. For a recent discussion of the notion that Jackson's administrations marked a golden age of participatory democracy, see Glenn C. Altschuler and Stuart M. Blumin's essay, "Limits of Political Engagement in Antebellum America: A New Look at the Golden Age of Participatory Democracy," in which the authors argue that "The claim that antebellum politics approximated the ideal of participatory democracy is now nearly a paradigm in American political history." *Journal of American History* 84, no. 3 (December 1997): 857. Similarly, Stanley Elkins and Eric McKitrick claimed that "'Democracy' was not to emerge as a fully legitimate cultural value in America, commanding more or less universal approval, until the 1830s, with the appearance of a national system of mass political parties." *The Age of Federalism: The Early American Republic, 1788–1800* (New York: Oxford University Press, 1993), 451.

2. Lucien Pye and Sidney Verba, *Political Culture and Political Development* (Princeton: Princeton University Press, 1965), 9; Robert D. Putnam, *Making Democracy Work: Civic Traditions in Modern Italy* (Princeton: Princeton University Press, 1993), 101. For historical applications of the idea of political culture, see Daniel Walker Howe, *The Political Culture of the American Whigs* (Chicago: University of Chicago Press, 1979); Kathryn Kish Sklar, *Florence Kelley and the Nation's Work: The Rise of Women's Political Culture, 1830–1900* (New Haven: Yale University Press, 1995); and Jean Fagan Yellin and John C. Van Horne, eds., *The Abolitionist Sisterhood: Women's Political Culture in Antebellum America* (Ithaca: Cornell University Press, 1994).

3. Wyatt-Brown, *The Shaping of Southern Culture*, 58, 66; William Lloyd Garrison, letter to Andrew Jackson, July 27, 1824, in *The Letters of William Lloyd Garrison*, ed. Walter M. Merrill and Louis Ruchames (Cambridge, Mass.: Harvard University Press, Belknap Press, 1971), 1:24. In Garrison's opinion, Jackson was driven by a "savage and domineering spirit," a "cold-blooded ferocity—a palpable ignorance of our constitution and laws—and a sacrifice of reason and common prudence, which could not otherwise than alarm and astound the nation"—impressions that he unfortunately shared with the general by letter (25). For an illuminating discussion of the links between personal volatility and the Southern culture that shaped Jackson's persona and his career, see Kenneth S. Greenberg, *Honor and Slavery* (Princeton: Princeton University Press, 1996).

4. Although Washington may not have been a member of the American Philosophical Society, he was a contributor. In 1800, for example, he donated $25 for one of the society's projects, while Hamilton and Jefferson each donated $12.50 out of the $128.25 that was collected. American Philosophical Society, Minutes, April 4, 1800, 298, Manuscript Collections, American Philosophical Society, Philadelphia. For the quest to develop a national university, see Leonard

C. Helderman, *George Washington: Patron of Learning* (New York: Century Co., 1932); and Edgar Bruce Wesley, *Proposed: The University of the United States* (Minneapolis: University of Minnesota Press, 1936). For the debates surrounding the proposal for a national university, see Annals of Congress, *Debates and Proceedings of the Congress of the United States* (Washington: Gales and Seaton, 1834–36), December 5, 1796; December 12, 1796; December 26–27, 1796; December 2, 1806; February 28, 1806; December 1810; December 5, 1815; March 1817; December 1817; January 14, 1822. For Madison's philanthropic activities, see Ralph Ketcham, *James Madison: A Biography* (Charlottesville: University Press of Virginia, 1990), chap. 22, "Retirement."

5. I am indebted to Adam Reichmann for his help in researching the material on the national university and Jackson's attitudes toward voluntary associations. Jackson did not leave any charitable bequests in his will. Van Buren, on the other hand, ostensibly made one donation during his lifetime, for a statue of Andrew Jackson.

6. Election figures are from Remini, *The Life of Andrew Jackson* (New York: Penguin Books, 1988), 168. Bertram Wyatt-Brown notes that most of Jackson's support came from the South in 1828. While Northern voters accorded him 49% of their electoral votes, he won a stunning 92% in the South. *The Shaping of Southern Culture*, 66.

7. For a discussion of Jackson's Indian policies, see Mary Hershberger, "Mobilizing Women, Anticipating Abolition: The Struggle against Indian Removal in the 1830s," *Journal of American History* 86, no. 1 (June 1999): 15–40; John A. Andrew III, *From Revivals to Removal: Jeremiah Evarts, the Cherokee Nation, and the Search for the Soul of America* (Athens: University of Georgia Press, 1992); William G. McLoughlin, *Cherokees and Missionaries, 1789–1839* (New Haven: Yale University Press, 1984), and *Cherokee Renascence in the New Republic* (Princeton: Princeton University Press, 1986); Michael Paul Rogin, *Fathers and Children: Andrew Jackson and the Subjugation of the American Indian* (New York: Vintage Books, 1976); Ronald Satz, *American Indian Policy in the Jacksonian Era* (Lincoln: University of Nebraska Press, 1975); Herman J. Viola, *Thomas L. McKenney: Architect of America's Early Indian Policy, 1816–1830* (Chicago: Swallow Press, 1974); Francis Paul Prucha, *The Great Father: The United States and the American Indians* (Lincoln: University of Nebraska Press, 1984), and "Andrew Jackson's Indian Policy: A Reassessment," *Journal of American History* 56 (December 1969): 527–39; William G. McLoughlin, "The Reverend Evan Jones and the Cherokee Trail of Tears, 1838–1839," *Georgia Historical Quarterly* 73, no. 3 (fall 1989): 559–83, and "Georgia's Role in Instigating Compulsory Indian Removal," *Georgia Historical Quarterly* 70, no. 4 (winter 1986): 605–23; Ronald N. Satz, "The Cherokee Trail of Tears: A Sesquicentennial Perspective," *Georgia Historical Quarterly* 73, no. 3 (fall 1989): 431–66; and Remini, *Andrew Jackson and His Indian Wars*.

8. Remini, *The Life of Andrew Jackson*, 68, 82, 85.

9. Remini, *The Life of Andrew Jackson*, 112; Andrew Jackson, letter to James Monroe, March 4, 1817, in *Correspondence of Andrew Jackson*, ed. John Spencer Bassett (Washington, D.C.: Carnegie Institution, 1926–33), 2:279–80.

10. R. Pierce Beaver, *Church, State and the American Indians: Two and a Half Centuries of Partnership between Protestant Missions and Government* (St. Louis, Concordia Publishing House, 1966), 64; Bernard W. Sheehan, *Seeds of Extinction: Jeffersonian Philanthropy and the American Indian* (New York: W. W. Norton, 1973).

11. James Monroe, letter to Andrew Jackson, October 5, 1815, in Correspondence of Andrew Jackson, 2:332.

12. John C. Calhoun, letter to Jedediah Morse, February 7, 1820, in *Report to the Secretary of*

War of the United States on Indian Affairs, by Jedediah Morse (New Haven: S. Converse, 1822), 12.

13. James Monroe, message to the Senate and House of Representatives of the United States, March 30, 1824, in *The Writings of James Monroe,* ed. Stanislaus Murray Hamilton (New York: G. P. Putnam's Sons, 1903), 7:15; John Calhoun, message to the Cherokee nation, January 30, 1824, *American State Papers: Indian Affairs* 2:473, quoted in Andrew, *From Revivals to Removal,* 125. According to Monroe, "there is no obligation to remove the Indians by force," in part because the "Indian title was not affected in the slightest circumstance by the compact with Georgia." Monroe felt that they could only be removed "when it may be done *peaceably* and on *reasonable* conditions in full proof that it was the clear and distinct understanding of both parties . . . that the Indians had a right to the territory, in the disposal of which they were to be regarded as free agents" (ibid.). On the Cherokee constitution, see in addition McLoughlin, "Georgia's Role."

14. Jackson quoted in Remini, *The Life of Andrew Jackson,* 219.

15. Feller, *The Jacksonian Promise,* 179; Andrew, *From Revivals to Removal,* 205; For a fuller account of women's roles in the petition campaigns, see Hershberger, "Mobilizing Women."

16. Petition from [the Ladies of] Lewis, New York, January 24, 1831, National Archives, Cherokee Removal Records, RG 233, HR 21A-G8.2; "Memorial from the Ladies of Steubenville, Ohio, Relating to Indian Removal," February 15, 1830, National Archives, HR21A, H1.1, RG 233.

17. Rebecca Gratz to Maria Gist Gratz, January 14, 1830, in *Letters of Rebecca Gratz,* ed. David Philipson (Philadelphia: Jewish Publication Society of America, 1929), 112–13.

18. Andrew Jackson, "State of the Union Address, December 6, 1830," reprinted in *The Cherokee Removal: A Brief History with Documents,* ed. Theda Perdue and Michael D. Green (New York: Bedford Books, 1995), 119–20.

19. Ibid., 120.

20. *United States Register of Debates in Congress* (Washington, D.C.: Gales and Seaton, 1830), vol. 6, pt. 1, 508.

21. American Board of Commissioners of Foreign Missions (ABCFM), Annual Report (1830), 76. For the administration's policies, see R. Pierce Beaver, *Church, State and the American Indians;* and Andrew, *From Revivals to Removal.*

22. Andrew, *From Revivals to Removal,* 217; Thomas L. McKenney, letter to Reverend Eli Baldwin, May 21, 1829, in *Documents and Proceedings* of Board for the Emigration, Preservation and Improvement of the Aborigines of America (New York, 1829), 3; John Eaton, letter to Reverend Eli Baldwin, August 25, 1829, in Board for the Emigration, Preservation and Improvement of the Aborigines of America, Annual Report, 1830, 45–46. See also Satz, *American Indian Policy;* Viola, *McKenney;* Adam Reichmann, "Andrew Jackson's Indian Removal Campaigns," paper delivered at seminar, Graduate Center, City University of New York, May, 2001.

23. ABCFM, Annual Report (1832), 90.

24. Ellis's evidence certainly bears out the extent to which the confrontation was cast as a state's rights issue in the Southern press. To quote one article: to yield would be to "acknowledge the supremacy of the Supreme Court, admit its right to control [Georgia's] criminal jurisdiction . . . stop the wheels of her lottery, [and] command her citizens to evacuate the Cherokee territory" under the threat of federal reprisals. As another commentator succinctly noted, "the contest was not between Georgia and the missionaries, but between Georgia and the Supreme Court." Richard E. Ellis, *The Union at Risk: Jacksonian Democracy, State's Rights and the Nullification Crisis* (New York: Oxford University Press, 1987), 113, 119; Anthony F. C. Wallace, *The*

Long, Bitter Trail: Andrew Jackson and the Indians (New York: Hill and Wang, 1993),76; Perdue and Green, *The Cherokee Removal*, 60. For a particularly nuanced interpretation of the standoff, see McLoughlin, *Cherokee Renascence*. The Congregationalists' *Boston Recorder*, which had warmly supported Evarts's petition campaign, noted impatiently that if the states could run the government by threatening to secede, "Then the General Government is only a tool for individual states to play the fool with." April 14, 1830, 57.

25. Remini, *Andrew Jackson and His Indian Wars*, 269, 270. According to Remini, the Cherokee removals constituted "one of the most disgraceful and heart-rending episodes in American history," executed "in total violation not only of American principles of justice and law, but of Jackson's own strict code of honor." *The Life of Andrew Jackson*, 218−19.

26. Richard R. John, *Spreading the News: The American Postal System from Franklin to Morse* (Cambridge, Mass.: Harvard University Press, 1995), 3. See also Richard R. John, "Taking Sabbatarianism Seriously: The Postal System, the Sabbath, and the Transformation of American Political Culture," *Journal of the Early Republic* 10 (winter 1990): 517−67; Robert H. Abzug, *Cosmos Crumbling: American Reform and the Religious Imagination* (New York: Oxford University Press, 1994), chap. 5; and Bertram Wyatt-Brown, "Prelude to Abolitionism: Sabbatarian Politics and the Rise of the Second Party System," *Journal of American History* 58 (September 1971): 316−41.

27. John, "Taking Sabbatarianism Seriously," 529.

28. Ibid., 541−42.

29. Ibid., 543, 547. The absence of women's petitions was confirmed by the author's random sampling of the Sabbatarian petitions at the National Archives.

30. New England Antislavery Society, Annual Report (1833), 17−18; Louis Filler, *The Crusade against Slavery, 1830−1860* (New York: Harper and Brothers, 1960), 67; Aileen S. Kraditor, *Means and Ends in American Abolitionism: Garrison and His Critics on Strategy and Tactics, 1834−1850* (New York: Pantheon, 1969), 6. Filler's figures, which have been adopted by other scholars, were based on the annual reports of the AAS. The Massachusetts Antislavery Society placed the number of auxiliaries at "not less than Two Thousand" in 1839, shortly after the movement had peaked, with "at least Two Hundred Thousand persons enrolled as members." Annual Report (1840), 3. On abolitionism more generally, see Paul Goodman, *Of One Blood: Abolitionism and the Origins of Racial Equality* (Berkeley: University of California Press, 1998); Paul Goodman, "The Manual Labor Movement and the Origins of Abolitionism," *Journal of the Early Republic* 13 (fall 1993): 355−88; Kraditor, *Means and Ends*; Lawrence Friedman, *Gregarious Saints: Self and Community in American Abolitionism, 1830−1870* (New York: Cambridge University Press, 1982); Gilbert Hobbs Barnes, *The Antislavery Impulse: 1830−1844* (New York: D. Appleton-Century Co., 1933); David Brion Davis, "Introduction," in *Antebellum Reform*, ed. David Brion Davis (New York: Harper and Row, 1967), 1−10; David Donald, "Toward a Reconsideration of the Abolitionists," in *Lincoln Reconsidered* (New York: Vintage Books, 1961), 19−36; James Brewer Stewart, *Holy Warriors: The Abolitionists and American Slavery* (New York: Hill and Wang, 1976); Ronald G. Walters, *The Antislavery Appeal: American Abolitionism after 1830* (Baltimore: Johns Hopkins University Press, 1976); Lewis Perry, *Radical Abolitionism: Anarchy and the Government of God in Antislavery Thought* (Ithaca: Cornell University Press, 1973); Lewis Perry and Michael Fellman, eds., *Antislavery Reconsidered: New Perspectives on the Abolitionists* (Baton Rouge: Louisiana State University Press, 1979); Paul Finkelman, ed., *His Soul Goes Marching On: Responses to John Brown and the Harpers Ferry Raid* (Charlottesville: University Press of Virginia, 1995); Yellin and Van Horne, *The Abolitionist Sisterhood;* and Deborah Gold Hansen, *Strained Sisterhood:*

Gender and Class in the Boston Female Antislavery Society (Amherst: University of Massachusetts Press, 1993).

31. *Encyclopedia of Associations* (Detroit: Gale Research Company, 2000), passim. The 2% figure is based on the country's population of approximately 13 million in 1830. That figure had risen to 17 million in 1840, but the lower figure was used to compensate for the fact that there were 2 million slaves in 1830, and nearly 2.5 million a decade later, all of whom were precluded from joining any nonreligious movement, and for the fact that the peak of the mobilization fell at mid-decade, for which reliable census data were not available. But even if the 1840 figures were used, the membership of the AAS would still have constituted approximately 1.5% of the total national population, which would make it larger on a percentage basis than all of the organizations mentioned except the Boy Scouts.

32. Massachusetts Antislavery Society, Annual Report (1835), 15; Mayer, *All on Fire,* 195.

33. Massachusetts Antislavery Society, Annual Report (1835), 18.

34. Andrew Jackson, "Message of the President of the United States" in *Unites States Register of Debates,* 24th Cong., 1st sess., appendix 11; Andrew Jackson, letter to Amos Kendall, August 9, 1835, in *Correspondence of Andrew Jackson* (1931), 5:360; Harriet Martineau, "The Martyr Age of the United States" (Boston: Weeks, Jordan and Co., 1839), 46. According to David Grimsted, Jackson "personally wished the abolitionists could be made to atone with their lives" (*American Mobbing, 1828–1861: Toward Civil War* [New York: Oxford University Press, 1998], 23), while Michael Holt records that "Jackson ordered his postmaster general to direct Southern postmasters to destroy abolitionist literature" (*The Rise and Fall of the American Whig Party: Jacksonian Politics and the Onset of the Civil War* [New York: Oxford University Press, 1999], 44). Jackson's Southern sympathies were also apparent in his appointment of three Southerners to the Supreme Court in 1835 and 1836, including Roger Taney, who handed down the infamous *Dred Scott* decision in 1857.

35. Russel B. Nye, *Fettered Freedom: Civil Liberties and the Slavery Controversy, 1830–1860* (East Lansing: Michigan State College Press, 1949), 56; William Leggett quoted in John, *Spreading the News,* 270; John Quincy Adams quoted in the *Boston Recorder,* May 26, 1836, 3. There have been many lively debates over the years concerning whether or not Jackson's administration was proslavery. For an overview, see Leonard L. Richards, "The Jacksonians and Slavery," in Perry and Fellman, *Antislavery Reconsidered,* 99–118. However, from the perspective of the Indian removals and the treatment of abolitionist petition and mail campaigns, the actions of the Jackson administration decidedly fell within the pro-Southern camp.

36. In reporting on a published report of the bounty placed on Phelps's head, the *Boston Recorder* angrily noted: "Why did the author not affix his name to it? Because he is a coward." April 19, 1836, 72; "An Account of the Interviews Which Took Place on the Eight of March, between a Committee of the Massachusetts Anti-slavery Society, and the Committee of the Legislature" (Boston, 1836), available on the Library of Congress's American Memory Web site.

37. Nye, *Fettered Freedom,* 137; American Antislavery Society (AAS), "To the People of the United States; or, To Such Americans as Value Their Rights, and Dare to Maintain Them" (1836), reprinted in *The Anti-slavery Examiner* 1, no. 1 (August 1836; reprint, Westport: Negro University Press, 1970), 1:2. My emphasis.

38. American Colonization Society, Annual Report (Washington, D.C., 1827); "Minutes of the Twenty-first Biennial American Convention for Promoting the Abolition of Slavery, and Improving the Condition of the African Race, Convened at the City of Washington, December 8, 1829." Library of Congress, American Memory Web site. There were several more female auxiliaries of the American Colonization Society by 1829, almost all of which were in the upper

South. However, these chapters still constituted only a fraction of the society's auxiliaries. American Colonization Society, Minutes and Ledgers, Manuscript Collections, Library of Congress. Elizabeth Varon notes women's fund-raising activities for Virginia colonization societies in the 1820s, and the creation of a female auxiliary in 1840, as well as female societies to aid Liberian education. She has also identified three female antislavery petitions that were submitted to the state legislature during the 1832 Virginia Debates on slavery that followed in the wake of the Turner rebellion. *We Mean to Be Counted: White Women and Politics in Antebellum Virginia* (Chapel Hill: University of North Carolina Press, 1998), chap. 2. Deborah Gold Hansen discusses the development of cross-class alliances within a single antislavery auxiliary in *Strained Sisterhood* and "The Boston Female Anti-slavery Society and the Limits of Gender Politics," in Yellin and Van Horne, *The Abolitionist Sisterhood,* 45–66. More significantly, female laborers were active in circulating petitions through groups such as the Lynne Female Anti-slavery Society. See Edward Magdol, *The Antislavery Rank and File: A Social Profile of the Abolitionists' Constituency* (New York: Greenwood Press, 1986), 37–38.

39. Angelina Grimké, speech at the Second Antislavery Convention of American Women, May 16, 1838, in *The Concise History of Woman Suffrage: Selections from the Classic Work of Stanton, Anthony, Gage and Harper,* ed. Mari Jo Buhle and Paul Buhle (Urbana: University of Illinois Press, 1978), 76; Angelina Grimké, "An Appeal to the Women of the Nominally Free States," American Antislavery Society (New York, 1836), reprinted in *Women's Rights Emerges within the Antislavery Movement, 1830–1870: A Brief History with Documents,* by Kathryn Kish Sklar (New York: Bedford/St. Martins, 2000), 102; Boston Female Antislavery Society, Annual Report (1836), 29. For the Grimkés' career, see Gerda Lerner, *The Grimké Sisters from South Carolina: Pioneers for Woman's Rights and Abolition* (New York: Schocken Books, 1971).

40. *Memoirs of John Quincy Adams, Comprising Portions of His Diary from 1795 to 1848,* ed. Charles Frances Adams (Philadelphia: J. B. Lippincott, 1871), 10:345; John Quincy Adams, letter to Charles Francis Adams, December 15–19, 1835, quoted in Leonard L. Richards, *The Life and Times of Congressman John Quincy Adams* (New York: Oxford University Press, 1986), 117.

41. Nye, *Fettered Freedom,* 49.

42. Adams quoted in the *Recorder,* May 26, 1836, 91. For a detailed account of Adams's role in the gag rule debates, see William Lee Miller, *Arguing about Slavery: John Quincy Adams and the Great Battle in the United States Congress* (New York: Vintage Books, 1995). Van Buren's role in the gag rule debates is discussed in Donald B. Cole, *Martin Van Buren and the American Political System* (Princeton: Princeton University Press, 1984).

43. "Memorial from the Women of Brookline, Massachusetts," February 14, 1838, National Archives, HR 26A H1.1, RG 233; "Petition, Ladies of Windsor Country, Vermont, 1840," HR 30A G5.1, RG 233. Although there is a strong possibility that the women who signed the anti-slavery petitions—even after the gag rule—were far more radical than the "benevolent ladies" and asylum directors like Gratz who promoted the anti-Indian-removal memorials, the change in the rhetorical tenor of female petitioning was striking. The 70% figure is Gerda Lerner's, the 59% figure comes from Paul Goodman's research in *Of One Blood,* 229. For a state-by-state breakdown of the gender balance in petition signatories in 1837, see table 6 on that page, which shows that the ratio varied from none in Michigan to 100% in Rhode Island and was 64%–70% in the states with the largest number of signatories, Massachusetts and Ohio. Interestingly, Pinckney sought to legitimize his argument for the gag rule by pointing out that two-fifths of the thirty-four thousand signatures on the 176 petitions before Congress at the time were by women. *Congressional Globe,* 24th Cong., 1st sess. (Washington, D.C.: Globe, 1836), 3:386.

44. James Forten, Jr., "Speech Delivered before the Philadelphia Female Anti-slavery Soci-

ety, April 14, 1836," in *The Black Abolitionist Papers,* ed. C. Peter Ripley (Chapel Hill: University of North Carolina Press, 1991), 2:158; AAS, "To the People of the United States," 1:7–8; William Jay quoted in Alice Felt Tyler, *Freedom's Ferment: Phases of American Social History from the Colonial Period to the Outbreak of the Civil War* (New York: Harper Torchbooks, 1944), 511.

45. Arthur Schlesinger, Jr., *The Age of Jackson* (1945; reprint, Boston: Little, Brown and Co., 1953), 350, 351, 354; Varon, *We Mean to Be Counted,* 82; Feller, "Politics and Society," 158. A great deal of historical attention has been devoted to parsing the intellectual and ideological differences between Jacksonian Democrats and anti-Jacksonians. For many historians, Whig coalitions seemed to symbolize many of the trends that fed the fires of reform: they delighted in voluntary associations, they backed the Benevolent Empire, and they eagerly promoted and just as enthusiastically benefited from the profound social and economic changes that permeated Jacksonian society. As Daniel Walker Howe explains, Whig culture actively embraced both moral and material progress and evangelical reform. Thus, "One reason why the Whigs were able to keep insisting on the evil of political parties is that the benevolent societies (mainly led by Whigs and promoting the kind of reform Whigs wanted) provided them with an alternative mode of organizing in pursuit of their social objectives. The rise of political parties, along with the danger that they would become patronage-oriented, could only tend to undercut the influence of the cause-oriented voluntary associations." *The Political Culture of the American Whigs,* 158; Daniel Walker Howe, "The Evangelical Movement and Political Culture in the North during the Second Party System," *Journal of American History* 77 (March 1991): 1216. The ideological differences that separated Jacksonians from the Whigs are still more sharply etched in Lawrence F. Kohl, *The Politics of Individualism: Parties and the American Character in the Jacksonian Era* (New York: Oxford University Press, 1989); Ellis, *The Union at Risk;* and Paul E. Johnson, *A Shopkeeper's Millennium: Society and Revivals in Rochester, New York, 1815–1837* (New York: Hill and Wang, 1978). For a detailed description of the party itself, see Holt, *The Rise and Fall of the American Whig Party.* According to Holt, Whigs were more likely to endorse temperance and educational reforms than their Democratic counterparts, who portrayed "Whigs as bigoted and self-righteous religious fanatics intent on imposing their ethical values on others" (68). However, Garrisonian abolitionists regarded both parties with equal suspicion. Thus, although the members of the Massachusetts Antislavery Society felt that "abolitionists [were] about equally divided among both political parties," they contended that both parties ultimately fell into "the pro-slavery category," noting the AAS's ban on "voting for such men as Tyler, or Clay, or Van Buren, or Calhoun." Massachusetts Antislavery Society, Annual Report (1839), 21, and Annual Report (1843), 30, 64.

46. Richards, *Adams,* 142.

47. Suzanne Lebsock, *The Free Women of Petersburg: Status and Culture in a Southern Town, 1784–1860* (New York: W. W. Norton and Co., 1984), xvii.

Chapter Seven

1. Arthur Tappan quoted in Bertram Wyatt-Brown, *Lewis Tappan and the Evangelical War against Slavery* (Cleveland: Press of Case Western Reserve University, 1969), 118, 119.

2. Ibid., 120.

3. For earlier interpretations of the abolitionist movement, see, for example, John L. Thomas, *The Liberator: William Lloyd Garrison* (Boston: Little, Brown and Co., 1963); David Brion Davis, *The Slave Power Conspiracy and the Paranoid Style* (Baton Rouge: Louisiana State University Press, 1969); David Donald, *Lincoln Reconsidered: Essays on the Civil War Era* (New

York: Alfred Knopf, 1965); and the more sympathetic volume edited by Martin Duberman, *The Antislavery Vanguard: New Essays on the Abolitionists* (Princeton: Princeton University Press, 1965). David Brion Davis's introduction to the volume he edited entitled *Antebellum Reform* (New York: Harper & Row, 1967) captures the language of these discourses. According to Davis, historians had been "put off" by the "reformers' extremism, fanaticism, eccentricity and contentiousness," as well as their "moral fundamentalism" (1). The literature on the antislavery movement is immense. See, among others, Aileen S. Kraditor, *Means and Ends in American Abolitionism: Garrison and His Critics on Strategy and Tactics, 1834–1850* (New York: Pantheon Books, 1969); James Brewer Stewart, *Holy Warriors: The Abolitionists and American Slavery* (New York: Hill and Wang, 1976); Ronald G. Walters, *The Antislavery Appeal: American Abolitionism after 1830* (Baltimore: Johns Hopkins University Press, 1976); Lawrence Friedman, *Gregarious Saints: Self and Community in American Abolitionism, 1830–1870* (New York: Cambridge University Press, 1982); Lewis Perry, *Radical Abolitionism: Anarchy and the Government of God in Antislavery Thought* (Ithaca: Cornell University Press, 1973); Ronald G. Walters, *American Reformers, 1815–1860* (New York: Hill and Wang, 1978, 1997), chap. 4; Benjamin Quarles, *Black Abolitionists* (New York: Oxford University Press, 1969); Edward Magdol, *The Antislavery Rank and File: A Social Profile of the Abolitionists' Constituency* (New York: Greenwood Press, 1986); Shirley J. Yee, *Black Women Abolitionists: A Study in Activism, 1828–1860* (Knoxville: University of Tennessee Press, 1992); Robert H. Abzug, *Cosmos Crumbling: American Reform and the Religious Imagination* (New York: Oxford University Press, 1994), chap. 6; Jean Fagan Yellin, *Women and Sisters: The Antislavery Feminists in American Culture* (New Haven: Yale University Press, 1989); Jean Fagan Yellin and John C. Van Horne, eds, *The Abolitionist Sisterhood: Women's Political Culture in Antebellum America* (Ithaca: Cornell University Press, 1994); Lori Ginzberg, *Women in Antebellum Reform* (Wheeling, Ill.: Harlan Davidson Co., 2000), chap. 4; Paul Goodman, *Of One Blood: Abolitionism and the Origins of Racial Equality* (Berkeley: University of California Press, 1998); Julie Roy Jeffrey, *The Great Silent Army of Abolitionism: Ordinary Women in the Antislavery Movement* (Chapel Hill: University of North Carolina Press, 1998); Debra Gold Hansen, *Strained Sisterhood: Gender and Class in the Boston Female Antislavery Society* (Amherst: University of Massachusetts Press, 1993); and Kathryn Kish Sklar, *Women's Rights Emerges within the Antislavery Movement, 1830–1870: A Brief History with Documents* (New York: Bedford/St. Martin's, 2000); as well as the biographies of individual abolitionists, such as Henry Mayer's *All on Fire: William Lloyd Garrison and the Abolition of Slavery* (New York: St. Martin's Press, 1998).

4. Leonard L. Richards, *"Gentlemen of Property and Standing": Anti-abolition Mobs in Jacksonian America* (New York: Oxford University Press, 1970) 12, 14, 77; David Grimsted, *American Mobbing, 1828–1861: Toward Civil War* (New York: Oxford University Press, 1998); Andrew Jackson, letter to Amos Kendall, August 9, 1935, in *The Correspondence of Andrew Jackson*, ed. John Spencer Bassett (Washington, D.C.: Carnegie Institution, 1926–33), 5:360.

5. Richards, *"Gentlemen of Property and Standing"*; Russell B. Nye, *Fettered Freedom: Civil Liberties and the Slavery Controversy: 1830–1860* (East Lansing: Michigan State College Press, 1949), 119, 116.

6. Kimberly K. Smith's arguments in *The Dominion of Voice: Riot, Reason, and Romance in Antebellum Politics* (Lawrence: University Press of Kansas, 1999) help to shed some light on these ideas by casting the Jacksonian mobs as the last gasp of the eighteenth-century tradition of rioting as a form of popular political discourse.

7. Andrew Jackson, "Message of the President of the United States" in *United States Register of Debates in Congress*, 24th Cong., 1st sess. (Washington, D.C.: Gale and Seton, 1835), ap-

pendix 11; Donald B. Cole, *Martin Van Buren and the American Political System* (Princeton: Princeton University Press, 1984), 272; *Albany Argus,* August 10, 1836. Van Buren's antiabolitionism is discussed in Cole, *Martin Van Buren,* chap. 9. Michael F. Holt notes that "Van Buren's friend, Silas Wright of New York, made a speech in the U.S. Senate praising antiabolitionist mobs as a true expression of Northern sentiment," citing this as additional evidence of the Democrats' "explicit proslavery position." *The Political Crisis of the 1850s* (New York: W. W. Norton and Co., 1978), 29. Richards also ties Van Burenite Democrats to the Albany mob. *"Gentlemen of Property and Standing,"* 87.

8. Richards, *"Gentlemen of Property and Standing,"* 148. Thus, he concluded, "political affiliation was probably *not* an independent variable."

9. See, for example, Leon Litwack, *North of Slavery: The Negro in the Free States, 1790–1860* (Chicago: University of Chicago Press, 1961), passim.

10. David Brion Davis, *The Problem of Slavery in the Age of Revolution, 1770–1823* (Ithaca: Cornell University Press, 1975); Charles Sellers, *The Market Revolution: Jacksonian America, 1815–1846* (New York: Oxford University Press, 1991), 128, 405.

11. Richards, *"Gentlemen of Property and Standing,"* 61, 48; Boston *Commercial Gazette,* August 16, 1836, quoted in Boston Female Antislavery Society, Annual Report (1836), 36–37.

12. Sklar, *Women's Rights Emerges,* 23, 21, 120; Boston Female Antislavery Society, Annual Report (1837), 34. For the Grimkés, see Gerda Lerner, *The Grimké Sisters from South Carolina: Pioneers for Woman's Rights and Abolition* (New York: Schocken Books, 1971). As Sklar points out, when the AAS sent copies of Angelina Grimké's "Appeal to the Christian Women of the South" to Charleston, they were burned, and friends warned that if she came home "she could not escape personal violence at the hands of the mob" (19).

13. Bruce Laurie, *Artisans into Workers: Labor in Nineteenth Century America* (1989; reprint, Urbana: University of Illinois Press, 1997), 59.

14. David R. Roediger, *The Wages of Whiteness: Race and the Making of the American Working Class* (New York: Verso, 1991); Michael Kaplan, "New York City Tavern Violence and the Creation of a Working Class Male Identity," *Journal of the Early Republic* 15, no. 4 (winter 1995): 614.

15. Emma Jones Lapsansky, "'Since They Got Those Separate Churches': Afro-Americans and Racism in Jacksonian Philadelphia," *American Quarterly* 32 (1980): 57. On racist rioting, see also Paul Goodman, "The Manual Labor Movement and the Origins of Abolitionism," *Journal of the Early Republic* 13 (fall 1993): 355–88; Carl E. Prince, "The Great 'Riot Year': Jacksonian Democracy and Patterns of Violence in 1834," *Journal of the Early Republic* 5 (spring 1985): 1–19; and Linda S. Kerber, "Abolitionists and Amalgamators: The New York City Race Riots of 1834," *New York History* 48, no. 1 (1967): 28–39.

16. The Philadelphia Female Anti-slavery Society is discussed in Jean Soderlund, "Priorities and Power," in Yellin and Van Horne, *The Abolitionist Sisterhood,* 67–88. For an excellent description of one of the major fairs, see Lee Chambers-Schiller, "'A Good Work among the People': The Political Culture of the Boston Antislavery Fair," ibid. The fairs are also discussed in Jeffrey, *The Great Silent Army,* chap. 3.

17. The schism is discussed in Walters, *The Antislavery Appeal,* chap. 1, "Divisions: Antislavery Unity and Disunity"; Stewart, *Holy Warriors,* chaps. 4 and 5: Walters, *American Reformers,* chap. 4; Kraditor, *Means and Ends;* Amy Swerdlow, "Abolition's Conservative Sisters: The Ladies' New York City Anti-slavery Societies, 1834–1840"; Debra Gold Hansen, "The Boston Female Anti-slavery Society and the Limits of Gender Politics"; Jean R. Soderlund, "Priorities and Power: The Philadelphia Female Anti-slavery Society," in Yellin and Van Horne, *The Abo-*

litionist Sisterhood, 31–90; Mayer, *All on Fire*, chap. 13, "Schism"; and Dorothy Sterling, *Ahead of Her Time: Abby Kelley and the Politics of Antislavery* (New York: W. W. Norton and Co., 1991), among others. The fortunes of the political wing are described in Eric Foner, *Free Soil, Free Labor, Free Men: The Ideology of the Republican Party before the Civil War* (New York: Oxford University Press, 1970); and William E. Geinapp, *The Origins of the Republican Party, 1852–1856* (New York: Oxford University Press, 1987).

18. The efforts of black and white female abolitionists are described in Debra Gold Hansen, "The Boston Female Anti-slavery Society," in Yellin and Van Horne, *The Abolitionist Sisterhood*, 45–65; Anne M. Boylan, "Benevolence and Antislavery Activity among African-American Women in New York and Boston, 1820–1840," ibid., 119–37; and Julie Roy Jeffrey, *The Great Silent Army*. See also Daniel C. Littlefield, "Blacks, John Brown, and a Theory of Manhood," in *His Soul Goes Marching On: Responses to John Brown and the Harpers Ferry Raid*, ed. Paul Finkelman (Charlottesville: University Press of Virginia, 1995), 67–97; Jane H. Pease and William H. Pease, *They Who Would Be Free: Blacks' Search for Freedom, 1830–1861* (New York: Atheneum, 1974); and Benjamin Quarles, *Black Abolitionists*. The notion of two abolitionisms is from Pease and Pease, *They Who Would Be Free*.

19. For a discussion of abolitionist imagery, see Yellin, *Women and Sisters*.

20. Edward W. Said, *Orientalism* (New York: Vintage Books 1979), 3.

21. Black Convention, Proceedings (1834), 28, in *The Black Abolitionist Papers*, ed. George E. Carter and C. Peter Ripley, microfilm edition, reel 1:475. For example, Prince Hall and more than seventy other Boston blacks petitioned the Massachusetts state legislature for transportation assistance for a colonization project in Africa in 1787. There were federal efforts, as well, beyond the work of the AAS. In 1833, for example, twelve hundred African Americans from Providence, Rhode Island, sent a petition reminding Jackson of the loyalty of his black troops in the Battle of New Orleans, where the general first made his reputation, and asking him on the basis of that record to abolish slavery in the capital and Southern territories in Florida and Arkansas. Black community leaders also tried their hand at economic boycotts, albeit with limited success. In 1831, a group of female parishioners at Bethel Church in Philadelphia launched one of the first female free produce associations, which was advertised in Garrison's *Liberator*. The idea that committed abolitionists should shun products produced through slave labor ultimately proved untenable when certifiably untainted products were not readily at hand. Nonetheless, each of the first five black conventions in the early 1830s formally endorsed the concept, urging "colored capitalists" to invest in free produce stores. Quoted in Quarles, *Black Abolitionists*, 74.

22. See, for example, Massachusetts Antislavery Society, Annual Reports, passim. Massachusetts passed its personal liberty law in 1843, backed by an eloquent report drafted by John Quincy Adams's son, Charles Francis, calling for legislation to separate "the people of Massachusetts from all connection to slavery," and a broadly based petition campaign that yielded 150 pounds of memorials bearing sixty-five thousand names. Eric Foner, *Free Soil*, 82; Mayer, *All on Fire*, 320.

23. Kenneth M. Stampp, *America in 1857: A Nation on the Brink* (1957; reprint, New York: Oxford University Press, 1990), 127; Massachusetts Antislavery Society, Annual Report (1845), 50. As N. P. Rogers, editor of the *New Hampshire Herald of Freedom* and a member of the New Hampshire Abolition Society, explained in response to charges that "Garrison is a no-human government man": "He is not . . . no-human government, nor have the advocates of the human right of government any right to be such, *as abolitionists*." Massachusetts Abolition Society, Annual Report (1841), 31. Conversely, Ronald Walters argues that "as Christian anarchists, they be-

lieved that the proper course of action was not to vote or to have anything else to do with human governments, which they regarded as inherently sinful." *American Reformers*, 89. Aileen Kraditor does a good job of parsing Garrisonian reactions to partisan politics in *Means and Ends*, chaps. 5 and 6. For a useful discussion of the nuances at the federal level, see Mayer, *All on Fire*, chap. 13, "Schism."

24. William Hamilton, "Why a Convention Is Necessary," keynote address to the Fourth Annual Convention of the Colored People, New York, June 2–13, 1834, in Foner and Branham, *Lift Every Voice*, 156. A long-standing ACS supporter, Henry Clay introduced his $12 million distribution bill to finance public education, internal improvements, and colonization via federal land sales in April 1832. Although it passed in both the House and the Senate, Jackson killed it with a pocket veto in December of the following year. Jackson's action was probably inspired by the arguments of Southern strict constructionists that such comprehensive national policymaking might provide precedents for the federal abolition of slavery, as well as by his glowering personal dislike of Clay. Liberia ultimately declared independence in 1847 and was finally recognized as an independent state by Lincoln in 1862. Clay's commitment remained unwavering, as evidenced by the stipulation in his will that the children of his slaves would be gradually emancipated and transported to Liberia. Merrill D. Peterson, *The Great Triumvirate: Webster, Clay and Calhoun* (New York: Oxford University Press, 1987), 488–89.

25. American Moral Reform Society, Minutes and Proceedings of the First Annual Meeting (Philadelphia, 1837), 4.

26. Black Convention, Proceedings (1834), 25; in Carter and Ripley, *Black Abolitionist Papers*, microfilm edition, 1:474; Linda M. Perkins, "Black Women and Racial 'Uplift' Prior to Emancipation," in *The Black Woman Cross-Culturally*, ed. Filomena Steady (Cambridge: Schenkman Publishing Co., 1981), 326. See also Yee, *Black Women Abolitionists;* and Willi Coleman, "Architects of a Vision: Black Women and Their Antebellum Quest for Political and Social Equality," in *African-American Women and the Vote, 1837–1965*, ed. Ann D. Gordon and Bettye Collier-Thomas (Amherst: University of Massachusetts Press, 1997), 24–40. As one spokesman noted, "Temperance societies are being made the order of the day, gaming and extravagance are being superseded by a judicious husbandry of finances, and idleness and levity are yielding precedence to industry and reflection. Day and Sabbath schools . . . have multiplied . . . literary societies and libraries have been established; lectures have been instituted and contributions levied for their support."

27. Perkins, "Black Women and Racial 'Uplift,'" 318–19.

28. *Colored American*, vol. 3 (May 18, 1839), quoted in Louis Filler, *The Crusade against Slavery, 1830–1860* (New York: Harper and Brothers, 1960), 144; *North Star*, September 29, 1848, in *The Life and Writings of Frederick Douglass: Early Years, 1817–1849*, ed. Philip S. Foner (New York: International Publishers, 1950), 1:335. Lewis Woodson, "the father of black nationalism," also made the link between drinking and squandered resources, estimating that the twenty-five thousand dollars spent annually by Pittsburgh's black citizens on alcohol could educate twenty-five hundred children for four years, build four churches, or establish a manual labor college. Donald Yacovone, "The Transformation of the Black Temperance Movement, 1827–1854: An Interpretation," *Journal of the Early Republic* 8 (fall 1988): 289. A number of related institutions also appeared, including a black temperance newspaper, the *Northern Star and Freedmen's Advocate*, published in the 1840s, and several temperance boardinghouses, restaurants, and emporiums. Unfortunately, the success of the black temperance movement provided an opening for at least one highly destructive racist clash. White rowdies launched a two-day rioting spree with an attack on Philadelphia's Moyamensing Temperance Society Parade in 1842, a melee

that culminated in the destruction of the Second Colored Presbyterian Church and the Smith Beneficial Hall, a frequent venue for black temperance meetings. Smith Hall was torched by the crowd, then demolished by city officials who explained that "the building, symbolizing the social and economic progress of the black community, would incite further outbursts" (Yacovone, "The Transformation," 294). The temperance riot highlighted one of the bitterest ironies of the black crusade for moral reform. The more avidly African American communities embraced racial uplift, the sharper working-class whites' antipathies became, as blacks sought to represent the bourgeois values that many white workers ostensibly rejected. By aspiring to mores and lifestyles associated with middle-class whites, black moral reformers ideologically distanced themselves from the working class, and the more they rose, the more imperative it became for racially motivated mobs to bring them down.

29. Pennsylvania Abolition Society, "Facts on Beneficial Societies and Schools for Negroes, 1823–1838," Manuscripts, reel 26, Historical Society of Pennsylvania, Philadelphia.

30. Colored Citizens of Philadelphia, "A Memorial to the Honorable Senate and House of Representatives of the Commonwealth of Pennsylvania" (Philadelphia, 1854), 6. Others invested in buildings, banks, real estate, and government bonds. Almost all of the larger associations developed investment strategies when they drafted their constitutions, a practice that clearly indicated their interest in communal capital accumulation. W. E. B. Du Bois placed the wealth of Philadelphia's sixteen black churches at $114,000 in 1838 and also used the financial holdings of various voluntary associations as a measure of communal progress and wealth in the 1890s. As he explained, "the Negro churches of Philadelphia raise nearly $100,000 a year. They hold in real estate $900,000 worth of property, and these are no insignificant element in the economics of the city." *The Philadelphia Negro: A Social Study* (New York: Benjamin Bloom, 1899), 200, 203.

31. Quarles, *Black Abolitionists*, 40, 200. Papers such as the *Colored American* also tracked instances of communal giving. See also Emmett D. Carson, *A Hand Up: Black Philanthropy and Self-Help in America* (Washington, D.C.: Joint Center for Political and Economic Studies, 1993). Interestingly, some individuals, churches, and benevolent institutions also raised money to purchase fugitive slaves in peril of being sent back south, or to enable people to purchase their family members. In one instance, Boston's Twelfth Baptist Church raised $1,300 (@ $17,000), a sizable sum, to buy the freedom of two of their deacons. And some groups generated capital to help fugitive slaves in their escape.

32. C. Peter Ripley, ed. *The Black Abolitionist Papers* (Chapel Hill: University of North Carolina Press, 1991), 3:32; *North Star*, December 3, 1847, and September 29, 1848, in *The Life and Writings of Frederick Douglass*, 1:280, 336. The national black conventions also urged their auxiliaries to "pay strict attention to the patronage and circulation of The Liberator, The Emancipator, and all other papers pledged to our interest." Proceedings of the National Black Convention, 1834. In Carter and Ripley, *Black Abolitionist Papers*, microfilm edition, 1:471.

33. For a fuller account of the black women's abolitionist movement, see Yee, *Black Women Abolitionists*. On vigilance societies, see Linda Perkins, "Black Women and Racial 'Uplift,'" 317–34. For the history of black women's organizations more generally, see Evelyn Brooks Higginbotham, "Beyond the Sound of Silence: Afro-American Women in History," *Gender and History* 1, no. 1 (spring 1989): 50–67; Anne Firor Scott, "Most Invisible of All: Black Women's Voluntary Associations," *Journal of Southern History* 56, no. 1 (1990): 2–22; and Darlene Clark Hine and Kathleen Thompson, *A Shining Thread of Hope: The History of Black Women in America* (New York: Broadway Books, 1998).

34. For black women's activities, see Yee, *Black Women Abolitionists*. For class and social dis-

tinctions among white women's organizations, see Nancy A. Hewitt, *Women's Activism and Social Change: Rochester, New York, 1822–1872* (Ithaca: Cornell University Press, 1984).

35. See also "Proceedings of a Meeting of the New York Committee of Vigilance" (1836), in Ripley, *Black Abolitionist Papers*, print version, 3:168–80; and "Annual Report of the Colored Vigilant Committee" (1843), ibid., microfilm edition, 1:397–402.

36. *Prigg v. Pennsylvania* is discussed in Don E. Fehrenbacher, *Slavery, Law and Politics: The Dred Scott Case in Historical Perspective* (1978; reprint, New York: Oxford University Press, 1981), 21–23. Some free blacks in Baltimore also engaged in petition campaigns. In 1839, fifty-five black citizens petitioned the city council to be exempted from the payment of school taxes, since they were barred from city schools. In 1844, they submitted a petition asking for a portion of the school tax to support two segregated schools in their own community, followed by a second petition on this theme six years later. All were rejected, leading Nelson Well, a black drayman, to bequeath $3,500 (@ $45,000 in 2000 dollars) for the education of "the poor free colored children" of Baltimore in the late 1850s. Baltimore blacks also mounted a petition drive to stalemate the Jacobs reenslavement bill in 1859. Christopher Phillips, *Freedom's Port: The African American Community of Baltimore, 1790–1860* (Urbana: University of Illinois Press, 1997), 227–33.

37. Lewis Tappan, quoted in Wyatt-Brown, *Lewis Tappan and the Evangelical War*, 329; Arthur Tappan, "The Fugitive Slave Bill: Its History and Unconstitutionality" (New York: William Harnad, 1850), preface; Frederick Douglass, speech at the American Antislavery Society meeting, May 11, 1847, in *Lift Every Voice: African-American Oratory, 1787–1900*, ed. Philip S. Foner and Robert James Branham (Tuscaloosa: University of Alabama Press, 1998), 248. For the growing militancy in the black community, see Pease and Pease, *They Who Would Be Free*, chap. 11, "The Uses of Violence"; Quarles, *Black Abolitionists*, chap. 10, "Shock Therapy and Crisis"; James Oliver Horton and Lois E. Horton, *In Hope of Liberty: Culture, Community and Protest among Northern Free Blacks, 1700–1860* (New York: Oxford University Press, 1997), chap. 10, "The Widening Struggle, Growing Militancy, and the Hope of Liberty for All"; James Oliver Horton and Lois E. Horton, *Black Bostonians: Family Life and Community Struggle in the Antebellum North* (1979; reprint, New York: Holmes and Meier, 1999), chap. 9, "A Decade of Militancy"; and Litwack, *North of Slavery*, chap. 8: "The Crisis of the 1850s." However, as Bertram Wyatt-Brown points out, the Tappans stood aloof from the growing endorsement of physical violence. See *Lewis Tappan and the Evangelical War*, chap. 17, "The Violent Decades."

38. Ripley, *Black Abolitionist Papers*, print version, 3:51. As Benjamin Quarles points out, blacks were barred from service in state militias under the Militia Act of 1792. It remained a controversial issue. While Rhode Island allowed a black company to use state arms, Massachusetts declined to endorse their petitions to legally form a militia unit. *Black Abolitionists*, 229, 230.

39. Pease and Pease, *They Who Would Be Free*, 222; Massachusetts Antislavery Society, Annual Report (1852), 11. Webster's role is discussed in Peterson, *The Great Triumvirate*, 480–83. Obstruction of the law was a federal offense punishable by up to one thousand dollars in fines and six months in jail.

40. *Frederick Douglass: Selected Speeches and Writings*, ed. Philip Foner (Chicago: Lawrence Hill Books, 1999), 179. When the rioters were charged with treason, Douglass labeled the charges an "absurdity.... Our government has virtually made every colored man in the land an outlaw, one who may be hunted by any villain who may think proper to do so, and if the hunted man ... shall lift his arm in his own defense ... he is arrested, arraigned, and tried for high treason, and if found guilty, he must suffer death! The basis of allegiance is protection ... to the government that destroys us, we owe no allegiance" (ibid., 181).

41. Holt, *The Political Crisis of the 1850s*, 193.

42. Garrison quoted in Mayer, *All on Fire*, 478; "Annual Meeting of the Massachusetts Anti-slavery Society: Sketches of the Discussions" *Liberator*, February 13, 1857, in *Documents of Upheaval: Selections from William Lloyd Garrison's "The Liberator," 1831–1865*, ed. Truman Nelson (New York: Hill and Wang, 1966), 222. Lawrence Friedman's *Gregarious Saints* is particularly good on growing radicalism among white abolitionists. See chap. 7, "Righteous Violence," as well as the annual reports of organizations such as the Massachusetts Antislavery Society. To quote Douglass's biographer, William S. McFeely, "Many antislavery leaders who had been pacific, in action if not always in rhetoric—Henry Ward Beecher, Gerrit Smith and Douglass himself among them—now called on their followers to send guns to the Kansas abolitionists." *Frederick Douglass* (New York: W. W. Norton and Co., 1991), 188. Douglass was ambivalent about the Harpers Ferry raid, but nonetheless passed along a twenty-five-dollar gift from James Gloucester (195). Various perspectives on John Brown's raid can be found in Finkelman, *His Soul Goes Marching On*. For Douglass's role in funding Brown, see Mayer, *All on Fire*, 476; and McFeely, *Frederick Douglass*, 195. Both Mayer (670) and Finkelman (6) contend that Brown's involvement in the Pottawatomie massacre was not well known in the East. Emerson's involvement is discussed in Robert D. Richardson, Jr., *Emerson: The Mind on Fire* (Berkeley: University of California Press, 1995), 498.

43. Ripley, *Black Abolitionist Papers*, print version, 3:54; Pease and Pease, *They Who Would Be Free*, 241. For the Dred Scott decision, see Fehrenbacher, *Slavery, Law and Politics*.

Chapter Eight

1. For an excellent discussion of the Eaton affair, see Kristin E. Wood, " 'One Woman So Dangerous to Public Morals': Gender and Power in the Eaton Affair," *Journal of the Early Republic* 17 (summer 1997): 237–75. See also Catherine Allgor, *Parlor Politics: In Which the Ladies of Washington Help Build a City and a Government* (Charlottesville: University Press of Virginia, 2000), chap. 5, "The Fall of Andrew Jackson's Cabinet."

2. Bruce Allen Dorsey, "City of Brotherly Love: Religious Benevolence, Gender and Reform in Philadelphia, 1780–1844" (Ph.D. diss., Brown University, 1993), 116, 120, 121. Transatlantic trends are discussed in Walter I. Trattner, *From Poor Law to Welfare State: A History of Social Welfare in America* (New York: Free Press, 1989), chap. 4; Priscilla Ferguson Clement, *Welfare and the Poor in the Nineteenth Century City: Philadelphia, 1800–1854* (Rutherford, N.J.: Fairleigh Dickinson University Press, 1985); and Christine Stansell, *City of Women: Sex and Class in New York, 1789–1860* (New York: Alfred A. Knopf, 1986), 34–35. As Amy Bridges explains, "The change in dramatis personae and government functions marked a redrawing of the line between public and private." *A City in the Republic: Antebellum New York and the Origins of Machine Politics* (Cambridge: Cambridge University Press, 1984), 1–2.

3. Lawrence F. Kohl, *The Politics of Individualism: Parties and the American Character in the Jacksonian Era* (New York: Oxford University Press, 1989), 117. See also David M. Schneider, *The History of Public Welfare in New York State, 1609–1866* (Chicago: University of Chicago Press, 1938). Josiah Quincy, who wrote the Boston report, noted that the city's poor relief rolls had risen by 60% between 1801 and 1820. Elected mayor that year, he presided over the construction of a thirty-five-thousand-dollar house of industry while cutting outdoor relief payments to the poor. See Thomas O'Connor, "To Be Poor and Homeless in Old Boston," in *Massachusetts and the New Nation*, ed. Conrad Edick Wright (Boston: New England University Press, 1992), 202–25. For a fuller discussion of the impact of changing municipal attitudes

about poverty during the 1820s, see Stansell, *City of Women*, 32–35; Dorsey, "City of Brotherly Love," chap. 3; Clement, *Welfare and the Poor in the Nineteenth Century City;* Raymond A. Mohl, *Poverty in New York, 1783–1825* (New York: Oxford University Press, 1971); Raymond A. Mohl, "Humanitarianism in the Preindustrial City: The New York Society for the Prevention of Pauperism, 1817–1823," *Journal of American History* 57, no. 3 (December 1970): 576–99; Robert E. Cray, Jr., *Paupers and Poor Relief in New York City and Its Rural Environs, 1700–1830* (Philadelphia: Temple University Press, 1988); Vincent Francis Bonelli, "The Response of Public and Private Philanthropy to the Panic of 1819 in New York City" (Ph.D. diss., Fordham University, 1976); and Bridges, *A City in the Republic.*

4. Dorsey, "City of Brotherly Love," 139; Joanna H. Mathews, *A Short History of the Orphan Asylum Society in the City of New York, Founded in 1806* (New York: Anson D. F. Randolph and Co., 1893), 34.

5. Anne Boylan, "Women and Politics in the Era before Seneca Falls," *Journal of the Early Republic* 10 (fall 1990): 378.

6. Philadelphia Orphan Society, Annual Report (1823), 8, Annual Report (1828), 6, Annual Report (1837), 8, Annual Report (1825), 6, and Annual Report (1829), 5; David Rothman, *The Discovery of the Asylum: Social Order and Disorder in the New Republic* (Boston: Little, Brown and Co., 1971).

7. Mathews, *A Short History*, 34, 46.

8. Female Hospitable Society, Annual Report (1828), 40–41.

9. For the role of female "influence" and political brokering in the development of female charities, see Lori Ginzberg, *Women and the Work of Benevolence: Morality, Politics, and Class in the Nineteenth-Century United States* (New Haven: Yale University Press, 1990), 77.

10. Clement, *Welfare and the Poor in the Nineteenth Century City:* 59. See also Rothman, *The Discovery of the Asylum;* Roy M. Brown, *Public Poor Relief in North Carolina* (Chapel Hill: University of North Carolina Press, 1928); Barbara L. Bellows, *Benevolence among Slaveholders: Assisting the Poor in Charleston, 1670–1860* (Baton Rouge: Louisiana State University Press, 1993).

11. Society for the Prevention of Juvenile Delinquency, Documents, 54 (House of Refuge [New York], Annual Report [1828]), 245; Robert S. Pickett, *House of Refuge: Origins of Juvenile Reform in New York State, 1815–1857* (Syracuse: Syracuse University Press, 1969); House of Refuge (Philadelphia), Annual Report (1829), 10; New York Dispensary, Annual Reports. See also Mohl, *Poverty in New York,* chap. 16. These patterns resoundingly belie the notion of a "gendered bargain" in which men monopolized politics while women assumed control of social welfare services in antebellum America. See Jeanie Attie, *Patriotic Toil: Northern Women and the American Civil War* (Ithaca: Cornell University Press, 1998).

12. Free School Society (later renamed Public School Society), Annual Report (1824), 66; House of Refuge (Philadelphia), Annual Report (1829), n.p., Annual Report (1832), 7; Schneider, *The History of Public Welfare,* 317–19. See also Carl F. Kaestle, *The Evolution of the Urban School System, 1750–1850* (Cambridge, Mass.: Harvard University Press, 1973). At least one women's group, the New York Female Association, did receive $1,075 in municipal funds for their educational work with the five to six hundred children of the poor they taught in 1824. New York Female Association, Annual Report (1824–25), 5, 6. At least one Catholic orphanage also continued to receive allocations for the instruction of its inmates.

13. House of Refuge (Philadelphia), Annual Report (1835), 5, 7, and Annual Report (1832), 26; Philadelphia Orphan Society, Annual Report (1829), 5. I have chosen to use the term "directresses" in lieu of more modern terms such as "directors" "or "trustees" because this is the language that the antebellum board members used to describe themselves.

14. Mathews, *A Short History*, 52; New York Colored Orphan Asylum, Annual Report (1839), 5; Female Society of Philadelphia for the Relief and Employment of the Poor, Annual Report (1835), 7.

15. See, for example, Paul Boyer, *Urban Masses and Moral Order in America, 1820–1920* (Cambridge, Mass.: Harvard University Press, 1978); Clifford Griffin, *Their Brothers' Keepers: Moral Stewardship in the United States: 1800–1860* (New York: H. Wolff, 1960); Charles I. Foster, *Errand of Mercy: The Evangelical United Front, 1790–1837* (Chapel Hill: University of North Carolina Press, 1960); Rothman, *The Discovery of the Asylum;* and Mohl, *Poverty in New York, 1783–1825.* For a dissenting view, see Lois W. Banner, "Religious Benevolence as Social Control: A Critique of an Interpretation," *Journal of American History* 68, no. 1 (June 1973): 23–41. Examples of more recent interpretations include Peregrine Horden and Richard Smith, eds., *The Locus of Care: Families, Communities, Institutions and the Provision of Welfare since Antiquity* (London: Routledge, 1998); and Peter Mandler, ed., *The Uses of Charity: The Poor on Relief in the Nineteenth-Century Metropolis* (Philadelphia: University of Pennsylvania Press, 1990). As Mandler points out, "the aims of charity are not necessarily the same as its uses." "We must put aside the assumption that charity played only a minor role in the working class economy ... looking with more discrimination on how working class families used and viewed charitable offerings in specific settings" (28, 16). See also Bruce Bellingham, "Waifs and Strays: Child Abandonment, Foster Care, and Families in Mid–Nineteenth Century New York," in Mandler, *The Uses of Charity*, 123–60; Clarke A. Chambers, "Toward a Redefinition of Welfare History," *Journal of American History* 73, no. 2 (September 1986): 422. Lawrence Kohl also criticizes the notion that "the world is torn between an independent, aggressive class of controllers and a passive class of the controlled," which "obscures a reality in which the controlled are rarely without their own resources to resist control and even to exert a degree of control over those who would seek to manipulate them." "The Concept of Social Control and the History of Jacksonian America," *Journal of the Early Republic* 5 (spring 1985): 33.

16. Stansell, *City of Women*, 54.

17. Ibid.; Society for the Reformation of Juvenile Delinquents, *Documents of the House of Refuge* (New York: Mahlon Day, 1832), 277–78, 248–49. See also House of Refuge (Philadelphia), Annual Reports, passim.

18. New York Children's Aid Society, Annual Report (1855), n.p.

19. New York Orphan Asylum, 1844 Bylaws, quoted in Mathews, *A Short History*, 56; Susan Lynne Porter, "The Benevolent Asylum—Image and Reality: The Care and Training of Female Orphans in Boston, 1800–1840" (Ph.D. diss., Boston University, 1984), 228; Society for the Relief of Poor Widows with Small Children, Minutes, n.d. (1830s), Manuscript Collections, New-York Historical Society, New York; New York Colored Orphan Asylum, Annual Report (1844), 7; *Colored American*, April 22, 1837; Rhoda G. Freeman, "The Free Negro in New York City in the Era before the Civil War" (Ph.D. diss., Columbia University, 1966).

20. Stansell, *City of Women*, 33; Priscilla Ferguson Clement, "Nineteenth Century Welfare Policy, Programs and Poor Women: Philadelphia as a Case Study," *Feminist Studies* 18, no. 1 (spring 1992): 37.

21. Stansell, *City of Women*, 111; Clement, "Nineteenth Century Welfare Policy," 42. See also Mandler, *The Uses of Charity;* and Amy Gilman, "From Widowhood to Wickedness: The Politics of Class and Gender in New York City Private Charity, 1799–1860," *History of Education Quarterly* 24 (spring 1984): 59–74. The role of charities in both sustaining and raising wages for seamstresses is discussed in Mari Jo Buhle, "Needlewomen and the Vicissitudes of Modern Life: A Study of Middle-Class Construction in the Antebellum Northeast," in *Visible Women:*

New Essays on American Activism, ed. Suzanne Lebsock and Nancy Hewitt (Urbana: University of Illinois Press, 1993), 145–65. The directors the Female Hospitable Society were extremely critical of "the low price of women's wages," which were less than twenty cents for sewing a complete shirt, a price that had declined over time. As they pointed out, even if a woman worked full time, she could produce only about twelve shirts per week, which was not enough to support a family. "What is to become of her children whilst the mother is thus *forced* to labor? . . . Oppressing the poor is the worst way,—*the way of injustice*." Annual Report (1828), 41.

22. For Irish women as donors to charities, see Hasia R. Diner, *Erin's Daughters in America: Irish Immigrant Women in the Nineteenth Century* (Baltimore: Johns Hopkins University Press, 1983). According to Diner, "women contributed the vast bulk of financial support for both parish maintenance and Catholic charitable work generally" (137).

23. Perhaps the strongest statement of the notion that women's voluntary associations were largely absent in the South is in Elizabeth Fox-Genovese, *Within the Plantation Household: Black and White Women of the Old South* (Chapel Hill: University of North Carolina Press, 1988). For countervailing views see Cynthia Kierner, *Beyond the Household: Women's Place in the Early South, 1700–1835* (Ithaca: Cornell University Press, 1998); Elizabeth R. Varon, *We Mean to Be Counted: White Women and Politics in Antebellum Virginia* (Chapel Hill: University of North Carolina Press, 1998); Suzanne Lebsock, *The Free Women of Petersburg: Status and Culture in a Southern Town, 1784–1860* (New York: W. W. Norton and Co., 1984); and Anne Firor Scott, *Natural Allies: Women's Associations in American History* (Urbana: University of Illinois Press, 1991).

24. Society for the Relief of Poor Widows with Small Children, Minutes, 1834, 1839, 1840, Manuscript Collections, New-York Historical Society, New York.

25. New York Colored Orphan Asylum, Annual Reports (1842, 1846, 1855); American Female Guardian Society and Home for the Friendless, Annual Report (1849), 19. New states, like California, also began to subsidize women's charities, including $5,000 [$70,000] allocations to San Francisco's Protestant Orphan Asylum in the 1850s. Roger W. Lotchin, *San Francisco, 1846–1856: From Hamlet to City* (Lincoln: University of Nebraska Press, 1974), 333.

26. Bellows, *Benevolence among Slaveholders*, 166. Elizabeth Varon in *We Mean to Be Counted* also suggests that petitions for public appropriations for Virginia's female asylums fell on deaf ears during the parsimonious 1830s. Conditions began to improve somewhat by the 1850s, as Baltimore's Home for the Friendless began to receive public funding and so did at least one female charity in Richmond, Virginia.

27. Kierner, *Beyond the Household*, 202; Varon, *We Mean to Be Counted*, 32, 48–52. Frederick A. Bode also found some female tract and charity groups in Georgia, but notes that for Southerners, religion was "a common sphere in which men and women frequently acted together to . . . perform works of benevolence." "A Common Sphere: White Evangelicals and Gender in Antebellum Georgia," *Georgia Historical Quarterly* 79, no. 4 (winter 1995): 779. Following Nat Turner's rebellion in Virginia in 1831, most Southern states passed legislation barring the assembly of even small groups of blacks, whether slave or free, without the presence of whites. The Virginia assembly outlawed preaching by both licensed and unlicensed black ministers, and all efforts to teach freedmen, mulattoes, or slaves to read and write were prohibited, which echoed legislation passed in other states. A few organizations, like the Brown Fellowship Society of Charleston, a wealthy mulatto group, managed to skirt these prohibitions, but most did not. The history of Charleston's African Methodist Episcopal Church is particularly telling. By 1818, the Charleston congregation was the second largest AME parish in the country. Shortly afterwards, in 1822, the city was rocked by an abortive slave rebellion led by Denmark Veysey. Sev-

eral members of the congregation were implicated in the plot, the pastor fled for his life, and the church was summarily demolished. Without the protections of a charter, and in the face of white wrath, the parishioners had no legal recourse against the destruction of their institution.

28. Stephanie McCurry," The Politics of Yeoman Households in South Carolina," in *Divided Houses: Gender and the Civil War,* ed. Catherine Clinton and Nina Silber (New York: Oxford University Press, 1992), 37. For Southern charities and social reform movements see Fox-Genovese, *Within the Plantation Household;* Jean Friedman, *The Enclosed Garden: Women and Community in the Evangelical South, 1830–1900* (Chapel Hill: University of North Carolina Press, 1985); Barbara L. Bellows, *Benevolence among Slaveholders,* and "Tempering the Wind: The Southern Response to Urban Poverty, 1850–1856" (Ph.D. diss., University of South Carolina, 1983); Lebsock, *The Free Women of Petersburg;* Varon, *We Mean to Be Counted;* Kierner, *Beyond the Household;* John W. Quist, *Restless Visionaries: The Social Roots of Antebellum Reform in Alabama and Michigan* (Baton Rouge: Louisiana State University Press, 1998), and "Slaveholding Operatives of the Benevolent Empire: Bible, Tract and Sunday School Societies in Antebellum Tuscaloosa, Alabama," *Journal of Southern History* 62 (August 1996): 481–526; and Ira Berlin, *Slaves without Masters: The Free Negro in the Antebellum South* (New York: Oxford University Press, 1974).

29. Fitzhugh quoted in Lee Ann Whites, "Rebecca Latimer Felton and the Problem of 'Protection' in the New South," in *Visible Women: New Essays on American Activism,* ed. Suzanne Lebsock and Nancy Hewitt (Urbana: University of Illinois Press, 1993), 43.

30. Bellows, "Tempering the Wind," 33; Charleston Orphan House, Rules for the Government of the Orphan House (Charleston, S.C., 1839). For an example of these practices in Georgia, see E. Merton Coulter, "Benjamin Braswell: Georgia Pioneer Philanthropist," *Georgia Historical Quarterly* 65, no. 2 (summer 1981): 67–81. At least one Charleston women's group, the Ladies Benevolent Society, did control substantial investments. However, their holdings were smaller than those of many Northern asylums run by women.

31. Don Harrison Doyle, *The Social Order of a Frontier Community: Jacksonville, Illinois, 1825–1870* (Urbana: University of Illinois Press, 1978), 68, 76; James Brown, *The History of Public Assistance in Chicago, 1833–1893* (Chicago: University of Chicago Press, 1941).

32. Kathleen D. McCarthy, *Noblesse Oblige: Charity and Cultural Philanthropy in Chicago, 1849–1929* (Chicago: University of Chicago Press, 1982), 20; Chicago Orphan Asylum, Annual Reports; Chicago Home for the Friendless, Annual Reports; Mamie Ruth Davis, "A History of Policies and Methods of Social Work in the Chicago Orphan Asylum" (master's thesis, University of Chicago, 1927); Marion Barnett Smith, "History of the Chicago Home for the Friendless" (master's thesis, University of Chicago, 1930).

33. McCarthy, *Noblesse Oblige,* 20; Chicago Reform School, Annual Reports, passim.

34. Elizabeth R. Varon, "Tippecanoe and the Ladies, Too: White Women and Party Politics in Antebellum Virginia," *Journal of American History* 82, no. 2 (September 1994): 494–521; Varon, *We Mean to Be Counted,* chap. 3.

35. For a discussion of the AFMRS, see Carroll Smith-Rosenberg, "Beauty, the Beast, and the Militant Woman," in *Disorderly Conduct: Visions of Gender in Victorian America* (New York: Oxford University Press, 1985), 109–28; Barbara J. Berg, *The Remembered Gate: Origins of American Feminism: The Woman and the City, 1800–1860* (New York: Oxford University Press, 1978); Flora L. Northrup, *The Record of a Century, 1834–1934* (New York: American Female Guardian Society and Home for the Friendless, 1934); Mary Ryan, "The Power of Women's Networks," in *Sex and Class in Women's History,* ed. Judith L. Newton et al. (London:

Routledge and Kegan Paul, 1983), 167–83; and Lori Ginzberg, *Women and the Work of Benevolence*, and *Women in Antebellum Reform* (Wheeling, Ill.: Harlan Davidson Co. 2000).

36. *Advocate for Moral Reform*, passim.

37. Ibid., April 1, 1843, 52.

38. E. P. Thompson, *The Making of the English Working Class* (1963; reprint, New York: Vintage Books, 1966), 832.

39. "An Appeal to the Worthy, Toiling Females of New England," *Voice of Industry*, November 20, 1846, reprinted in *The Factory Girls*, ed. Philip S. Foner (Urbana: University of Illinois Press, 1977), 149; Lowell Female Labor Reform Association, "Factory Tract #1: Factory Life as it Is," ibid., 132; "Preamble and Constitution of the Lowell Female Labor Reform Association," ibid., 105. For the history of the Lowell women, see Thomas Dublin, *Women at Work: The Transformation of Work and Community in Lowell, Massachusetts, 1826–1860* (New York: Columbia University Press, 1979).

40. Jama Lazerow, "Religion and the New England Mill Girl: A New Perspective on an Old Theme," *New England Quarterly* 60 (1987): 434; Pittsburgh *Spirit of Liberty*, November 15, 1845, quoted in Foner, *The Factory Girls*, 252. For the role of female factory workers in funding abolitionist campaigns, see David A. Zonderman, *Aspirations and Anxieties: New England Factory Workers and the Mechanized Factory System, 1815–1850* (New York: Oxford University Press, 1992), 117.

41. Sarah Bagley, Speech at the New England Workingmen's Association, May 27, 1845, in Foner, *The Factory Girls*, 109.

42. Bagley quoted in *Voice of Industry*, January 9, 1846, in Foner, *The Factory Girls*, 243.

43. Judith Wellman, "The Seneca Falls Women's Rights Convention: A Study of Social Networks," *Journal of Women's History* 3, no. 1 (spring 1991): 18.

44. Ibid. See also Ellen Carol DuBois, *Feminism and Suffrage: The Emergence of an Independent Women's Movement in America, 1848–1869* (Ithaca: Cornell University Press, 1978).

45. See, for example, David Grimsted, *American Mobbing, 1828–1861: Toward Civil War* (New York: Oxford University Press, 1998); Tyler Anbinder, *Nativism and Slavery: The Northern Know Nothings and the Politics of the 1850s* (New York: Oxford University Press, 1992).

46. For a very different interpretation, see Ginzberg, *Women and the Work of Benevolence*.

47. Kathryn Kish Sklar, *Catharine Beecher: A Study in American Domesticity* (New Haven: Yale University Press, 1973), xiv; Thomas J. Brown, *Dorothea Dix: New England Reformer* (Cambridge, Mass.: Harvard University Press, 1998), 77.

48. Dorothea Dix, "Memorial to the Legislature of Massachusetts, 1843" (Boston, January 1843); Thomas J. Brown, *Dorothea Dix*, 89.

49. Dix, "Memorial," 4, 24–25; Thomas J. Brown, *Dorothea Dix*, 94. Dix brilliantly manipulated what Karen Halttunen has termed "the pornography of pain." "Humanitarianism and the Pornography of Pain in Anglo-American Culture," *American Historical Review* 100, no. 2 (April 1995): 303–34.

50. David Gollaher, *Voice for the Mad: The Life of Dorothea Dix* (New York: Free Press, 1995), 162; Horace Mann quoted in Helen Marshall, *Dorothea Dix: Forgotten Samaritan* (New York: Russell and Russell, 1937), 147.

51. Franklin Pierce, veto message to the Senate, May 3, 1854, in *A Compilation of the Messages and Papers of the Presidents, 1789–1897*, ed. James D. Richardson (Washington, D.C.: Government Printing Office, 1897), 5:248–49. For Pierce's career, see Larry Gara, *The Presidency of Franklin Pierce* (Lawrence: University of Kansas Press, 1991).

52. Clinton and Silber, *Divided Houses*, 2.

Conclusion

1. For a fuller discussion of the concept of "third party government," see Lester Salamon, *Partners in Public Service: Government-Nonprofit Relations in the Modern Welfare State* (Baltimore: Johns Hopkins University Press, 1995).

2. Kathryn Kish Sklar, "The Historical Foundations of Women's Power in the Creation of the American Welfare State, 1830–1930," in *Mothers of a New World: Maternalist Politics and the Origins of Welfare States*, ed. Seth Koven and Sonya Michel (New York: Routledge, 1993), 43–93.

3. Charles J. Stillé, *History of the United States Sanitary Commission: Being the General Report of Its Work during the War of the Rebellion* (Philadelphia: J. B. Lippincott, 1866), 172–73. For other firsthand accounts of the commission's work see Mary Livermore, *My Story of the War: A Woman's Narrative of Four Years Personal Experience* (Hartford: A. D. Worthington, 1889); L. P. Brockett and Mary C. Vaughan, *Woman's Work in the Civil War: A Record of Heroism, Patriotism and Patience* (Philadelphia: Zeigler, McCurdy, 1867); and Katherine Prescott Wormeley, *The Other Side of War* (Boston: Ticknor and Co., 1889). The literature on the social history of the Civil War, and particularly women's roles in the war, has grown in recent years. For earlier secondary accounts of the Sanitary Commission, see Robert Bremner, *The Public Good: Philanthropy and Welfare in the Civil War Era* (New York: Alfred A. Knopf, 1980); George M. Fredrickson, *The Inner Civil War: Northern Intellectuals and the Crisis of the Union* (New York: Harper and Row, 1965); and Mary Elizabeth Massey, *Women in the Civil War* (1944; reprint, Lincoln: University of Nebraska Press, 1994). More recent works include Maris Vinovskis, "Have Social Historians Lost the Civil War? Some Preliminary Demographic Speculations," *Journal of American History* 76 (June 1989): 34–58; Jeanie Attie, *Patriotic Toil: Northern Women and the American Civil War* (Ithaca: Cornell University Press, 1998); Catherine Clinton and Nina Silber, eds., *Divided Houses: Gender and the Civil War* (New York: Oxford University Press, 1992); Drew Gilpin Faust, *Mothers of Invention: Women of the Slaveholding South in the American Civil War* (Chapel Hill: University of North Carolina Press, 1996); George C. Rable, *Civil Wars: Women and the Crisis of Southern Nationalism* (Urbana: University of Illinois Press, 1989); Elizabeth D. Leonard, *Yankee Women: Gender Battles in the Civil War* (New York: W. W. Norton and Co., 1994); Judith Ann Giesberg, *Civil War Sisterhood: The U.S. Sanitary Commission and Women's Politics in Transition* (Boston: Northeastern University Press, 2000); Anne Firor Scott, *Natural Allies: Women's Associations in American History* (Urbana: University of Illinois Press, 1991), chap. 3; and Lori Ginzberg's highly insightful chapter, "A Passion for Efficiency," in *Women and the Work of Benevolence: Morality, Politics, and Class in the Nineteenth-Century United States* (New Haven: Yale University Press, 1990).

4. Wormeley, *The Other Side of War*, 7. According to Stillé, the women who convened the group included Mrs. William H. Aspinwall, Mrs. Judge Roosevelt, Mrs. William Cullen Bryant, Mrs. G. L. Schuyler, Mrs. Peter Cooper, Mrs. R. B. Chandler, Mrs. G. Stuyvesant, Mrs. Abraham S. Hewitt, Mrs. Samuel F. B. Morse, Mrs. John Sherwood, and Mrs. Henry W. Bellows. Stillé, *History of the United States Sanitary Commission*, 525.

5. Stillé, *History of the United States Sanitary Commission*, 44, 43, 58.

6. Ibid., 87, 104. For Gilded Age and Progressive Era male philanthropy, see, for example, Ellen Condliffe Lagemann, *Private Power for the Public Good: A History of the Carnegie Foundation for the Advancement of Teaching* (Middletown, Conn.: Wesleyan University Press, 1983); Ellen Condliffe Lagemann, *The Politics of Knowledge: The Carnegie Corporation, Philanthropy, and Public Policy* (Chicago: University of Chicago Press, 1989); Barry D. Karl and Stan-

ley N. Katz, "American Private Philanthropic Foundations and the Public Sphere, 1890–1930," *Minerva* 19 (1981): 336–70; Frank Ninkovich, "The Rockefeller Foundation, China, and Cultural Change," *Journal of American History* 70 (March 1984): 799–820; Kathleen D. McCarthy, *Women's Culture: American Philanthropy and Art, 1830–1930* (Chicago: University of Chicago Press, 1991), chap. 5; James A. Smith, *The Idea Brokers: Think Tanks and the Rise of the New Policy Elite* (New York: Free Press, 1991); Ron Chernow, *Titan: The Life of John D. Rockefeller, Sr.* (New York: Random House, 1998); Kathleen D. McCarthy, "Patronage of the Arts," in *Encyclopedia of the United States in the Twentieth Century*, ed. Stanley I. Kutler, Robert Dallek, David A. Hollinger, and Thomas McCraw (New York: Charles Scribner's Sons, 1996), 6:1725–42; and the articles and bibliography in Ellen Condliffe Lagemann, ed., *Philanthropic Foundations: New Scholarship, New Possibilities* (Indianapolis: Indiana University Press, 1999).

7. George Templeton Strong, *The Diary of George Templeton Strong: The Civil War, 1860–1865*, ed. Allan Nevins and Milton Halsey Thomas (New York: Macmillan, 1952), 165. For Dix's role in the war, see Thomas J. Brown, *Dorothea Dix: New England Reformer* (Cambridge, Mass.: Harvard University Press, 1998); and David Gollaher, *Voice for the Mad: The Life of Dorothea Dix* (New York: Free Press, 1995).

8. Stillé, *History of the United States Sanitary Commission*, 168; Wormeley, *The Other Side of War*, 11; Livermore, *My Story*, quoted in Ginzberg, "A Passion for Efficiency," in *Women and the Work of Benevolence*, 155.

9. Robert E. Reigel, "Mary Livermore," in *Notable American Women*, ed. Edward T. James (Cambridge, Mass.: Harvard University Press, Belknap Press, 1971), 2:411.

10. "Metropolitan Fair in Aid of the United States Sanitary Commission" (New York: Charles O. Jones, 1864), p. 5; Stillé, *History of the United States Sanitary Commission*, 483; 241. Figures vary on the actual amounts that were raised by the fairs, including the Northwestern Sanitary Fair. See, for example, Ginzberg, *Women and the Work of Benevolence*, 167–68, which places the figures considerably higher than Stillé. Interestingly, the Sanitary Commission brought Midwestern women like Livermore into partnerships with the federal government that had eluded them at the state and local level in their antebellum charities. There apparently was also a fair in Baltimore. See Robert W. Schoeberlein, "A Fair to Remember: Maryland Women in Aid of the Union," *Maryland Historical Magazine* 90, no. 4 (winter 1995): 467–88.

11. Jacqueline Jones, *Soldiers of Light and Love: Northern Teachers and Georgia Blacks, 1865–73* (Chapel Hill: University of North Carolina Press, 1980), 78, 62; W. E. B. Du Bois, *Black Reconstruction in America, 1860–1880* (New York: Russell and Russell, 1909), 648. Newspaper references to black soldier's aid and contraband relief associations can be found in George E. Carter and C. Peter Ripley, eds., *The Black Abolitionist Papers*, microfilm edition. See also Bremner, *The Public Good;* and Julie Roy Jeffrey, *The Great Silent Army of Abolitionism: Ordinary Women in the Antislavery Movement* (Chapel Hill: University of North Carolina Press, 1998). To quote Eric Foner, although "northern benevolent societies, the Freedmen's Bureau, and after 1868, state governments provided most of the funding for black education during Reconstruction . . . the initiative often lay with blacks themselves. Urban blacks took immediate steps to set up schools, sometimes holding classes temporarily in abandoned warehouses, billiard rooms, or, in New Orleans and Savannah, former slave markets. . . . Throughout the South, blacks in 1865 and 1866 raised money to purchase land, build schoolhouses, and pay teachers' salaries. . . . Blacks donated their labor to construct schoolhouses, and black families offered room and board to teachers to supplement their salaries. By 1870, blacks had expended over $1 million on education." *A Short History of Reconstruction, 1863–1877* (New York: Harper and Row, 1990), 43–44.

12. Jones, *Soldiers of Light and Love,* 224. See also Linda M. Perkins, "The Black Female American Missionary Association Teacher in the South, 1861–1870," in *Black Americans in North Carolina and the South,* ed. Jeffrey J. Crow and Flora J. Hatley (Chapel Hill: University of North Carolina Press, 1984); and Willie Lee Rose, *Rehearsal for Reconstruction: The Port Royal Experiment* (New York: Oxford University Press, 1964). Selected educational efforts are also briefly discussed in Leon F. Litwack, *Been in the Storm So Long: The Aftermath of Slavery* (New York: Vintage Books, 1979); James M. McPherson, *The Struggle For Equality: Abolitionists and the Negro in the Civil War and Reconstruction* (Princeton: Princeton University Press, 1964); and Eric Foner's monumental *Reconstruction: America's Unfinished Devolution, 1863–1877* (New York: Harper and Row, 1988). For a highly critical assessment of the educational efforts, see James D. Anderson, *The Education of Blacks in the South, 1860–1935* (Chapel Hill: University of North Carolina Press, 1988).

13. Jones, *Soldiers of Light and Love,* 90. Du Bois's figures are strikingly different, placing the Freedmen's Bureau's contributions at $5.5 million, and the private contributions at $1.6 million for a far larger number of schools. However, since Jones compiled her figures from an extensive reading of various state and federal documents, I have opted to use her figures. For Du Bois's estimates, see W. E. B. Du Bois, *Black Reconstruction in America,* 667.

14. Du Bois, *Black Reconstruction in America,* 648.

15. Scott, *Natural Allies:* 69; Faust, *Mothers of Invention:* 24.

16. For Texas, see Elizabeth York Enstam, *Women and the Creation of Urban Life: Dallas, Texas, 1843–1920* (College Station: Texas A & M University Press, 1998). For women in other areas of the South, see Scott, *Natural Allies;* and Faust, *Mothers of Invention.*

17. Rable, *Civil Wars,* 288; Anne Firor Scott, *The Southern Lady: From Pedestal to Politics, 1830–1930* (Chicago: University of Chicago Press, 1971), 82–102; Varon, *We Mean to Be Counted: White Women and Politics in Antebellum Virginia* (Chapel Hill: University of North Carolina Press, 1998), 176. Faust, *Mothers of Invention.* On Gilded Age and Progressive Era associations, see, for example, Enstam, *Women and the Creation of Urban Life;* Elizabeth Hayes Turner, *Women, Culture and Community: Religion and Reform in Galveston, 1880–1920* (New York: Oxford University Press, 1997); Marjorie Spruill Wheeler, *New Women of the New South* (New York: Oxford University Press, 1991);and Judith N. McArthur, *Creating the New Woman: The Rise of Southern Women's Progressive Culture in Texas, 1893–1918* (Urbana: University of Illinois Press, 1998); as well as important earlier works such as Jacquelyn Dowd Hall, *Revolt against Chivalry: Jessie Daniel Ames and the Women's Campaign against Lynching* (New York: Columbia University Press, 1974).

18. Faust, *Mothers of Invention,* 254. For black women's organizations, see Glenda Gilmore, *Gender and Jim Crow: Women and the Politics of White Supremacy in North Carolina, 1896–1920* (Chapel Hill: University of North Carolina Press, 1996); Evelyn Brooks Higginbotham, *Righteous Discontent: The Women's Movement in the Black Baptist Church, 1880–1920* (Cambridge, Mass.: Harvard University Press, 1993); Darlene Clark Hine and Kathleen Thompson, *A Shining Thread of Hope: The History of Black Women in America* (New York: Broadway Books, 1998); Deborah Gray White, *Too Heavy a Load: Black Women in Defense of Themselves, 1894–1994* (New York: W. W. Norton, 1999); and Linda O. McCurry, *To Keep the Waters Troubled: The Life of Ida B. Wells* (New York: Oxford University Press, 1998).

19. See, for example, Leonard, *Yankee Women,* chap. 2, which details Wittenmyer's career. For Josephine Shaw Lowell, see Joan Waugh, *Unsentimental Reformer: The Life of Josephine Shaw Lowell* (Cambridge, Mass.: Harvard University Press, 1997).

20. Ginzberg, *Women and the Work of Benevolence;* Paula Baker, "The Domestication of Pol-

itics: Women and American Political Society, 1780–1920," *American Historical Review* 89, no. 3 (June 1984): 636. For discussions of some of the ways in which this played out, see Theda Skocpol, *Protecting Soldiers and Mothers: The Political Origins of Social Policy in the United States* (Cambridge, Mass.: Harvard University Press, 1991); and Kathleen D. McCarthy, "Women, Politics, Philanthropy: Some Historical Origins of the Welfare State," in *The Liberal Persuasion: Arthur Schlesinger, Jr., and the Challenge of the American Past*, ed. John Patrick Diggins (Princeton: Princeton University Press, 1997), 142–50. These patterns differed markedly in the South, where religious imperatives and the enduring prerogatives of white women's moral and maternal authority continued to hold sway through organizations like the Women's Christian Temperance Union. Varon, Scott, and others have noted the upsurge of women's missionary societies in Southern states during the Gilded Age and emphasize the centrality of the WCTU. Francis Willard, the union's president, made a highly successful recruitment sweep through the Southern states in 1881, building her organization into a national edifice. Rather than "scientific" reforms, evangelical Protestantism continued to be the driving force of civil society activities among both black and white women in the South until the 1890s. Scott, *Natural Allies;* Varon, *We Mean to Be Counted.* For a particularly strong statement about the role of black evangelical networks in mobilizing Southern African American women, see Higginbotham, *Righteous Discontent.*

21. According to survey data gathered by Independent Sector, Americans still give and volunteer in significant numbers at all levels of the economic structure, and households in the lowest brackets (those with an annual income of ten thousand dollars or less) statistically give more as a percentage of household income than upper-middle-class households. *Giving and Volunteering in the United States* (Washington, D.C.: Independent Sector, published biennially). The only groups that seem to be entirely absent from antebellum nonprofit activities—except as clients—were slaves, the Northern white working-class women depicted by Christine Stansell in *City of Women: Sex and Class in New York, 1789–1860* (New York: Alfred A. Knopf, 1986), and the Irish laborers examined by Peter J. Way in *Common Labour: Workers and the Digging of North American Canals, 1780–1860* (Cambridge: Cambridge University Press, 1993). However, far more work needs to be done, particularly on laborers' religious activities, to determine whether native-born working-class white women or Irish workmen were significantly less inclined to give and volunteer than African Americans or Irish women, as well as the consequences of these trends in terms of their larger social, political, and economic roles.

22. For an excellent discussion of the concept of women's political culture, see Kathryn Kish Sklar, *Florence Kelley and the Nation's Work: The Rise of Women's Political Culture, 1830–1900* (New Haven: Yale University Press, 1995).

Bibliography

Primary Sources

Adams, Abigail, and John Adams. *The Book of Abigail and John: Selected Letters of the Adams Family, 1762–1784.* Edited by L. H. Butterfield, Marc Friedlaender, and Mary-Jo Kline. Cambridge, Mass.: Harvard University Press, 1975.

Adams, John Quincy. *Memoirs of John Quincy Adams, Comprising Portions of His Diary from 1795 to 1848.* Edited by Charles Frances Adams. Philadelphia: J. B. Lippincott, 1871.

The Adams Family Papers. Edited by L. H. Butterfield, Wendell Garrtt and Marjorie Sprague. Cambridge, Mass.: Harvard University Press, Belknap Press, 1963.

Advocate for Moral Reform.

African Methodist Episcopal Church of the City of Philadelphia. Articles of Association. Philadelphia, 1799.

Albany Argus.

Allen, Richard. *The Life, Experience, and Gospel Labours of the Rt. Rev. Richard Allen.* Philadelphia: Martin and Boden, 1833.

Alvord, J. W. "Schools and Finances of Freedmen." Washington, D.C.: Government Printing Office, 1868.

American Academy of Arts and Sciences. *Memoirs.* Boston: Adams and Nourse, 1785.

American Antislavery Society (AAS). Annual Reports.

———. *Constitution and Declaration of the National Antislavery Convention, 1833.* New York, 1838.

———. "Declaration of Sentiments." New York: 1833.

American Bible Society. Annual Reports.

———. Board of Managers' Minutes. American Bible Society Manuscript Collections. American Bible Society, New York.

American Board of Commissioners of Foreign Missions. Annual Reports.

American Colonization Society. Annual Reports.

———. Manuscript Collections. Library of Congress.

American Education Society. Annual Reports.

American Female Guardian Society and Home for the Friendless. Annual Reports. New York, 1849.

———. Our Golden Jubilee: A Retrospect. New York, 1884.

American Free Produce Association. Constitution. 1838.

American Missionary Association. Annual Reports.

———. History of the American Missionary Association with Facts and Anecdotes Illustrating Its Work in the South. New York: S. W. Green, 1874.

American Moral Reform Society. Minutes and Proceedings of the First Annual Meeting. Philadelphia, 1837.

American Philosophical Society. Manuscript Collections. American Philosophical Society, Philadelphia.

———. Early Proceedings of the American Philosophical Society, 1744–1838. Philadelphia, 1884.

———. Year Book, 1937. Philadelphia, 1938.

American Society of Free Persons of Colour. Constitution. Philadelphia, 1830.

———. Constitution and Proceedings of the Convention. Philadelphia, 1831.

American Society for Meliorating the Condition of the Jews. Annual Reports.

American Sunday School Union. Annual Reports.

American Tract Society. Annual Reports.

Andrews, Charles C. History of the New-York African Free Schools. New York: Mahlon and Day, 1830.

Annals of the First African Church in United States of America, Now Styled the African Episcopal Church of St. Thomas. Philadelphia: King and Baird, 1862.

Association for the Benefit of Colored Orphans (New York). Annual Reports.

Association for the Care of Colored Orphans (Philadelphia). Annual Reports.

Association for the Relief of Jewish Widows and Orphans of New Orleans. Annual Reports.

Bacon, Benjamin G., and Charles Gardner. "Committee to Visit the Colored People: Census and Facts." 1838. Pennsylvania Abolition Society Manuscripts. Reel 26. Historical Society of Pennsylvania, Philadelphia.

Baltimore Beneficial Society. Constitution and By-Laws. Baltimore, 1818.

Baltimore Home for the Friendless. Annual Reports.

Benevolent Sons of Bethel Church. Minutes, 1826–1844. Mother Bethel African Methodist Episcopal Church Manuscripts. Historical Society of Pennsylvania, Philadelphia.

Bethel Church. Articles of Association of the African Methodist Episcopal Church of the City of Philadelphia. Philadelphia: John Ormrod, 1799.

Bethune, George Washington. Memoirs of Mrs. Joanna Bethune. New York: Harper and Brothers, 1863.

Bethune, Joanna. The Power of Faith: Exemplified in the Life and Writings of Mrs. Isabella Graham of New York. New York: J. Seymour, 1816.

———. The Power of Faith: Exemplified in the Life and Writings of Mrs. Isabella Graham of New York. New York: J. Seymour, 1817.

Board for the Emigration, Preservation and Improvement of the Aborigines of America. Annual Reports.

———. Documents and Proceedings. New York, 1829.

Boston Female Antislavery Society. Annual Reports.

Boston Female Asylum. *An Account of the Rise, Progress, and Present State of the Boston Female Asylum.* Boston: Russell and Cutler, 1810.

—————. Annual Reports.

Boston Seaman's Aid Society. Annual Reports.

Boston Society for the Diffusion of Useful Knowledge. Annual Reports.

Brockett, L. P., and Mary C. Vaughan. *Woman's Work in the Civil War: A Record of Heroism, Patriotism and Patience.* Philadelphia: Zeigler, McCurdy, 1867.

Buckingham, Joseph T. *Annals of the Massachusetts Charitable Mechanic Association.* Boston: Crocker and Brewster, 1853.

Carey, Mathew. *Essays on the Public Charities of Philadelphia.* Philadelphia: J. Clarke, 1829.

Carter, George E., and C. Peter Ripley, eds. *The Black Abolitionist Papers.* Microfilm edition.

Catholic Indigent Orphan Institute. *History.* New Orleans, 1916.

"A Catholic Layman." "Brief Address to the Roman Catholic Congregation Worshiping at St. Mary's on the Approaching Election for a Board of Trustees." Philadelphia: n.p., 1822.

Charitable Mechanic Association. Addresses. Boston, 1810.

Charleston Orphan House. Rules for the Government of the Orphan House. Charleston, S.C., 1839.

Chicago Home for the Friendless. Annual Reports.

Chicago Orphan Asylum. Annual Reports.

Chicago Reform School. Annual Reports.

Colored Citizens of Philadelphia. "A Memorial to the Honorable Senate and House of Representatives of the Commonwealth of Pennsylvania." Philadelphia, 1854.

Commons, John R., Ulrich B. Phillips, Eugene A. Gilmore, Helen L. Sumner, and John B. Andrews, eds. *A Documentary History of American Industrial Society.* New York: Russell and Russell, 1958.

"The Constitution of the Roman Catholic Churches of the States of North Carolina, South Carolina, and Georgia, Which Are Comprised in the Diocese of Charleston and Province of Baltimore." Charleston, S.C.: Office of the Seminary, 1826.

Daughters of Africa. Order Book, 1821–29. American Negro Historical Society. Manuscripts. Historical Society of Pennsylvania, Philadelphia.

Defoe, Daniel. "An Essay upon Projects." 1697. Reprinted in *Selected Poetry and Prose of Daniel Defoe,* edited by Michael F. Shugrue. New York: Holt, Rinehart and Winston, 1968.

Dix, Dorothea. "Memorial to the Legislature of Massachusetts, 1843." Boston, January 1843.

"Documents Relating to the Ursuline Convent in Charlestown." Boston: Samuel N. Dickinson, 1842.

"Documents Relative to the Present Distressed State of the Roman Catholic Church in the City of Charleston, South Carolina." Charleston, S.C., 1818.

Douglass, Frederick. *The Life and Writings of Frederick Douglass: Early Years, 1817–1849.* Edited by Philip S. Foner. New York: International Publishers, 1950.

—————. *Frederick Douglass: Selected Speeches and Writings.* Edited by Philip S. Foner. Chicago: Lawrence Hill Books, 1999.

Du Bois, W. E. B. *Black Reconstruction in America.* New York: Russell and Russell, 1909.

Earle, Thomas. "The Right of States to Annul Charters, Considered and the Decisions of the Supreme Court of the United States Thereon Examined." Philadelphia: Carey and Lea et al., 1823.

Farrar, Timothy. *Report on the Case of the Trustees of Dartmouth College against William Woodward.* Portsmouth, N.H.: John W. Foster, 1819.

Female Association of Philadelphia for the Relief of Women and Children in Reduced Circumstances. Annual Reports.

———. Constitution. Philadelphia, 1803.

Female Association of the City of New York. Annual Reports.

Female Bible Society of Philadelphia. Annual Reports.

Female Friendly Institution of the City and Liberties of Philadelphia. Constitution and By-Laws. Philadelphia, 1830.

Female Hebrew Benevolent Society. Constitution. Philadelphia, 1825, 1858.

Female Hospitable Society. Annual Reports.

———. "The Nature and Design of the Hospitable Society." Philadelphia, 1803.

———. "Reports . . . since Its Commencement in 1808." Philadelphia: Lydia R. Bailey, 1831.

Female Society of Philadelphia for the Relief and Employment of the Poor. Reports.

Fitzhugh, George. *Cannibals All! Slaves without Masters*. Richmond, Va.: A Morris, 1857.

Foner, Philip S., ed. *The Factory Girls*. Urbana: University of Illinois Press, 1977.

———, ed. *The Democratic-Republican Societies, 1790–1800: A Documentary Sourcebook of Constitutions, Declarations, Addresses, Resolutions and Toasts*. Westport: Greenwood Press, 1976.

Foner, Philip S., and Robert James Branham, eds. *Lift Every Voice: African-American Oratory, 1787–1900*. Tuscaloosa: University of Alabama Press, 1998.

Foner, Philip S., and George E. Walker, eds. *Proceedings of the Black State Conventions, 1840–1865*. Philadelphia: Temple University Press, 1979.

Forten, James, Jr. "An Address Delivered before the Ladies' Antislavery Society of Philadelphia." Philadelphia: Merrihew and Gunn, 1836.

Franklin, Benjamin. *The Autobiography of Benjamin Franklin*. 1793. Reprint, New Haven: Yale University Press, 1964.

———. *Benjamin Franklin: Writings*. Edited by J. A. Leo Lemay. New York: Library of America, 1987.

———. *The Papers of Benjamin Franklin*. Edited by Eric W. Labaree and Whitfield J. Bell, Jr. New Haven: Yale University Press, 1959–.

———. *The Writings of Benjamin Franklin*. Edited by Albert Henry Smyth. 10 vols. New York: Haskell House Publishers, 1970.

Freedman's Journal.

Free School Society (later renamed Public School Society). Annual Reports.

Friendly Society of St. Thomas's African Church of Philadelphia. Constitution and Rules. Philadelphia, 1797.

Garrison, Wendell Phillips. *William Lloyd Garrison*. 4 vols. Boston: Houghton Mifflin, 1894.

Garrison, William Lloyd. "An Address Delivered before the Free People of Color in Philadelphia and New York." Boston: Stephen Foster, 1831.

———. *The Letters of William Lloyd Garrison*. Vols. 1–4. Edited by Walter M. Merrill and Louis Ruchames. Cambridge, Mass.: Harvard University Press, Belknap Press, 1971.

———. "The Maryland Scheme of Expatriation Examined." Boston: Garrison and Knapp, 1834.

———. "Sentiments of the People of Color." In *Thoughts on African Colonization*. Boston: Garrison and Knapp, 1832.

———. *Thoughts on African Colonization*. Boston: Garrison and Knapp, 1832.

General Society of Mechanics and Tradesmen of the City of New York. Annual Reports.

———. Charter and By-Laws.

The Globe.

Graham, Isabella. *The Unpublished Letters and Correspondence of Mrs. Isabella Graham.* Edited by Joanna Bethune. New York: John S. Taylor, 1838.

Gratz, Rebecca. *Letters of Rebecca Gratz.* Edited by David Philipson. Philadelphia: Jewish Publication Society of America, 1929.

Gratz, Rebecca. "Report on Hebrew Sunday School." February 25, 1838. Reprinted in *Four Centuries of Jewish Women's Spirituality,* edited by Willem M. Umansky. Boston: Beacon Press, 1992.

Hamilton, Alexander, James Madison, and John Jay. *The Federalist Papers.* 1787–88. Reprint, New York: New American Library, 1961.

Harvard University. *Endowment Funds at Harvard University.* Cambridge, Mass.: Harvard University, 1948.

Hebrew Society for the Visitation of the Sick and Mutual Assistance. Constitution and By Laws. Philadelphia, 1824.

Hebrew Sunday School Society. *Celebration of the Seventy-fifth Anniversary.* Philadelphia: Hebrew Sunday School Society, 1913.

———. Constitution and By-Laws. Philadelphia, 1859.

———. *Proceedings of the Commemorative Celebration of the Fiftieth Anniversary of the Founding of the Hebrew Sunday Schools of America.* Philadelphia: Hebrew Sunday School Society, 1888.

Historical Catalogue of the University of Mississippi, 1849–1909. Nashville: Marshall and Bruce Co., 1910.

House of Refuge (Cincinnati). Annual Reports.

House of Refuge (New York). Annual Reports.

House of Refuge (Philadelphia). Annual Reports.

Indigent Widows and Single Women's Society of Philadelphia. Annual Reports.

Jackson, Andrew. *The Correspondence of Andrew Jackson.* Edited by John Spencer Bassett. Washington, D.C.: Carnegie Institution, 1926–33.

Jefferson, Thomas. *The Portable Thomas Jefferson.* Edited by Merrill D. Peterson. New York: Penguin Books, 1975.

———. *Public and Private Papers.* New York: Vintage Books, Library of America, 1990.

———. *The Writings of Thomas Jefferson.* Edited by Albert Ellery Bergh. Washington, D.C.: Thomas Jefferson Memorial Association, 1907.

Jones, Absalom. "A Thanksgiving Sermon Preached January 1, 1808 . . . on Account of the Abolition of the African Slave Trade." Philadelphia: St. Thomas African Episcopal Church, 1808.

———. "Memoir." In *Annals of the First African Church in the United States of America, Now Styled the African Episcopal Church of St. Thomas.* Philadelphia: King and Baird, 1862.

Jones, Absalom, and Richard Allen. "An Address to Those Who Keep Slaves, and Approve the Practice." Philadelphia, 1794.

———. "A Narrative of the Proceedings of the Black People during the Late Awful Calamity in Philadelphia in the Year 1793: And a Refutation of Some Censures Thrown upon Them, in Some Late Publications." Philadelphia, 1794.

———. "To the Free People of Color." Philadelphia, 1794.

Ladies of the Sanitary Committee of St. Thomas Episcopal Church. "Fair for the Sick and Wounded Soldiers." Philadelphia, 1864.

"A Layman of the Congregation." "An Inquiry into the Causes Which Led to the Dissensions Actually Existing in the Congregation of St. Mary's." Philadelphia: n.p., 1821.

Leamy, John, et. al. "Address of the Committee of St. Mary's Church of Philadelphia to Their Brethren of the Roman Catholic Faith." New York: J. Kingsland and Co., 1821.

Livermore, Mary. *My Story of the War: A Woman's Narrative of Four Years Personal Experience*. Hartford: A. D. Worthington, 1889.

Madison, James. *The Writings of James Madison*. Edited by Gaillard Hunt. G. P. Putnam's Sons, 1904.

Martineau, Harriet. "The Martyr Age of the United States." Boston: Weeks, Jordan and Co., 1839.

Massachusetts Antislavery Society. Annual Reports.

Mather, Cotton. *Bonifacious: An Essay upon the Good*. 1710. Reprint, Cambridge, Mass.: Harvard University Press, Belknap Press, 1955.

Mathews, Joanna H.. *A Short History of the Orphan Asylum Society in the City of New York, Founded 1806*. New York: Anson D. F. Randolph and Co., 1893.

"Metropolitan Fair in Aid of the United States Sanitary Commission." New York: Charles O. Jones, 1864.

"Minutes of the Twenty-first Biennial American Convention for Promoting the Abolition of Slavery, and Improving the Condition of the African Race, Convened at the City of Washington, December 8, 1829." Library of Congress, American Memory Web site.

Monroe, James. Message to the Senate and House of Representatives of the United States, March 30, 1824. In *The Writings of James Monroe*, edited by Stanislaus Murray Hamilton. New York: G. P. Putnam's Sons, 1903.

Morse, Jedediah. *Report to the Secretary of War of the United States on Indian Affairs*. New Haven: S. Converse, 1822.

Mother Bethel African Episcopal Church. Manuscript Collections. Historical Society of Pennsylvania, Philadelphia.

Nelson, Truman, ed. *Documents of Upheaval: Selections from William Lloyd Garrison's "The Liberator," 1831–1865*. New York: Hill and Wang, 1966.

New England Antislavery Society. Annual Reports.

New Hampshire Cent Institution. Report. Concord, N.H., 1814.

New York African Society for Mutual Relief. Constitution and Certificate of Incorporation. New York, 1886.

New York African Society for Mutual Relief. Manuscript Collections. Schomburg Center for Research in Black Culture, New York.

New York Association for the Relief of Respectable Aged Indigent Females. Annual Reports.

New York Children's Aid Society. Annual Reports.

New York Colored Orphan Asylum. Annual Reports.

New York Committee of Vigilance. First Annual Report. New York, 1837.

New York Dispensary. Annual Reports.

New York Female Association. Annual Reports.

New York Female Benevolent Society. Annual Reports.

New York Female Society for the Promotion of Sabbath Schools. Annual Reports.

————. Constitution and By-Laws.

New York Magdalen Society. Annual Reports.

"An Observer." "The Battle of St. Mary's." Philadelphia, n.p., 1822.

The Occident.

Orphan Asylum Society of the City of New York. Annual Reports.

Paine, Thomas. *The Complete Writings of Thomas Paine*. Edited by Philip Foner. New York: Citadel Press, 1945.

"Pastoral Letter of the Most Reverend Archbishop of Baltimore of the Roman Catholic Church of the United States to the Roman Catholic Clergy of the United States of America." Baltimore, 1829.

Pennsylvania Abolition Society. "Facts on Beneficial Societies and Schools for Negroes, 1823–1838." Manuscripts. Reel 26. Historical Society of Pennsylvania, Philadelphia.

———. Manuscript Collections. Historical Society of Pennsylvania, Philadelphia.

Pennsylvania General Assembly. Report of the Committee Appointed to Investigate the Affairs of the Philadelphia Savings Institution. Harrisburg, 1836.

Pennsylvania Society for Promoting the Abolition of Slavery. "Memorials Presented to the Congress of the United States of America by the Different Societies Instituted for Promoting the Abolition of Slavery." Philadelphia: Francis Bailey, 1792.

Perdue, Theda, and Michael D. Green, eds. The Cherokee Removal: A Brief History with Documents. New York: Bedford Books, 1995.

Petition from [the Ladies of] Lewis, New York, January 24, 1831. National Archives, Cherokee Removal Records, RG 233, HR 21A-G8.2.

Philadelphia Association for the Care of Colored Orphans. Annual Reports.

Philadelphia Female Antislavery Society. Annual Reports.

Philadelphia Orphan Society. Annual Reports.

Philadelphia Saving Fund Society. The Act to Incorporate. Philadelphia, 1835.

———. Articles of Association, With an Explanation of the Principles of the Institution and Its Objects. Philadelphia, 1817.

Philadelphia Society for the Establishment and Support of Charity Schools. Annual Reports.

———. Constitution. Philadelphia, 1801.

Poughkeepsie Sanitary Fair. "Brochure." Poughkeepsie, N.Y., 1864.

Public School Society of New York. (previously named Free School Society). Annual Reports.

The Recorder (also known as the Boston Recorder). Boston.

Record of the Bethel African Methodist Episcopal Church. New York: Carlton and Porter, 1864.

"Report on the Free Colored Poor of the City of Charleston." Charleston, S.C., 1842.

"A Reporter." "A Graphic Account of the Alarming Riots at St. Mary's Church in April, 1822." Philadelphia, 1822.

Richardson, James D., ed. A Compilation of the Messages and Papers of the Presidents, 1789–1897. Washington, D.C.: Government Printing Office, 1897.

Ripley, C. Peter, ed. The Black Abolitionist Papers. Chapel Hill: University of North Carolina Press, 1991.

Roman Catholic Society of St. Joseph for the Educating and Maintaining of Poor Orphan Children. Report. Philadelphia, 1844.

Roman Catholic Sunday School Society. Constitution. Philadelphia, 1816.

Ross, Chief John. Papers. Vol. 1, 1807–1839. Edited by Gary E. Moulton. Norman: University of Oklahoma Press, 1978.

Seaman's Friend Society (Boston). Annual Reports.

Seton, Elizabeth. Selected Writings. Edited by Ellen Kelly and Annabelle Melville. New York: Paulist Press, 1987.

Simpson, Stephen. Biography of Stephen Girard. Philadelphia: Thomas Bonsal, 1832.

Société Catholique pour l'instruction des orphelins dans l'indigence. Constitution. New Orleans, 1849.

Society for the Prevention of Juvenile Delinquency. Documents. In New York House of Refuge Annual Report, 1828.

Society for the Prevention of Pauperism. Annual Reports.

Society for the Reformation of Juvenile Delinquents. Documents of the House of Refuge. New York: Mahlon Day, 1832.

Society for the Relief of Poor Widows with Small Children. Annual Reports.

———. Constitution and By Laws.

———. Minutes. Manuscript Collections, New-York Historical Society, New York.

State Papers and Publick Documents of the United States. Boston: T. B. Wait and Sons, 1817.

Stillé, Charles J. *History of the United States Sanitary Commission: Being the General Report of Its Work during the War of the Rebellion.* Philadelphia: J. B. Lippincott, 1866.

Stirling, Dorothy. *We Are Your Sisters: Black Women in the Nineteenth Century.* New York: W. W. Norton, 1984.

Strong, George Templeton. *The Diary of George Templeton Strong: The Civil War, 1860–1865.* Edited by Allan Nevins and Milton Halsey Thomas. New York: Macmillan, 1952.

Sunday School Union Society of Charleston, S.C. Report. Charleston, S.C.: 1823.

Tappan, Arthur. "The Fugitive Slave Bill: Its History and Unconstitutionality." New York: William Harnad, 1850.

Tappan, Lewis. *The Life of Arthur Tappan.* London: Sampson Low and Marston, 1870.

Temperance Beneficial Association. Charter and By-Laws. Philadelphia, 1837.

Temperance and Benevolent Association (Philadelphia). Annual Reports.

The Colored American.

The Liberator.

The Occident.

Tocqueville, Alexis de. *Democracy in America.* 1835–41. Reprint, New York: Modern Library, 1981.

Union Beneficial Society of Journeymen and Bricklayers. Constitution and By-Laws. Philadelphia, 1836.

Union Benevolent Association (Philadelphia). Annual Reports.

United States Bureau of the Census. *Historical Statistics of the United States, Colonial Times to 1957.* Washington, D.C.: 1960.

United States Congress. *Abridgements of the Debates of Congress, from 1789 to 1856.* 16 vols. New York: D. Appleton, 1857–61.

———. *Annals of the Congress of the United States, 1789–1824.* 42 vols. Washington, D.C.: United States Government, 1803.

———. *Congressional Globe.* 46 vols. Washington, D.C.: Globe, 1834–73.

United States Register of Debates in Congress. Washington, D.C.: Gales and Seaton, Printers, 1830.

United States Sanitary Commission. "A Report to the Secretary of War." Washington, D.C., 1861.

———. "A Visitor's Guide to the Great Central Fair." Philadelphia, 1864.

———. "Origin, Struggles and Principles of the United States Sanitary Commission." New York, 1864.

———. "To the Loyal Women of America." New York, 1861.

———Women's Pennsylvania Branch. Annual Report. Philadelphia, 1864.

"A View of the Application for an Amendment of the Charter of Incorporation of St. Mary's Church." Harrisburg: William White, 1823.

Washington, George. *The Writings of George Washington from the Original Manuscript Sources.* Edited by John C. Fitzpatrick. Washington, D.C.: United States Government Printing Office, 1940.

White, Charles I. *Life of Mrs. Eliza A. Seton.* New York: Edward Dunigan and Brother, 1852.

————. *Life of Mrs. Eliza A. Seton.* 3d ed. New York: Kelly Publishing Co., 1879.

Woman's Central Relief Association. Annual Reports.

Workingmen's Beneficial Society. Annual Reports.

Wormeley, Katherine Prescott. *The Other Side of War.* Boston: Ticknor and Co., 1889.

————. *The United States Sanitary Commission.* Boston: Little, Brown and Co., 1863.

Secondary Sources

Abbott, Richard H. *Cotton and Capital: Boston Businessmen and Antislavery Reform, 1854–1868.* Amherst: University of Massachusetts Press, 1991.

Abend, Rosemary. "Constant Samaritans: Quaker Philanthropy in Philadelphia, 1680–1799." Ph.D. diss., University of California, Los Angeles, 1988.

Abzug, Robert H. *Cosmos Crumbling: American Reform and the Religious Imagination.* New York: Oxford University Press, 1994.

Adams, Donald R. "The Bank of Stephen Girard." *Journal of Economic History* 32, no. 4 (1972): 841–59.

Adams, Henry. *History of the United States of America during the Administrations of Thomas Jefferson.* 1889–91. Reprint, New York: Library of America, 1986.

Ahlstrom, Sydney E. *A Religious History of the American People.* New Haven: Yale University Press, 1972.

Akers, Charles W. *Abigail Adams: An American Woman.* Boston: Little, Brown and Co., 1980.

Alexander, John K. *Render Them Submissive: Responses to Poverty in Philadelphia, 1760–1800.* Amherst: University of Massachusetts Press, 1980.

Alexander, Ruth M. "'We Are Engaged as a Band of Sisters': Class and Domesticity in the Washingtonian Temperance Movement." *Journal of American History* 75, no. 3 (December 1988): 763–85.

Alley, Robert S., ed. *James Madison on Religious Liberty.* Buffalo: Prometheus Books, 1985.

Allgor, Catherine. *Parlor Politics: In Which the Ladies of Washington Help Build a City and a Government.* Charlottesville: University Press of Virginia, 2000.

Alter, George, Claudia Goldin, and Elyce Rotella. "The Savings of Ordinary Americans: The Philadelphia Saving Fund Society in the Mid–Nineteenth Century." *Journal of Economic History* 54, no. 4 (December 1994): 735–67.

Altschuler, Glenn C., and Stuart M. Blumin. "Limits of Political Engagement in Antebellum America: A New Look at the Golden Age of Participatory Democracy." *Journal of American History* 84, no. 3 (December 1997): 855–85.

Ammon, Harry. *James Monroe: The Quest for National Identity.* Charlottesville: University Press of Virginia, 1990.

Anbinder, Tyler. *Nativism and Slavery: The Northern Know Nothings and the Politics of the 1850s.* New York: Oxford University Press, 1992.

Anderson, James D. *The Education of Blacks in the South, 1860–1935.* Chapel Hill: University of North Carolina Press, 1988.

Andrew, John A., III. *From Revivals to Removal: Jeremiah Evarts, the Cherokee Nation, and the Search for the Soul of America.* Athens: University of Georgia Press, 1992.

Appleby, Joyce. *Capitalism and a New Social Order: The Republican Vision of the 1790s.* New York: New York University Press, 1984.

————. *Inheriting the Revolution: The First Generation of Americans.* Cambridge, Mass.: Harvard University, The Belknap Press, 2000.

————. "The Popular Sources of American Capitalism." *Studies in American Political Development* 9 (fall 1995): 432–57.

————. "Republicanism and Ideology." *American Quarterly* 37 (fall 1985): 461–73.

————. "Republicanism in Old and New Contexts." *William and Mary Quarterly* 43 (1986): 20–34.

————. "What Is Still American in the Political Philosophy of Thomas Jefferson?" *William and Mary Quarterly* 39, no. 2 (April 1982): 287–309.

Ashton, Dianne C. "Rebecca Gratz and the Domestication of American Judaism." Ph.D. diss., Temple University, 1986.

Atack, Jeremy, and Peter Passell. *A New Economic View of American History from Colonial Times to 1940.* 2d ed. New York: W. W. Norton and Co., 1985.

Attie, Jeanie. *Patriotic Toil: Northern Women and the American Civil War.* Ithaca: Cornell University Press, 1998.

Baatz, Simon, "Patronage, Science, and Ideology in an American City: Patrician Philadelphia, 1800–1860." Ph.D. diss., University of Pennsylvania, 1986.

Bailyn, Bernard. *The Ideological Origins of the American Revolution.* Cambridge, Mass.: Harvard University Press, 1967.

Baker, Jean Harvey. *Affairs of Party: The Political Culture of Northern Democrats in the Mid–Nineteenth Century.* Ithaca: Cornell University Press, 1983.

————. "Politics, Paradigms and Public Culture." *Journal of American History* 84, no. 3 (December 1997): 894–99.

Baker, Paula. "The Domestication of Politics: Women and American Political Society, 1780–1920." *American Historical Review* 89, no. 3 (June 1984): 620–47.

Baltzell, E. Digby. *Puritan Boston and Quaker Philadelphia.* Boston: Beacon Press, 1979.

Banner, Lois W. "Religious Benevolence as Social Control: A Critique of an Interpretation." *Journal of American History* 68, no. 1 (June 1973): 23–41.

Banning, Lance. "Jeffersonian Ideology Revisited: Liberal and Classical Ideas in the New American Republic." *William and Mary Quarterly* 60 (1988): 1–20.

Barnes, Gilbert Hobbs. *The Antislavery Impulse: 1830–1844.* New York: D. Appleton-Century Co., 1933.

Bauman, Mark K. "The Emergence of Jewish Social Service Agencies in Atlanta." *Georgia Historical Quarterly* 69, no. 4 (winter 1985): 488–508.

Beaver, R. Pierce. *Church, State and the American Indians: Two and a Half Centuries of Partnership between Protestant Missions and Government.* St. Louis: Concordia Publishing House, 1966.

Becker, Dorothy G. "Isabella Graham and Joanna Bethune: Trailblazers of Organized Women's Benevolence." *Social Service Review* 61, no. 2 (June 1987): 319–36.

Bell, Marion L. *Crusade in the City: Revivalism in Nineteenth Century Philadelphia.* Lewisburg: Bucknell University Press, 1977.

Bellingham, Bruce. "Waifs and Strays: Child Abandonment, Foster Care, and Families in Mid–Nineteenth Century New York." In *The Uses of Charity: the Poor on Relief in the Nineteenth Century Metropolis,* edited by Peter Mandler, 123–60. Philadelphia: University of Pennsylvania Press, 1990.

Bellows, Barbara L. *Benevolence among Slaveholders: Assisting the Poor in Charleston, 1670–1860.* Baton Rouge: Louisiana State University Press, 1993.

————. "Tempering the Wind: The Southern Response to Urban Poverty, 1850–1865." Ph.D. diss., University of South Carolina, 1983.

Bender, Thomas. "Wholes and Parts: The Need for Synthesis in American History." *Journal of American History* 73 (June 1986): 120–36.

———, ed. *The Antislavery Debate: Capitalism and Abolitionism as a Problem in Historical Interpretation.* Berkeley: University of California Press, 1992.

Benson, Lee. *The Concept of Jacksonian Democracy: New York as a Test Case.* Princeton: Princeton University Press, 1961.

Benson, Susan Porter. "Business Heads and Sympathizing Hearts: Women and the Providence Employment Society." *Journal of Social History* 71 (1984): 497–524.

Berg, Barbara J. *The Remembered Gate: Origins of American Feminism: The Woman and the City, 1800–1860.* New York: Oxford University Press, 1978.

Berger, Peter L., and Richard John Neuhaus. *To Empower the People: The Role of Mediating Structures in Public Policy.* Washington, D.C.: American Enterprise Institute, 1977.

Berkhofer, Robert J., Jr. *The White Man's Indian: Images of the American Indian to the Present.* New York: Vintage Books, 1978.

Berlin, Ira. *Many Thousands Gone: The First Two Centuries of Slavery in North America.* Cambridge, Mass.: Harvard University Press, 1998.

———. *Slaves without Masters: The Free Negro in the Antebellum South.* New York: Oxford University Press, 1974.

Bernhard, Virginia. "Cotton Mather and the Doing of Good: A Puritan Gospel of Wealth." *New England Quarterly* 49 (June 1976): 225–41.

Beyan, Amos J. *The American Colonization Society and the Creation of the Liberian State: A Historical Perspective, 1822–1900.* Lanham: University Press of America, 1991.

Billington, Ray Allen. "The Burning of the Charlestown Convent." *New England Quarterly* 10 (March 1937): 4–24.

———. *The Protestant Crusade: 1800–1860: A Study of the Origins of American Nativism.* New York: Macmillan Co., 1938.

Blassingame, John W. *Black New Orleans.* Chicago: University of Chicago Press, 1961.

Blight, David W. *Frederick Douglass's Civil War: Keeping Faith in Jubilee.* Baton Rouge: Louisiana State University Press, 1989.

Blumin, Stuart. *The Emergence of the Middle Class: Social Experience in the American City, 1760–1900.* New York: Cambridge University Press, 1989.

Bode, Frederick A. "A Common Sphere: White Evangelicals and Gender in Antebellum Georgia." *Georgia Historical Quarterly* 79, no. 4 (winter 1995): 775–809.

Bodenhorn, Howard. "Capital Mobility and Financial Integration in Antebellum America." *Journal of Economic History* 52, no. 3 (September 1992): 585–603.

Bodo, John. *The Protestant Clergy and Public Issues, 1812–1848.* Princeton: Princeton University Press, 1954.

Bogin, Ruth. "Petitioning and the New Moral Economy of Post-revolutionary America." *American Quarterly*, 3d ser., 45, no. 3 (July 1988): 391–425.

Bolton, Sarah Knowles. *Famous Givers and Their Gifts.* 1896. Reprint, Freeport, N.Y.: Books for Libraries Press, 1971.

Bonelli, Vincent Francis. "The Response of Public and Private Philanthropy to the Panic of 1819 in New York City." Ph.D. diss., Fordham University, 1976.

Bonomi, Patricia U. *Under the Cope of Heaven: Religion, Society, and Politics in Colonial America.* New York: Oxford University Press, 1986.

Boydston, Jean. "The Woman Who Wasn't There: Women's Market Labor and the Transition to Capitalism in the United States." *Journal of the Early Republic* 16 (summer 1996): 183–206.

Boyer, Paul. *Urban Masses and Moral Order in America, 1820–1920.* Cambridge, Mass.: Harvard University Press, 1978.

Boylan, Anne M. "Benevolence and Antislavery Activity among African-American Women in New York and Boston, 1820–1840." In *The Abolitionist Sisterhood: Women's Political Culture in Antebellum America,* edited by Jean Fagan Yellin and John C. Van Horne, 119–37. Ithaca: Cornell University Press, 1994.

———. *Sunday School: The Formation of an American Institution, 1790–1880.* New Haven: Yale University Press, 1988.

———. "Timid Girls, Venerable Widows and Dignified Matrons: Life Cycle Patterns among Organized Women in New York and Boston, 1797–1840." *American Quarterly* 38 (winter 1986): 779–97.

———. "Women and Politics in the Era before Seneca Falls." *Journal of the Early Republic* 10 (fall 1990): 363–82.

———. "Women in Groups: An Analysis of Women's Benevolent Organizations in New York and Boston, 1797–1840." *Journal of American History* 71, no. 3 (December 1984): 497–515.

Brands, H. W. *The First American: The Life and Times of Benjamin Franklin.* New York: Doubleday, 2000.

Brant, Irving. "Madison: On the Separation of Church and State." *William and Mary Quarterly,* 3d ser., 8, no. 1 (January 1951): 3–24.

Breen, T. H. "An Empire of Goods: The Anglicization of Colonial America, 1690–1776." *Journal of British Studies* 25 (October 1986):467–99.

———. "Narrative of Commercial Life: Consumption, Ideology and Community on the Eve of the American Revolution." *William and Mary Quarterly,* 3d ser., 50, no. 3 (July 1993): 471–501.

Bremner, Robert H. *American Philanthropy.* Chicago: University of Chicago Press, 1988.

———. *From the Depths: The Discovery of Poverty in the United States.* New York: New York University Press, 1956.

———. *The Public Good: Philanthropy and Welfare in the Civil War Era.* New York: Alfred A. Knopf, 1980.

Bridenbaugh, Carl. *Cities in Revolt: Urban Life in America, 1743–1776.* New York: Alfred A. Knopf, 1955.

———. *Cities in the Wilderness, 1652–1742.* New York: Ronald Press Co., 1938.

Bridges, Amy. *A City in the Republic: Antebellum New York and the Origins of Machine Politics.* Cambridge: Cambridge University Press, 1984.

Brown, James. *The History of Public Assistance in Chicago, 1833–1893.* Chicago: University of Chicago Press, 1941.

Brown, Roy M. *Public Poor Relief in North Carolina.* Chapel Hill: University of North Carolina Press, 1928.

Brown, Thomas J. *Dorothea Dix: New England Reformer.* Cambridge, Mass.: Harvard University Press, 1998.

Bruce, Philip Alexander. *History of the University of Virginia, 1819–1919.* 5 vols. New York: Macmillan Co., 1920.

Bruchey, Stuart. *The Roots of American Economic Growth, 1607–1861.* New York: Harper Torchbooks, 1965.

Buckley, Thomas E. "After Disestablishment: Thomas Jefferson's Wall of Separation in Antebellum Virginia." *Journal of Southern History* 41, no. 3 (August 1995): 445–80.

———. "Evangelicals Triumphant: The Baptists' Assault on the Virginia Glebes, 1786–1801." *William and Mary Quarterly*, 3d ser., 45, no. 1 (January 1988): 33–69.

Buhle, Mari Jo. "Needlewomen and the Vicissitudes of Modern Life: A Study of Middle-Class Construction in the Antebellum Northeast." In *Visible Women: New Essays on American Activism*, edited by Suzanne Lebsock and Nancy Hewitt, 145–65. Urbana: University of Illinois Press, 1993.

Buhle, Mari Jo, and Paul Buhle, eds. *The Concise History of Woman Suffrage: Selections from the Classic Work of Stanton, Anthony, Gage and Harper*. Urbana: University of Illinois Press, 1978.

Butler, Jon. *Awash in a Sea of Faith: Christianizing the American People*. Cambridge, Mass.: Harvard University Press, 1990.

Cahn, Frances, and Valeska Bary. *Welfare Activities of Federal, State and Local Governments in California, 1850–1934*. Berkeley: University of California Press, 1936.

Callcott, George H. *A History of the University of Maryland*. Baltimore: Maryland Historical Society, 1966.

Carey, Patrick W. *People, Priests and Prelates: Ecclesiastical Democracy and the Tensions of Trusteeism*. Notre Dame: University of Notre Dame Press, 1987.

Carlson, Douglas W. "'Drinks He to His Own Undoing': Temperance Ideology in the Deep South." *Journal of the Early Republic* 18 (winter 1998): 659–91.

Carson, Emmett D. *A Hand Up: Black Philanthropy and Self-Help in America*. Washington, D.C.: Joint Center for Political and Economic Studies, 1993.

Carwardine, Richard J. *Evangelicals in Antebellum America*. New Haven: Yale University Press, 1993.

Chambers, Clarke A. "Toward a Redefinition of Welfare History." *Journal of American History* 73, no. 2 (September 1986): 407–33.

Chambré, Susan. "Philanthropy." In *Jewish Women in America: An Historical Encyclopedia*, edited by Paula E. Hyman and Deborah Dash Moore, 2:1049–55. New York: Routledge, 1997.

Chandler, Alfred D., Jr. "Patterns of Railroad Finance, 1830–1850." *Business History Review* 28: 248–63.

Chernow, Ron. *Titan: The Life of John D. Rockefeller, Sr.* New York: Random House, 1998.

Clark, Christopher. *The Roots of Rural Capitalism: Western Massachusetts, 1780–1860*. Ithaca: Cornell University Press, 1990.

Clement, Priscilla Ferguson. "Nineteenth Century Welfare Policy, Programs, and Poor Women: Philadelphia as a Case Study." *Feminist Studies* 18, no. 1 (spring 1992): 35–58.

———. "The Response to Need, Welfare and Poverty in Philadelphia." Ph.D. diss., University of Pennsylvania, 1977.

———. *Welfare and the Poor in the Nineteenth Century City: Philadelphia, 1800–1854*. Rutherford, N.J.: Fairleigh Dickinson University Press, 1985.

Clinton, Catherine, and Nina Silber, eds. *Divided Houses: Gender and the Civil War*. New York: Oxford University Press, 1992.

Cohen, Jean L., and Andrew Arato. *Civil Society and Political Theory*. Cambridge, Mass.: MIT Press, 1994.

Coburn, Carol K., and Martha Smith. *Spirited Lives: How Nuns Shaped Catholic Culture and American Life, 1836–1920*. Chapel Hill: University of North Carolina Press, 1999.

Cole, Donald B. "The Age of Jackson: After Forty Years." *Reviews in American History* 14 (March 1986): 149–59.

————. *Martin Van Buren and the American Political System.* Princeton: Princeton University Press, 1984.

————. *The Presidency of Andrew Jackson.* Lawrence: University Press of Kansas, 1993.

Coleman, Willi. "Architects of a Vision: Black Women and Their Antebellum Quest for Political and Social Equality." In *African-American Women and the Vote, 1837–1965,* edited by. Ann D. Gordon and Bettye Collier-Thomas, 24–40. Amherst: University of Massachusetts Press, 1997.

Coll, Blanche D. "The Baltimore Society for the Prevention of Pauperism, 1820–1822." *American Historical Review* 61, no. 1 (October 1955): 77–87.

Cornell, Saul. *The Other Founders: Anti-Federalism and the Dissenting Tradition in America, 1788–1828.* Chapel Hill: University of North Carolina Press, 1999.

Cosgrove, John L. "The Hibernian Society of Charleston, South Carolina." *Journal of the American Irish Historical Society* 27 (1926): 150–58.

Cott, Nancy F. *The Bonds of Womanhood: "Woman's Sphere" in New England, 1780–1835.* New Haven: Yale University Press, 1977.

Coulter, E. Merton. "Benjamin Braswell: Georgia Pioneer Philanthropist." *Georgia Historical Quarterly* 65, no. 2 (summer 1981): 67–81.

————. *College Life in the Old South.* New York: Macmillan Co., 1928.

Cray, Robert E., Jr. *Paupers and Poor Relief in New York City and Its Rural Environs, 1700–1830.* Philadelphia: Temple University Press, 1988.

Cross, Whitney. *The Burned Over District: A Social and Intellectual History of Enthusiastic Religion in Western New York, 1800–1850.* Ithaca: Cornell University Press, 1950.

Cunningham, Noble E., Jr. *In Pursuit of Reason: The Life of Thomas Jefferson.* New York: Ballantine Books, 1987.

————. *The Presidency of James Monroe.* Lawrence: University Press of Kansas, 1996.

Curran, Christopher, and Jack Johnston. "The Antebellum Money Market and the Economic Impact of the Bank War: A Comment." *Journal of Economic History* 39, no. 2 (June 1979): 461–74.

Curry, Leonard P. *The Free Black in Urban America, 1800–1850: The Shadow of the Dream.* Chicago: University of Chicago Press, 1981.

Curti, Merle, and Roderick Nash. *Philanthropy in the Shaping of American Higher Education.* New Brunswick: Rutgers University Press, 1965.

Cutler, William W., III. "Status, Values and the Education of the Poor: The Trustees of the New York Public School Society, 1805–1853." *American Quarterly* 24, no. 1 (March 1972): 69–85.

Dalzell, Robert F., Jr. *Enterprising Elite: The Boston Associates and the World They Made.* Cambridge, Mass.: Harvard University Press, 1987.

Davis, Cyprian. *The History of Black Catholics in the United States.* New York: Crossroad, 1990.

Davis, David Brion. *The Problem of Slavery in the Age of Revolution, 1770–1823.* Ithaca: Cornell University Press, 1975.

————. *The Slave Power Conspiracy and the Paranoid Style.* Baton Rouge: Louisiana State University Press, 1969.

————, ed. *Antebellum Reform.* New York: Harper and Row, 1967.

Davis, Mamie Ruth. "A History of Policies and Methods of Social Work in the Chicago Orphan Asylum." Master's thesis, University of Chicago, 1927.

Dervin, Joseph I. *Mrs. Seton: Foundress of the American Sisters of Charity.* New York: Farrar, Strauss and Giroux, 1968.

Diggins, John Patrick. "Comrades and Citizens: New Mythologies in American Historiography." *American Historical Review* 90, no. 3 (1985): 614–38.

di Giacomantonio, William C. "'For the Gratification of a Volunteering Society': Antislavery and Pressure Group Politics in the First Federal Congress." *Journal of the Early Republic* 15 (summer 1995): 169–97.

Diner, Hasia R. *Erin's Daughters in America: Irish Immigrant Women in the Nineteenth Century.* Baltimore: Johns Hopkins University Press, 1983.

———. *A Time for Gathering: The Second Migration, 1820–1880.* Baltimore: Johns Hopkins University Press, 1992.

Dolan, Jay. *The American Catholic Experience: A History from Colonial Times to the Present.* Garden City, N.Y.: Doubleday and Co., 1985.

Donald, David. *Lincoln Reconsidered: Essays on the Civil War Era.* New York: Knopf, 1965.

Dorsey, Bruce Allen. "City of Brotherly Love: Religious Benevolence, Gender and Reform in Philadelphia, 1780–1844." Ph.D. diss., Brown University, 1993.

———. "Friends Becoming Enemies: Philadelphia Benevolence and the Neglected Era of American Quaker History." *Journal of the Early Republic* 18 (fall 1998): 395–428.

Doyle, Don Harrison. *The Social Order of a Frontier Community: Jacksonville, Illinois, 1825–1870.* Urbana: University of Illinois Press, 1978.

Dreisbach, Daniel. "A New Perspective on Jefferson's Views on Church-State Relations: The Virginia Statute for Establishing Religious Freedom in Its Legislative Context." *American Journal of Legal History* 35 (April 1991): 192–204.

Duberman, Martin, ed. *The Antislavery Vanguard: New Essays on the Abolitionists.* Princeton: Princeton University Press, 1965.

Dublin, Thomas. *Women at Work: The Transformation of Work and Community in Lowell, Massachusetts, 1826–1860.* New York: Columbia University Press, 1979.

DuBois, Ellen Carol. *Feminism and Suffrage: The Emergence of an Independent Women's Movement in America, 1848–1869.* Ithaca: Cornell University Press, 1978.

Du Bois, W. E. B. *The Philadelphia Negro: A Social Study.* New York: Benjamin Bloom, 1899.

Dwight, Henry Otis. *The Centennial History of the American Bible Society.* New York: Macmillan Co., 1916.

Eberly, Wayne J. "The Pennsylvania Abolition Society, 1775–1830." Ph.D. diss., Pennsylvania State University, 1973.

Egerton, Douglas R. "'Its Origin Is Not a Little Curious': A New Look at the American Colonization Society." *Journal of the Early Republic* 5 (winter 1985): 463–80.

———. "Markets without a Market Revolution: Southern Planters and Capitalism." *Journal of the Early Republic* 16 (summer 1996): 207–21.

Elazar, Daniel J. *Community and Polity: The Organizational Dynamics of American Jewry.* Philadelphia: Jewish Publication Society of America, 1976.

Elkins, Stanley, and Eric McKitrick. *The Age of Federalism: The Early American Republic, 1788–1800.* New York: Oxford University Press, 1993.

Ellis, Joseph J. *American Sphinx: The Character of Thomas Jefferson.* New York: Vintage Books, 1998.

———. *Passionate Sage: The Character and Legacy of John Adams.* New York: W. W. Norton and Co., 1993.

Ellis, Richard E. *The Union at Risk: Jacksonian Democracy, State's Rights and the Nullification Crisis.* New York: Oxford University Press, 1987.

Encyclopedia of Associations. Detroit: Gale Research Co., 2000.

Enstam, Elizabeth York. *Women and the Creation of Urban Life: Dallas, Texas, 1843–1920.* College Station: Texas A & M University Press, 1998.

Ernst, Robert. *Immigrant Life in New York City, 1825–1863.* New York: Octagon Books, 1979.

Faber, Eli. *A Time for Planting: The First Migration, 1654–1820.* Baltimore: Johns Hopkins University Press, 1992.

Fabian, Ann. *Card Sharps, Dream Books, and Bucket Shops: Gambling in Nineteenth-Century America.* Ithaca: Cornell University Press, 1990.

Faust, Drew Gilpin. *Mothers of Invention: Women of the Slaveholding South in the American Civil War.* Chapel Hill: University of North Carolina Press, 1996.

Fehrenbacher, Don E. *The Slaveholding Republic: An Account of the United States Government's Relations to Slavery.* New York: Oxford University Press, 2001.

————. *Slavery, Law and Politics: The Dred Scott Case in Historical Perspective.* 1978. Reprint, Oxford University Press, 1981.

Feller, Daniel. "A Brother in Arms: Benjamin Tappan and the Antislavery Democracy." *Journal of American History* 88, no. 1 (June 2001): 48–74.

————. *The Jacksonian Promise: America, 1815–1840.* Baltimore: Johns Hopkins University Press, 1995.

————. "Politics and Society: Toward a Jacksonian Synthesis." *Journal of the Early Republic* 10 (summer 1990): 135–61.

Filler, Louis. *The Crusade against Slavery, 1830–1860.* New York: Harper and Brothers, 1960.

Finkelman, Paul, ed. *His Soul Goes Marching On: Responses to John Brown and the Harpers Ferry Raid.* Charlottesville: University Press of Virginia, 1995.

Finnegan, Margaret. *Selling Suffrage: Consumer Culture and Votes for Women.* New York: Columbia University Press, 1999.

Fisher, Terry K. "Lending as Philanthropy: The Philadelphia Jewish Experience, 1847–1954." Ph.D. diss., Bryn Mawr College, 1967.

Fitchett, E. Horace, "The Free Negro in Charleston, South Carolina." Ph.D. diss., University of Chicago, 1950.

Flexner, Eleanor. *Century of Struggle: The Women's Rights Movement in the United States.* Cambridge, Mass.: Harvard University Press, Belknap Press, 1959.

Fogel, Robert William. *Without Consent or Contract: The Rise and Fall of American Slavery.* New York: W. W. Norton and Co., 1989.

Folks, Homer. *The Care of Destitute, Neglected and Delinquent Children.* New York: Macmillan and Co., 1902.

Foner, Eric. *Free Soil, Free Labor, Free Men: The Ideology of the Republican Party before the Civil War.* New York: Oxford University Press, 1970.

————. *Reconstruction: America's Unfinished Devolution, 1863–1877.* New York: Harper and Row, 1988.

————. *A Short History of Reconstruction, 1863–1877.* New York: Harper and Row, 1990.

————. *The Story of American Freedom.* New York: W. W. Norton and Co., 1998.

Forbes, Ella. "African-American Resistance to Colonization." *Journal of Black Studies* 21, no. 2 (December 1990): 210–23.

Foster, Charles I. *Errand of Mercy: The Evangelical United Front, 1790–1837.* Chapel Hill: University of North Carolina Press, 1960.

Foucault, Michel. *Power/Knowledge: Selected Interviews and Other Writings by Michel Foucault.* Edited by Colon Gordon. New York: Pantheon Books, 1972.

Fox-Genovese, Elizabeth. *Within the Plantation Household: Black and White Women of the Old South.* Chapel Hill: University of North Carolina Press, 1988.

Frasca, Ralph. "From Apprentice to Journeyman to Partner: Benjamin Franklin's Workers and the Growth of the Early American Printing Trade." *Pennsylvania Magazine of History and Biography* 114, no. 2 (1990): 229–48.

Frederickson, George M. *The Black Image in the White Mind: The Debate on Afro-American Character and Destiny, 1817–1914.* Middletown, Conn.: Wesleyan University Press, 1987.

———. *The Inner Civil War: Northern Intellectuals and the Crisis of the Union.* New York: Harper and Row, 1965.

Freehling, William W. *Prelude to Civil War: The Nullification Controversy in South Carolina, 1816–1836.* New York: Oxford University Press, 1966.

Freeman, Rhoda G. "The Free Negro in New York City in the Era before the Civil War." Ph.D. diss., Columbia University, 1966.

Friedman, Jean. *The Enclosed Garden: Women and Community in the Evangelical South, 1830–1900.* Chapel Hill: University of North Carolina Press, 1985.

Friedman, Lawrence. *Gregarious Saints: Self and Community in American Abolitionism, 1830–1870.* New York: Cambridge University Press, 1982.

Fukuyama, Francis. *Trust: The Social Virtues and the Creation of Prosperity.* New York: Free Press, 1995.

Fullinwider, Robert, ed. *Civil Society, Democracy and Civic Renewal.* New York: Rowman and Littlefield, 1999.

Gallay, Alan. "The Origins of Slaveholders' Paternalism: George Whitefield, the Bryan Family, and the Great Awakening in the South." *Journal of Southern History* 53, no. 3 (August 1987): 369–94.

Gara, Larry. *The Presidency of Franklin Pierce.* Lawrence: University of Kansas Press, 1991.

Gaustad, Edwin S. *Faith of Our Fathers: Religion and the New Nation.* New York: Harper and Row, 1987.

———. *Sworn on the Altar of God: A Religious Biography of Thomas Jefferson.* Grand Rapids: William B. Eerdmans Publishing Co., 1996.

Geinapp, William E. *The Origins of the Republican Party, 1852–1856.* New York: Oxford University Press, 1987.

Genovese, Eugene D. *The Political Economy of Slavery: Studies in the Economy and Society of the Slave South.* New York: Vintage Books, 1967.

George, Carol V. R. *Segregated Sabbaths: Richard Allen and the Emergence of Independent Black Churches, 1760–1840.* New York: Oxford University Press, 1973.

Giesberg, Judith Ann. *Civil War Sisterhood: The U.S. Sanitary Commission and Women's Politics in Transition.* Boston: Northeastern University Press, 2000.

Gilje, Paul A. *Rioting in America.* Bloomington: Indiana University Press, 1996.

———. "The Rise of Capitalism in the Early Republic." *Journal of the Early Republic* 16 (summer 1996): 159–81.

Gilje, Paul A., and Howard B. Rock, eds. *Keepers of the Revolution: New Yorkers at Work in the Early Republic.* Ithaca: Cornell University Press, 1992.

Gilman, Amy. "From Widowhood to Wickedness: The Politics of Class and Gender in New York City Private Charity, 1799–1860." *History of Education Quarterly* 24 (spring 1984): 59–74.

Gilmore, Glenda. *Gender and Jim Crow: Women and the Politics of White Supremacy in North Carolina, 1896–1920.* Chapel Hill: University of North Carolina Press, 1996.

Ginzberg, Lori. *Women and the Work of Benevolence: Morality, Politics, and Class in the Nine-teenth-Century United States.* New Haven: Yale University Press, 1990.

———. *Women in Antebellum Reform.* Wheeling, Ill.: Harlan Davidson Co., 2000.

Gollaher, David. *Voice for the Mad: The Life of Dorothea Dix.* New York: Free Press, 1995.

Gongaware, George. *The History of the German Friendly Society of Charleston, South Caro-lina, 1766–1916.* Richmond: Garrett and Massie, 1935.

Goodman, Paul. "The Manual Labor Movement and the Origins of Abolitionism." *Journal of the Early Republic* 13 (fall 1993): 355–88.

———. *Of One Blood: Abolitionism and the Origins of Racial Equality.* Berkeley: University of California Press, 1998.

Gramsci, Antonio. *Selections from the Prison Notebooks.* Translated and edited by Quintin Hoare and Geoffrey Nowell-Smith. London: Lawrence and Wishart, 1971.

Greenberg, Kenneth S. *Honor and Slavery.* Princeton: Princeton University Press, 1996.

Greene, Jack P. "Interpretive Frameworks: The Quest for Intellectual Order in Early American History." *William and Mary Quarterly* 48 (1991): 515–30.

Griffin, Clifford. *Their Brothers' Keepers: Moral Stewardship in the United States: 1800–1860.* New York: H. Wolff, 1960.

———. "Religious Benevolence as Social Control, 1815–1816." *Mississippi Valley Historical Review* 45 (December 1957): 423–44.

Grimsted, David. *American Mobbing, 1828–1861: Toward Civil War.* New York: Oxford University Press, 1998.

Grinstein, Hyman. *The Rise of the Jewish Community in New York, 1654–1860.* New York: Jewish Publication Society of New York, 1945.

Habermas, Jurgen. *The Structural Transformation of the Public Sphere.* Cambridge, Mass.: MIT Press, 1989.

Hall, Jacquelyn Dowd. *Revolt against Chivalry: Jessie Daniel Ames and the Women's Campaign against Lynching.* New York: Columbia University Press, 1974.

Hall, John. *Civil Society: Theory, History, Comparison.* Cambridge: Polity Press, 1995.

Hall, Peter Dobkin. *"Inventing the Nonprofit Sector" and Other Essays on Philanthropy, Volun-tarism and Nonprofit Organizations.* Baltimore: Johns Hopkins University Press, 1992.

———. "The Model of Boston Charity: A Theory of Charitable Benevolence and Class Devel-opment." *Science and Society* 38, no. 4 (1974): 464–77.

———. *The Organization of American Culture, 1700–1900: Private Institutions, Elites, and the Origins of American Nationality.* New York: New York University Press, 1982.

———. "Religion and the Origins of Voluntary Associations in the United States." Working Paper 213. New Haven: Program on Nonprofit Organizations, Yale University, 1994.

———. "What the Merchants Did with Their Money: Charity and Testamentary Trusts in Massachusetts, 1800–1880." Working Paper 214. New Haven: Program on Nonprofit Orga-nizations, Yale University, 1995.

Halttunen, Karen. "Humanitarianism and the Pornography of Pain in Anglo-American Cul-ture." *American Historical Review* 100, no. 2 (April 1995): 303–34.

Hammack, David, ed. *Making the Nonprofit Sector in the United States: A Reader.* Bloomington: Indiana University Press, 1998.

Handlin, Oscar, and Mary Flug Handlin. *Commonwealth: A Study of the Role of the Govern-ment in the American Economy: Massachusetts, 1774–1861.* 1947. Reprint, Cambridge, Mass.: Harvard University Press, 1969.

Hansen, Deborah Gold. *Strained Sisterhood: Gender and Class in the Boston Female Antislavery Society.* Amherst: University of Massachusetts Press, 1993.

Harlow, Ralph Volney. *Gerrit Smith: Philanthropist and Reformer.* New York: Henry Holt and Co., 1939.

Harmon, Judd Scott. "Marriage of Convenience: The United States Navy in Africa, 1820–1843." *American Neptune* 32, no. 3 (July 1972): 264–76.

Harris, Katherine. "The United States, Liberia and Their Foreign Relations to 1847." Ph.D. diss., Cornell University, 1982.

Harris, Robert L., Jr. "Early Black Benevolent Societies, 1780–1830." *Massachusetts Review* 20, no. 3 (1979): 603–25.

Harrold, Stanley. *The Abolitionists and the South, 1831–1861.* Lexington: University Press of Kentucky, 1995.

Haskell, Thomas L. "Capitalism and the Origins of the Humanitarian Sensibility." Parts 1 and 2. *American Historical Review* 90, no. 2 (April 1985): 339–61; no. 3 (June 1985): 547–66.

Hatch, Nathan O. *The Democratization of American Christianity.* New Haven: Yale University Press, 1989.

Haviland, Margaret Morris. "Beyond Women's Sphere: Young Quaker Women and the Veil of Charity in Philadelphia, 1790–1810." *William and Mary Quarterly,* 3d ser., 51, no. 3 (July 1994): 419–46.

Heale, M. J. "Patterns of Benevolence: Associated Philanthropy in the Cities of New York, 1830–1860." *New York History* 57 (January 1976): 53–79.

Healey, Robert M. *Jefferson on Religion in Public Education.* New Haven: Yale University Press, 1962.

Helderman, Leonard C. *George Washington: Patron of Learning.* New York: Century Co., 1932.

Henretta, James A. *The Evolution of American Society, 1700–1815.* London: D. C. Heath and Co., 1973.

———. *The Origins of American Capitalism: Collected Essays.* Boston: Northeastern University Press, 1991.

Hershberger, Mary. "Mobilizing Women, Anticipating Abolition: The Struggle against Indian Removal in the 1830s." *Journal of American History* 86, no. 1 (June 1999): 15–40.

Hewitt, Nancy A. *Women's Activism and Social Change: Rochester, New York, 1822–1872.* Ithaca: Cornell University Press, 1984.

Heyrman, Christine L. "A Model of Christian Charity: The Rich and Poor in New England, 1630–1730." Ph.D. diss., Yale University, 1977.

———. *Southern Cross: The Beginnings of the Bible Belt.* Chapel Hill: University of North Carolina Press, 1997.

Higginbotham, Evelyn Brooks. "Beyond the Sound of Silence: Afro-American Women in History." *Gender and History* 1, no. 1 (spring 1989): 50–67.

———. *Righteous Discontent: The Women's Movement in the Black Baptist Church, 1880–1920.* Cambridge, Mass.: Harvard University Press, 1993.

Hine, Darlene Clark, and Kathleen Thompson. *A Shining Thread of Hope: The History of Black Women in America.* New York: Broadway Books, 1998.

Hirrell, Leo P. *Children of Wrath: New School Calvinism and Antebellum Reform.* Lexington: University of Kentucky Press, 1998.

Hirsch, Susan E. *The Roots of the American Working Class.* Philadelphia: University of Pennsylvania Press, 1978.

Hofer, Frank William. *Counties in Transition: A Study of Public and Private Welfare Adminis-tration in Virginia.* Charlottesville: Institute for Research in the Social Sciences, University of Virginia, 1929.

Hoff, Joan. *Law, Gender and Injustice: A Legal History of U.S. Women.* New York: New York University Press, 1991.

Hofstadter, Richard. *The American Political Tradition and the Men Who Made It.* New York: Vintage Books, 1948.

Hoganson, Kristin. "Garrisonian Abolitionists and the Rhetoric of Gender, 1850–1860." *American Quarterly* 45, no. 4 (December 1993): 558–95.

Holt, Michael F. *The Political Crisis of the 1850s.* New York: W. W. Norton and Co., 1978.

———. *The Rise and Fall of the American Whig Party: Jacksonian Politics and the Onset of the Civil War.* New York: Oxford University Press, 1999.

Horne, H. Oliver. *A History of Savings Banks.* London: Oxford University Press, 1947.

Horden, Peregrine, and Richard Smith, eds. *The Locus of Care: Families, Communities, Institu-tions and the Provision of Welfare since Antiquity.* London: Routledge, 1998.

Horton, James Oliver, and Lois E. Horton. *Black Bostonians: Family Life and Community Strug-gle in the Antebellum North.* 1979. Reprint, New York: Holmes and Meier, 1999.

———. *In Hope of Liberty: Culture, Community and Protest among Northern Free Blacks, 1700–1860.* New York: Oxford University Press, 1997.

Howe, Daniel Walker. "The Evangelical Movement and Political Culture in the North during the Second Party System." *Journal of American History* 77 (March 1991): 1216–39.

———. *The Political Culture of the American Whigs.* Chicago: University of Chicago Press, 1979.

Hoyt, William D., Jr. "The Papers of the Maryland State Colonization Society." *Maryland His-torical Magazine* 32 (September 1937) 247–71.

Hutton, Frankie. "Economic Considerations in the American Colonization Society's Early Effort to Emigrate Free Blacks to Liberia, 1816–1836." *Journal of Negro History* 68, no. 4 (fall 1983): 376–89.

Ingersoll, Thomas N. "Free Blacks in a Slave Society: New Orleans, 1718–1812." *William and Mary Quarterly.* 3d ser., 48 (1991): 173–200.

Innes, Stephen. *Creating the Commonwealth: The Economic Culture of Puritan New England.* New York: W. W. Norton, 1995.

Isenberg, Nancy. *Sex and Citizenship in Antebellum America.* Chapel Hill: University of North Carolina Press, 1998.

Jacoby, George Paul. *Catholic Child Care in Nineteenth Century New York.* New York: Arno Press, 1974.

James, Frances Godwin. "Charity Endowments as Sources of Local Credit in Seventeenth and Eighteenth Century England." *Journal of Economic History* 8 (1948): 153–70.

James, Sidney V. *A People among Peoples: Quaker Benevolence in Eighteenth Century America.* Cambridge, Mass.: Harvard University Press, 1963.

Jarvis, William. "Mother Seton's Sisters of Charity." Ph.D. diss., Columbia University, 1984.

Jeffrey, Julie Roy. *The Great Silent Army of Abolitionism: Ordinary Women in the Antislavery Movement.* Chapel Hill: University of North Carolina Press, 1998.

———. "Permeable Boundaries: Abolitionist Women and Separate Spheres." *Journal of the Early Republic* 21, no. 1 (spring 2001): 79–94.

Johansen, Mary Carroll. "'Intelligence, Though Overlooked': Education for Black Women in the Upper South, 1800–1840." *Maryland Historical Magazine* 93, no. 4 (winter 1998): 443–65.

John, Richard R. *Spreading the News: The American Postal System from Franklin to Morse.* Cambridge, Mass.: Harvard University Press, 1995.

————. "Taking Sabbatarianism Seriously: The Postal System, the Sabbath, and the Transformation of American Political Culture." *Journal of the Early Republic* 10 (winter 1990): 517–67.

Johnson, Michael P., and James L. Roark. "'A Middle Ground': Free Mulattos and the Friendly Moralist Society of Antebellum Charleston." *Southern Studies* (1982): 246–62.

Johnson, Paul E. *A Shopkeeper's Millennium: Society and Revivals in Rochester, New York, 1815–1837.* New York: Hill and Wang, 1978.

Johnson, Whittington B. "Free African-American Women in Savannah, 1800–1860: Affluence and Autonomy Amid Diversity." *Georgia Historical Quarterly* 76, no. 2 (summer 1992): 26.

Jones, Alice Hanson. "Wealth and Growth of the Thirteen Colonies: Some Implications." *Journal of Economic History* 44, no. 2 (June 1984): 239–54.

————. "Wealth Estimates for the New England Colonies about 1770." *Journal of Economic History* 32, no. 1 (1972): 98–127.

Jones, Jacqueline. *Soldiers of Light and Love: Northern Teachers and Georgia Blacks, 1865–73.* Chapel Hill: University of North Carolina Press, 1980.

Jordan, W. K. *Philanthropy in England, 1480–1660: A Study of the Changing Pattern of English Social Aspirations.* London: G. Allen and Unwin, 1959.

Jordan, Winthrop D. *White over Black: American Attitudes toward the Negro, 1550–1812.* 1968. Reprint, New York: W. W. Norton, 1977.

Kaestle, Carl F. *The Evolution of the Urban School System, 1750–1850.* Cambridge, Mass.: Harvard University Press, 1973.

Kaplan, Michael. "New York City Tavern Violence and the Creation of a Working Class Male Identity." *Journal of the Early Republic* 15 (winter 1995): 591–617.

————. "The World of the B'hoys: Urban Violence and the Political Culture of Antebellum New York City, 1825–1860." Ph.D. diss., New York University, 1996.

Karl, Barry D., and Stanley N. Katz, "American Private Philanthropic Foundations and the Public Sphere, 1890–1930." *Minerva* 19 (1981): 336–70.

Katz, Michael. *In the Shadow of the Poorhouse.* New York: Basic Books, 1986.

Keane, John, ed. *Civil Society and the State: New European Perspectives.* London: University of Westminster Press, 1988.

————. *Democracy and Civil Society.* London: University of Westminster Press, 1988.

Kelso, Robert. *The History of Public Poor Relief in Massachusetts, 1620–1920.* Montclair, N.J.: Patterson Smith, 1969.

Kerber, Linda K. "The Republican Ideology of the Revolutionary Generation." *American Quarterly* 37:4 (fall 1985): 474–95.

————. "The Republican Mother: Women and the Enlightenment—an Historical Perspective." *American Quarterly* 28 (summer 1976): 187–205.

————. *Women of the Republic: Intellect and Ideology in Revolutionary America.* Chapel Hill: University of North Carolina Press, 1980.

Kerber, Linda K., et al. "Beyond Roles, Beyond Spheres: Thinking about Gender in the Early Republic." Forum in *William and Mary Quarterly* 46, no. 3 (July 1989): 565–85.

Kerber, Linda K. "Abolitionists and Amalgamators: The New York City Race Riots of 1834." *New York History* 48, no. 1 (1967): 28–39.

Ketcham, Ralph. *James Madison: A Biography.* 1971. Reprint, Charlottesville: University Press of Virginia, 1990.

Kierner, Cynthia. *Beyond the Household: Women's Place in the Early South, 1700–1835*. Ithaca: Cornell University Press, 1998.

Kohl, Lawrence. "The Concept of Social Control and the History of Jacksonian America." *Journal of the Early Republic* 5 (spring 1985): 21–34.

———. *The Politics of Individualism: Parties and the American Character in the Jacksonian Era*. New York: Oxford University Press, 1989.

Kraditor, Aileen S. *Means and Ends in American Abolitionism: Garrison and His Critics on Strategy and Tactics, 1834–1850*. New York: Pantheon, 1969.

Kramer, Lloyd S. *Paine and Jefferson on Liberty*. New York: Continuum, 1988.

Kulikoff, Alan. *The Agrarian Origins of American Capitalism*. Charlottesville: University Press of Virginia, 1992.

———. "The Transition to Capitalism in Rural America." *William and Mary Quarterly* 46 (1989): 120–44.

Kuykendall, John W. *Southern Enterprize: The Work of National Evangelical Societies in the Antebellum South*. Westport: Greenwood Press, 1982.

Lagemann, Ellen Condliffe. *The Politics of Knowledge: The Carnegie Corporation, Philanthropy, and Public Policy*. Chicago: University of Chicago Press, 1989.

———. *Private Power for the Public Good: A History of the Carnegie Foundation for the Advancement of Teaching*. Middletown, Conn.: Wesleyan University Press, 1983.

———, ed. *Philanthropic Foundations: New Scholarship, New Possibilities*. Indianapolis: Indiana University Press, 1999.

Lambert, Frank. "'Pedlar in Divinity': George Whitefield and the Great Awakening, 1737–1745." *Journal of American History* 77, no. 3 (1990): 812–37.

———. *Pedlar in Divinity: George Whitefield and the Transatlantic Revivals, 1737–1770*. Princeton: Princeton University Press, 1994.

———. "Subscribing for Profits and Piety: The Friendship of Benjamin Franklin and George Whitefield." *William and Mary Quarterly*, 3d ser., 50, no. 3 (July 1993): 529–54.

Lamoreaux, Naomi R. "Banks, Kinship and Economic Development: The New England Case." *Journal of Economic History* 66, no. 3 (1986): 647–67.

———. *Insider Lending: Banks, Personal Connections, and Economic Development in Industrial New England*. Cambridge: Cambridge University Press, 1994.

Lapsansky, Emma Jones. "'Since They Got Those Separate Churches': Afro-Americans and Racism in Jacksonian Philadelphia." *American Quarterly* 32 (1980): 54–78.

Lapsansky, Phillip. "Graphic Discord: Abolitionist and Antiabolitionist Images." In *The Abolitionist Sisterhood: Women's Political Culture in Antebellum America*, edited by Jean Fagan Yellin and John C. Van Horne, 201–30. Ithaca: Cornell University Press, 1994.

Larson, David M. "Benevolent Persuasion: The Art of Benjamin Franklin's Philanthropic Papers." *Pennsylvania Magazine of History and Biography* 110 (1986): 196–218.

Larson, Rebecca. *Daughters of Light: Quaker Women Preaching and Prophesying in the Colonies and Abroad, 1700–1775*. New York: Alfred A. Knopf, 1999.

Laurie, Bruce. *Artisans into Workers: Labor in Nineteenth Century America*. 1989. Reprint, Urbana: University of Illinois Press, 1997.

———. *Working People of Philadelphia, 1800–1850*. Philadelphia: Temple University Press, 1980.

Lazerow, Jama. "Religion and the New England Mill Girl: A New Perspective on an Old Theme." *New England Quarterly* 60 (1987): 429–53.

————. *Religion and the Working Class in Antebellum America*. Washington, D.C.: Smithsonian Institution Press, 1995.

————. "Rethinking Religion and the Working Class in Antebellum America." *Mid-America* 75, no. 1 (January 1993): 85–104.

Lears, T. J. Jackson. "The Concept of Cultural Hegemony: Problems and Possibilities." *American Historical Review* 90, no. 3 (June 1985): 567–93.

Lebsock, Suzanne. *The Free Women of Petersburg: Status and Culture in a Southern Town, 1784–1860*. New York: W. W. Norton and Co., 1984.

Lemay, J. A. Leo., ed. *Reappraising Benjamin Franklin: A Bicentennial Perspective*. Newark: University of Delaware Press, 1993.

Leonard, Elizabeth D. *Yankee Women: Gender Battles in the Civil War*. New York: W. W. Norton and Co., 1994.

Lerner, Gerda. *Black Women in White America: A Documentary History*. New York: Vintage Books, 1973.

————. *The Grimké Sisters from South Carolina: Pioneers for Woman's Rights and Abolition*. New York: Schocken Books, 1971.

Lieby, James. *Charity and Correction in New Jersey: A History of State Welfare Institutions*. New Brunswick: Rutgers University Press, 1967.

Light, Dale. "The Reformation of Philadelphia Catholicism, 1830–1860." *Pennsylvania Magazine of History and Biography* 112, no. 3 (July 1988): 375–405.

————. *Rome and the New Republic: Conflict and Community in Philadelphia Catholicism between the Revolution and the Civil War*. Notre Dame: University of Notre Dame Press, 1996.

Lincoln, C. Eric, and Lawrence H. Mamiya. *The Black Church in the African-American Experience*. Durham: Duke University Press, 1990.

Link, Eugene Perry. *Democratic-Republican Societies, 1790–1800*. New York: Columbia University Press, 1942.

Littlefield, Daniel C. "Blacks, John Brown, and a Theory of Manhood." In *His Soul Goes Marching On: Responses to John Brown and the Harpers Ferry Raid*, edited by Paul Finkelman, 67–97. Charlottesville: University Press of Virginia.

Litwack, Leon F. *Been in the Storm So Long: The Aftermath of Slavery*. New York: Vintage Books, 1979.

————. *North of Slavery: The Negro in the Free States, 1790–1860*. Chicago: University of Chicago Press, 1961.

Lotchin, Roger W. *San Francisco, 1846–1856: From Hamlet to City*. Lincoln: University of Nebraska Press, 1974.

Lumpkin, Wilson. *The Removal of the Cherokee Indians from Georgia, 1827–1841*. 2 vols. 1907. Reprint, New York: August M. Kelley, Publisher, 1971.

Mabee, Carleton. *Black Education in New York State from Colonial to Modern Times*. Syracuse: Syracuse University Press, 1979.

Magdol, Edward. *The Antislavery Rank and File: A Social Profile of the Abolitionists' Constituency*. New York: Greenwood Press, 1986.

Maier, Pauline. *American Scripture: Making the Declaration of Independence*. New York: Alfred A. Knopf, 1997.

————. "The Debate over Incorporations: Massachusetts in the Early Republic." In *Massachusetts and the New Nation*, edited by Conrad Edick Wright, 73–117. Boston: Northeastern University Press, 1992.

————. *From Resistance to Revolution: Colonial Radicals and the Development of American Opposition to Britain, 1765–1776.* New York: Alfred A. Knopf, 1972.

————. "The Revolutionary Origins of the American Corporation." *William and Mary Quarterly,* 3d ser., 50, no. 1 (January 1993): 51–84.

Malone, Dumas. *Jefferson: The Sage of Monticello.* Boston: Little, Brown and Co., 1977.

Mandler, Peter, ed. *The Uses of Charity: The Poor on Relief in the Nineteenth-Century Metropolis.* Philadelphia: University of Pennsylvania Press, 1990.

Marshall, Helen. *Dorothea Dix: Forgotten Samaritan.* New York: Russell and Russell, 1937.

Massey, Mary Elizabeth. *Women in the Civil War.* 1944. Reprint, Lincoln: University of Nebraska Press, 1994.

Masur, Louis P. "Age of the First Person Singular: The Vocabulary of the Self in New England, 1780–1850." *Journal of American Studies* 25 (1991): 189–211.

————. *1831: Year of Eclipse.* New York: Hill and Wang, 2001.

Matejasic, Thomas D. "Whig Support for African Colonization: Ohio as a Test Case." *Mid-America* 66, no. 2 (1984): 79–92.

Mathews, Donald G. *Religion in the Old South.* Chicago: University of Chicago Press, 1977.

Mayer, Henry. *All on Fire: William Lloyd Garrison and the Abolition of Slavery.* New York: St. Martin's Press, 1998.

McArthur, Judith N. *Creating the New Woman: The Rise of Southern Women's Progressive Culture in Texas, 1893–1918.* Urbana: University of Illinois Press, 1998.

McCarthy, Kathleen D. "The History of Philanthropy and Nonprofits." *Third Sector Review* (Australia) 4, no. 2 (1998): 7–22.

————. *Noblesse Oblige: Charity and Cultural Philanthropy in Chicago, 1849–1929.* Chicago: University of Chicago Press, 1982.

————. "Parallel Power Structures: Women and the Voluntary Sphere." In *Lady Bountiful Revisited: Women, Philanthropy and Power,* edited by Kathleen D. McCarthy, 1–31. New Brunswick: Rutgers University Press, 1990.

————. "Patronage of the Arts." In *Encyclopedia of the United States in the Twentieth Century,* edited by Stanley I. Kutler, Robert Dallek, David A. Hollinger, and Thomas McCraw, 6:1725–42. New York: Charles Scribner's Sons, 1996.

————. "Women, Politics, Philanthropy: Some Historical Origins of the Welfare State." In *The Liberal Persuasion: Arthur Schlesinger, Jr., and the Challenge of the American Past,* edited by John Patrick Diggins. Princeton: Princeton University Press, 1997.

————. *Women's Culture: American Philanthropy and Art, 1830–1930.* Chicago: University of Chicago Press, 1991.

————, ed. *Lady Bountiful Revisited: Women, Philanthropy and Power.* New Brunswick: Rutgers University Press, 1990.

————, ed. Special Issue on Women and Philanthropy. *Voluntas* 7, no. 4 (December 1996).

————, ed. *Women, Philanthropy and Civil Society.* Bloomington: Indiana University Press, 2001.

McCoy, Drew R. *The Elusive Republic: A Political Economy in Jeffersonian America.* Chapel Hill: University of North Carolina Press, 1980.

————. *The Last of the Fathers: James Madison and the Republican Legacy.* New York: Cambridge University Press, 1989.

McCurry, Linda O. *To Keep the Waters Troubled: The Life of Ida B. Wells.* New York: Oxford University Press, 1998.

McCurry, Stephanie. *Masters of Small Worlds: Yeoman Households, Gender Relations, and the*

Political Culture of the Antebellum South Carolina Low Country. New York: Oxford University Press, 1995.

———. "The Two Faces of Republicanism: Gender and Proslavery Politics in Antebellum Society." *Journal of American History* (March 1992): 1245–64.

McDonald, Robert M. S. "Thomas Jefferson's Changing Reputation as Author of the Declaration of Independence: The First Fifty Years." *Journal of the Early Republic* 19, no. 2 (summer 1999): 169–96.

McFeely, William S. *Frederick Douglass.* W. W. Norton and Co., 1991.

McGraw, Marie Tyler. "Richmond Free Blacks and African Colonization, 1816–1832." *Journal of American Studies* 21 (1987): 207–24.

McLoughlin, William G. *Cherokee Renascence in the New Republic.* Princeton: Princeton University Press, 1986.

———. *Cherokees and Missionaries, 1789–1839.* New Haven: Yale University Press, 1984

———. "Georgia's Role in Instigating Compulsory Indian Removal." *Georgia Historical Quarterly* 70, no. 4 (winter 1986): 605–23.

———. "The Reverend Evan Jones and the Cherokee Trail of Tears, 1838–1839." *Georgia Historical Quarterly* 73, no. 3 (fall 1989): 559–83.

McPherson, James M. *The Struggle For Equality: Abolitionists and the Negro in the Civil War and Reconstruction.* Princeton: Princeton University Press, 1964.

Miller, Howard. *The Legal Foundations of American Philanthropy, 1776–1844.* Madison: State Historical Society of Wisconsin, 1961.

Miller, John Chester. *The Wolf by the Ears: Thomas Jefferson and Slavery.* Charlottesville: University Press of Virginia, 1991.

Miller, Nathan. *The Enterprise of a Free People: Aspects of Economic Development in New York State during the Canal Period, 1792–1838.* Ithaca: Cornell University Press, 1962.

Miller, Randall M., and Jon L. Wakelyn, eds. *Catholics in the Old South: Essays on Church and Culture.* Macon: Mercer University Press, 1983.

Miller, William Lee. *Arguing about Slavery: John Quincy Adams and the Great Battle in the United States Congress.* New York: Vintage Books, 1995.

Mintz, Stephen. *Moralists and Modernizers.* Baltimore: Johns Hopkins University Press, 1995.

Mohl, Raymond A. "Humanitarianism in the Preindustrial City: The New York Society for the Prevention of Pauperism, 1817–1823." *Journal of American History* 57, no. 3 (December 1970): 576–99.

———. *Poverty in New York: 1783–1825.* New York: Oxford University Press, 1971.

Morison, Samuel Eliot. *Three Centuries of Harvard, 1636–1936.* Cambridge, Mass.: Harvard University Press, 1936.

Moses, Wilson J. "Black Communities in Antebellum America: Buttressing Held Views." *Reviews in American History* 25, no. 4 (December 1997): 557–63.

Myers, Marvin. *The Jacksonian Persuasion: Politics and Belief.* Palo Alto: Stanford University Press, 1957.

Myrdal, Gunnar. *An American Dilemma: The Negro Problem and Modern Democracy.* New York: Harper and Row, 1944.

Nash, Gary B. *Forging Freedom: The Formation of Philadelphia's Black Community: 1720–1840.* Cambridge, Mass.: Harvard University Press, 1988.

———. "New Light on Richard Allen: The Early Years of Freedom." *William and Mary Quarterly,* 3d ser., 46, no. 2 (1989): 332–40.

———. "Poverty and Poor Relief in Pre-revolutionary Philadelphia." *William and Mary Quarterly* 33 (1976).

———. *The Urban Crucible: Social Change, Political Consciousness and the Origins of the American Revolution.* Cambridge, Mass.: Harvard University Press, 1979.

Nash, Margaret. "Rethinking Republican Motherhood: Benjamin Rush and the Young Ladies' Academy of Philadelphia." *Journal of the Early Republic* 17 (summer 1997): 171–91.

Nash, Michael. "Research Note: Searching for Working Class Philadelphia in the Records of the Philadelphia Saving Fund Society." *Journal of Social History* 29, no. 3 (spring 1996): 683–87.

Newman, Richard S. "Prelude to the Gag Rule: Southern Reaction to Antislavery Petitions in the First Federal Congress." *Journal of the Early Republic* 16 (winter 1996): 571–99.

Ninkovich, Frank. "The Rockefeller Foundation, China, and Cultural Change." *Journal of American History* 70 (March 1984): 799–820.

Nodyne, Kenneth R. "The Role of De Witt Clinton and the Municipal Government in the Development of Cultural Organizations in New York City, 1803–1817." Ph.D. diss., New York University, 1969.

Norris, James D. *R. G. Dun and Company, 1841–1900: The Development of Credit-Reporting in the Nineteenth Century.* Westport: Greenwood Press, 1978.

North, Douglass C. *The Economic Growth of the United States, 1790–1860.* New York: W. W. Norton and Co., 1966.

Northrup, Flora L. *The Record of a Century, 1834–1934.* New York: American Female Guardian Society and Home for the Friendless, 1934.

Norton, Mary Beth. *Liberty's Daughters: The Revolutionary Experience of American Women, 1750–1800.* Boston: Little, Brown and Co., 1980.

Nye, Russel B. *Fettered Freedom: Civil Liberties and the Slavery Controversy, 1830–1860.* East Lansing: Michigan State College Press, 1949.

Oakes, James. *The Ruling Race: A History of American Slaveholders.* New York: Vintage Books, 1983.

Oates, Mary J. *The Catholic Philanthropic Tradition in America.* Bloomington: Indiana University Press, 1995.

O'Connell, Neil J. "George Whitefield and Bethesda Orphan-House." *Georgia Historical Quarterly* 54 (1970): 41–62.

O'Connor, Thomas, "To Be Poor and Homeless in Old Boston." In *Massachusetts and the New Nation,* edited by Conrad Edick Wright, 202–25. Boston: Northeastern University Press, 1992.

O'Grady, John. *Catholic Charities in the United States: History and Problems.* 1930. Reprint, New York: Arno Press, 1971.

Olaskey, Marvin. *The Tragedy of American Compassion.* Washington, D.C.: Regnery, 1995.

Olmstead, Alan L. "Investment Constraints and New York City Mutual Savings Bank Financing of Antebellum Development." *Journal of Economic History* 32, no. 3 (1972): 811–41.

———. "New York City Mutual Savings Bank Portfolio Management and Trustee Objectives." *Journal of Economic History* 34, no. 4 (December 1974): 815–34.

———. *New York City Mutual Savings Banks, 1819–1861.* Chapel Hill: University of North Carolina Press, 1976.

Owen, David. *English Philanthropy, 1660–1960.* Cambridge, Mass.: Harvard University Press, Belknap Press, 1964.

Palaudan, Phillip Shaw. *"A People's Contest": The Union and the Civil War, 1861–1865*. New York: Harper and Row, 1988.

Payne, Peter L., and Lance Edwin Davis. *The Savings Bank of Baltimore, 1818–1866: A Historical and Analytical Study*. Baltimore: Johns Hopkins University Press, 1956.

Pease, Jane H., and William H. Pease. *Ladies, Women and Wenches: Choice and Constraint in Antebellum Charleston and Boston*. Chapel Hill: University of North Carolina Press, 1991.

———. *They Who Would Be Free: Blacks' Search for Freedom, 1830–1861*. New York: Atheneum, 1974.

Perkins, Linda M. "The Black Female American Missionary Association Teacher in the South, 1861–1870." In *Black Americans in North Carolina and the South*, edited by Jeffrey J. Crow and Flora J. Hatley, 122–36. Chapel Hill: University of North Carolina Press, 1984.

———. "Black Women and Racial 'Uplift' Prior to Emancipation." In *The Black Woman Cross-Culturally*, edited by Filomena Steady, 317–34. Cambridge, Mass.: Schenkman Publisher, 1981.

Perry, Lewis. *Radical Abolitionism: Anarchy and the Government of God in Antislavery Thought*. Ithaca: Cornell University Press, 1973.

Perry, Lewis, and Michael Fellman, eds. *Antislavery Reconsidered: New Perspectives on the Abolitionists*. Baton Rouge: Louisiana State University Press, 1979.

Pessen, Edward. *Jacksonian America: Society, Personality, and Politics*. Urbana: University of Illinois Press, 1985.

———. *Riches, Class and Power before the Civil War*. New York: D. C. Heath, 1973.

Peterson, Merrill D. *The Great Triumvirate: Webster, Clay and Calhoun*. New York: Oxford University Press, 1987.

———. *Thomas Jefferson and the New Nation: A Biography*. New York: Oxford University Press, 1970.

Phillips, Christopher. *Freedom's Port: The African American Community of Baltimore, 1790–1860*. Urbana: University of Illinois Press, 1997.

Phillips, Clifton Jackson. *Protestant America and the Pagan World: The First Half Century of the American Board of Commissioners for Foreign Missions, 1810–1860*. Cambridge, Mass.: East Asian Research Center, Harvard University, 1969.

Pickett, Robert S. *House of Refuge: Origins of Juvenile Reform in New York State, 1815–1857*. Syracuse: Syracuse University Press, 1969.

Pierson, Michael D. "Guard the Foundation Wall: Antebellum New York Democrats and the Defense of Patriarchy." *Gender and History* 7, no. 1 (April 1995): 25–40.

Pocock, J. G. A. *The Machiavellian Moment*. Princeton: Princeton University Press, 1975.

———. "Virtue and Commerce in the Eighteenth Century." *Journal of Interdisciplinary History* 3 (summer 1972): 119–34.

Poe, William A. "Lott Cary: Man of Purchased Freedom." *Church History* 39, no. 1 (March 1970): 49–61.

Porter, Susan Lynne. "The Benevolent Asylum—Image and Reality: The Care and Training of Female Orphans in Boston, 1800–1840." Ph.D. diss., Boston University, 1984.

Potter, David M. *The Impending Crisis: 1848–1861*. New York: Harper Torchbooks, 1976.

Powell, John Harvey. *Bring Out Your Dead: The Great Plague of Yellow Fever in Philadelphia in 1793*. Philadelphia: University of Pennsylvania Press, 1949.

Prince, Carl E. "The Great 'Riot Year': Jacksonian Democracy and Patterns of Violence in 1834." *Journal of the Early Republic* 5 (spring 1985): 1–19.

Prucha, Francis Paul. "Andrew Jackson's Indian Policy: A Reassessment." *Journal of American History* 56 (December 1969): 527–39.

———. *The Great Father: The United States and the American Indians.* Lincoln: University of Nebraska Press, 1984.

Prude, Jonathan. "Capitalism, Industrialization, and the Factory in Post-revolutionary America." *Journal of the Early Republic* 16 (summer 1996): 237–55.

Putnam, Robert. *Bowling Alone: The Collapse and Revival of American Community.* New York: Simon and Schuster, 2000.

———. *Making Democracy Work: Civic Traditions in Modern Italy.* Princeton: Princeton University Press, 1993.

———. "The Prosperous Community: Social Capital and Public Life." *American Prospect* 13 (spring 1993): 35–42.

Pye, Lucien, and Sidney Verba. *Political Culture and Political Development.* Princeton: Princeton University Press, 1965.

Quarles, Benjamin. *Black Abolitionists.* New York: Oxford University Press, 1969.

Quist, John W. *Restless Visionaries: The Social Roots of Antebellum Reform in Alabama and Michigan.* Baton Rouge: Louisiana State University Press, 1998.

———. "Slaveholding Operatives of the Benevolent Empire: Bible, Tract and Sunday School Societies in Antebellum Tuscaloosa, Alabama." *Journal of Southern History* 62 (August 1996): 481–526.

Rable, George C. *Civil Wars: Women and the Crisis of Southern Nationalism.* Urbana: University of Illinois Press, 1989.

Raboteau, Albert J. *Slave Religion: The "Invisible Institution" in the Antebellum South.* New York: Oxford University Press, 1978.

Raphael, Marc Lee. *Jews and Judaism in a Midwestern Community: Columbus, Ohio, 1840–1975.* Columbus: Ohio Historical Society, 1979.

Reed, Harry. *Platform for Change: The Foundations of the Northern Free Black Community, 1775–1865.* East Lansing: Michigan State University Press, 1994.

Reichmann, Adam. "Andrew Jackson's Indian Removal Campaigns." Seminar paper. Graduate Center, City University of New York, May 2001.

Reigel, Robert E. "Mary Livermore." In *Notable American Women*, edited by Edward T. James, 2:410–12. Cambridge, Mass.: Harvard University Press, Belknap Press, 1971.

Remer, Rosiland. *Printers and Men of Capital: Philadelphia Book Publishers in the New Republic.* Philadelphia: University of Pennsylvania Press, 1996.

Remini, Robert V. *Andrew Jackson and His Indian Wars.* New York: Viking, 2001.

———. *The Life of Andrew Jackson.* New York: Penguin Books, 1988.

Rice, Charles E. *Freedom of Association.* New York: New York University Press, 1982.

Richards, Leonard L. *"Gentlemen of Property and Standing": Anti-abolition Mobs in Jacksonian America.* New York: Oxford University Press, 1970.

———. "The Jacksonians and Slavery." In *Antislavery Reconsidered: New Perspectives on the Abolitionists*, edited by Lewis Perry and Michael Fellman, 99–118. Baton Rouge: Louisiana State University Press, 1975.

———. *The Life and Times of Congressman John Quincy Adams.* New York: Oxford University Press, 1986.

Richardson, Joe M. *Christian Reconstruction: The American Missionary Association and Southern Blacks, 1861–1890.* Athens: University of Georgia Press, 1986.

Richardson, Robert D., Jr. *Emerson: The Mind on Fire*. Berkeley: University of California Press, 1995.

Risch, Erna. "Immigrant Aid Societies before 1820." *Pennsylvania Magazine of History and Biography* 60, no. 1 (January 1836): 15–33.

Robertson, David. *Denmark Vesey: The Buried History of America's Largest Slave Rebellion and the Man Who Led It.* New York: Alfred A. Knopf, 1999.

Rock, Howard B. *Artisans of the New Republic: Tradesmen of New York City in the Age of Jefferson*. New York: New York University Press, 1984.

Rodgers, Daniel T. "Republicanism: The Career of a Concept." *Journal of American History* 79, no. 1 (1992): 11–38.

Roeber, A. G. "J. H. C. Helmuth, Evangelical Charity, and the Public Sphere in Pennsylvania, 1793–1800." *Pennsylvania Magazine of History and Biography* 121 (1997): 77–100.

Roediger, David R. *The Wages of Whiteness: Race and the Making of the American Working Class*. New York: Verso, 1991.

Rogin, Michael Paul. *Fathers and Children: Andrew Jackson and the Subjugation of the American Indian*. New York: Vintage Books, 1976

Rose, Willie Lee. *Rehearsal for Reconstruction: The Port Royal Experiment*. New York: Oxford University Press, 1964.

Rothenberg, Winifred. "The Emergence of a Capital Market in Rural Massachusetts, 1730–1830." *Journal of Economic History* 45, no. 4 (December 1985): 781–808.

Rothman, David. *The Discovery of the Asylum: Social Order and Disorder in the New Republic*. Boston: Little, Brown and Co., 1971.

Rotundo, E. Anthony. *American Manhood: Transformations in Masculinity from the Revolution to the Modern Era*. New York: Basic Books, 1993.

Rousseve, Charles Barthelemy. *The Negro in Louisiana: Aspects of His History and His Literature*. New Orleans: Xavier Press, 1937.

Rozier, John. "William Terrell: Forgotten Benefactor." *Georgia Historical Quarterly* 65, no. 2 (summer 1981): 92–103.

Rury, John L. "Philanthropy, Self-Help, and Social Control: The New York Manumission Society." *Phylon* 46, no. 3 (1995): 231–41.

Russell, John H. *The Free Negro in Virginia, 1619–1865*. Baltimore: Johns Hopkins University Press, 1913.

Ryan, Mary. *Cradle of the Middle Class: The Family in Oneida County, New York, 1790–1865*. New York: Cambridge University Press, 1981.

———. "The Power of Women's Networks." In *Sex and Class in Women's History*, edited by Judith L. Newton et. al., 167–86. London: Routledge and Kegan Paul, 1983.

———. "A Women's Awakening: Evangelical Religion and the Families of Utica, New York, 1800–1840." In *Women in American Religion*, edited by Janet Wilson James, 89–110. Philadelphia: University of Pennsylvania Press, 1980.

Said, Edward W. *Orientalism*. New York: Vintage Books, 1979.

Salamon, Lester M. *America's Nonprofit Sector: A Primer*. New York: Foundation Center, 1999.

———. *Partners in Public Service: Government-Nonprofit Relations in the Modern Welfare State*. Baltimore: Johns Hopkins University Press, 1995.

Salamon, Lester M., and Helmut Anheier. *The Emerging Sector: An Overview*. Baltimore: Institute for Policy Studies, Johns Hopkins University, 1994.

Sander, Kathleen Waters. *The Business of Charity: The Woman's Exchange Movement, 1832–1900.* Urbana: University of Illinois Press, 1998.

Sanford, Charles B. *The Religious Life of Thomas Jefferson.* Charlottesville: University Press of Virginia, 1984.

Sarna, Jonathan. "The American Jewish Response to Mid–Nineteenth Century Christian Missions." *Journal of American History* 68, no. 1 (June 1981): 35–51.

Satz, Ronald. *American Indian Policy in the Jacksonian Era.* Lincoln: University of Nebraska Press, 1975.

———. "The Cherokee Trail of Tears: A Sesquicentennial Perspective." *Georgia Historical Quarterly* 73, no. 3 (fall 1989): 431–66.

Sayre, Ruth Ann. "A Study of the Changes in Structure and Function of the Board of Managers of the Chicago Home for the Friendless, 1858–1933." Master's thesis, University of Chicago, 1945.

Schlenther, Boyd Stanley. "'To Convert the Poor People in America': Bethesda Orphanage and the Thwarted Zeal of the Countess of Huntingdon." *Georgia Historical Quarterly* 77, no. 2 (summer 1994): 225–56.

Schlesinger, Arthur. *The Age of Jackson.* Boston: Little, Brown and Co., 1945.

Schneider, David M. *The History of Public Welfare in New York State, 1609–1866.* Chicago: University of Chicago Press, 1938.

Schneider, Eric C. *In the Web of Class: Delinquents and Reformers in Boston, 1810s–1930s.* New York: New York University Press, 1992.

Schoeberlein, Robert W. "A Fair to Remember: Maryland Women in Aid of the Union." *Maryland Historical Magazine* 90, no. 4 (winter 1995): 467–88.

Schoenbachler, Matthew. "Republicanism in the Age of Democratic Revolution: The Democratic-Republican Societies of the 1790s." *Journal of the Early Republic* 18 (spring 1998): 237–61.

Schweikart, Larry. "Southern Banks and Economic Growth in the Antebellum Period: A Reassessment." *Journal of Southern History* 53, no. 1 (February 1987): 19–36.

Scott, Anne Firor. "Most Invisible of All: Black Women's Voluntary Associations." *Journal of Southern History* 56, no. 1 (1990): 2–22.

———. *Natural Allies: Women's Associations in American History.* Urbana: University of Illinois Press, 1991.

———. *The Southern Lady: From Pedestal to Politics, 1830–1930.* Chicago: University of Chicago Press, 1971.

Scott, Donald M. *From Office to Profession: The New England Ministry, 1750–1850.* Philadelphia: University of Pennsylvania Press, 1978.

Sears, Jesse Brundage. *Philanthropy in the History of American Higher Education.* 1922. Reprint, New Brunswick: Transaction Publishers, 1990.

Seligman, Adam B. *The Idea of Civil Society.* Princeton: Princeton University Press, 1992.

Sellers, Charles. *The Market Revolution: Jacksonian America, 1815–1846.* New York: Oxford University Press, 1991.

Shalhope, Robert E. "Republicanism and Early American Historiography." *William and Mary Quarterly* 39, no. 2 (1982): 334–56.

Sheehan, Bernard W. *Seeds of Extinction: Jeffersonian Philanthropy and the American Indian.* New York: W. W. Norton, 1973.

Shiels, Richard D. "The Feminization of American Congregationalism, 1730–1835." *American Quarterly* 33 (spring 1980): 46–62.

Sidbury, James. *Ploughshares into Swords: Race, Rebellion, and Identity in Gabriel's Virginia, 1730–1810*. New York: Cambridge University Press, 1997.

Sklar, Kathryn Kish. *Catharine Beecher: A Study in American Domesticity*. New Haven: Yale University Press, 1973.

———. *Florence Kelley and the Nation's Work: The Rise of Women's Political Culture, 1830–1900*. New Haven: Yale University Press, 1995.

———. "The Historical Foundations of Women's Power in the Creation of the American Welfare State, 1830–1930." In *Mothers of a New World: Maternalist Politics and the Origins of Welfare States*, edited by Seth Koven and Sonya Michel, 43–93. New York: Routledge, 1993.

———. *Women's Rights Emerges within the Antislavery Movement, 1830–1870: A Brief History with Documents*. New York: Bedford/St. Martins, 2000.

Skocpol, Theda. *Protecting Soldiers and Mothers: The Political Origins of Social Policy in the United States*. Cambridge, Mass.: Harvard University Press, 1991.

Slaughter, Thomas. *The Whiskey Rebellion: Frontier Epilogue to the American Revolution*. New York: Oxford University Press, 1986.

Smith, Billy G. "Inequality in Late Colonial Philadelphia: A Note on Its Nature and Growth." *William and Mary Quarterly*, 3d ser., 41, no. 4 (October 1984): 629–45.

———. *The "Lower Sort": Philadelphia's Laboring People, 1750–1800*. Ithaca: Cornell University Press, 1990.

Smith, James A. *The Idea Brokers: Think Tanks and the Rise of the New Policy Elite*. New York: The Free Press, 1991.

Smith, Kimberly K. *The Dominion of Voice: Riot, Reason, and Romance in Antebellum Politics*. Lawrence: University Press of Kansas, 1999.

Smith, Marion Barnett. "History of the Chicago Home for the Friendless." Master's thesis, University of Chicago, 1930.

Smith, Rogers M. *Civic Ideals: Conflicting Visions of Citizenship in U.S. History*. New Haven: Yale University Press, 1997.

Smith-Rosenberg, Carroll. "Beauty, the Beast, and the Militant Woman." In *Disorderly Conduct: Visions of Gender in Victorian America*, 109–28. New York: Oxford University Press, 1985.

———. *Religion and the Rise of the American City: The New York City Mission Movement, 1812–1870*. Ithaca: Cornell University Press, 1971.

Soltow, Lee. "Economic Inequality in the United States in the Period from 1790 to 1860." *Journal of Economic History* 31, no. 4 (1974): 822–39.

Stampp, Kenneth M. *America in 1857: A Nation on the Brink*. 1957. Reprint, New York: Oxford University Press, 1990.

Stansell, Christine. *City of Women: Sex and Class in New York, 1789–1860*. New York: Alfred A. Knopf, 1986.

Staudenraus, P. J. *The African Colonization Movement, 1816–1865*. 1961. Reprint, New York: Octagon Books, 1980.

Stebbins, Giles Badger. *Facts and Opinions Touching the Real Origin, Character and Influence of the American Colonization Society*. New York: Negro Universities Press, 1961.

Sterling, Dorothy. *Ahead of Her Time: Abby Kelley and the Politics of Antislavery*. New York: W. W. Norton and Co., 1991.

Stewart, James Brewer. "The Emergence of Racial Modernity and the Rise of the White North, 1790–1840." *Journal of the Early Republic* 18 (spring 1998): 183–217.

————. *Holy Warriors: The Abolitionists and American Slavery.* New York: Hill and Wang, 1976.

Story, Ronald. *Harvard and the Boston Upper Class: The Forging of an Aristocracy, 1800–1870.* Middletown, Conn.: Wesleyan University Press, 1980.

Stott, Richard. "Artisans and Capital Development." *Journal of the Early Republic* 16 (summer 1996): 257–71.

Sushka, Mary Elizabeth. "The Antebellum Money Market and the Economic Impact of the Bank War." *Journal of Economic History* 36, no. 4 (December 1976): 809–35.

Teaford, Jon C. *The Municipal Revolution in America: Origins of Modern Urban Government, 1650–1825.* Chicago: University of Chicago Press, 1975.

Temin, Peter. *The Jacksonian Economy.* New York: W. W. Norton and Co., 1969.

Thelen, David, ed. *Memory and American History.* Bloomington: Indiana University Press, 1989.

Thernstrom, Stephen. *Progress and Poverty: Social Mobility in a Nineteenth Century City.* Cambridge, Mass.: Harvard University Press, 1964.

Thomas, John L. *The Liberator: William Lloyd Garrison.* Boston: Little, Brown and Co., 1963.

————. "Romantic Reform in America, 1816–1865." *American Quarterly* 17, no. 4 (1965): 656–81.

Thomas, Lamont D. *Rise to Be a People: A Biography of Paul Cuffe.* Urbana: University of Illinois Press, 1986.

Thompson, E. P. *The Making of the English Working Class.* 1963. Reprint, New York: Vintage Books, 1966.

Tobias, Thomas J. *The Hebrew Orphan Society of Charleston, South Carolina.* Charleston, S.C.: Hebrew Orphan Society, 1957.

Trattner, Walter I. *From Poor Law to Welfare State: A History of Social Welfare in America.* New York: Free Press, 1989.

Turner, Elizabeth Hayes. *Women, Culture and Community: Religion and Reform in Galveston, 1880–1920.* New York: Oxford University Press, 1997.

Tyborg-Penn, Rosalyn. *African-American Women in the Struggle for the Vote.* Bloomington: Indiana University Press, 1998.

Tyler, Alice Felt. *Freedom's Ferment: Phases of American Social History from the Colonial Period to the Outbreak of the Civil War.* New York: Harper Torchbooks, 1944.

Umansky, Ellen M., and Dianne Ashton, eds. *Four Centuries of Jewish Women's Spirituality.* Boston: Beacon Press, 1992.

Van Doren, Carl. *Benjamin Franklin.* New York: Viking Press, 1938.

Van Horne, John C. "Collective Benevolence and the Common Good in Franklin's Philanthropy." In *Reappraising Benjamin Franklin: A Bicentennial Perspective,* edited by J.A. Leo Lemay. Newark: University of Delaware Press, 1993.

Varon, R. Elizabeth. "Tippecanoe and the Ladies, Too: White Women and Party Politics in Antebellum Virginia." *Journal of American History* 82, no. 2 (September 1994): 494–521.

————. *We Mean to Be Counted: White Women and Politics in Antebellum Virginia.* Chapel Hill: University of North Carolina Press, 1998.

Vinovskis, Maris. "Have Social Historians Lost the Civil War? Some Preliminary Demographic Speculations." *Journal of American History* 76 (June 1989): 34–58.

Viola, Herman J. *Thomas L. McKenney: Architect of America's Early Indian Policy, 1816–1830.* Chicago: Swallow Press, 1974.

Wade, Richard C. *The Urban Frontier: Pioneer Life in Early Pittsburgh, Cincinnati, Lexington, Louisville and St. Louis.* Chicago: University of Chicago Press, 1959.

Waldstreicher, David. *In the Midst of Perpetual Fetes: The Making of American Nationalism, 1776–1820.* Chapel Hill: University of North Carolina Press, 1997.

Wallace, Anthony F. C. *The Long, Bitter Trail: Andrew Jackson and the Indians.* New York: Hill and Wang, 1993.

Walters, Ronald G. *American Reformers, 1815–1860.* New York: Hill and Wang, 1978, 1997.

———. *The Antislavery Appeal: American Abolitionism after 1830.* Baltimore: Johns Hopkins University Press, 1976.

———. "Comment." Forum on Racial Modernity. *Journal of the Early Republic* 18 (spring 1998): 228–36.

Ward, John William. *Andrew Jackson: Symbol for an Age.* New York: Oxford University Press, 1955.

Warner, Amos G. *American Charities.* New York: Thomas Y. Crowell Co., 1894.

Watkinson, James D. "'Fit Objects of Charity': Community, Race, Faith, and Welfare in Antebellum Lancaster County, Virginia, 1817–1860." *Journal of the Early Republic* 21, no. 1 (spring 2001): 41–70.

Watson, Harry. *Liberty and Power: The Politics of Jacksonian America.* New York: Hill and Wang, 1990.

Waugh, Joan. *Unsentimental Reformer: The Life of Josephine Shaw Lowell.* Cambridge, Mass.: Harvard University Press, 1997.

Way, Peter J. *Common Labour: Workers and the Digging of North American Canals, 1780–1860.* Cambridge: Cambridge University Press, 1993.

———. "Evil Humors and Ardent Spirits: The Rough Culture of Canal Construction Laborers." *Journal of American History* 79, no. 4 (March 1993): 1397–1428.

Weber, Max. *The Protestant Ethic and the Spirit of Capitalism.* Translated by Talcott Parsons. New York: Charles Scribner's Sons, 1958.

Weil, François. "Capitalism and Industrialization in New England, 1815–1845. *Journal of American History* 84, no. 4 (March 1998): 1334–54.

Wellman, Judith. "The Seneca Falls Women's Rights Convention: A Study of Social Networks." *Journal of Women's History* 3, no. 1 (spring 1991): 9–37.

Wesley, Edgar Bruce. *Proposed: The University of the United States.* Minneapolis: University of Minnesota Press, 1936.

West, John G., Jr. *The Politics of Revelation and Reason: Religion and Civic Life in the New Nation.* Lawrence: University of Kansas Press, 1996.

Wheeler, Marjorie Spruill. *New Women of the New South.* New York: Oxford University Press, 1991.

White, Deborah Gray. *Too Heavy a Load: Black Women in Defense of Themselves, 1894–1994.* New York: W. W. Norton, 1999.

White, Gerald T. *A History of the Massachusetts Hospital Life Insurance Company.* Cambridge, Mass.: Harvard University Press, 1955.

Whitehead, John S. "How to Think about the Dartmouth College Case." *History of Education Quarterly* 26, no. 3 (fall 1986): 333–49.

———. *The Separation of College and State: Columbia, Dartmouth, Harvard and Yale, 1776–1876.* New Haven: Yale University Press, 1973.

Whites, Lee Ann. "Rebecca Latimer Felton and the Problem of 'Protection' in the New South."

In *Visible Women: New Essays on American Activism*, edited by Suzanne Lebsock and Nancy Hewitt, 41–61. Urbana: University of Illinois Press, 1993.

Whitescarver, Keith. "Creating Citizens for the Republic: Education in Georgia, 1776–1810." *Journal of the Early Republic* 13 (winter 1993): 435–79.

Wiberly, Stephen. "Four Cities: Public Poor Relief in Urban America, 1700–1775." Ph.D. diss., Yale University, 1975.

Wiebe, Robert H. *The Search for Order*. New York: Hill and Wang, 1967.

———. *Self-Rule: A Cultural History of American Democracy*. Chicago: University of Chicago Press, 1995.

Wildes, Harry Emerson. *Lonely Midas: The Story of Stephen Girard*. New York: Farrar and Rinehart, 1943.

Wilentz, Sean. *Chants Democratic: New York and the Rise of the American Working Class, 1788–1850*. New York: Oxford University Press, 1984.

Willcox, James M. *A History of the Philadelphia Saving Fund Society, 1816–1916*. Philadelphia: J. B. Lippincott, 1916.

Williams, Howell W. "Benjamin Franklin and the Poor Laws." *Social Service Review* 18, no. 1 (1944): 77–91.

Williams, William. "The 'Industrious Poor' and the Founding of the Pennsylvania Hospital." *Pennsylvania Magazine of History and Biography* 97, no. 4 (October 1973): 431–43.

Wills, Gary. *Inventing America: Jefferson's Declaration of Independence*. New York: Vintage Books, 1979.

Winch, Julie. *Philadelphia's Black Elite: Activism, Accommodation, and the Struggle for Autonomy*. Philadelphia: Temple University Press, 1988.

Wolf, Edwin, II, and Maxwell Whiteman. *The History of the Jews of Philadelphia from Colonial Times to the Age of Jackson*. Philadelphia: Jewish Publication Society of America, 1975.

Wood, Gordon S. *The Creation of the American Republic: 1776–1787*. New York: W. W. Norton and Co., 1969.

———. "The Enemy Is Us: Democratic Capitalism in the Early Republic." *Journal of the Early Republic* 16 (summer 1996): 293–308.

———. "The Greatness of George Washington." *Virginia Quarterly Review* 68, no. 2 (spring 1992): 189–207.

———. *The Radicalism of the American Revolution*. New York: Vintage Books, 1993.

———. "The Significance of the Early Republic." *Journal of the Early Republic* 8 (spring 1988): 1–20.

Wood, Kristin E. "'One Woman So Dangerous to Public Morals': Gender and Power in the Eaton Affair." *Journal of the Early Republic* 17 (summer 1997): 237–75.

Woods, Sister Frances Jerome. "Congregations of Religious Women in the Old South." In *Catholics in the Old South: Essays on Church and Culture*, edited by Randall M. Miller and Jon L. Wakelyn, 99–123. Macon: Mercer University Press, 1983.

Wosh, Peter J. "Bibles, Benevolence, and Emerging Bureaucracy: The Persistence of the American Bible Society, 1816–1890." Ph.D. diss., New York University, 1988.

———. *Spreading the Word: The Bible Business in Nineteenth Century America*. Ithaca: Cornell University Press, 1994.

Wright, Conrad Edick. *The Transformation of Charity in Postrevolutionary New England*. Boston: Northeastern University Press, 1992.

Wright, Esmond. *Franklin of Philadelphia*. Cambridge, Mass.: Harvard University Press, Belknap Press, 1986.

Wyatt-Brown, Bertram. "God and Dun and Bradstreet, 1841–1851." *Business History Review* 40, no. 4 (winter 1966): 432–50.

———. *Lewis Tappan and the Evangelical War against Slavery.* Cleveland: Press of Case Western Reserve University, 1969.

———. "Prelude to Abolitionism: Sabbatarian Politics and the Rise of the Second Party System." *Journal of American History* 58 (September 1971): 316–41.

———. *The Shaping of Southern Culture: Honor, Grace, and War, 1760s–1880s.* Chapel Hill: University of North Carolina Press, 2001.

Wyllie, Irwin G. "The Search for an American Law of Charity." *Mississippi Valley Historical Review* 46 (1959): 203–21.

Yacovone, Donald. "The Transformation of the Black Temperance Movement, 1827–1854: An Interpretation." *Journal of the Early Republic* 8 (fall 1988): 281–97.

Yee, Shirley J. *Black Women Abolitionists: A Study in Activism, 1828–1860.* Knoxville: University of Tennessee Press, 1992.

Yellin, Jean Fagan. *Women and Sisters: The Antislavery Feminists in American Culture.* New Haven: Yale University Press, 1989.

Yellin, Jean Fagan, and John C. Van Horne, eds. *The Abolitionist Sisterhood: Women's Political Culture in Antebellum America.* Ithaca: Cornell University Press, 1994.

Yenawine, Bruce Harley. "Benjamin Franklin's Legacy of Virtue: The Franklin Trusts of Boston and Philadelphia." Ph.D. diss., Syracuse University, 1995.

Zagarri, Rosemarie. "Morals, Manners, and the Republican Mother." *American Quarterly* 44, no. 2 (June 1992): 192–215.

Zboray, Ronald J., and Mary Saracino Zboray. "Whig Women, Politics and Culture in the Campaign of 1840: Three Perspectives from Massachusetts." *Journal of the Early Republic* 17 (summer 1997): 277–315.

Zonderman, David A. *Aspirations and Anxieties: New England Factory Workers and the Mechanized Factory System, 1815–1850.* New York: Oxford University Press, 1992.

Zuckerman, Michael. "Doing Good by Doing Well: Benevolence and Self-Interest in Franklin's Autobiography." In *Reappraising Benjamin Franklin: A Bicentennial Perspective*, edited by J. A. Leo Lemay, 441–51. Newark: University of Delaware Press, 1993.

———. "The Selling of the Self: From Franklin to Barnum." In *Benjamin Franklin, Jonathan Edwards and the Representation of American Culture*, edited by Barbara Oberg and Harry S. Stout. New York: Oxford University Press, 1993.

Index